Exploring Human Communication

Sue DeWine
Ohio University

Melissa K. Gibson
Western Michigan University

Matthew J. Smith
Indiana University South Bend

Roxbury Publishing Company
Los Angeles, California

Library of Congress Cataloging-in-Publication Data

DeWine, Sue, 1944-
Exploring human communication / Sue DeWine, Melissa K. Gibson,
   Matthew J. Smith.
      p. cm.
   Includes bibliographical references and index.
   ISBN 1-891487-10-8
1. Communication—Social aspects. 2. Interpersonal communication.
I. Gibson, Melissa K., 1969–. II. Smith, Matthew J., 1971–. III. Title.
HM258.D39   2000
302.2—DC21

98-19381
CIP

EXPLORING HUMAN COMMUNICATION

Publisher and Editor: Claude Teweles
Copy Editor: Elsa van Bergen
Supervising Editor: Dawn VanDercreek
Production Coordinator: C. Max-Ryan
Typography: Rebecca Evans
Cover Design: Marnie Kenney
Illustrations: Benjamin Alan Davies

Photo Credits: Chapter 1: PNI (Picture Network International); Chapter 2: Roxbury; Chapter 3: Carl Wilson; Chapter 4: Charles Kuo/*Daily Bruin*; Chapter 5: Roxbury; Chapter 6: Roxbury; Chapter 7: Justin Warren/*Daily Bruin*; Chapter 8: Roxbury; Chapter 9: Roxbury; Chapter 10: © 1992 KU University Relations; Chapter 11: Feminist Majority Foundation; Chapter 12: Roxbury; Chapter 13: Justin Warren/*Daily Bruin*; Chapter 14: Jon Ferrey/*Daily Bruin*; Chapter 15: Roxbury; Chapter 16: Index Stock Imagery; Chapter 17: SMART Technologies Inc.

Printed on acid-free paper in the United States of America. This paper meets the standards for recycling of the Environmental Protection Agency.

ISBN: 1-891487-10-8

ROXBURY PUBLISHING COMPANY
P.O. Box 491044
Los Angeles, California 90049-9044
Tel: (310) 473-3312 • Fax: (310) 473-4490
E-mail: roxbury@crl.com
Web site: www.roxbury.net

*To my family, colleagues, and former
students who continue to inspire me to
write about our relationships*—SD

*To my parents, Howard and Kathy, and my brother,
Jason, for their empowering love; to my friends and
colleagues for their unceasing support; and to my students
for reminding me every day why I teach*—MKG

*To Sue and Melissa, true mentors
and truer friends*—MJS

Contents

Preface

The authors of this text have taught the basic communication course for many years. We tried several different basic textbooks but felt they were all missing three crucial elements: (1) a view of communication from the *student's* perceptive; (2) interesting case studies with stories from students facing communication problems; and (3) a strong *applied* focus with strategies that could actually be put to use while students read the book. *Exploring Human Communication* is our effort at providing what we thought was missing from other texts.

Along with emphasizing traditional competencies in areas such as interpersonal, small group, and organizational communication, we have also incorporated coverage of topics not usually found in basic texts, but ones that are increasingly central to human communication: understanding legal communication, communicating with new technologies, and using communication principles on the job.

We have designed this book to be an applications-oriented approach to the discipline, helping students internalize concepts by applying them to real-world situations and contexts both inside *and* outside the classroom. In order to make this material more accessible, we have included numerous activities, illustrations, and student-centered stories.

In special boxes throughout the text, we integrate the themes of communication across cultures and ethical dilemmas in communication. These *Spotlight on Diversity* and *Spotlight on Ethics* boxes encourage you to think critically about the concepts introduced in each chapter. In addition, our *Mission: Possible* activities suggest specific, attainable ways in which you can apply those concepts to your own life.

Each chapter also features a number of student-centered stories. By reading these examples and considering your own experiences, we hope that you will be able to relate the content of this text to you own life.

In striving to create a text that would meet the above goals, we benefited from the contributions of other communication educators. We would iike to thank the following individuals who were kind enough to review the first draft and earlier proposal of this book. Their comments were extremely helpful. They are:

Melissa L. Beall (University of Northern Iowa)
Nancy Buerkel-Rothfuss (Central Michigan State University)
Thomas G. Endres (University of St. Thomas)
Dale Gauthreaux (Akron University)
Deborah Hefferin (Broward Community College)
Lawrence W. Hugenberg (Youngstown State University)
Terry M. Perkins (Eastern Illinois University)

Kristi Schaller (Georgia State University)
Deanna Sellnow (North Dakota State University)

As teachers and former students ourselves, we know that students often find college textbooks rather dry. We sincerely hope you will find this book readable and even enjoyable. Good luck to you as you take this journey with us to more effective communication and better interpersonal relationships.

Sue DeWine
Melissa K. Gibson
Matthew J. Smith

About the Authors

Sue DeWine has, for over 25 years, been a professor and a consultant to small manufacturing companies, government agencies, educational institutions, and Fortune 500 companies. In addition to teaching and writing, she has been the Director of the School of Interpersonal Communication at Ohio University for the past 11 years. She has published over 30 articles, 5 books, and presented over 100 professional papers in organizational communication, consulting, and relationships in the workplace. DeWine has traveled and taught extensively in Asia. She and her husband, Mike, have two children, Leigh Anne and James.

Melissa Gibson received her M.A. and Ph.D. from Ohio University and is currently an Assistant Professor at Western Michigan University. Her research interests focus on blue-collar workers and power in the workplace. She attributes her teaching style to her father's work ethic and her mother's wit. She is a very successful teacher, winning the Central States Communication Association Young Teacher's Award and Outstanding Teaching Award at WMU in her first two years as a faculty member.

Matthew Smith received his Ph.D. from Ohio University and is currently an Assistant Professor at Indiana University South Bend. His research focus is computer-mediated communication. He teaches in the areas of rhetoric, organizational communication, and mediated communication. He received the Claude E. Kanter Fellowship while at Ohio University, which recognizes outstanding research.

Part One

Fundamentals of Human Communication

CHAPTER 1

Introducing the Importance of Communication

As the television camera pulls back, the viewer sees an aerial shot of the crash site on the side of the mountain. It had taken rescue workers eight hours to reach what was left of American Airlines flight 965. Of the 160 passengers and crew, only five survived, including a six-year-old New Jersey girl, Michelle DuSan, and her father. Her mother and brother both died in the crash in the Andes Mountains.

In the hospital Michelle asks her father, "When we go home, I won't have to ride on another airplane, will I? Please don't tell me I must."

The scene switches to airline consultant John Nann who concludes: "What we had here was a classic example of miscommunication and an inability of two parties to communicate in aviation language. This was a lack of communication." The pilot thought he was cleared for one route, while the air controller thought the plane was traveling another. The auto pilot turned the plane directly into the side of a mountain.

Broadcast in December 1995 on the television show *20/20*, this newscast served as a dramatic reminder of the possibly serious consequences of everyday encounters. Pilots and air controllers communicate every day without tragic results. And yet, this time, two of them misunderstood each other. Everyday encounters can serve as the threads that hold our lives together or the ball of string that unravels to bring our lives into a series of serious consequences. Saying "hello" to an acquaintance you met in class, fighting with siblings or your own child, convincing your boss to provide more financial support for you, getting someone you like to like you back, talking with a professor about a grade, giving an oral report in class, or sharing an evening with a good friend—these are all everyday encounters. But they are not ordinary or automatic. They do not happen without thought or effort.

Everyday encounters have significant impact on our lives. The acquaintance you met today may become one of your best friends in the months to come. The person you dated last weekend could become your future spouse. A classmate may end up being a professional colleague. To navigate your way through these encounters successfully—all the while maintaining a positive image of yourself—takes highly developed communication skills. This book should help you identify and develop those skills.

As the authors of this text we will use our own everyday encounters as examples. We will also use stories provided by students in a class we jointly taught on human communication. Both our own and our students' stories are real. These are not hypothetical examples. These life events happened to us or to people we know. The students' stories have enriched our understanding of the communication problems facing college students today. Some of these college students were living away from home for the first time, and some were adults with jobs and families they had to manage in addition to attending classes as nontraditional students. We found their own stories to be poignant, sometimes sad, sometimes funny, but always real. We hope you will find them the same way.

This chapter serves as the beginning of what we hope will be an adventure of self-discovery. As you read this book, try to keep your own personal relationships in mind and think about the effect your own communication style might have on others. We have already begun to look at the importance of our patterns of communication; in the balance of this chapter we will talk about:

- The definitions of communication.
- Characteristics of the communication process.
- The myths of communication.
- An historical perspective on the field of human communication studies.

You will notice, as you read, that we combine expert opinion with the opinion of college students, like yourself.

My roommate and I drove to school separately, with our parents, but conveniently arrived at the same time. Once everything was in our room, we noticed that we had two of all the major appliances—and that our parents had already left. We had all these things, nowhere to put it all, and no way to get rid of it. For one week, we had to keep all this stuff lying around, and then we each had to go home to drop off the extra computer, answering machine, television, and stereo. We had to spend our first real weekend of college at home. It was awful. That, I think, is a good example of how communication plays an important role in every day life. If Val and I had communicated better about our plans about what to take, we would not have had to deal with all those inconveniences.

— Jenny, first-year college student

Jenny learned very early in her relationship with her roommate how important communication was to making her life less stressful. Another one of our students also explained the importance of communication to his life:

I try to have a lot of interaction with my daughter. Typically we talk in the evenings before she goes to bed. Recently I had a sore throat and couldn't really talk much, so I had to listen while she talked. She started talking about school and since I didn't interrupt with my usual battery of questions she kept right on talking in great detail. As I listened I learned she was having trouble with another child in her class. It took her a long time to get to that point in her story, but since I never interjected my own thoughts or questions she finally got to the point she wanted to talk about. Because she brought it up it gave me an opportunity to help her come up with some strategies for dealing with this difficult situation. I wonder if I ever would have heard about it had I not had a sore throat. It certainly reminded me of how important it is just to listen to your children.

— Phil, nontraditional student

As a nontraditional student, Phil has to adapt his communication to a variety of settings: as a student, a dad, a husband, and an employee, to name just a few of his roles. His communication patterns change with each new setting and each new role he assumes. Thus, he makes hundreds of decisions every day about the appropriateness of his messages.

We know from many years of research that we spend about 75 percent of each day engaged in some form of communication, which means we daily make countless decisions about how to communicate effectively. Those decisions involve not only the message but the method we choose to deliver that message. More and more of our communication is mediated, meaning it is done through technology: E-mail, writing papers on computers, voice mail, interactive video games, etc. Regardless of the method, the challenge is to figure out how to ensure your message will be received as intended, and consciously to select the best method of sending it. Blaming misunderstandings on the listener, "Oh, you misunderstood," is not good enough. Whether you intended it or not, the message still had a certain impact. Because of the many consequences of our communication efforts, we need to increase our understanding of how the communication process works. We begin by working our way toward a basic definition of communication.

Definitions of Human Communication

Nearly 30 years ago one well-known communication scholar reviewed scholarly articles and textbooks and identified 95 different definitions of human communication (Dance, 1970). The number has probably more than doubled in the past two decades. The reason there are so many definitions of communication is the complex nature of this process. The art of expressing yourself involves many complicated physical as well as psychological skills. Therefore, we want to take some time to understand some of these processes.

Some of the common concepts included in Frank Dance's review of definitions are the following: a verbal process by which we understand others and reduce uncertainty through the use of symbols. Other definitions suggest that communication must be intentional. Although all of these concepts are important considerations, for the purpose of this text we will define human communication as shared meaning between two or more individuals using a symbol system. First of all, human communication is sharing or reaching a common understanding of a message between two or more people. (We will be discussing *intra*personal communication, or communication with your inner self, in Chapter 5, and group and organizational communication in Chapters 7 and 8, but for the most part we are interested in communication between two or more individuals). Second, human communication is based on the use of some sort of symbol system. We use symbols that have common meanings only because we have agreed that certain words will stand for the objects or ideas they represent.

In Figure 1.1 the process of communication is represented as intersecting circles. As humans move through their routines, they are constantly "bumping up against" other persons. It is when our lives touch each other that there is a chance for shared meaning. Each of our "bubbles" is made up of experiences, training or education, and individual background. The occurrence of successful interaction with another individual depends to some extent on the degree to which these "bubbles" intersect. That is why successful communicators are always looking for ways to find common links to the person(s) with

Figure 1.1 Communication Model   ❖ ❖ ❖ ❖

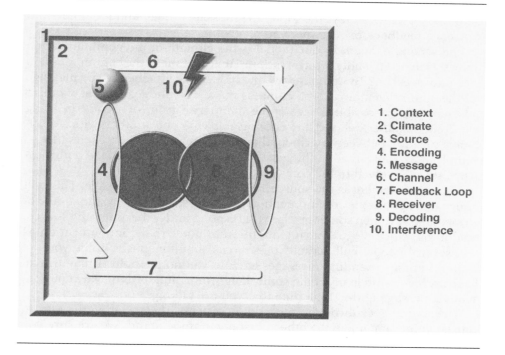

1. Context
2. Climate
3. Source
4. Encoding
5. Message
6. Channel
7. Feedback Loop
8. Receiver
9. Decoding
10. Interference

whom they are talking. The more we can connect on common topics, the greater the chance you will understand me when I introduce an uncommon or unfamiliar topic.

The message travels through a channel, or pathway, that includes written memos, a face-to-face conversation, electronic mail, television, and bulletin board postings. The sender of the message encodes the message: He delivers a thought or idea through some recognized symbol system, which the listener then must decode or translate into some meaningful message. The sender's and the receiver's level of experience, education, and training affects the encoding and decoding process. Accomplishing this process through the mass media (Chapter 9) or through some form of mediated communication (Chapter 15) is a large part of the human communication process today. The basic process is, however, pretty much the same as shown in the model.

The first element we focus on is the context of the communication. Everything else is affected by the type of relationship in which the communication is occurring. The context might be one person talking to one other person—a private, personal conversation that no one else overhears. That is certainly a form of communication different from a public speech, which is intended for a large audience and made accessible to anyone who wants to listen. Even in a small group, you are attempting to communicate simultaneously within several relationships at the same time. For example, if the group is made up of five people (Person A, Person B, Person C, Person D, and Person E), you could be attempting to maintain multiple relationships. You are Person A and you have separate relationships with each of the other people (i.e., A & B, A & C). There are also triads: you & B & C; you & C & D. And so on. Of course there are also pairs and triads that do not include you (B, C, & D). There are many conversations you are trying to maintain at one time. Therefore, the context for the communication will affect the topic, the message, the channel chosen, and how much feedback or response you receive.

The second element in our model is the climate of the communication context. Is this a "friendly" conversation? Or is the tone of the communication tense and stressful? By "climate" we mean feelings attached to the message and the communicators. Some climates make communication easy; others make it next to impossible. For example, compare a group of friends spending an evening together, relaxed and comfortable with one another, with a disciplinary meeting between a principal and a truant student. In each of these examples, the context will influence the tone of voice used and the body posture of those involved in the conversation.

The third element is the source, or the sender of the message. This will change throughout the communication event. First, you may be the source of the message and then someone else will respond and he becomes the source. In addition, since we are paying attention to nonverbal communication as well, several people will actually be sources simultaneously. While you are talking, I am also sending messages back to you nonverbally. I may frown, shake my head, shift in my chair, smile, laugh, or in hundreds of ways communicate a message at the same time that you are talking.

The source goes through an encoding process of translating the idea in your head into language the other person will understand. We are sure you have had the experience of knowing what you wanted to say but not being able to find the words to say it. You were experiencing an encoding problem.

We have already indicated that the message may be verbal or nonverbal, but it could also be mental. You may say "I'm glad to meet you," but you are looking away and acting nervous. In this case your message is being sent both through the words you speak and your actions. You may also have had occasions when you felt you were communicating with someone without actually saying the message out loud—you just knew what the person was thinking. As a society we have not fully explored our use of mental translation of messages, but there are certainly individuals among us who would claim that this is a very normal and common way to communicate.

The channel you select will have a dramatic impact on the message you are sending. You might use a memo, a phone call, face-to-face conversation, a meeting, a public forum, E-mail, or mass media. Choosing the wrong channel can have disastrous results. For example, a young man intends to ask his girlfriend to marry him. If he's not sure of her answer, proposing on the loud speaker at the halftime of a basketball game may prove quite embarrassing for both of them. Likewise, congratulating someone only via E-mail for a significant accomplishment may actually insult the individual. Nothing takes the place of a warm smile and a firm handshake. So, carefully select the channel that best matches the message your are sending.

The receiver goes through a process of decoding the message by translating it into his or her world experiences. The language of the message may have different meanings based on our life experiences. Our belief system, our values, our education, family background—in fact, everything that makes each of us a unique individual—shapes our encoding process and determines how we will interpret the message. Have you ever had the experience of paying a compliment to someone only to find out the person thought you were

being critical? In your experience, saying "Let's get together sometime" may
mean you are interested in spending time with the other person. But what
if that person has just broken up with a boyfriend who said, "I'm sure we
can be friends and even get together sometime"? Suddenly the phrase takes
on the meaning of a brush-off. Being sensitive to others' interpretations
of our messages is one of the most important skills demonstrated by effective
communicators.

The *feedback loop* occurs when you receive responses to your message.
Your memo may ask an individual to respond in writing; your smile and nod
of your head may indicate you'd like to hear what the other person thinks in
response to your statement; or your phone call may include the following
comment: "So, what do you think?" It may be difficult to communicate in a
large crowd because the feedback loop may be delayed. For example, the
authors have team-taught a class of 450 students. Feedback from students
may come days or weeks after a lecture. Even though we work hard at actually "engaging" the class, with that many people we hear from only a small
fraction of the students in any one class session. As mentioned earlier, feedback is often spontaneous and not specifically invited—or even welcome.
Some communication scholars refer to a "cough index" as indication of a
restless, unengaged audience.

Messages are always subject to interference. Interference may be physical, like loud distracting sounds, or psychological, for example when you are
worried about something else and are not really listening to the speaker. The
environment itself may interfere with the communication process. For example, you may be talking to a friend on the street corner and you are very cold
(physical interference). You would like to stay and talk, but you are missing
most of what is being said because all you can think about is how cold you are.
We also know that the size, shape, and color of the room you are in will affect
the content and the process of communicating. You may also be worried
about what a listener thinks of you and how he or she will interpret your
responses (psychological interference).

Finally, *timing* will have a dramatic impact on the communication process. If you are late meeting someone and a friend stops you to talk about a
project, you are probably only picking up part of the message. Or, if you have
just eaten a big meal, you may be sleepy and so the message may not come
through clearly. Therefore, the timing of the conversation, given all the other
things going on in your life, is critical. It would probably be more honest to
say to someone that you're not able to listen than to pretend to hear the message. Invite the person to talk with you at some other predetermined time.

In addition to these basic *elements* of the communication event there are
unique *characteristics* of the process that make it difficult to analyze precisely.
We will discuss these characteristics of communication next.

Characteristics of Human Communication

First of all, it is very difficult to discuss communication as if we could stop it in
process, hold it still for a few moments, analyze it, and then let it start again.
Three of the most obvious characteristics of communication are that the process is continuous, ongoing, and dynamic. This means the process never

stops. Even while we are analyzing a conversation we just had with someone we are already communicating a new message.

The process is constantly changing because who you were a few moments ago is not the same person you are at this moment. Each new fact or experience changes us in some way. From the moment we are born we exchange messages with other human beings. To be accurate, although it might be somewhat cumbersome, we should begin every sentence with "and," indicating that everything we say is actually a continuation of the previous message. We can never know a person totally because we cannot know what all that previous "talk" was.

Second, communication begins with the self. We cannot hope to communicate with others unless we understand ourselves and are comfortable with our own identity. *intra*personal communication (which is discussed in Chapter 5) is the study of our inner perceptions and self-concepts. The communication process begins with our view of ourselves and our place in this world.

Third, communication is irreversible or inerasable. This means once the communication event has occurred it will "color" all our future interactions. Did you ever wonder why lawyers introduce evidence that the judge immediately rules as inadmissible? Certainly one would expect that a properly trained lawyer would know full well what kind of evidence should not be introduced, but they do it anyway. That is because the jury hears it and retains it even though the judge tells them to disregard it. Can you look at a picture and then pretend you never saw it? Of course not. It has registered in your brain whether you want it to or not. Lawyers know this.

One of your authors recalls experiences where erasing the communication would have been desirable:

I can remember many occasions when I would have liked literally to "wipe the slate clean," hoping the person would forget what I had just said. For example, a friend of mine once congratulated a mutual friend on her pregnancy when she had actually simply gained a good deal of weight. All three of us were embarrassed and would have welcomed eliminating that remark from our memory. I also remember very clearly the day I saw an acquaintance of mine walking down the street with a limp. I had known this person for several years and I was surprised to see him limping. So, I said, "What happened to your leg, Jack?" and he replied, "It's just my bum leg, I've always had trouble walking." I had just not noticed before, or simply had not been in a position to observe his walking all the years I had known him. My thoughtless comment made him embarrassed and more uncomfortable. But there was nothing I could do to erase that comment. He and I had to live with it. I could add more comments or change the topic, but I could not eliminate from his memory the fact that I had noticed his limp.

Fourth, communication is reciprocal. When one person talks, this act stimulates a reaction from another person. It is very difficult to ignore talk directed at you. Try talking to someone in a context where people usually do not talk to each other: in an elevator (where everyone usually stares at the floor indicator and tries to avoid contact), waiting in line at the bank, or in the waiting room of an airport. If one person talks, the other responds. The process is reciprocal. Teenagers on a first date often have not learned this principle. As a consequence, the partners sit silently waiting for the other person to say something. When one of them finally has the courage to "break the ice" what a sense of relief they both experience. If I simply talk about things that interest me and ask the other person about him or herself the rest will take care of itself.

Fifth, communication is unrepeatable. It cannot be "staged" again. Have you ever tried to explain to someone a funny event that happened to you and you get a blank stare? Often we end such attempts by saying, "You had to be there." And we're right! You do have to "be there" to fully appreciate and understand the communicative event. We cannot recreate the experience for someone else. Telling of the experience pales in comparison to the actual experience. That is why teachers are frustrated when a student asks: "Did I miss anything when I was absent?" Of course you missed something!

Finally, communication is transactional. This means that it is going in multiple directions at all times. You are both a sender and receiver of the message at the same time. While I am talking you may be frowning, indicating that you do not understand or do not agree, which is a strong message even though you are not talking. A speaker is listening for signs of disinterest or feedback coming from the person to whom he or she is speaking. The process involves at least two people simultaneously performing the roles of speaker and listener. You are "listening" while you are speaking and the other person is "speaking" while you are listening.

Communication does not take place in a vacuum. It occurs in some kind of context or setting. There are four typical contexts in which you will engage in communication.

*Inter*personal communication is communication between two people—a dyad (Chapter 6). *Inter*personal relationships include best friends, dating partners or spouses, or you and a parent. You probably have hundreds of *inter*personal relationships ranging from those that are very close to you to those that are only acquaintances.

Group communication is communication among three or more people who have some common purpose (see Chapter 7). Any club or student organization you belong to probably fits this definition of a small group, as would a group of friends. In addition, you could consider your family a small group.

Organizational communication involves the human communication processes that occur in an organized hierarchy with common goals and individualized tasks. Your university is an organization, and your future employment will probably be in an organization of some size. As we will discover in Chapter 8, many complex relationships exist in organizations—including working relationships, friendships, reporting relationships, and co-worker connections.

Mass communication is communication by some sort of media such as television, newspapers, or the Internet. All of these contexts are affected by cultural differences. This may mean international differences or cultures within one country. At the same time, these contexts affect the content and the method of sharing meanings across and within cultures. Clearly the context can have a dramatic influence on how effective the message is.

All of the elements discussed are present in any transmission of a message. They actually help determine when communication has taken place. We would not support the view that all behavior is communication (i.e., a grumbling stomach may "communicate" that someone is hungry but it certainly is not a message intentionally sent by the "speaker"). We agree with G. Cronkhite "that there is a distinction between interpretation of nonsymbolic behavior . . . and communication achieved by symbols and the symbolic aspects of rituals" (1986, p. 236). In this text we will focus on symbolic behavior that is *pragmatic*, or has an intended purpose, and the effects those messages have on others. Thus, nonverbal behaviors that are arbitrary and have no intended meaning are not what we would call communication.

Even when valid communication takes place, it is not necessarily successful communication. Poor communication occurs when there is no intersecting of common experiences or meanings. Communication failures have been blamed for the breakup of marriages, world wars, and the increase in malpractice cases against doctors. A series of myths about the communication process contribute to these communication failures.

Communication Myths

There is one major obstacle to improving our communication behaviors: We all think we're pretty good communicators already! "I've been talking all my life, haven't I?" If that's the case, then why do we fight with friends? How is it that your parents accuse you of not listening? Why do some of us get overcome with stage fright before giving a speech? The answer is, there are commonly held myths about communication that inhibit our ability to improve.

Myth #1: As long as two people are talking, they should be able to understand each other.

Not true. Being able to "talk" is not the same thing as being able to communicate. Understanding occurs only when individuals share in it, or attribute the same or similar meaning to the messages. The word "communicate" actually comes from the Latin word *"communicare,"* which means "to make common." This means making the idea or message commonly understood among people.

Think of the times you have heard words but weren't listening to the message: a long church sermon, a boring class lecture, a political candidate engaging in political "babble," or an acquaintance who carries on a monologue. This is talk, not shared meaning or communication. Just because something is spoken doesn't mean anyone has actually heard it. The following dialogue illustrates this point:

Sue (to her son): "James, I really need some help around the house."

James: "OK."

Sue: "How about working on the kitchen with me."

James: "Um." (staring at the TV)

Sue: "Or, you could work outside in the yard and I could work on the kitchen."

James: "Um." (still watching TV)

Effective communication can make our lives less stressful and more fulfilling.

Sue: "I think we could get it all done in about an hour, OK?"

James: (no response)

Sue: "James, are you listening to me?"

James: "What?"

Sue: "Are you going to help or not?"

James: "Why are you always yelling at me?"

You can imagine where the rest of that conversation went. At no point was there any "shared understanding" although Sue was doing a lot of talking. Does this dialogue sound at all familiar to you? How many times each day do we "talk past" each other? How often have you tried to express your feelings to someone, but the message just didn't seem to get through? We should not assume that because "talk" has taken place any kind of understanding has resulted. It may take several messages, on several different occasions, with some dramatic attention-getting statement, to capture the other person's interest. It takes a great deal of work to ensure understanding.

Myth #2: As long as you have the 'right' message, it doesn't matter how you send it.

This is an incorrect assumption. When we are in a hurry we are most likely to believe this myth. We think that just getting the message out there means we have communicated and that it doesn't really matter how we have gone about sending the message. Instead, each of us needs to think carefully about the means of sending the message. We may have the "right" message but be sending it the "wrong" way. You may desire to send a message via E-mail because it's fast, but perhaps it is the kind of message that should be sent face-to-face (i.e., a change in job requirements.) Too many times we are more interested in getting the message to someone than in making sure the message is sent in a way that will generate the results we want.

For example, some of the least effective memos begin by providing a detailed history or background of the problem. By the time readers get to the main point they have lost interest. Worse still are memos that never clearly indicate what action the author wants the reader to take as a consequence of reading the memo. These memos usually end up in the "circular file" (the trash can). Getting the message out does not eliminate the sender's responsibility for shared meaning. The sender must consider very carefully the medium, or method, to be used to send a message. A memo may not be the most effective way to emphasize the importance of the message.

In one study on mediated communication, one of the authors interviewed corporate executives about the impact of computer-generated messages on *inter*personal relationships (Compton, White, & DeWine, 1991). One senior-level executive was retiring after 25 years with the company and became angry with his boss because he felt there was little recognition of his contributions over the years. "You mean there was no acknowledgment of your retirement?" the interviewer asked. "Oh sure, he thanked me for my service. But he did it by E-mail. He didn't even have the courtesy to walk into my office and shake my hand." For this individual, the inappropriateness of the medium negated the message that was meant to be a positive statement about his work. He left the corporation with no feelings of attachment or loyalty to the company. His self-image was negatively affected as well. All because he wanted a handshake instead of a computer-generated message. The message was right; the method was wrong.

Myth # 3: You can decide to send no message at all.

P. Watzlawick, J. Beavin, and D. Jackson (1967) proposed that there is no such thing as nonbehavior. They suggested that one cannot say that a message is only sent when it is intentional, conscious, successful, or when mutual understanding occurs. Consequently, when you are making a comment to one roommate, and another roommate overhears it, you are sending a message to that other person whether you intended to or not. When you attempt not to say anything, you are in fact sending a very loud message that you really don't want to talk! This is not communication as we have defined it in this book, but it *is* a message. In fact, as Michael Motley (1990) has pointed out, once we accept the fact that communication (1) is interactive, (2) involves encoding, (3) involves the exchange of symbols, and (4) has a range of high- to low-quality messages, then we must conclude that an individual can choose not to communicate. However, it is a myth to believe that you can decide to send no message. Sending a message is not the same thing as communicating. Communicating implies some form of shared understanding.

Your nonverbal behavior reveals messages constantly without your even being aware of them. Lawyers have perfected the art of detecting when witnesses are lying by watching their faces. It is by watching the witness' face, eyes, and body movement, that the lawyer can tell if he or she is uneasy. Therefore, you must be sensitive to the unintended messages you send as well as to the conscious ones.

Myth #4: More communication is always a good thing.

Too often the solution to a problem is defined as "more communication." Simply increasing the frequency of interactions does not guarantee success. Many times more communication is not helpful. When more angry words will be said and later regretted, when one person is already suffering from information overload, when the demands of the situation are such that individuals must respond quickly to a crisis, additional communication can be distracting and unhelpful.

Think of a time when you lost something precious to you. It may have been a family pet or even a loved one. Perhaps words seemed inadequate to express your grief. There are times when more talk does not communicate. Are there times when you just want to be left alone? It may be because you need time to "cool off" or to think. There are those individuals who believe more talk is always a good thing. We can think of individuals who constantly chat. There are times when we would like to shake them or yell at them to stop talking. Those are the moments when more talk is not a good thing.

Myth #5: Words have meaning.

The idea that words have meaning is incorrect. Words have meaning only because we agree that they have that meaning. The word itself does not have meaning and does not represent its referent (the object the word symbolizes) unless we arbitrarily agree to that representation. Instead of calling this object we sit on a "chair" we could just as easily decide to name it "siton." The word has no meaning in and of itself since the meanings are assigned in an arbitrary process. Therefore, there is great room for misunderstanding. Take the phrase, "I love you." The word "love" could mean:

- "I am attracted to you physically."
- "I am attracted to you psychologically."
- "I think of you as a brother."
- "You are really funny and I admire your creativity."
- and so on.

As you can imagine, these different interpretations can have huge effects on relationships.

Myth #6: Communication is a natural process.

The act of speaking is taught from the first words spoken to a baby. However, the art of communicating must be learned and practiced. We are not born with these skills as if they are some type of automatic reflex. Some of us are better than others at communicating our feelings and responding to others. But all of us can improve our skill at dealing with others and communicating clearly to them. That is the ultimate goal of this book and of the course in which you are currently enrolled.

History of Communication

Helping individuals communicate effectively has been the goal of communication scholars for hundreds of years. The human race established a system of communication that supported the development of society. Communication, as a field, began to emerge in ancient times and still serves as the foundation for much of what we believe about how human beings interact. Knowing something about these early writers will help you understand the principles outlined in this book. We invite you to imagine another time and place when the field of communication was just beginning.

Ancient Greece

The field of communication traces its history back over 2,500 years to ancient Greece when the spoken word was the dominant form of communication. Oral presentations were the most efficient way of spreading information and presenting legal and political arguments.

Imagine yourself in the following setting.

You cross the busy central marketplace in Athens, to attend the Lyceum, a school founded by Aristotle. Aristotle is a well-known philosopher and author on classical rhetoric, or the study of persuasion. You are training for public life, where you will defend your arguments in public in the ancient form of democratic government. Individual citizens must defend themselves in court without benefit of lawyers, so in a sense, each citizen must be a practicing lawyer.

However, if you are a woman, it is not appropriate for you to speak in public, and you are not allowed to attend schools of higher learning. There is a slight possibility you studied with Aspasia, the only known ancient Greek teacher of philosophy and rhetoric who was a woman. Allusions to her by other writers "help to confirm that Aspasia was indeed a real person, a teacher of rhetoric who shared her knowledge and political skill with [others]" (Jarratt & Ong, 1995, p. 10). Some scholars feel we cannot overestimate how extraordinary such behavior was for a woman in fifth-century, B.C., although women in earlier and later periods of history played a more public role.

If you are attending one of these schools, you listen to the philosopher/teachers' lectures in the open arena and you discuss philosophy, logic, ethics, and rhetoric with your classmates. Nearby, other contemporaries are engaged in athletic events and practice for war games because war is a dominant preoccupation in these times.

Aristotle, in his famous book *The Rhetoric*, defined rhetoric as having five
distinct parts:

- *Invention*, or finding all the available means of argument.
- *Arrangement*, or the way in which a speaker organizes the main points of the speech.
- *Style*, which is the use of language and phrasing.
- *Delivery*, or the presentation of the material and all the voice inflections and gestures.
- *Memory*, the ability to remember all the major points without the use of notes.

Attention to audience analysis began here. Insisting that the speaker
adapt what is said to the particular audience being addressed is a critical
canon of rhetoric. Storytelling, dramatic performances, and poetry readings
by actors and orators became dominant forms of entertainment. These individuals were honored and respected (see Cooper, 1932).

In ancient Greece the status of a speaker was just as important as what
was said. The Greeks often confused authority with being right: because you
were in a position of authority, you were right. Conley (1990) suggested that
"public discussion, where options were debated and consensus sought, was
evidently the traditional way in which decisions were reached" (1990, p.2).
However, it was not only the argument that counted. "The status of the
speaker who presented the argument is all important" (p. 2). So, while we like
to refer to ancient Greece as the birthplace of democracy, all men and women
were certainly not equal.

There were those who argued for more equality. Plato, for example,
implemented two basic principles that placed rhetoric, or the art of persuasion, at the forefront of Greek public life. He argued that (1) power should
reside in the people as a whole and (2) high offices should go to those who are
selected by the citizens as the best individuals for the job. These were revolutionary ideas that ultimately placed persuasive speech at the center of the new
democracy.

> In civil disputes, persuasion established claims where no clear truth was
> available. Persuasive speech, too, could depose or empower tyrants,
> determine public policy, and administer laws. The public speaker was
> inseparable from the business of government and civic affairs, and early
> on some enterprising orators turned to teaching the art of persuasive
> speech as well as practicing it. (Bizzell & Herzberg, 1990, p. 2)

These "enterprising orators" were called Sophists. They were intinerant,
or part-time travelling teachers. When a democratic form of government was
implemented in 450 B.C. they were in great demand. The typical political
structure built around clans and families was replaced with a system of representative government, which cut across all former barriers of influence.
These teachers traveled from one town to the next teaching the skill of argument. They were severely criticized for not seeking the truth and instead practicing what some saw as the tricks of persuading others. However, the Sophists saw themselves as problem solvers.

❖ ❖ ❖ ❖   ## The Roman Empire

The Roman Empire actually copied much from the Greek culture in establishing Roman court systems and laws. Cicero emerged during the time of the Roman Empire as one of Rome's most famous orators. After Aristotle, Cicero is known as the next great rhetorician in the classical tradition. His work, *De Inventione*, is probably the most widely read book next to Aristotle's work. In this book he describes how one might use amplification and heightened emotion in the political arena. He had a reputation as a brilliant lawyer in Rome. Although he was not a teacher, he became known as a prolific writer, producing seven treatises on rhetoric during his lifetime.

Quintilian was the last prominent classical philosopher. He is well known for his definition of rhetoric as "A good man speaking well." Note the emphasis on the "goodness" of the individual speaking as well as the quality of the address. He made his name as an outstanding teacher. His book *The Institutes of Oratory* was the most widely used text from the Roman period. During these classical times rhetoric was central to each citizen's life, but as we move into the medieval period we find rhetoric and argument receiving far less attention.

Medieval Rhetoric

The Middle Ages refers to the period from the fall of the Roman Empire to the Renaissance. During this time public deliberations disappeared and those in power made most decisions. Augustine, a bishop, was well trained in the classical tradition and applied it to the teaching of Christianity. His famous work, *De Doctrina Christiana*, was one of the best known books from this period. For the most part the rhetorical teachings from Greek times were lost during the medieval period and only the Christian Church maintained some interest in intellectual pursuits. Later in this period the study of grammar emerged and an interest in language was expressed in the form of letter writing.

Renaissance Rhetoric

During the Renaissance, from the fourteenth to the seventeenth centuries, city-states developed, and some of the central principles of political rhetoric were restored along with them. Rhetoric and science were emerging as new fields of study. By the end of this period people seemed less interested in the eloquence of language and more interested in how arguments were constructed. Humanism, which focused on the importance of philosophy and human achievement, taught citizens to combine philosophy and political ideals in their writing and oratory. Humanism spread throughout Italy, France, and England. Sir Thomas More led this movement in England. Sir Francis Bacon, a sixteenth-century philosopher and courtier, wrote on acquiring knowledge for its own sake. He helped renew interest in democratic argument which flourished during the seventeenth to nineteenth centuries.

Enlightenment Rhetoric and Twentieth-Century Rhetoric

In the seventeenth to the nineteenth centuries knowledge greatly expanded in the areas of science, philosophy, and politics. The elocution movement focused on delivery, supplied instruction in pronunciation, and began the focus on nonverbal language. A focus on persuasion again emerged. Literary societies began in the early eighteenth century, and at some universities belonging to such a society became a graduation requirement. Students were encouraged to participate in declamation (public speech), composition, debate, and the modes of conducting business in deliberative assemblies. These events were sponsored by the literary societies, which were early forms of debating societies, where issues of a more historical nature were discussed and debated. One university "felt so strongly about the importance of student participation in these societies that it said as late as 1904 that 'no student will receive a diploma who has not been a member of these societies at least a year'" (Boase & Carlson, 1989). Later, debating societies tackled current events and argued as teams. Well-known authors of Enlightenment rhetoric include John Locke, George Campbell, Hugh Blair, and Richard Whately. A Whately scholar, R. E. McKerrow, has noted, "Whately's *Elements of Rhetoric* is well known for its classification of argument types, its doctrines of presumption and burden of proof, and its forceful defense of the 'natural manner' of delivery" (1988, p. 211).

As we move into the 1920s and 1930s, English and speech departments were separated as the interests in both fields began to diverge, and research in the areas of rhetoric and persuasion flourished. I. A. Richards, a scholar of language, became required reading, and his book *The Philosophy of Rhetoric* continues to be a key work in the area of language and symbol systems. Kenneth Burke, in his well-known books *A Grammar of Motives* and *A Rhetoric of Motives*, discussed how discourse influences motives. Chaim Perelman and Richard Weaver became leading rhetorical scholars of the 1950s and focused on the ethics of argument. Perelman, in particular, identified the structure of argument as claims, supporting evidence, conditions, and assumptions. With his structural outline one could develop a sound argument.

Today, college English departments are developing a renewed interest in teaching writing as the public demands that college graduates increase their skill in writing. Speech departments still maintain the study of rhetoric as their base but have developed new areas of study:

- Organizational communication, which focuses on the human potential in organizations through human resources management.
- *Inter*personal communication, which examines communication patterns in the family, the dyad, and small groups.
- Legal communication, leading to the study of law or as communication consultants to the legal profession.
- Health communication, or the study of communication within the health-care context.

All of these new areas of study have as their base the analysis of all available forms of persuasion and the impact of messages on both the sender and the receiver.

In the last century we have experienced dramatic revolutions in the workplace. The transistor, photocopier, and personal computer changed just about everything at work, as well as at home. These inventions happened at work, often while groups were looking for answers to entirely different problems. Warren Bennis of the University of Southern California argues that "one is too small a number to produce greatness" when revolutionary inventions are designed. At DuPont it takes up to 250 ideas to generate one major, marketable new product. At Pfizer Inc., the yield is one new drug out of 100 possibilities. Success therefore, takes risk-takers, shared information, and communication among and between all types of employees. At 3M the scientists and engineers can spend up to 5 percent of company time on their own projects, without ever telling managers what they're up to. DuPont researchers may pursue their blue-sky ideas one day a week and Xerox has instituted mandatory weekly meetings where everyone takes turns describing their ideas.

— *Newsweek*, Winter, 1997, p.26

What do you think?

- *What kind of environment limits your creativity?*
- *What policies might be put in place to insure that the myths of communication discussed earlier in this chapter do not interfere with creativity?*
- *How does interacting with others help you come up with new ideas and creative solutions to problems?*

In this book you will be introduced to all the above-mentioned areas of communication study and practice. We will discuss intended and unintended communication in verbal communication (Chapter 2) and nonverbal communication (Chapter 3). A series of skills to encourage effective listening will be discussed (Chapter 4) and how perception affects our understanding of others is developed (Chapter 5). This material lays the groundwork for a series of chapters on various communication contexts: *inter*personal relationships (Chapter 6), small groups (Chapter 7), organizational communication (Chapter 8), and mass communication (Chapter 9). Understanding cultural differences is an important concept that changes communication in all of those contexts (Chapter 10). Other communication skills include resolving *inter*personal conflicts (Chapter 11), understanding reported research (Chapter 12), preparing public presentations (Chapters 13 and 14), communication and technology (Chapter 15), communicating in the courtroom (Chapter 16), and applying all these communication skills on the job (Chapter 17).

From Greek times to the present, it is critical that each person be able to articulate ideas to others in written or oral form. Those who cannot meet this challenge can be severely limited in today's society. This need to be articulate will only increase with the challenges of the twenty-first century, when information dissemination will become a dominant career field. This book should help you meet the challenge of the twenty-first century.

Summary

Communication is shared meaning between two or more individuals using a symbol system. The model of communication presented in this chapter included context, climate, source, message, channel, feedback, receiver, interference, and timing. Communication is continuous and ongoing, begins with the self, and is irreversible, reciprocal, unrepeatable, and transactional. Communication contexts covered in this book include *inter*personal, small group, organizational, mass media, and cultural. A number of myths of communication interfere with successfully getting the message across: as long as people are talking, they should be able to understand each other; as long as you have the "right" message, it doesn't matter how you send it; you can decide to send no message at all; more communication is always a good thing; words have meanings; and communication is a natural process.

A brief history of the field of communication begins with ancient Greece and a famous philosopher, Aristotle. The five parts of rhetoric were discussed: invention, arrangement, style, delivery, and memory. Cicero and Quintilian were well-known authors of the Roman Empire, and Augustine's rhetorical teachings developed during the medieval period. During the Renaissance, Sir Thomas More and Sir Francis Bacon led the Humanism movement in England. The Enlightenment period and the twentieth century produced a number of rhetorical writers who are still used today as foundation for further study of rhetoric and communication.

At Your Bookstore

Adams, S. (1996). *The Dilbert Principle*. New York: Harper Business.

Griffin, E. (1991). *A First Look at Communication Theory*. New York: McGraw-Hill.

Kavanagh, K. H., & Kennedy, P. H. (1992). *Promoting Cultural Diversity*. Newbury Park, CA: Sage.

Tannen, D. (1990). *You Just Don't Understand*. New York: Ballantine Books.

Tedford, T. L. (1985). *Freedom of Speech in the United States*. New York: Random House.

CHAPTER 2

Communicating Verbally

At the difficult age of 12, I found myself in a foreign land. My father had accepted a position at the University of Illinois, and we decided to move our family to the United States. Having grown up in a small town in Scotland, I was a little overwhelmed by the thought of moving to such a strange place.

Upon arrival, I embarked on the hardest task of my life to date. I had to learn to adjust my way of life so that it would fit into my new environment. Of all the adjustments to be made, something as simple as the way I spoke proved to be the hardest transition. This was something that I really hadn't given much thought to; it seemed trivial to me. But not so for all the other eighth graders.

I recall my first day at my new school. The teacher took attendance, but my name wasn't on the attendance sheet. She asked if anyone's name wasn't called. I raised my hand, she asked me my name, and pandemonium broke out as the other students laughed. Oh no, that guy is different; he's not like us! It sounds silly now, but in eighth grade, it isn't cool to be different. Here I was, trying to fit in, and before anyone judges me, I am condemned to unpopularity by an accent.

I think this had a huge impact upon my life. I immediately became self-conscious about my dialect and practically said nothing to anyone. As a result of my seclusion, I missed out on so many things. . . . Anyone who's moved to a new town might be able to understand the hardships of trying to fit into a different school. Not to mention that this town was in a different country.

— Dave, second-year college student

The rock band **INXS** (1987) once noted that "words are weapons, sharper than knives," knowing all too well that the things we say can be used to hurt others. Dave learned the hard way that people are likely to judge others both by what they say and by *how* they say it. Speaking a particular dialect did not seem to matter to Dave until it made him distinct from his American classmates. Unfortunately, scenes like this one are common. As students of communication, we need to understand how the verbal message affects the communication process. When communication scholars talk about verbal communication, they are referring to a number of things, including the words we use when we talk and the marks we use to communicate through writing. As you examine some of the underlying concepts in verbal communication in this chapter, consider how the judgments we make about how others speak or write are based upon each of our own imperfect experiences with language. Perhaps if Dave's classmates had thought more about how conditional or variable their own language usage was, they would have been less likely to judge him so quickly. In order to help you think about the variable nature of language and its impact on verbal communication, this chapter:

- Introduces concepts surrounding the nature of language.
- Points out some concrete strategies for reducing confusion.
- Suggests ways to make responsible and sensitive choices in your own language usage.

Figure 2.1 Symbol Communicating Access for Those Who Use Wheelchairs or Are Otherwise Differently Abled

Understanding the Nature of Language

Words Are Symbols

The first thing we need to be aware of is that words are symbols. A symbol is something that stands for something else. Symbols are tools humans have invented to convey meaning. Consider the symbol of a stick figure sitting on a semicircle (Figure 2.1). To a person who uses a wheelchair, this symbol placed on the door of a restroom means that a facility is accessible to someone who is differently abled. To a driver, this symbol painted on an empty parking space means that he will have to keep driving around the lot. To a small child who has never had this icon explained to her, this symbol might have no significance initially. As you can see, a symbol can have more than one meaning to more than one person.

Of course, the same symbol can have more than one meaning to the same person. Drivers are taught that a red traffic light means to stop, and most drivers consistently agree on this meaning. However, does a yellow traffic light always get the same interpretation? When faced with a traffic signal that has turned yellow, some drivers speed up so that they can pass through the intersection before the signal turns to red. Yet if a police cruiser were following the same driver, he might slow to a stop. Why? Obviously, conditions influenced the driver's interpretation of the symbol, even though the symbol itself was the same. As this example further illustrates, a variety of meanings are possible with a given symbol.

Cultures throughout the world, including the American, are filled with all kinds of symbols, including traffic signs, hand gestures, and horns—all of which communicate meanings. For now, we will focus on the nature of meaning within language. Even as the traffic light, the high five, and the alarm clock are human inventions, so are words. In short, words are the symbols that have been developed by cultures to represent objects, concepts, actions, characteristics, and conditions. We call a collection of words, and the accompanying ways in which they are interrelated, language. There are several characteristics of language you need to be aware of in order to understand how people shape meaning through it.

Language Is Arbitrary

How much do you dread getting a paper back from your professor with numerous red marks scrawled across it? Few of us look forward to having our language skills criticized, and yet we accept the authority of instructors to enforce a standard of usage. Culturally accepted practices such as this encourage within us a bias that there is one right way to use language, and, typically, we as individuals haven't mastered it. Institutions such as our schools convince us that we need to distinguish between the right way and the wrong way to pronounce, use, and spell words. In actuality, no one "right" way exists in language. Instead, what we observe are the conventions of a particular language.

Language conventions are the socially determined practices of usage. Such conventions are achieved whenever a culture agrees to follow a particular set of rules. People have no compelling reason to call the nocturnal insect that produces a soft light either a firefly or a lightning bug. Either term, *firefly* or *lightning bug*, is arbitrary. The only reason we call it one or the other instead of calling it a *bright bug* is because groups of people have agreed upon one name or another. People who live in the southern portions of the United States tend to call it a *firefly* while those in the northern states typically call it a *lightning bug*. No biological difference exists between those bugs in the South and those in the North, but the name of the luminescent creature differs because of differing language conventions.

Meanings Are in People

Words, then, are essentially empty vessels waiting to be filled by people who assign meaning to them. *Firefly* is merely a collection of sounds uttered or letters on a printed page until a person mentally relates the word with the glowing insect.

The tenuous nature among a thing, the idea of the thing, and the word is explained in I. A. Richards and C. K. Ogden's triangle of meaning. Within the triangle, which shows the relationship between an object and how we think and speak, *firefly* is a symbol. When you hear or read the symbol, your mind links the idea of the thing to the reference that is stored in your memory. Ideally, this reference corresponds with the thing, in this case the firefly.

However, as your own experience with language can probably confirm, not all symbols prompt a reference to the intended thing. A visitor from the South who has never heard a firefly called a lightning bug will not know what you are talking about without further elaboration. Thus, the relationship between a symbol and the thing is represented by a dotted and not a solid line in Figure 2.2. Often we are frustrated when the words we use do not convey the meanings we intend. This is because meanings are found in the people who assign them to symbols and not in the symbols themselves.

Figure 2.2 Ogden and Richards' Triangle of Meaning

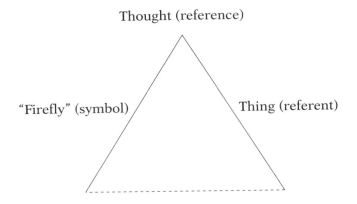

Source: I. A. Richards and C. K. Ogden (1946). *The Meaning of Meaning.* Harcourt Brace & World.

Thus, no word has an inherent meaning. Even onomatopoeic words, which attempt to imitate the sound of a natural phenomenon, can represent more than one referent. For example, the word *buzz*, used to describe the sound made by a bee, can be used to describe the sound made by an alarm clock, even though the two sounds have obvious distinctions to the ear. Likewise, many other words have multiple meanings, some of them as a matter of language convention and others as a matter of group or personal association.

The accepted meaning a word has for the majority of the population is its denotation. It is helpful to think of a denotation as a meaning that would appear in the dictionary. For instance, the word *mass* is used later in this textbook to talk about a large number of people. However, words can have multiple denotations. *Mass* can also refer to the amount of matter an object possesses, or to a religious ceremony. That words can have more than one agreed-upon meaning can be a source of confusion for communicators.

The meanings of words can be further complicated by the connotations, or the particular associations that people have with a word. Connotations arise when an individual or a group begins to associate a meaning or attitude with a word. This connotative meaning may or may not have anything to do with its denotative meaning. The word *broccoli* denotes a green vegetable, one that connotatively suggests a healthy treat or an unpalatable plant, depending on your personal disposition. People often describe connotations in terms of a positive, neutral, or negative response. Some people assign a negative connotation to the phrase *mass media* because they associate television, radio, and print with commercial interests that want to encourage greed and consumption among the public. Other people who do not view the mass media as quite so devious think of this as a neutral term. Obviously, connotations differ from individual to individual, but their effects can undermine the denotative meanings over time.

Such a transformation took place with the word *gay*. During the last several centuries of its use, *gay* was an adjective used to describe qualities of happiness and lightness. Popular sentiment dubbed the last decade of the nineteenth century "the gay 90s" because of the carefree nature of those times.

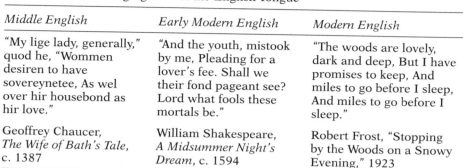

Figure 2.3 The Changing Face of the English Tongue

Middle English	Early Modern English	Modern English
"My lige lady, generally," quod he, "Wommen desiren to have sovereynetee, As wel over hir housebond as hir love."	"And the youth, mistook by me, Pleading for a lover's fee. Shall we their fond pageant see? Lord what fools these mortals be."	"The woods are lovely, dark and deep, But I have promises to keep, And miles to go before I sleep, And miles to go before I sleep."
Geoffrey Chaucer, *The Wife of Bath's Tale*, c. 1387	William Shakespeare, *A Midsummer Night's Dream*, c. 1594	Robert Frost, "Stopping by the Woods on a Snowy Evening," 1923

During the latter half of the twentieth century, however, people began to assign the connotative meaning of "homosexual" to the word. Even though most dictionaries still list "carefree" as a possible definition for *gay*, most people would agree that the dominant denotative meaning is now "homosexual," and more specifically, male homosexual.

Language Changes

The above example is just one illustration of how every living language is in the process of change. Not only are meanings subject to change, but users are constantly adding and abandoning words, altering meanings, refining pronunciations, and changing spellings within their language. Just compare the language used in the most recent episode of your favorite sitcom to the language used in any one of William Shakespeare's comedies to see what drastic changes English has undergone in the last 500 years. Forsooth, *Seinfeld*, a show about naught, wouldst sound odd indeed in the tongue of an Elizabethan.

Even the conventions of language undergo transformation over time. During the last century the standards of English grammar have demanded that when referring to a person of unknown gender, the unspecified individual should be referred to with the masculine pronoun *he*. This was not always the case. Sharon Zuber and Ann M. Reed (1993) note that prior to the nineteenth century, use of the pronoun *they* was acceptable as a gender-neutral term. *They*, grammarians insisted, was the plural pronoun and thus unacceptable to use by the rule that pronouns should agree in number with their antecedents. In 1850 the British Parliament passed an act that made *he* the preferred pronoun in such cases. Today, scholars are questioning this standard because it excludes the participation of well over half the population. Singular *they* is already a feature of our oral language, and despite the protests of some staunch grammarians, might ultimately become acceptable in written forms as well.

Language Is Guided by Rules

Despite the fact that it is dynamic, language is also governed by rules. In other words, even though we have seen how words change over time, the structures that govern their use follow certain rules that are less likely to change in short periods of time. Here we are not referring to the arbitrary rules established by academics such as "*i* before *e* except after *c*" but those rules that guide the formation of a collection of words into a structured statement. Syntax is the arrangement of words in statements. Despite the fact that words vary a great deal among persons, places, and times, syntax is comparatively regular within language families.

Steven Pinker (1994) suggests that language is an instinct to acquire an art. Normally functioning human beings are born with the ability to learn a language, what some have called the Language Acquisition Device, but people must be fostered in one particular language before they reach adolescence if they are to grasp all the intricacies of a given language. Thus, Rumanian orphans adopted in their infancy by American parents will grow up to speak Standard American English. The way that a child's mind organizes the structures of language is influenced by interaction with those around her. From the time humans are in the womb, communication is influencing the way we think about reality.

Even though much of what Shakespeare wrote in the sixteenth century may sound strange to the twentieth-century ear, the formations behind Shakespeare's statements are essentially the same as those that guide us today. In English, as in most other Western languages, one typical pattern consists of a subject, or a doer, and a predicate, or an action: "The firefly glows."

This underlying pattern can be adapted to countless applications, none of which the user needs to rehearse. In other words, when you learned to use language, you did not memorize every possible sentence you ever intended to use. When you learned to speak, for instance, you could not have memorized all the sentences necessary to talk about the World Wide Web—in no small part because the technology had not even been introduced yet. Before you could surpass the state of being a "newbie" and develop your own "homepage," you had to learn some new terminology. You are able to incorporate new words into your syntax, or sentence arrangement, because you learned the *structure* of your language and not just its *vocabulary*.

Every Language Possesses a Structure

The structure of one language may not parallel that of another. Such is the case with Ebonics, a variety of American English once called Black English. In 1996 the Oakland, California, school system announced that it would begin offering courses in Ebonics, and critics stepped forward to challenge the decision. Some believed that teaching Ebonics contributed to the deterioration of Standard American English (SAE). However, as we have already discussed, language doesn't deteriorate, it merely changes. Other critics—among them civil rights activist Jesse Jackson—voiced a different concern: They felt that legitimizing Ebonics could prevent African American youths from learning SAE and keep them from having access to careers where a mastery of SAE would be expected.

Jackson and his supporters had a legitimate point: Language is often associated with power. Historically, the people who have had the most power in a given society have also determined what counts as proper language. Those who lacked the standardized vocabulary and pronunciations were considered illiterate, uneducated, or simply unintelligent. Given such a practice of linguistic discrimination, people who were not educated by the powerful classes could rarely gain access to jobs that would allow them to transcend their poverty.

Such is the case with the development of grammar in England. The British aristocracy, worried that the growing merchant class threatened their social position, imposed a complex system of rules and regulations upon the English language in order to keep the lower classes from having access to the social position afforded by mastery of the standard. Early grammarians superimposed the rules of Latin grammar upon English and thus justified arbitrary rules that still plague English speakers today. For instance, in Latin, because of the way words combine, it is impossible to have a preposition at the end of a sentence. However, native speakers know that English allows for such a placement without losing any meaning. Winston Churchill, the prime minister of Great Britain during World War II, mocked this arbitrary rule when he purposely contorted his syntax to quip, "That is something up with which I shall not put."

The arbitrary rules of class-based grammar have been perpetuated in America. Americans wish to believe that they are a classless society. However, linguistic prejudices are as prevalent in America as those concerning race, religion, or gender. Part of this problem stems from the myth that there is a "standard" American English. In fact, no language has a standard, and everyone is speaking a dialect. A dialect is a variation of a given language spoken by a group of people.

For instance, individuals who grew up in Boston, Dallas, and Los Angeles all pronounce the simple word *car* in noticeably different ways. Different parts of North America were settled by different nationalities. As each nationality adopted American English, it subtly influenced the pronunciation of words within a given geographic area and enriched the American lexicon, or collection of words, with new contributions. The Appalachian mountains, for example, were settled primarily by Scots. Today many Appalachian natives omit the terminal *g* in some words in their speech so that *talking* is pronounced *talkin'* and *walking* is *walkin'*. But these speakers have not *dropped* a letter from their pronunciation: Their Scottish forebears never got around to adding it. While a dialect may be indicative of a person's geographic background, it actually tells you very little about a person's intelligence. Our stereotypes about dialects handicap our ability to make more accurate assessments of people's abilities.

Spoken Language Differs From Written Language

Part of the reason we believe in a standard is because English is a written as well as a spoken language. However, it is a mistake to assume that the standards imposed upon written language need to apply to spoken language. The misconception that the two should coincide emerges from a belief that because writing is more permanent than an oral utterance, language can be fixed, or set, for all time. But we know that even though written language has changed little since the invention of the printing press, spoken language has continued to evolve. Although we still spell the word *knight* as our English-speaking predecessors did, we no longer pronounce the *k*, *g*, or *h*, as they once did. As we have seen, words not only change over time, they also change over space. People from Boston, Dallas, and Los Angeles might agree to spell *car* the same, but they certainly aren't obliged to say it the same.

Another misconception suggests that written language is superior to spoken language. However, of the world's more than 6,700 languages, most have not been committed to writing (Grimes, 1996). Are those languages without writing systems inferior to those who have them? Certainly not. Obviously, a number of cultures have been able to use the technology of writing to assist them in developing their cultures in a specific way. Walter Ong (1982) notes that in print-based cultures such as ours, people tend to be more individually focused and linear in thinking. *Oral* cultures tend to be more group-focused and recursive or circular in thinking. Our perception of print-based superiority is rooted in the fact that we come from a print-based culture, but both approaches have their merits.

In communication studies, you will find that you will be studying both oral and written language. Understanding what people have to say to one another at a party, trying to get information about a bank account, or consoling a friend—these are important parts of connecting with others. Likewise, understanding how someone says something matters, too. Communication studies as a social science focuses on these kinds of verbal issues. But communication studies address other forms of symbolic communication as well. We call any collection of symbols a text, and that includes written memos circulated within a company, a movie like *Independence Day*, or even an event like a parade or a place like Disneyland. Rhetorical studies within the field of communication pay attention to a variety of texts to see how people communicate using both words and other symbolic forms of communication. Ideally, neither written nor spoken language should be privileged above the other. Instead, we should look at *all* forms of symbolic communication as having merit and being worthy of our investigation.

One example of a text filled with symbolic meaning is found in the powerful impact of the original location for the movie *Field of Dreams*. Following the movie's popularity at the box office, thousands of people from across the nation visited the site in Dyersvukkem, Iowa. Surprisingly, the over 25,000 people who visit the site yearly do so without the site being advertised or having a charge for admission. In fact, the site is not closely supervised.

> Instead, the site is left much as it appeared in the film save for some wearing down of the grass and the presence of two souvenir shacks operated by the friends and family of the owners of the fields. Visitors make their own parking spots, create their own "tours" of the site, and spend as much time as they want doing whatever they want, whether it be playing ball, visiting the cornfield, or sitting in the bleachers enjoying the activity. (Aden, Rahoi, & Beck, 1995)

These visitors are connecting to a place, to a text that carries for them rich, symbolic meaning.

Reducing Confusion With Verbal Messages

Communicators can express a multitude of emotions through verbal messages. The words we choose can comfort or condemn, alarm or allay, inspire or incense. Negotiating how we can make our language work for us is perhaps one of the earliest lessons we learn. Most children quickly understand that their cries will get their parents' attention. As we grow older, and our symbolic communication grows more complex, we tend to develop other strategies to communicate our needs to the world around us. However, what may be perfectly clear to us may be confusing to another. The use of devices such as abstraction, euphemism, idiom, jargon, and slang can confound the verbal messages we want others to receive. We need to be aware that these subtle miscommunications can impede our ability to make successful connections with others. Let's look at each of these in turn.

Abstraction Increases Uncertainty

One of the best ways to clarify your intended meaning when communicating with verbal symbols is to be aware that language operates at several levels of abstraction. The more abstract or removed from concrete, specific reality a word is, the greater the opportunity for slippage in the interpretation of meaning. If I mention having read a "book" I could be referring to any one of millions of titles. You are left wondering if I read a textbook, a novel, a biography, or some other form of printed material. *Book* is a far more abstract term than say, *Chicken Soup for the Soul*. If a friend confides in you that she just met a cute guy, there are a significant number of interpretations for you to make about this guy. Is he short or tall? Is he pale or tanned? Does he wear eyeglasses or not? The abstractness of the word *guy* doesn't help you identify the individual very well. Abstraction operates like a telescope. An abstract term, like a telescope with a big picture of the sky, is open to a wide field of vision. However, if you were to sharpen the focus on the telescope to get a better view of a particular star, it would be like narrowing your terms to restrict slippage in meaning.

To compensate for abstract language, skillful communicators use descriptive language. The key to descriptive language is that it is rich with details. Instead of the abstract "guy" she met, your friend could have described, "Sean, a 22-year-old political science major from New Jersey who looks just like George Clooney." Obviously, being more concrete, or specific, in your language choices has benefits in professional situations as well. Microsoft reports that numerous computer users call their help lines because they are unable to find an "any" key when prompted to "press any key."

Euphemisms Color Language

In some cases, abstraction is intentional. Euphemisms are used with the intent not to offend others with harsh words. We use euphemisms when discussing topics that cause fear or embarrassment. Euphemisms substitute for a number of controversial topics such as death (*departed*), sex (*sleeping with*), and firing (*downsizing*). Hugh Rawson (1995) indicates several principles that guide the formation of euphemisms, among them:

- Foreign phrasings sound finer (thus we eat "filet mignon" not "charred meat").

- Bad words are not so bad when abbreviated (thus you can BS with an SOB).

- Indirection is better than direction (thus you wear *unmentionables* beneath your street clothes).

A friend who declares, "I'm all tied up," does not mean to be taken literally.
She is using an idiom, a phrase in which the words' collective meaning
differs from their individual meanings.

Although euphemisms serve a purpose in attempting to uphold the sensibilities of polite society, the act of abstracting from the source can make meaning unclear. Because they perpetuate the limitation of knowledge, euphemisms frustrate the effective communication of ideas.

Idioms Are Greater Than the Sum of Their Parts

Sometimes, the confusion caused by a lack of communication clarity is humorous, as in this case reported by an exchange student:

I arrived in the United States two years ago thinking I could communicate spoken English with no problem. However, it took me a short time to realize how wrong I was. Coming from Buenos Aires, Argentina, where Spanish is the first language, I never learned slang.

Only 10 minutes after arriving to the airport, a couple of Argentinean students and I met our ride. He smiled and said, "What's up?" We all looked up at the ceiling, and without finding anything, we replied, "Not much."

> After going through numerous situations like this, I realized how important it is to know the everyday language as well as the culture of a place when you need to establish intercultural communication.
>
> — Sebastian, a third-year college student

As you will see again in subsequent chapters, communicating across cultures can be particularly challenging. Even people who take the time to learn the vocabulary and syntax of another language can still be frustrated by the idiom of another tongue, just as Sebastian was. Idioms are those phrases whose meaning cannot be understood by the meanings of their separate words. If you've ever studied with a foreign exchange student, you know that idioms can be a source of confusion and humor for these second-language users. Recognizing that your invitation to "hit the books" implies studying—rather than pounding on your textbooks—comes with greater immersion in a language.

Idioms are just one of the ways in which both the variety and arbitrariness of language use can complicate human communication. A native speaker of American English knows full well what he intends to communicate when he suggests his friend "hit the books," but his foreign colleague may not fully understand what the American is trying to convey. Like most of us, the American student cannot recognize the peculiarities of his language choices until his foreign colleague asks for clarification or points out the humor in such a statement. The more familiar we are with a particular language, the more difficult it is for us to express its more subtle meanings with those outside our linguistic community.

Jargon Limits Access to Messages

A linguistic community is any distinct group of language users. You don't have to visit a foreign country to observe different linguistic communities interacting. The people all around you are embedded within linguistic communities. Consider the specialized vocabulary, or jargon, of any professional. Healthcare, legal, and finance professionals all have specialized vocabularies they use when communicating with others in their profession. Truck drivers are another example of a linguistic community which shares a specialized vocabulary. To the uninitiated, terms such as *smokey* and *hammer down* hold little relation to the concepts of *police* and *speeding*, but they are easily recognized by those familiar with the trucking industry. It should be noted that people who are members of any one linguistic community can simultaneously be members of other linguistic communities as well.

A truck driver, for instance, can also be familiar with the jargon of chess players and heavy metal fans. However, on the radio with a fellow trucker, he is less than likely to use terms such as *pawn* or *checkmate*. But when he arrives at a chess tournament, he will readily set aside his trucker jargon for the more formal style of a chess competitor. The process of changing one's language use from one linguistic community to another is called code-switching.

You could think of people who code-switch as being bidialectic. After all, they are able to speak two or more versions of the same language. One of these languages might be for talking around the house with family members and

C. B. operators are among those groups that have developed their own specialized language, or jargon, for communicating among themselves.

the other for talking around the construction site with co-workers. Code-switching is characterized by a number of factors, including differences among the words used (vocabulary), the way words are pronounced (phonology), the arrangement of words (syntax), and the topics discussed. People who have grown up in economically depressed communities but have gone on to improve their socioeconomic standing have learned how to code-switch. Someone who can discuss the virtues of the latest Andrew Lloyd Weber production on Broadway but still "play the dozens" in Harlem has mastered code-switching.

Almost everyone engages in code-switching at some point. After all, few people communicate exactly the same way in all situations. For example, competent communicators rarely talk with their significant other as they do with a police officer. Code-switching is a communication strategy in which we use language to negotiate our social relationships.

Slang Frequently Changes Meaning

Another type of specialized, and characteristically informal, language is slang. Slang tends to be less enduring than other contributions to language. Some slang terms do end up as part of vocabulary, and others fade after a short period of use. In the 1980s you could hear numerous primary school

MISSION: POSSIBLE

From your family to your fraternity, every group you are a part of is its own linguistic community. If we accept that the Sapir-Whorf Hypothesis is right and that language helps shape our perceptions, then each of these groups is contributing to how you see the world.

Beginning with your primary social unit, your family, and continuing through your various scholastic, social, and community affiliations, list as many different linguistic communities as you can recall. Then return to your list and record at least one word or phrase used that is unique to each.

When you have done this, ask yourself: Would the phrase recorded in one column be understood by members of another group of which I am a member? How have you mastered the techniques of code-switching in each group?

students exclaiming, "Cowabunga!", a slang term introduced by surfers and made popular through the Teenage Mutant Ninja Turtles. Needless to say, few people are still chanting "Cowabunga!" today. Many people mistakenly label nonstandard words as slang. For instance *ain't* is not a slang word. Although its usage may be considered nonstandard, according to the *Oxford English Dictionary* the word itself has been a part of the English language since at least 1778. Slang terms may be regarded as nonstandard, but unlike some other nonstandard terms, slang is always in the process of change. What had been considered *hot* in the 1950s had become *cool* in the 1960s, as slang meanings changed to suit the definitions assigned by one generation after another.

A second characteristic of slang is that it, like jargon, limits inclusion. The slang of one group within a culture may not be used by another. College students make up one group, which develops its own slang. Terms for the processes of socializing and dating recognizable among people attending college are often unrecognizable to those in different life situations. Although a sophomore may think that a particular classmate is a "hottie," an older "townie" may not understand that she thinks that a person who dates a lot is attractive. That each generation of young adults tries to create new words for dating and socializing indicates these words' importance to that particular culture.

The Sapir-Whorf hypothesis suggests that cultures develop language in ways that prioritize relevant experiences to them (Pinker, 1994). College students use far more terms to describe their dating experience than do senior citizens, because college students feel dating is more of a priority than senior citizens do. This does not mean that senior citizens can't understand what their grandchildren are talking about, but the Sapir-Whorf hypothesis suggests that they are less likely to develop their language on that topic simply because it isn't as much of a priority to them.

As familiar as we are with our own verbal practices, it frustrates us when we fail to make connections with other people who speak the same language we do. Even though languages are shared among numerous people, they are used by individuals who shape them according to their own needs and desires. In your efforts to become a more effective communicator, you should understand the potential pitfalls that exist within language structures and strive not to misuse abstraction, euphemism, idiom, jargon, and slang in your verbal messages.

Developing Cultural Sensitivity Through Verbal Decisions

The recent move toward politically correct language reflects this same concern for establishing and carrying forward cultural priorities through language. Political correctness has gained a negative connotation among those who think it is an attempt to abridge the freedom of speech. Satirical comments such as James Finn Garner's *Politically Correct Bedtime Stories* (1994) point out the absurdity of attempting to reshape language to extremes. It seems impractical and wordy to call a short person "vertically challenged." *Political correctness* has become such a loaded term that its objectives have largely been forgotten.

Perhaps a better way to conceptualize the objective of respecting other people's identities through language can be expressed as cultural sensitivity. Culturally sensitive people respect the linguistic identity of other cultures and co-cultures, especially when considering how these groups wish to be viewed and described through language. A co-culture is any group of people existing within a dominant culture. Thus, your religious affiliation, ethnicity, and even your own family are co-cultures existing within the larger American culture. At the minimum, cultural sensitivity means choosing not to refer to different races, lifestyles, or genders by derogatory names or slurs. You could probably cite a dozen or more derogatory names for females, such as "chicks." By electing to refer to women as "chicks," an individual contributes to the perpetuation of a view of women as weak and dependent upon another—just as a young chick is upon a hen. Women such as Maya Angelou, Diane Feinstein, and Oprah Winfrey are certainly neither weak nor dependent on another. To call these or any women "chicks" undermines what women have accomplished in the arts, politics, and communication. In addition, such a label is insensitive in that most women are fully aware of the connotations this word carries with it and would not choose to be called by it.

Language Is Power

The power to name is one of the key ways in which the powerful enforce their domination over the powerless. By calling people of African decent African Americans rather than Negroes, we demonstrate a sensitivity—a respect if you will—for the identity they have chosen for themselves. Consider how you might feel if someone you never met misnamed you. Suppose your name was William, and you went by Bill but absolutely hated to be called Willie. How would you then feel if someone you just met started calling you Willie? Now imagine if instead of your name, people were mislabeling you according to your home town. Such insensitivity hurts the receiver of such messages and erects barriers to more effective communication. By sharing the power to name among people, and acknowledging everyone's right to fix his or her own identity, we express the principle of cultural sensitivity and thereby promote good will among communicators.

Figure 2.4 The American Sign Language representation for *man* features a gesture near the forehead while that for *woman* is near the mouth.

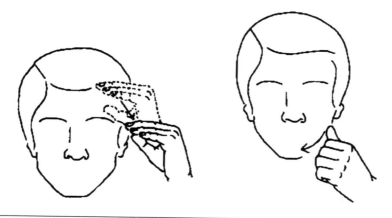

Sexist Language Undermines Equality

One way in which we can all demonstrate greater cultural sensitivity is to be aware of choices we make. Obviously, we all make mistakes, sometimes without even realizing it. That's why an important part of developing cultural sensitivity has to do with learning more about people who are different from us. Another is to be aware that American English is filled with biased terminology.

A lot of familiar phrases reinforce sexist language—language that perpetuates stereotypes about people's genders. Sexist language does not always appear as blatantly as a term like "chick." Instead, it can work upon our collective psyches in a far more subtle manner. One can even find examples of sexist language's subtleties in American Sign Language (see Figure 2.4). References to anything masculine is signed near the area of the head closest to the brain, but feminine references are designated closest to the mouth. Presuming that men are smarter and that women are more talkative subtly encourages the belief that stereotypes are accurate.

In general, the repetitious use of sexist language reinforces the notion that fundamental differences exist between the genders and that these differences make one gender superior to the other. Thus, although advice such as "boys don't cry" and "girls just want to have fun" may not be intended to promote inequality between males and females, the gradual repetition of literally hundreds of such statements ultimately convinces some people that difference and subordination are natural.

Culturally sensitive users of language monitor their statements to check for such differences. While there are many references to women, like "cookie," "tomato," and "peach," few such consumable references exist for men. These terms are blatantly sexist, and even phrases which portray themselves as gender-neutral are not. The generic use of "man" to describe all *Homo Sapiens* does not suggest "womankind" in its use. Thus, job descriptions have evolved into more inclusive forms: *fireman* has been changed to *firefighter* and *policeman* to *police officer*.

Strategies Can Compensate for Bias

As a competent communicator moving into the twenty-first century, you will want to be particularly sensitive to the choices you make. Consider using some of the following strategies when adapting your communication to non-sexist standards.

1. In either your speaking or writing, seek gender-neutral pronoun references when dealing with non-gender-specific individuals. The simplest way to accomplish this is to make your examples plural: "Students should submit their homework on time" rather than "Every student should submit his homework on time."

2. Substitute inclusive terms for gender-specific ones. A great deal of progress has already been made turning *mail men* into *letter carriers* and substituting "Men at work" signs for "Workers ahead" signs. Be conscious of the fact that no job is suited for one gender over another. Let your language choices reflect that men can be nannies and women can be professional wrestlers.

3. Do not assume that any task, activity, or condition is exclusive to either gender. Is road construction, quilting, or a headache the prerogative of one gender more than of the other? Some women are perfectly capable of doing "men's work," and football great Rosie Greer knits. As you communicate with others, let them know that you think accomplishment is something achieved through individual character and not determined by someone's sex.

4. Resist the temptation to assume you know the gender of an individual. Whether you are in the process of composing a letter to a potential employer, or in the midst of a conversation, rather than assume the gender of an individual, ask for clarification. If you are writing to a person you have not met, call that person's office and ask for the proper form of address. However, you can rarely go wrong by addressing someone by his or her job title, such as director, coordinator, or vice president, rather than gender-specific Mr. or Ms. In less formal situations, ask your conversation partner if someone named "Pat" is female or male rather than assume the gender.

5. Avoid loaded terms that demean human dignity. No one wants to be referred to as an animal or an anatomical feature. Demeaning men to "beef" and women to "broads" robs them of their individual dignity and makes you appear disrespectful to others.

Unlike our nonverbal communication, some of which is unconscious activity, we have a great deal of control over our verbal communication. Knowing that sexist language perpetuates social injustice, we can all be more aware of the choices we make in everyday communication situations. The power of language is something we are all influenced by and use to influence others. But because every power bestows upon the user a responsibility, it falls to you to strive for greater clarity, concern, and compassion in your verbal messages.

Summary

Verbal communication is concerned with the way in which we use words, either spoken or written. Words are symbols, representations of something else. Even though we recognize certain conventions among users of the same language, all meaning is in people, not in the words they use. We can identify denotative meanings shared by the majority of a population, but we cannot know all the connotative associations people individually ascribe to words. Given time, of course, the usage of language changes. Yet even though the superficial rules of a language might change, all language is governed by rules, guided in its arrangement and construction by mechanisms in the mind. This results in a recognizable structure though not necessarily the one prescribed by grammar handbooks. Moreover, spoken language differs from written language.

Given the mutable nature of language, competent communicators strive to reduce confusion in their verbal messages. Needless abstractions reduce the accuracy of what a speaker says and should be replaced with more descriptive language. Euphemisms color messages, idioms frustrate those unfamiliar with them, and jargon limits access to those uninitiated into a particular linguistic group. Learning to code-switch when moving from group to group helps one to compensate for specialized languages like jargon and slang. The Sapir-Whorf hypothesis suggests people prioritize relevant experiences through language.

Realizing that power relations are reflected through our verbal messages should encourage us to move toward greater cultural sensitivity, respecting the linguistic identities of others. By monitoring the biased terminology in our own language and by adopting strategies that purposefully counter sexism, we can avoid demonstrating disrespect for others through sexist language.

At Your Bookstore

Eble, C. C. (1996). *Slang and Sociability: In-group Language Among College Students*. Chapel Hill, NC: University of North Carolina Press.

Elgin, S. H. (1993). *Genderspeak: Men, Women and the Gentle Art of Verbal Self-defense*. New York: John Wiley & Sons.

Hulit, L. M., & Howard, M. R. (1997). *Born to Talk: An Introduction to Speech and Language Development* (2nd ed.). Boston, MA: Allyn & Bacon.

Milroy, L., & Muysken, P. (Eds.). (1995). *One Speaker, Two Languages: Cross-disciplinary Perspectives on Code-switching*. New York: Cambridge University Press.

CHAPTER 3

Communicating Nonverbally

In my many years of participating in various athletic events, I have witnessed many examples of communication, both verbal and nonverbal. The best example of communication and its importance is in baseball. Baseball involves a great deal of communication without spoken words.

In baseball, the majority of the coaching is done through motions and nonverbal messages. For example, the act of touching the bill of a baseball hat may be a signal from coach to player to steal a base. These actions vary in order to relay different messages. It is these signals that enable the coaches to communicate with one another and the players on the field.

Another example of this unspoken tongue is when the coach or manager goes to the pitcher's mound and touches his right arm and points toward the bullpen. This signal indicates that the bullpen coach is to send in the right-handed pitcher. These unspoken signs are a very effective form of communication, even though the conventional thought is that communication involves words.

— Ramon, third-year college student

As Ramon explains, our communication is not limited to words only. Just as coaches and players in a baseball game rely on hand gestures and signals to communicate information across a playing field, we too rely on nonverbal messages to create common connections with others. Nonverbal communication refers to all nonword messages that we transmit from person to person. In many ways, nonverbal communication is the most powerful form of communication that we, as human beings, have at our disposal.

The old cliché, "A picture is worth a thousand words" illustrates this point. Remember back to the women's gymnastics competition of the 1996 Olympic Games. As the last gymnast on the United States team left to compete, Kerri Strug needed to complete the vault to give her team the gold medal. The world watched as on her first attempt she severely injured her leg on a maneuver. With one more run to go, the world waited breathlessly as she hopped in agony to the end of the mat, completed the run despite being in excruciating pain, and earned her team the gold. Did Kerri Strug need to explain to you the pain, shock, and pressure she was feeling? No, it was evident in her posture and facial expressions. And even though she later talked about what she experienced with reporters, we needed only to look at her grimaced face and see her tear-filled eyes to understand her pain. Sometimes words just can't communicate enough of what we're really feeling.

When you use nonverbal methods to send messages, you are using the most basic—and often the most believed—form of communication available. Imagine that your friend asks you how you're coping with the loss of your grandparent. Although you reply "Just fine," a tear silently trickles down your face. This nonverbal message—a tear—says something very different. However, even though they may have more impact than verbal messages, nonverbal messages may also be the most ambiguous. Can a tear communicate more than just sadness? Of course, tears are used to communicate a variety of feelings in human beings, from sadness to frustration to outright happiness.

In this chapter, we'll look more closely at this powerful but implicit form of communication that involves more than just words.

- First, we'll begin by discussing the similarities and differences between verbal and nonverbal messages.
- Then, we'll see how nonverbal messages function in our everyday communication.
- We'll study different types of nonverbal messages including how distance and space, body movement, touch, objects, and clothing have the potential to send very important messages. Even silence is indeed golden in its power to communicate.

Verbal vs. Nonverbal Messages

Similarities Between Verbal and Nonverbal Messages

In the previous chapter, you gained a better understanding of verbal communication and language. Perhaps the best way to help you understand nonverbal communication is by comparing it to what you have already learned about verbal messages.

How is nonverbal communication similar to verbal communication? First, both forms of communication are generally considered symbolic although not all communication researchers agree upon this entirely. If you say that you have a small tan dog named Abby, you're using symbols to stand for a pet you own. The words you use to describe your pet—small, tan, and dog—have agreed-upon symbolic meanings that paint a picture in your mind of what Abby is and looks like. J. K. Burgoon and T. J. Saine (1978) explain that nonverbal messages become symbolic when they represent an abstraction. When you see someone smiling (nonverbal act) and attach meaning that the person is happy, a symbolic link has been created because the nonverbal act has served to represent the abstract thought "happiness."

Another similarity between verbal and nonverbal messages is that they are both individually produced. The messages that we send are, in a sense, personal and subjective. The rhythmic tapping of your feet when you're excited is individually produced. In another person, this same tapping may be a nonverbal gesture done to indicate boredom or frustration. Interestingly, research on twins and triplets shows that they often develop a language of their own: The verbal messages that they devise are subjective and personal to them and their siblings.

Finally, both verbal and nonverbal messages are subject to interpretation. In both message forms, what you say and what you do must be interpreted by others. The people we interact with attach meaning to our verbal and nonverbal messages and alter their behavior accordingly. If a woman tells her fiancé that she has called off the wedding (verbal message) and he begins to cry (nonverbal message), they are both interpreting messages and acting accordingly. In these ways, it is possible to see the characteristics that verbal and nonverbal messages share. Both are symbolic, individually produced, and subject to interpretation.

How Nonverbal Messages Differ From Verbal Messages

Although nonverbal communication is similar to verbal communication in certain respects, it is also quite different in important ways (see Figure 3.1). Nonverbal communication is:

- More primitive.
- More uncontrollable.
- More believable.
- Continuous.
- Unstructured.
- More widely understood.

Nonverbal communication is a more primitive form of message-sending than is verbal communication (Hickson & Stacks, 1985). Some researchers believe that nonverbal communication is innate, that we are born with certain nonverbal understandings. For example, usually it takes a baby a year or longer to learn simple utterances like "Da Da" or "Ma Ma." To learn verbal communication, a child needs advanced muscle development and socialization. This is not the case with nonverbal communication. From the moment babies are born, they begin to communicate nonverbally through smiles, cries, yawns, and shrieks. Is the ability to smile when happy or frown when sad learned through imitation of parents and other adults, or is it an innate ability? Does anyone ever tell a child how to smile or how to frown? Not really, so perhaps nonverbal communication is an innate form of communication.

To further back up the claim that nonverbal communication is innate is the fact that biological forces govern many of our nonverbal actions. In many—but obviously not all—instances, our nonverbal messages are often more uncontrollable than our verbal communications (Hickson & Stacks, 1985). If a rude stranger cuts in front of you in the checkout line at the grocery, what can you do? When faced with a situation like this, you have several options. You could politely ask her to move or you could swear at her loudly. Generally, you have more control over these verbal actions than over the nonverbal messages you might be sending. Even if you remained silent, your clenched hands and blushing face indicate that you are really angry with that stranger. Although you may have chosen to do nothing to communicate your anger to this person, many of your nonverbal actions—like shaking, blinking, blushing, and trembling—can communicate loudly despite your intentions.

Nonverbal messages have considerable impact and can be more believable than verbal messages. When verbal and nonverbal messages contradict each other, you are more likely to believe the nonverbal message. Psychologists and counselors must practice this every day in their jobs. When individuals seek a professional to hear their problems and concerns, they are expecting the psychologist or counselor to be an attentive listener. If the counselor is avoiding eye contact, drawing pictures in a notebook, and turning away from the patient, the patient may believe the nonverbal message ("I'm not interested in what you're saying") over the verbal promise that the counselor made ("I'm here to listen to your concerns").

Another characteristic of nonverbal communication is that it is a relatively continuous process, whereas verbal communication is more discontin-

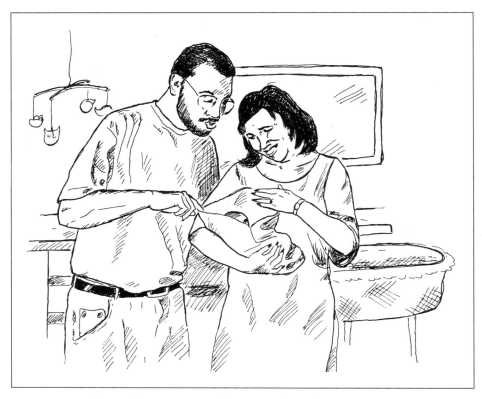

*Nonverbal messages are the primary form of communication
for infants until they develop verbal skills.*

uous. Verbal communication is composed of disconnected units broken down into words, phrases, and sentences. Each word and sentence has a distinct beginning and end. Unfortunately, it is not quite as easy to turn off nonverbal messages. We cannot turn off nonverbal messages being sent, such as when we wear certain clothing or have body odor. Someone who is speaking loudly in the library can quit speaking instantaneously, but someone with foul body odor on a hot humid day in a crowded subway car will continue to send that message until he or she leaves your physical presence.

Another interesting characteristic of nonverbal communication is its unstructured nature as compared to that of verbal communication. Language follows a specific linguistic structure, such as rules of grammar. As children, we must be taught that in English a verb follows a noun. It takes us a while to understand this and you can often hear young children confusing the sentence structure saying, "Go I to the store." The structured nature of language is readily apparent if you try to learn a new language. For example, when English speakers learn Spanish, they may be confused by the grammatical rule that adjectives follow the word they describe. In English, the adjective *red* would precede the noun *book* to say "the red book." However in Spanish, the adjective *rojo* would usually follow the noun *el libro* to say "el libro rojo." On the other hand, nonverbal communication tends to be more unstructured. There really is no book of grammar for nonverbal communication. For example, waving to someone does not follow the same structure or rules of grammar as a verbal message does. Waving your hand could mean that you are say-

Figure 3.1 Similarities and Differences in Nonverbal Communication

Characteristic	Verbal Messages	Nonverbal Messages
Symbolic	X	X
Individually produced	X	X
Subject to interpretation	X	X
More primitive		X
More uncontrollable		X
More believable		X
Continuous		X
Unstructured		X
Widely understood		X

ing hello, or that you are saying goodbye, or maybe even that you are flagging someone down for help. In this sense, we can't assume that waving your hand has a predictable pattern of meaning for a community of people.

Lastly, nonverbal messages are often more widely understood than verbal messages. Sometimes, nonverbal messages help us understand one another when other forms of communication fail. In particular, when we do not speak the same language, nonverbal methods may be the only hope for communication. Two communicators with different language backgrounds can still communicate through nonverbal gestures, expressions, and messages. Like a game of charades, it is possible to communicate your thoughts and feelings without uttering a word. Sometimes verbal messages are just not understood. For example, in the following story a student discovered that nonverbal messages helped her communicate when verbal messages were ineffective:

This past summer I lived in Virginia and taught a special education summer school session for autistic, severely retarded, preschool crack babies and emotionally disturbed children. Due to the fact that the majority of my students could not communicate verbally, I had to find other ways to communicate effectively with them. I quickly learned that eye contact was important. The students needed direct attention and contact in order for them to understand that I was talking to them.

I also learned other physical cues to help the students understand my requests. I learned to get through language barriers effectively. I realized how important it is to have different approaches to explaining something in order for different audiences to understand your point.

— Alyson, second-year college student

As Alyson discovered, she was able to communicate a mountain of information to her vocally and psychologically challenged students using nonverbal means (Heimlich & Mark, 1990). In this case, nonverbal messages were able to reach an audience that could not comprehend and decode language.

❖ ❖ ❖ ❖   ## The Functions of Nonverbal Messages

Now that we've talked about some of the similarities and differences between verbal and nonverbal communication, let's examine how nonverbal messages function in our everyday lives. Researchers believe that nonverbal communication serves several purposes in our communication (Burgoon & Saine, 1978). Nonverbal messages serve the following functions:

- To repeat.
- To complement.
- To contradict.
- To substitute.
- To regulate.

Sometimes, nonverbal messages work alongside verbal messages; other times nonverbal messages work entirely alone to generate meaning. For example, one way that nonverbal communication is used in our lives is to repeat or reinforce a verbal message. Repetition is used to clarify or explain a verbal message better. An example of this can be found when speaking to a child. If you ask a child how old he is, he will often give his age and hold up his stubby fingers to emphasize the point. A three-year-old will reply "Three" with three fingers. The gesture of holding up three fingers clarifies how old the child is and repeats the verbal message. However, this nonverbal message could stand alone. When asked how old he is, the child could simply hold up three fingers without a verbal accompaniment.

In a similar way, nonverbal messages may also work to complement the verbal message. Unlike the repeating function, nonverbal complements cannot stand apart from verbal messages, but rather they accentuate or add information to the verbal message. If you tenderly reach for your loved one's hand and look deeply in his or her eyes after proclaiming "I love you," you are using a nonverbal complement. The nonverbal gesture of reaching for someone's hand and making direct eye contact accentuates your verbal expression of affection. Even technological advancements in communication have not stopped us from using nonverbal signs and symbols to communicate. An entire code of symbols has been devised by Internet users to explain their words in cyberspace with more emphasis and feeling. For example, if you write in an Internet chat room that you're happy about your current relationship, you might follow it up with an appropriate symbol like :) to indicate your internal happiness. Complementing through a nonverbal message adds information or impact to a verbal message.

Sometimes our nonverbal messages contradict our verbal messages. As we've already discussed, when your nonverbal and verbal messages are contradictory, listeners are more likely to believe the nonverbal message. In this way, the nonverbal message may negate the verbal one. A fourth-grade teacher of one of the authors was a master of nonverbal contradiction. When the class was disruptive, the teacher would turn his back to the chalkboard and wait silently. To break the uneasy silence, a student might ask, "Mr. Fuller, are you angry with us?" to which he would always respond in a normal tone, "No, I'm not upset." However, nonverbal cues would lead the class to believe otherwise. Mr. Fuller's jaw would be clenched tightly and the veins on his neck would grow purplish in color. Although he verbally stated that he wasn't angry, the author and her classmates knew they were in big trouble and had better quiet down quickly.

❖ ❖ ❖ ❖

What other functions do nonverbal messages provide for us? Nonverbal messages may also serve as substitutes for verbal messages. In many instances, nonverbal messages are substituted for verbal messages because of the environment or noise level. For example, if you've ever attended a public auction, you've seen substitution in action. Whether the auction was to sell cars, Van Gogh paintings, or household furnishings, bidders at an auction substitute nonverbal gestures for verbal statements. The reason for this is purely practical. If an auctioneer has 300 people in attendance, it would be quite chaotic and disorderly to have each person call out a bid. Other bidders wouldn't be able to hear above all the noise. Instead, bidders use paddles or their hands and face to bid: The nonverbal substitution might come in the form of raised fingers for one bidder and a head nod for another bidder. Whatever the preferred nonverbal gesture is, the bidders have indicated their interest to the auctioneer, who visually manages all of these nonverbal messages in a more systematic way than if everyone were to call out their bid.

Another function of nonverbal communication is to regulate verbal communication situations. In a conversation, how do you know when you should talk? Often, the other person may use nonverbal cues to give you "permission" to speak. Nodding the head encourages someone to keep talking, indicating that you are listening to his or her ideas and thoughts. Attorneys understand this principle quite well. Sometimes in courtroom questioning, attorneys will use nonverbal movements to regulate a witness' testimony. If an attorney wants a short, abrupt answer from the witness, he or she might say, "Thank you" while turning away from the witness at just the right moment. The verbal message, combined with the direct body movement, stops the witness and cuts the testimony off at a strategic point.

As we've discussed in this section, nonverbal communication plays an important role in our lives. Because it is our most basic form of communication, we rely on nonverbal messages heavily. Even though language may be considered a more sophisticated form of communication, we still cannot help using nonverbal messages to repeat, complement, contradict, substitute for, and regulate our verbal messages. In these ways, verbal and nonverbal communication may work together as people try to make those common connections and strive to understand one another better. In the next section, we will talk about specific codes in nonverbal communication and how you communicate using each of these codes on a daily basis.

Communicating Through Space and Distance

Proxemic Communication

How far do you stand from someone at a party? If you whisper in the ear of a friend at a party, are you communicating your interest in that person or telling a secret you don't want anyone else to hear? The messages that you are sending may be interpreted differently from what you intend. You may just be passing a juicy rumor, but your conversation partner suddenly thinks that you are romantically interested. How could such a miscommunication occur? We

Breaking norms of behavior can be exhilarating, embarrassing, and even dangerous. But you can test the concept of territoriality and space by breaking norms of behavior in acceptable ways. For example, you can test territoriality norms in your college class. About halfway through the semester, observe where people sit in the classroom. After a few days of observation, you'll probably notice that you and other students tend to sit in the same general area and even the same seat day after day. If you arrive early once and sit in the seat of someone who appears to be particularly used to sitting in that same chair, watch the reaction that person has when he or she enters the classroom and sees you. Unless you have assigned seats, there really isn't any reason why anyone should feel territorial about a particular seat, but we do. You could even tell the person afterwards about your "social experiment" just to get his or her perception of why they sit in the same seat and how the person felt seeing you in "his" or "her" seat.

Figure 3.2 Categories of Distance

Category	Distance	Example
Intimate Distance	0–18 inches	Two close friends greeting each other
Personal Distance	18 inches–4 feet	Colleagues eating lunch together
Social Distance	4 feet–12 feet	Manager conducting formal business
Public Distance	12 feet+	Speaker addressing an audience

Source: Adapted from Hall, E. T. (1969). *The Hidden Dimension*. Garden City, NY: Anchor Press/Doubleday.

could say that it occurred because of differences in perceptions of space. The study of how people use space and distance to communicate is called proxemics. Proxemics refers to how space and distance act as a nonverbal code in human communication encounters. Does it make a difference whether you stand two inches or four feet away from a prospective employer during an interview? Of course it does and in this section we'll be talking about why a two-inch distance and a four-foot distance would send very different messages.

Edward Hall's (1969) interest in how people use space and distance to communicate resulted in a classic description of four categories of distance:

- Intimate.
- Personal.
- Social.
- Public.

These spaces apply primarily to communicators in the United States, although co-cultural group variation will exist (see Figure 3.2).

First, let's look at intimate distance. Hall believed that people maintain an intimate space around them (0–18 inches). This space is reserved for only those people who are relationally close to you such as your closest friends,

SPOTLIGHT ON DIVERSITY

When students from other countries attend college in the United States, they are often puzzled by Americans' behavior when they talk to them. They don't understand why Americans may take a step backward or walk away during conversations. The reason for this behavior involves the concept of personal space. The personal space, or distance that we use for conversation with a companion, varies according to culture. In India, Hindus stand about 3 to 3 1/2 feet apart when talking. Ecuadorans and Argentineans have a closer conversation distance than do people from the United States and Canada, often talking with their hands on the other person's clothing or shoulder. And, if the listener were to step backward to increase the distance, the Ecuadoran or Argentinean would likely step forward to close the distance and maintain proximity. What if someone from Argentina and someone from Canada were speaking to each other, but were unaware of the differences in personal space in the respective cultures? What comes to mind is a peculiar dance of two people engaged in frantic stepping backwards and forward, each in an attempt to maintain what the other perceives as appropriate personal space.

What do you think?

1. *Have you ever noticed cultural differences in perceptions of space when communicating with others*
2. *What occurs when people are uncomfortable with the distances that their conversation partner is maintaining?*

family members, and romantic partners. You'll let your romantic partner enter your intimate space without much thought because you have certain feelings and attractions to that person that you don't have for other people. By allowing someone into that space you're conveying a certain level of intimacy and comfort. That is why it would be highly inappropriate to walk up to a potential employer and stand two inches away. Not only could it lose the job for you, but the employer might think you were a little unstable for "getting in her face" like that. There are times, however, when we allow people with whom we don't have a personal relationship to enter our intimate space. For very practical reasons, we let our hair stylist, physician, and shoe salesperson enter our intimate space at will.

The next smallest space we occupy is our personal space. Personal space is the distance used for conversation and nonintimate communication (18 inches–4 feet). Personal space is the bubble of space you keep around you. It is the distance you maintain between you and other people. A 1994 episode of *Seinfeld* made light of the concept of personal space in a humorous way. In the episode Julia Louis-Dreyfus' character Elaine has a new beau, played by Judge Reinhold, whom she named the "Close Talker" because of his habit of invading her personal space and talking very close to her face. As Elaine discovered, this bubble of space is very important to human beings and we protect this space ferociously. Think about the last time you were at the library. If you were seated at a table, you probably spread out your books, papers, and backpack in a circle around you, indicating to others that this is "your space." In doing this, you have indicated to others thinking about sitting next to you that you need to have this much space around you to be comfortable.

Hall's other levels of distance refer to the distances that you maintain in more formal and less personal situations. Social space is the 4-12 feet space that you use with strangers, or other people you might interact with at the store, the office, or in school. Imagine again how far you would stand from a potential employer. Norms of your culture would dictate how far you would stand from that employer. The norm in the United States would be to not stand too close to a personnel manager or boss that you've just met. Instead, the most comfortable distance for communicating with a potential employer you just met would fall somewhere between 4 and 12 feet.

And finally, public distance (over 12 feet) is the space that occurs in larger communication contexts, such as the communication that exists with a lawyer arguing in a courtroom or a professor speaking to a class. Public distance connotes less personalization and more formality on the part of speaker and listener.

Territoriality

Another interesting component of proxemic communication that we hinted at above is the concept of territoriality. Territoriality is the tendency to stake out a space or territory that you believe is your own, just as an animal stakes out its territory. Dogs urinate on trees and fire hydrants to leave odor-laden messages about their status, sex, and age. They tell other dogs to stay out of their territory. While human beings don't usually go around marking their territory in the same way, we do use nonverbal messages to stake our claim. Do you sleep on the same side of the bed each night, and refuse to let your bed partner switch sides with you? Do you sit in the same seat in class day after day? If so, you're expressing territoriality.

A good example of territoriality occurs when two people move in and live together in common housing, whether through assignment in a residence hall or through marriage or other relationships. Individuals use territoriality in these situations to establish their own identity and communicate that identity to others. A student living in a residence hall might cover every inch of her side of the room with neon green paint, posters, and pictures. A newlywed might be angered by his wife's desire to move his Michael Jordan life-size poster from the living room to the basement. The message being communicated in these cases is clear: "These possessions are part of my identity and this is my territory!"

Communicating Through Body Movement

Facial expressions and gestures are among the most important nonverbal communication tools we have. Just as a picture is worth a thousand words, so too is the smile on a child's face after winning first prize in a computer contest, or the OK sign flashed when an astronaut returns safely from the latest space shuttle expedition. Our faces and bodies have great communicative power. Kinesics is the study of the potential that posture, movement, gestures and facial expressions have for communication purposes (Birdwhistell, 1970). Some people refer to kinesic communication as "body language." But just as we learned about verbal communication, the language of the body is not easily read and understood.

People demonstrate their territoriality by spreading out their belongings, laying claim to their personal space.

P. Ekman and W. V. Friesen (1969) categorized body movements into five types:

- Emblems.
- Adaptors.
- Regulators.
- Affect displays.
- Illustrators.

Emblems are substitutes for words. The sign that an angry motorist flashes you when you cut him off is an emblem. The "OK" sign, with the thumb and forefinger curled together, is an emblem. And the "V" for victory, or peace sign, is an emblem. In the large introductory communication course that the authors have taught together, an emblem was created to help students communicate more easily with members of the class. Because it was impossible to know all of the 400 students in the class, a "101" hand sign for students (the number standing for Interpersonal Communication 101) was introduced for use when students saw each other and the authors outside of class. The emblem is made by holding up the index finger, then curling the thumb and index fingers into a circle and then holding up the index finger again to resemble "101." When students use this emblem, they are using a sign that needs no verbal reinforcement. Emblems such as those just described can all stand alone; they need no verbal accompaniments to be understood. However, as

SPOTLIGHT ON DIVERSITY

Imagine that you're on a worldwide tour of several countries. You've decided to check into a hotel for the evening, and while at the hotel register, the clerk asks you how your trip is progressing. Smiling, you reply "OK" and use your thumb and forefinger curled in an "O" shape to reinforce what you've just said. What is the clerk's reaction? Well, it depends on which country you're in. If you're in the United States or Canada, the thumb and curled forefinger gesture means that everything is fine. If you're in Japan, this same gesture means "money." If you're in France, you've just indicated that your trip has been a "zero." If you were in Colombia, the thumb and curled forefinger gesture is only part of a commonly used gesture. Colombians would then place the circular gesture overtop their noses when explaining that someone is a homosexual. And, your gesture may even get you in a little trouble in Brazil, Belarus, or Denmark. In each of these cultures, the thumb and curled forefinger is totally unacceptable. In effect, it is an extremely rude and vulgar insult. So, if you're planning an international trip, it's important to understand the meanings attributed to common gestures. If you're not careful, a seemingly harmless gesture in your culture may have a very different meaning in another culture.

What do you think?

1. *Is understanding the nonverbal gestures of a culture one of the most difficult parts of traveling? Have you had any experiences in other cultures where your nonverbal gestures were misunderstood?*

2. *Are people of other cultures tolerant of communication mistakes made by those unfamiliar with the culture, slang, and language?*

you will read in the Spotlight on Diversity, emblems can differ in very dramatic ways from culture to culture.

Adaptors are movements that reveal our internal states. We use these movements when we are anxious or aroused. Essentially adaptors tell others about our internal states or feelings. Ekman and Friesen's (1969) research of psychiatric patients found that adaptors increase when people feel psychological discomfort. Imagine the adaptors that people use when speaking in public. Think for a moment about adaptors that *you* use when speaking. Do you twirl your hair when talking in a group meeting? Do you bite your fingers before talking to a superior or manager at work? Or do you sway back and forth when delivering a public speech? In such potentially anxious situations, nonverbal movements are a reflection of the nervousness and the need to feel more comfortable.

Regulators are nonverbal movements that control communication. College instructors all too often understand nonverbal regulators. An interesting phenomenon across college campuses nationwide occurs when the end of a class period nears. Students yawn, close their books, and look anxiously at the clock. The "leave-taking" behaviors of students send a clear message to the instructor—Stop! It's time to leave. In conversations, we also use regulating nonverbal cues to tell our partners when to keep talking, when to elaborate, and when to stop. S. Duncan and D. C. Fiske (1977) describe this as a "turn system," or a series of nonverbal signals used by a speaker and a listener to direct a conversation.

The messages that we send through facial expressions such as scowling, frowning, and smiling are known as affect displays. Affect displays are movements of the body and face to show emotion. Some researchers argue that we have a universal ability to detect emotional states through affect displays. Is a smile a smile in Australia and in Austria? Is a frown a frown in Borneo as well as in Brazil? To some degree, it is. In research studies, people have great success in detecting emotions across cultures. However, there does seem to be a documented difference in when and how emotions are displayed. For example, in Italy it may be a norm of behavior for people to express their grief and sadness intensely, whereas in England the culture demands a "stiff upper lip" from its natives. And, in Asian cultures, individuals often smile and nod even when they disagree.

The last type of nonverbal movement described by Ekman and Friesen is an illustrator. Illustrators are nonverbal movements that help to reinforce verbal messages. Nodding your head when saying "yes" is an example of a nonverbal illustrator. Waving goodbye when you're saying "See you later" is also an illustrator. Like meanings of words, illustrators can change as the culture changes. Can you think of any illustrators that have emerged in the last 10 or 20 years? Snapping is an example of a contemporary illustrator that was developed by a co-culture and then adopted by the larger culture. E. P. Johnson (1995) explains that snapping, or a wide sweeping arm motion that ends with the thumb and middle finger making a snapping sound, originated with African American women and African American gay men. Snapping is often used to reinforce a message in playful, ridiculing ways. For example, snapping might follow a degrading comment made by someone to tease someone who was wearing a pair of shoes purchased at a low-quality store. The act of snapping reinforces the comments being made by the speaker, indicating intent and intensity.

Communicating Through Touch

Tactile communication is communication through touching. Tactile communication could be the most taken-for-granted, misunderstood, and misused form of nonverbal communication. Scientific studies have revealed the need for touch and companionship. In laboratory studies in which baby monkeys were isolated from the touch of researchers, the monkeys failed to thrive, resulting in a higher disease and mortality rate than was the case with monkeys who were not isolated. Recent interest in the social plight of children in Romania and North Korea brings us reminders of the human need for human touch as well. Children who were placed in orphanages and basically abandoned because of a lack of government funding in these countries were found lying in their cribs craving attention and human interaction. Not surprisingly, the mortality rate was extremely high for these infants when compared to infants of comparable age not in these settings. Failure to thrive is as much a social problem as it is a physical deprivation.

What makes tactile communication so difficult to interpret and understand? To some degree, the norms of acceptable behavior and the context of the situation govern when touch is appropriate. Think for a minute about all the norms of behavior around touching someone. Toddlers are taught never to touch their genitals. Young children are taught the difference between "good touches" and "bad touches" to prevent molestation from adults. Adults, particularly men, are taught to shake hands firmly for fear of being considered "wimpy." Unfortunately, nowhere is there a dictionary of touching. These norms are both taught and observed.

Another difficulty with tactile communication is the context of the situation. What does a pat on the behind mean? It could mean great affection for a lover. It could be a form of discipline for a disruptive toddler. It could also be a form of congratulations from one football player to another. And in yet another context, it could be a form of sexual harassment from a boss to an employee. Touching is based on the intent of the message and the perceptions of those involved. Because of these two factors, touch can communicate messages that the sender did not intend.

Touch varies on a continuum from very impersonal types to full sexual intimacy (Winter, 1976). A functional-professional type of touch is an impersonal but necessary form of touch. It is used by physicians, optometrists, hair stylists, and nurses. The touch used by these individuals is meant to be impersonal and nonintimate. A social-polite touch is a form of acknowledging the presence of others. Shaking hands is a very common form of greeting in many cultures. In other cultures, kissing is the social-polite form of touching. Friendship-warmth functions of touch are designed to show affection for those around us whom we consider relationally close. A hug, pat on the back, or kiss might be used to show affection for others, although there is great cultural variability as to how friendship or warmth is displayed. The final functions of touch—love-intimacy and sexual arousal—are used for only the most personal of situations. Touch in these situations is used to show the deepest levels of affection and commitment.

Communicating Through Objects and Clothing

We are what we wear. No matter where you go in the world, clothing and personal objects are important to different cultures. The power that your clothing and objects have for the purposes of communication is significant (DeVito & Hecht, 1989). Objectics is the display of clothing, ornaments, jewelry, glasses, and other artifacts that have communicative potential. Do you feel differently when you're dressed in a well-tailored business suit than you do in a pair of baggy sweat pants and T-shirt? You might feel more confident, walk more formally, and talk differently in a business suit. Also, other people are likely to interact with you in reaction to the way you are dressed. You would probably be taken more seriously and spoken to more formally when you wear your business suit.

Clothing and artifacts tell us a lot about ourselves and our environment. Clothing, jewelry, and other ornaments send important messages about our likes, dislikes, beliefs, attitudes, and values. If your hair is colored purple and protruding in long spikes, you are sending a message about who you are, just as does the person who wears only Versace clothing and carries a Gucci bag.

Why is it that some people become immediately tense and better behaved around a person dressed in a blue uniform with a gold badge strolling down the street? The answer is that this uniform indicates the person is a police officer. In U.S. society, we have designated specific clothing to certain occupations. Nurses, physicians, police officers, and restaurant servers usually have

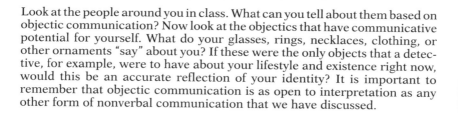

MISSION: POSSIBLE

Look at the people around you in class. What can you tell about them based on objectic communication? Now look at the objectics that have communicative potential for yourself. What do your glasses, rings, necklaces, clothing, or other ornaments "say" about you? If these were the only objects that a detective, for example, were to have about your lifestyle and existence right now, would this be an accurate reflection of your identity? It is important to remember that objectic communication is as open to interpretation as any other form of nonverbal communication that we have discussed.

specific uniforms to communicate status, position, and authority. Even organizations develop unspoken codes of appearance. For years, IBM employees could be seen dressed only in dark suits with white shirts. Organizational stories focus on employees who were sent home to change because they came to work wearing cream-colored rather than white shirts. Employees realized that the fast track to success at IBM included a closet full of dark suits and white shirts.

Contemporary Applications of Research: Nonverbal Communication in Gangs

Because nonverbal communication is such an important part of our lives, researchers have been studying and classifying nonverbal cues for decades. An interesting example of contemporary research in nonverbal communication is the work done by Dwight Conquergood (1994). He studied Chicago gangs from 1987 until 1992 by living in their neighborhoods and befriending gang members. He found that gangs rely on unique nonverbal codes for survival and to bind gang members together. Let's look at this work more closely as an example of how different types of nonverbal communication function in a current example.

First, Conquergood found that gang members use kinesic communication to reveal whether members were part of a Folks Nation or a Peoples Nation gang. Throughout the United States, many youth gangs are affiliated under either the Folks Nation or Peoples Nation, just as people might be affiliated under either the Republican or Democratic party. Conquergood found that posture was one indicator of whether the gang member belonged to a gang affiliated with either the Folks Nation or the Peoples Nation. For example, Peoples Nation gang members stand with their left foot tilted out to the left because the left side is the privileged side of the body for the Peoples Nation gangs. Folks Nation gangs stand with their shoulders and feet to the right.

Another form of kinesic communication that is prevalent in gang communication is the use of gestures. Gestures are equal to posture in indicating gang status. When gang members meet, they "rep" (represent) to indicate their identity and respect for other members. A member of a Folks Nation gang "reps" his or her identity with the hand turned upside down to symbolize a pitch fork—an icon of the Folks Nation. In the Latin Kings gang, "shaking on the crown" is an elaborate series of co-performed hand gestures that represent the Latin King crown or the national salute. Both members throw their right fists on their hearts, kiss their fingertips, and tap their hearts with the tips of the fingers extended in the shape of the crown. These gestures are performed when greeting and leaving other gang members.

Conquergood's research also reveals how gangs use proxemic communication to communicate through the use of space and distance. One of the main ways in which Chicago gang members communicate is through the use of visual icons such as graffiti. Graffiti is used to mark the boundaries of a gang's turf as well as to send messages. To outsiders, graffiti looks like gibberish, but to gang members it establishes territory. Think about the graffiti you've seen on a subway or city street wall. Could you understand what any of it meant? Gang graffiti is based on an elaborate communication system of underground symbols, icons, and logos. Conquergood tells of a gang who painted a "death mural" on the walls, postal boxes, and buildings in the gang's territory. To outsiders, the only recognizable symbol on the mural was that of a tombstone. In reality, the death mural was an elaborate and complicated story about a 16-year-old gang member who was beaten to death in the alley. Through the use of nonword symbols and signs, the members were able to communicate their territory and the story of their lives on the streets of Chicago.

Lastly, research on gangs indicates the importance of objectics for communicating information from member to member, as you may have seen in the movie *Colors*. For the Chicago gang members Conquergood studied, clothing was probably the most important nonverbal communication tool. In gangs, the color of clothing could mean life or death. To one gang, the color red symbolized membership; to another gang the color blue was a symbol of membership. Wearing the color blue in a neighborhood frequented by gangs symbolized by the color red could be potentially dangerous. For gang members, certain colors identify other members and create cohesion among those members. Conquergood also found that the tilt of a baseball cap indicates gang status, as well as the brand or style of lacing of sneakers. For example, members of the Peoples Nation gangs wear Converse sneakers because of the five-point star logo on the heel that is symbolic of their gang logo.

As this research shows, nonverbal communication is part of life for all human beings. Some groups, such as the gangs of Chicago, use unique and often secretive forms of nonverbal communication. Perhaps this is what is so interesting about nonverbal communication. As we've discovered in this chapter, nonverbal codes are probably the oldest and most primitive form of communicating we have. However, nonverbal codes are also the most open to interpretation. Just like the gangs of Chicago, people must give meaning to nonverbal codes. These meanings can change from person to person, group to group.

Summary

Nonverbal communication, or all nonword messages, is the most basic form of communication that we, as human beings, have to interact with each other. This doesn't mean that nonverbal communication is any easier to comprehend or understand than is verbal communication. In many ways, nonverbal messages are similar to verbal messages in that they are both symbolic, individually produced, and subject to interpretation. However, nonverbal messages differ in that they are more primitive, often uncontrollable, more believable, continuous, unstructured, and more widely understood. Nonverbal communication performs many functions for us in our everyday communication. Nonverbal messages may repeat, complement, contradict, substitute for, and regulate verbal messages.

Many categories of nonverbal communication exist. Proxemic communication concerns the study of space and distance. Hall categorizes space into four levels: intimate, personal, social, and public space. Territoriality refers to the way in which we communicate to others how much space we need to feel comfortable. Kinesics refers to how posture, movements, gestures, and facial expressions have communicative potential. Ekman and Friesen categorize gestures as emblems, adaptors, regulators, affect displays, and illustrators. Tactile communication focuses on how touch sends messages to those we interact with. How touch is interpreted is contextually bound. Tactile communication ranges from functional-professional touches such as the nonintimate touch that a physician uses with a patient, all the way to the most personal sexual touches that we give to those we are intimately involved with. The final category of nonverbal communication we discussed was objectic communication. The clothing, jewelry, and artifacts that we wear communicate volumes about us to others. Of course, our interpretation of any nonverbal message is based not only on personal perception but also on cultural perception. In these ways, we can see how nonverbal communication permeates every part of our interaction with others.

At Your Bookstore

Joseph, N. (1986). *Uniforms and Nonuniforms: Communication Through Clothing*. Westport, CT: Greenwood Publishing Group.

Josipovici, G. (1996). *Touch: An Exploration*. New Haven, CT: Yale University Press.

McNeill, D. (1992). *Hand and Mind: What Gestures Reveal About Thought*. Chicago: University of Chicago Press.

Morris, D. (1995). *Bodytalk: The Meaning of Human Gestures*. New York: Crown Publishing Group.

CHAPTER 4

Listening
for Improved
Communication

❖ ❖ ❖ ❖

This past summer I held a job as a teacher at a day-care facility in Fort Worth, Texas. I was assigned to a classroom of 16 five-year-olds, and sometimes added "drop-ins." I had always assumed that this type of job would be a piece of cake. I could just sit back, tell the kids what to do, and let them go about their business. Well, it didn't take long to discover that I was entirely wrong! Kids this age are just begging for interaction and approval; they want to be read to, played with, and above all, they ask a billion questions.

I began to realize how important it was to communicate with these children, not only by answering their questions and reading them stories, but by listening to them as well. If I really listened I found out that they had a lot to say. Each day I found myself becoming more and more skilled at encouraging them to talk to me. I feel that at least for a short time, I played an important role in preparing these children to interact with others. Not only did I learn the importance of communication, but I believe they did as well.

I think we all learned that if we listened to what one another had to say, we could all get along better. And for the times when some of them couldn't get along . . . well, we needed communication then too. I needed to listen to countless stories of opposite sides when it came time to break up an argument, and then decide on the fair thing to do. It wasn't always the easiest thing to try and explain to a five-year-old that what they were doing was wrong. However, with a lot of patience, listening, and talking, I think they learned a lot about communicating and I did, too.

— Leticia, second-year college student

As Leticia quickly learned, small children demand that you listen to them. They are absolutely insistent on it. As adults we hope for the same kind of attention, but we are less likely to scream and more likely to pout if we don't get it.

In today's society the family unit is no longer available for conferences. Our lives are fast-paced, both parents usually work outside the home, and people change hometowns frequently so that old friends aren't always available. The art of listening is lost and in its place we hire counselors to listen to us, and use computer screens to establish relationships.

Think of the last time someone took time to listen wholeheartedly as you talked about something important to you. Most of us try to do two things at once: listen to a friend and go on watching TV at the same time, for example. When we do this, the nonverbal message we send, whether we intend to or not, is: "This show is more important than you are." The greatest gift you can give another person is your full attention to his needs and concerns. To enter someone's world for a few moments and set aside all your own personal issues is easier talked about than done. This chapter will give you some concrete techniques for becoming a better listener. You will learn a lot more by listening than by talking.

Listening can be defined as a combination of hearing sound and giving meaning to the speaker's message. Listening is as demanding as speaking. We must convert each sound into a message and give it meaning. This takes a great deal more effort than sitting back and passively absorbing what you are hearing. Have you ever had the experience of listening really closely to a friend while she talked through a problem? Perhaps you have had the experience of paying careful attention to a difficult lecture? In these instances listening is hard work.

The word *listening* is derived from two Anglo-Saxon words: *hylstan*, meaning "hearing", and *hlosnian*, meaning "to wait in suspense". "Listening is a combination of hearing sound and waiting in suspense for psychological involvement with the speaker or source generating the message. Consequently, it goes beyond simply hearing sound waves to include psychological involvement with the speaker and his or her message" (DeWine, 1994, p. 140).

Even when we think we are listening we are hearing the stimulus in ways that support what we already believe. A group meeting can go something like this:

- *Summarizer*: "So, we all agree the new policy will require two signatures on requisitions from executive committee members of the sorority before any purchases for the house can be made."

- *Person who disagrees with the policy* hears: This will simply be a rubber stamp and any two signatures will do.

- *Person who agrees with the policy* hears: At last we will be firm about getting two committee members' signatures before any purchase is approved—we're finally cracking down.

We hear what we want to hear. No one wants to listen to bad news. The phrase, "Don't kill the messenger" comes from the Greek period when the unfortunate messenger who had to deliver bad news to the king (i.e., "Your kingdom is being attacked") was beheaded! We have a unique filtering system that allows us to filter out those messages that do not conform to our view of the world. We have to work hard to overcome these poor listening habits.

This chapter will discuss:

- The importance of listening, myths of listening, and why we are often poor listeners.

- Types of listening including pleasurable, informational, critical, and empathic.

We will suggest some techniques for improving your listening and for providing feedback to others.

The Importance of Listening

Being a good listener is clearly identified with good management skills. A survey of personnel directors in 300 organizations found effective listening was ranked highest among the skills defined as important in becoming a manager (Robbins, 1989). Tom Peters, internationally known consultant to business and coauthor of the best-selling book, *In Search of Excellence: Lessons from American's Best Run Companies*, described how important he thinks listening is:

My correspondence occupies many a file cabinet after years of dealing with managers in turbulent conditions. The most moving letters by far are the hun-

Figure 4.1 How We Spend Our Communication Time

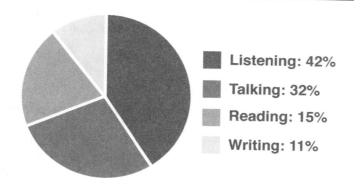

Listening: 42%

Talking: 32%

Reading: 15%

Writing: 11%

dreds about "simple listening." In fact, if I had a file labeled "religious conversion"—that is, correspondence from those whose management practices have truly been transformed—I suspect that 50 percent of its contents would deal with just one narrow topic: going out anew, with a "naive" mind-set, and listening to customers. (Peters, 1988, p. 16)

One review of research suggests that we spend about 75 percent of each day in some form of communication. Of all the communication behaviors, more time is engaged in listening than in all the others (see Figure 4.1).

Another study reports that listening takes up more of a person's day than all other communication behaviors combined. In another study, college students were reported to be engaged in some form of listening each day; on average 53 percent of a college student's day is spent listening (Baker et al., 1981).

Compare these figures with the way in which children are educated. We spend a great deal of time teaching students how to read and write. We spend very little time teaching them how to speak (usually public speaking classes are not available until high school) and virtually no time teaching students to listen. There are very few colleges offering courses in listening, even fewer high schools or elementary schools. This implies that people think as long as a person's hearing is not impaired he or she can listen. Listening is an art, like any other form of communication, and must be cultivated. First, we have to understand the difference between hearing and listening.

Hearing and Listening

Hearing and listening are two different functions with completely different outcomes. Hearing is the process of receiving sound and is a *physiological activity*. We are able to receive many sounds at the same time. As you read this book there are probably many sounds around you: a roommate making noise, TV in the background, shuffling feet, lawnmower, bells, clocks, all of which you are trying to ignore in order to retain the information you are reading. Listening is receiving and interpreting aural or heard stimuli and assigning meaning to those stimuli. It also includes the process of storing those messages for retrieval at a later date. Listening is a *psychological activity* that involves a higher-order thinking process. Even though we know that listening is important, that we spend more time engaged in that communication activity than in any other, and that it involves a more difficult process to master, we spend little or no time learning how to do it. We naturally go through a number of developmental stages as our listening skills change and adapt to life events.

Developmental Listening

Basically there are five stages in one's development into an effective listener. Initially individuals may learn to listen because "they have to." This is described as a "desire to comply with authority . . . and a desire to differentiate oneself from others" (Phillips, Lipson, & Basseches, 1994, p. 307). The second developmental stage is described as a desire to fit in with others. Early in our development we have a strong need to fit in, and we may be more influenced by our peers. Individuals are more motivated to learn the information they are hearing if it is somehow sanctioned by peers.

The third stage of listening development is listening to do well. Listening is seen as mastering a set of skills in order to achieve personal goals.

Later we come to see listening as a way of seeing people as individuals. We begin to see connections between our experiences and those of others. At this stage the "individual has come to appreciate that 'truth' depends on one's perspective, and one's context plays a primary role in determining that perspective" (Phillips et al., p. 310).

Finally, we begin to use listening as a way to develop complex relationships. Simple curiosity has given way to an ability to embrace others' differences and separate identities.

Depending on our stage of development as a listener, we may be more or less ready to engage in active listening. The stage of our development will also determine our ability to recognize some of the myths of listening and how these myths are preventing us from becoming effective listeners.

Myths of Listening

There are a number of myths about our listening ability that result in little attention being paid to this important communication skill.

Myth #1: We believe we can listen well already.

We think that because we can hear the words being spoken we are listening. After all, we've been doing it all our lives. This myth allows us to believe we don't have to pay much attention to this skill because it comes to us naturally. In fact, it is a very difficult skill that requires a great deal of energy and ability, which most people do not have.

Myth #2: Listening is a passive activity.

Appearances are deceptive. When we are listening it may appear that we are not physically "engaged" in the communication process, that all we have to do is passively sit back and absorb whatever comes our way. In fact, effective

Effective listening is not a passive activity.

listeners are physically as well as psychologically involved in the communication process. As your level of attention increases, there is a corresponding slight increase in your heart beat and body temperature. Being an effective listener means intense psychological activity as well: You are focused only on the other person and what she is trying to communicate. Being a fully engaged listener takes at least as much energy as speaking.

Myth #3: Learning to read is more important than listening.

The supreme importance of reading is what we are taught in school. We spend most of our education increasing our reading and writing skills, and yet we spend more time learning by listening to others—through conversations, class lectures, or the media—than we do by reading. Thus, in many ways we should be spending time learning to listen, just as we do in reading and writing.

Myth #4: Listening means agreement.

In the middle of an argument, we get this sudden impulse to answer the other person faster than he can talk. We may feel that our silence will be taken as agreement. This myth leads to defensive conversations. Often the other person only wants to be heard before listening to your argument. We are much better off listening quietly—without nodding our head or in any way indicating that we agree—and indicating simply that we are willing to listen to the other person's side of the issue. We should not feel compelled to answer immediately every argument presented. Give the other person a chance. Remember you can learn more by listening than by talking and you may discover, as you listen, that your views and the other person's views are not in as much conflict as you originally thought.

Myth #5: The speaker is totally responsible for the success of any oral interaction.

If we believe this myth of the speaker's total responsibility for success, then you are likely to blame any misunderstanding on the speaker. However, we know it is just as much the responsibility of the listener as the speaker to be clear, to understand, and to work at shared meaning.

Types of Listening

The five myths discussed above get in the way of effective listening. They allow us to ignore any responsibility or need to be engaged in the communication process as a listener. When we do this we are not being fair to the speaker. As listeners we must assume some of the burden for the continuous flow of messages. However, the level of responsibility shifts somewhat with the type of listening we are engaged in. Two researchers have identified at least four distinct types of listening:

- Pleasurable.
- Informational.
- Critical.
- Empathic and therapeutic. (Wolvin & Coakley, 1992)

Pleasurable Listening

There are many times when you listen for pure enjoyment: A concert, a walk in the woods, rain falling on a roof top, and children laughing are just a few examples. This type of listening is for entertainment and socializing. You do not need to remember facts or make notations of what you hear. Nor must you evaluate the quality of the sound. You listen because you enjoy the sound. The only requirement is to relax and absorb the message in a way that enriches your life.

Informational Listening

Your goal in listening to a classroom lecture is to retain information and to learn. Informational listening requires concentration and a desire to understand and remember what you are hearing. Unfortunately, sometimes a student's motivation may be low, or the material is not relevant to that individual, which makes informational listening tedious. We suggest that you assume the attitude that you might as well make this information useful to you. Unless you're willing to embarrass yourself and the speaker by walking out, you are basically a captive audience member. So why not make the information work for you? Relate it to something that does have meaning for you, or go over the information in your mind so you remember it without having to

Spotlight on Ethics

When you are listening to a speaker you should be attempting to determine if the information being presented should be believed. Unfortunately, unethical practices are too common. As a critical listener you must judge the rightness or wrongness of others' claims. Imagine a speaker using some of the following statements. How would you go about determining if these statements are true?

1. When Ronald Reagan was shot by John Hinckley, the President came within five minutes of dying (used in a speech supporting handgun legislation).

2. The first person to lose his life in the American War of Independence was an African American named Crispus Attucks (used in a speech to make people aware of the contributions of African Americans in American history).

3. The classic film *Citizen Kane* is based on the life of William Randolph Hearst (stated during a speech on film history).

4. Retired Supreme Court Justice Thurgood Marshall died on January 24, 1993 (an opening statement in an informative presentation on the impact of Marshall on the Supreme Court).

5. Overeating is the leading cause of heart disease (a persuasive appeal to entice individuals to join a diet club).

— Gouran, Wiethoff, & Doelgar, 1994

Think about the method you would use to verify each of the above statements. Some are true, some are not. Some could be used to persuade you to buy a product or believe in a concept. As a critical listener, you must be able to distinguish fact from fiction.

The answers to the above questions are found at the end of this chapter as well as a description of how one student found the answers. She discovered that three of the statements were false and two were true. She checked both the Internet and library sources and in one case found the Internet source to be incorrect. The time it took to verify these claims ranged from two minutes to one and one-half hours. Read carefully the report of how this student used both Internet and library sources. Was the process she used similar to the one you thought you would use? Did she identify any sources you did not think of? In Chapter 12 we will discuss in more detail how to investigate subjects and conduct library searches. For now, remember that as a critical listener, you are attempting to verify the accuracy of what you are hearing. This may take some investigation on your part after you have listened to the message.

review it again. Give yourself a goal as you listen. For example, if the lecture is on accounting and you have no plans to be an accountant, try to relate the information to your personal finances.

Critical Listening

Critical listening is suspicious listening. You are challenging the speaker's message and evaluating the accuracy of what you are hearing. Your job as a listener in this situation is to determine its meaningfulness and utility. You need to be able to capture detailed information and establish standards by which to judge that information. Ask yourself, "What is the speaker's point?" and compare the facts presented to experiences you have already had or information you have already acquired. Ask these questions about the information being presented: How, where, and when was this information collected? What is it being used for? In order to be an informed consumer you should also know something about basic statistics, enough to determine when statistics are being used in an unethical way to support an invalid argument.

Critical listening is not necessarily negative. It simply means you are thinking carefully about what you are hearing and applying good standards of evaluation to the information. This is particularly important when you are listening to advertising appeals or political candidates asking for your vote.

As you evaluate factual information you will be assessing various methods of support—how a communicator makes and backs up a point. We will be discussing these methods in greater detail in Chapter 12, but you should be alert to them now as you work to improve your listening ability. For example, analogy is comparing one thing to another for clarity; an *example* is using a specific item or story to explain an idea; *statistics* is the use of numbers for describing ideas; and testimony is the use of a well-known person to endorse an idea.

These methods of proof can be used to provide any of the three basic appeals used in public speaking:

- *Emotional appeal* (playing on the sympathies of the listener).
- *Logical appeal* (using facts and numbers to back up a claim).
- *Personal* or *ethical appeal* (using your own good name or reputation to support an idea).

We accept an idea because our emotions have been stirred, because the facts seem logical, or because we have faith in, or believe in, the speaker. You will learn more about basic appeals in public speaking in Chapter 12.

Empathic or Therapeutic Listening

Empathic means seeing something from the other person's point of view. Therapeutic means healing. Thus, empathic or therapeutic listening, is trying to help another individual cope with some problem by attempting to see the problem from his or her point of view and provide support while he or she struggles for solutions. This type of listening takes the greatest amount of skill and training in order to be effective. When someone turns to you for help, will you have the right words to say? Will she sense you are truly listening to her problem? In this type of listening you are "reading between the lines" by watching nonverbal signals and listening for themes that may run throughout a person's narrative. Here you seek to understand another human being rather than judge the rightness or wrongness of her actions or ideas. It takes great deal of energy and patience to refrain from judgment.

When someone needs an empathic listener she needs attention without interruption. She is trying to arrive at a clearer understanding of her own

To be an empathic listener you need to enter the other person's world wholeheartedly.

feelings. Even though she may ask for solutions, often she is not ready to listen to ideas about actions she can take to resolve her dilemma until she has had a chance to express her deep feelings of frustration, anger, or sadness. When someone tells you a family member is very ill, he needs time to express his fears and concerns before being able to listen to ideas about how to cope with this crisis. If you make a suggestion, and the response you get is, "Ya, but . . . " (i.e., "Yes, but you don't really understand," or "yes, but that wouldn't work") you know you have offered solutions too early in the process. This is the "yes, but," syndrome

As an empathic listener you need only to use minimal encouragement (i.e., "um hum") to let the speaker know you are listening to him and want him to continue talking. Your job is to listen intently to what he is saying and remain silent when he pauses. If you "fill in the gaps" for him, then you have solved the problem and it becomes your solution, not his. If you provide the solution for him and it doesn't work, then he can blame you. After all, it was your idea. That is a trap you don't want to fall into.

Another trap is wanting to share with the speaker a similar experience you have had. Telling your own story is inappropriate when your goal as an empathic listener is to focus on the other person 100 percent. It is very tempting to tell your story, especially if you feel you handled a similar problem successfully. Resist the urge to do this. It may make you feel good, but it is unlikely to help the other person come up with a solution that will work for her. Your primary task is to keep the person on track while she sorts through her feelings and to identify possible alternatives.

The difference between empathic listening on the one hand, and pleasurable, informative, and critical listening on the other, is that the latter types are all for our own intrinsic (internal) benefit: to enjoy, to learn, to believe. Empathic listening is for the extrinsic (outside of ourselves) benefit of another person: Our goal is to help the other person grow and profit from our encounter with him or her. The listener is demonstrating *empathy*—an intimate understanding of the other person's feelings and thoughts. There are specific steps one should take in the empathic listening process.

Steps to Empathic Listening

First, you need to assess your ability to listen. Are you in a frame of mind that will allow you to devote your full attention to another person? If your day has been very difficult, if you are not feeling well, if you have major problems of your own that prevent you from giving another person your full attention, then it would be more honest to admit this to the person seeking your help rather than pretend to listen. You might be able to suggest another time or another person who could provide this help.

Second, you should assess the immediacy of the problem. In other words, is this something that can "keep" until a later time when you are less busy, or is it something so critical that you should drop everything and sit down to help this person? You make this assessment by looking carefully for nonverbal cues like sad facial expressions or body posture. And you ask, "Is it important to talk now? If it is, I want us to take the time right now. If not, maybe we can set a time that would be good for both of us." If this critical question is not asked and nonverbal cues are missed, it is possible that a serious problem could be brushed aside. Because she was due to be somewhere else, one of your authors immediately suggested another time to meet a friend when that person really needed to talk right then. There will be times in your life when talking to a good friend about a problem he is facing is more important than anything else you had planned to do at that moment. You need to be prepared to recognize those moments.

Third, you should to get ready to listen physically and psychologically. Physically you must position yourself so that you can see the other person and respond to him without any distractions in your way (i.e., not talking over a desk with papers and memos scattered across the top). Your body language will indicate the degree to which you are listening. Your eye contact and leaning toward the other person, "tune you in" to the other person. Getting ready psychologically means "clearing your mental desk." You'll need to wipe your mind free of issues important to you, tasks you must complete, and demands on your time, so that you can devote yourself to this other person for this one moment in time. It's as if you are pushing everything off your mental desk in order to listen intently.

Fourth and fifth, you should listen for feelings and then listen for content. You must pay attention to the feelings the person is expressing before you ask questions about the content of the problem. Imagine you are feeling really bad about a course you are taking and thinking you may fail it. You want your friend to listen to you while you express your fears and doubts about your abilities. You may not be ready to jump into answering questions about what your grades have been, whether you have gone to study sessions, and if you read the textbook.

Let the person have the freedom to express her feelings first. This is difficult to do, especially when we feel bad about someone else's problem. It is uncomfortable for us to listen to people we like saying negative things about themselves. When someone says, "I just can't get math," our impulse is to say, "Of course you can. I'm sure you can do it." Although this may, on the surface sound like encouragement, what you are really doing is judging that person's feelings. In a sense you are saying, "You shouldn't feel that way." It is as if we do not allow her to express how she is really feeling.

This does not imply that self-pity should be a way of life. It does imply that the empathic listener will respond with paraphrasing (repeating what the individual has said in your own words), to let the speaker know the listener heard her and that she should continue to talk. "It sounds like you're really upset with yourself." If the person says "yes" and goes on talking, then you know you have identified the emotion she is expressing. If you have not accurately identified that emotion, then this gives her a chance to say so and correct your assumption. Only after the person has had a chance to fully express how she is feeling should you move to the next step of identifying the content of the problem.

Helping the person to identify the problem means listening with such attentiveness that you can summarize for her what you've heard. "So, you're afraid you may have failed your math class and what is really bothering you is how your parents will react. Is that right?" What you should *not* do is paraphrase using the word *why*. "Why are you so worried about your parents?" or "Why do you feel that way?" This requires the individual to defend herself and her feelings. Try not to ask "why" questions.

At this point you need to assess whether this individual needs to talk with someone who is a trained counselor. All you are doing is being an empathic listener and allowing the person to identify the problem. You are a sounding board. If the person needs psychological advice, you need to help her find someone with the credentials to help her on a longer-term basis. However, usually friends turn to friends first, so the way in which you respond may make a big difference in the individual's ability to cope with the problem successfully. There are a variety of factors that can affect how well you are able to handle this listening role.

Factors Affecting Listening Ability

You may have poor listening habits that have been developed over years. Some factors that influence your listening are within your control and others may not be.

The time of day and your mental alertness are big factors in your ability to listen. We know that people are not as attentive right after lunch. With a full stomach you are likely to get sleepy. Some people are not morning people and require an hour or two to really "wake up." Later in the afternoon, when people are hungry may be a difficult time to hold their attention as well. Is it any wonder that faculty and students would like to offer all classes between the hours of 10 A.M.–12 P.M. and 2–4 P.M.?

If you have a physiological hearing problem it will interfere with your ability to listen; however, it will not make it impossible. One of our colleagues is hearing-impaired and reads lips quite well. She is a very attentive listener, and when talking with her people have a sense of confidence that she is really paying attention to what they are saying.

There may be physical distractions that make it difficult to hear, much less pay attention. The authors have attended many luncheon meetings in a small dining room on our campus. The air vent in this room, which we are told cannot be turned off, is so noisy that if you sit in one corner of the room you must strain to hear. Unless the information is critically important to you, it is very easy to "fade." Large lecture rooms in the university environment can also lead to students "fading."

Of course the environment has a major impact both on the ability to communicate and on the capacity to listen. If someone feels he is in a private space, he will be much more comfortable speaking and you will be much less worried about someone interrupting the conversation. We also know the size of the room may affect how intimate the conversation may become. People tend to feel more comfortable talking about personal issues in a smaller room. A larger room, even if you are sitting in one corner of it, tends to make people more uncomfortable.

Mental distractions can be even more difficult to overcome. When you have something on your mind, an issue you are worried about, it is very difficult to set it aside and enter into the communication process wholeheartedly.

Your level of apprehension may also affect your ability to listen. If you are worried about how well you will do listening to someone else, you are likely to focus more attention on that concern than on the speaker. In Chapter 12 we will talk about communication apprehension, but for the time being you should be aware that the degree to which you are comfortable talking with individuals and groups will affect your comprehension skills as well as your self-confidence (which we will discuss in greater detail in the next chapter).

Semantic distractions—having any understanding for a word different from that of the speaker as well as factual distractions—when the facts you are listening to are at odds with the information you know to be true—can lead to poor listening behavior. You can easily be sidetracked into your own mental discussion and when you tune back in you discover that the speaker has moved on to another point.

You may have an overload of stimuli, meaning that too much information is coming at you at once. Perhaps you are watching a TV murder mystery that is about to reveal "whodunnit," while your roommate is telling you where you can meet him later tonight, when the phone rings with a classmate trying to give you information relevant to an exam you will be taking soon. Trying to focus on all of these stimuli at the same time will obviously make you less effective. You will probably only hear part of each message.

Poor Listeners

In the final analysis, there are some individuals who are poor listeners no matter what the conditions are when they are asked to be attentive. Some listeners with poor listening habits have become very skilled at "covering" them. Be sure you aren't one of these characters in the "nightmare of conversations":

- *The Great Pretender* is the person who seems to be taking in every word while her mind is somewhere else. College students have become very good at this technique. There is usually a student sitting in the front row, hanging on every word of the instructor, nodding her head, and yet when she is asked a question about the material says, "Huh?"

- *The Dominator* does not listen except to his own voice. This listener talks more than he listens. He dominates the conversation and makes it difficult for others to get into the conversation. He hasn't learned when to be silent and consequently others avoid being with him.

- *The Flighty* is a restless listener. She has trouble staying with a conversation for a sustained period of time. She may shift in her seat or rock back and forth on the balls of her feet, always appearing to be about to flee the scene. Her mind flits from one idea to another without spending much time on any one thought.

- *The Scribe* is often found in the classroom. This student is so worried about getting down each word that he misses the main point. Have you ever had the experience of trying hard to take notes in a class and then later looking at words that make no sense? You have probably fallen victim to "the scribe syndrome." Remember that your retention of information will be enhanced if you have a context in which to place the information you have recorded. Listen for the big picture first, then fill in the details.

Enhancing Your Listening Ability

Poor listeners and everyone wishing to become a really effective listener could be helped by the following suggestions for improving basic listening ability.

Before you begin to listen to someone, move to a place that provides some privacy and comfort for the person talking with you. In private conversations, people want to feel secure that the intended listener is the only listener. This may be something as simple as closing a door or moving to a quieter part of a large room. Ask the other person whether she is comfortable talking where you are or would prefer to move elsewhere.

> ### Tips for Improving Listening
>
> 1. *Decide to listen* and establish a specific goal for listening. Your purpose in listening may be to do better on the next exam, to follow driving instructions, to enjoy the details of a story, or to evaluate the quality of the message. Keep that purpose in mind when you begin to get distracted. If the communication event is important enough, you will find that you can only do one thing at a time. Turn off the TV, put down the book, focus on one person at a time.
>
> 2. *Don't hesitate to ask that the information be repeated.* If you want to be certain that you understand the information, it's better to ask that it be repeated. Speakers are flattered that you care enough to get it right.
>
> 3. *Restate the information* to make sure you understood what was said. "Did I get this correctly? . . . you said . . ." This allows the speaker to correct you if your understanding is incomplete. It also allows you to hear the information again. Research suggests that facts need to be repeated three times before you will remember them. When you first meet someone, the best way to remember her name is to use the name in a sentence immediately. "So, Sue, you're interested in golf?"
>
> 4. *Attend to the message*, not the speaker himself or what he's wearing or other distractions in the room. Focus your attention on the content of his message first. Avoid mental distractions that prevent you from retaining the message being sent.
>
> 5. *Use the extra time to summarize.* Researchers have found that people can think about four times faster than anyone can talk. Talk time is about 150 words per minute while "think time" is about 400 words per minute. If you have ever listened to "compressed speech," or speech with all pauses and some sounds removed, you will find that you can still easily comprehend what's being said. So you have extra time to summarize what you are hearing, anticipate what the person will say next, or apply what is being said to something that makes sense for you.

Listen with intensity, empathy, acceptance, and willingness to take responsibility for completeness rather than listening to argue a point of view that may or may not be consistent with your own set of values. Empathy is not the same thing as sympathy. Rather than feeling sorry for someone, you are simply trying to place yourself in the other person's position—not to agree or disagree—but merely to understand his point of view.

You need to check on your general listening behavior. Ask others if you are a good listener or if you tend to interrupt. Be prepared to accept their answers without feeling you must defend yourself. Ask others if you dominate small groups and how often you play the role of "interviewer" in a two-way conversation. If you don't like the answers you get, read this chapter again!

Feedback

The other half of the listening process is providing feedback once you have listened carefully to what another person has said. This takes as much skill as being an active listener. There are basically three types of feedback:

Evaluative feedback lets the other person know what you think is right or wrong about that person's behavior. You are judging the behavior according

MISSION: POSSIBLE

Take the following listening quiz to determine your listening awareness. Each statement is true or false. *Mark your choice.*

1. People tend to pay attention to what interests them.
2. People tend to expect or anticipate what they are familiar with.
3. Sometimes people distort things so they hear what they want to hear.
4. Listening is a natural process.
5. A person's training, experience, and knowledge affect what that person perceives.
6. Listening is a skill.
7. Hearing and listening are the same.
8. Most people have a short attention span and have difficulty concentrating on the same thing for too long.
9. Listening requires little energy. It is easy.
10. The speaker is totally responsible for the success of communication.
11. An effective speaker keeps an open, curious mind.
12. Speaking is a more important part of the communication process than listening.
13. When a listener's emotional level is high, he or she will be an effective listener.
14. When a person is involved with internal distractions, he or she will not be able to listen to what the speaker is saying.
15. Being critical and judging a speaker is not an effective listening skill.

The correct answers are at the end of this chapter. How many questions did you get correct?

to your own set of standards. "You are not dependable because you are always late to class." Here the speaker has made a judgment about the person based on the speaker's observation.

Interpretive feedback attempts to explain the observed behavior. "If you weren't staying out late each night, you wouldn't miss class so often." The speaker is analyzing the behavior and attributing some motive for the behavior based on his assessment of the situation. This places the speaker in the position of being the analyst.

Descriptive feedback simply describes the behavior without judging it or analyzing it. "In the past two weeks you have been late to class four times. I am concerned about the information you are missing." The speaker has observed the behavior and shared her concern about it without judging it to be right or wrong and without analyzing why the other person might be behaving this way.

Descriptive feedback causes less defensiveness and allows you to provide observations, and your concern about them, without going another step toward actual judgment. Feedback is more acceptable when it is:

- *Descriptive* ("You have missed several meetings" rather than "You're not dependable").

- *Specific* ("You've missed two out of the last three meetings" rather than "You always miss meetings").

- *Directed toward behavior rather than personalities* ("You were 15 minutes late today" rather than "I just can't count on you").

- *Well timed* (an hour before the event, saying, "Let's try to leave early" rather than as you're going out the door, saying, "We really should have left earlier").

- *Responsive to the needs of the other person* ("I know this information will be important to you so I'm concerned when you miss a meeting" rather than "I'm depending on you and you let me down").

If I provide feedback at a time when you cannot put it to good use, then it is harmful. For example, if Melissa's husband tells her in the middle of an evening out that he thinks another outfit would look better on her, she can't do anything about it then and there. He hasn't provided useful feedback and has only made her feel bad about how she looks. A better time to provide feedback is when she is making the decision about what to wear. She can choose to pay attention to the feedback or to ignore it.

A successful communicator is both a careful listener and a responsive communicator who looks for opportunities to provide feedback. Being able to listen carefully and provide feedback without causing the other person to be defensive are probably two of the most important skills you can have as a communicator. These two skills are also the most difficult to acquire.

Summary

Listening is an important part of the communication process. Most of us think we already know how to listen, and indeed, very little time is spent training us to listen in spite of the fact that we spend more time listening than in any other communication activity (writing, reading, or speaking). There are four types of listening described in this chapter: pleasurable, informational, critical, and empathic/therapeutic.

Poor listeners are likely to pay more attention to either mental or physical distractions than to the message. Semantic and factual distractions, as well as an overload of stimuli, may cause you to become one of the poor listeners: the great pretender, the dominator, the flighty, or the scribe. To improve your listening you should: get ready to listen, ask that information be repeated, restate the information yourself as well, attend to the message, and use the extra thinking time to summarize what you have heard. The other half of the listening process is providing feedback. Work to provide descriptive feedback, not evaluative or interpretive feedback.

At Your Bookstore

Atwater, E. (1992). *I Hear You: A Listening Skills Handbook*. New York: Walker and Co.

Bechler, C., & Weaver, R. (1994). *Listen to Win: A Manager's Guide to Effective Listening*. Portland, OR: Master Media.

Fromm, E., & Funk, R. (Eds.) (1994). *The Art of Listening*. New York: Continuum Publishing Group.

Helgesen, M., & Brown, S. (1994). *Active Listening: Building Skills for Understanding*. New York: Cambridge University Press.

Peters, T. (1988, Spring). "Learning to Listen." *Hyatt Magazine*, pp. 16-18.

Robertson, A. K. (1994). *Listen for Success: A Guide to Effective Listening*. New York: Irwin Professional Publishing.

Wolvin, A., & Coakley, C. (1992). *Listening* (4th ed.). Dubuque: Wm. C. Brown.

Answers to Spotlight on Ethics Problems

1. **When John Hinckley shot Ronald Reagan, the president came within five minutes of dying (used in a speech supporting handgun legislation).**

On the Internet:

Using keywords *Ronald Reagan, Hinckley, attempted, assassination,* and *medical reports* and conducting a search of Lycos, Yahoo, Excite, and Infoseek, I was unable to find the information within a one-hour time frame. I did find conflicting reports however on the date of the shooting, one website reporting 1982 while some other websites reported March 30, 1981, and still others reported March 31, 1981.

In the Library:

First, I needed to substantiate the date, so I looked in *Collier's Encyclopedia* under "Ronald Reagan." The date of the assassination attempt was March 30, 1981. Then, I looked at the *New York Times Index*. On page 899, it lists several articles covering the topic of the attempted assassination of Ronald Reagan. On March 31, 1981 (1: 1), the *New York Times* quoted Dean Dennis S. O'Leary, Clinical Affairs at the university hospital where Reagan was taken immediately following the attempt, as saying the "prognosis is excellent. He is alert and should be able to make decisions by tomorrow." O'Leary gave a detailed description of the wounds and the surgery as he revealed that the surgeons removed a .22 caliber bullet that struck Reagan's seventh rib, penetrated his left lung three inches, and collapsed the lung causing him pain. It is also reported his "vital organs were stable throughout the ordeal." Surgeons were doctors Benjamin Larry Aaron and Joseph Martin Giodano.

Next, I looked to the *Washington Post Index* to further verify the accurateness.

However, the *Washington Post* has no abstracts included, merely headlines and one-line descriptions.

For the next step, I went to the computer for a listing of full-text publications and newspapers on the Internet but was unable to access several newspaper records for 1981 without a subscription to the newspaper or paying a fee to have it mailed.

Finally, I decided to backtrack and went downstairs to look at the microfiche archives of the *Washington Post*. Their accounts were similar to those reported in the *New York Times*. Additionally, they quoted O'Leary as saying, "At no time was he [the president] in serious danger."

Conclusion

The statement made by the speechmaker is false. I found no evidence to substantiate his claim.

Time used in library: 45 minutes

---

2. **The first person to lose his life in the American War of Independence was an African American named Crispus Attucks (used in a speech to make people aware of the contributions of African Americans in American history).**

On the Internet:

Using keyword *Crispus Attucks* and conducting a search of Lycos, Yahoo, Excite, and Infoseek, I found references to the Boston Massacre (March 5, 1770) that named five victims: Samuel Gray, Samuel Maverick, James Caldwell, Crispus Attucks, and Patrick Carr, whose names are all included on the Crispus Attucks Monument. The story on the Internet described the massacre as a gathering of a crowd which jeered at British officers, who fired into the crowd. Eleven people were shot and five died. Some accounts claim Attucks struck the British officer, Hugh Montgomery, which led to shots being fired. This is the only information found within a 45-minute time frame.

In the Library:

I went first to the *Who's Who of African Americans*. There was no listing for Crispus Attucks.

I looked then at a book located nearby, *Reference Library of Black America*. In this book, there are several different small sections about Attucks listed in the index. On page 9, it describes the Boston Massacre in a chronology and states, "Crispus Attucks was shot and killed during the Boston Massacre, becoming one of the first casualties of the American Revolution." On page 105, however, under the heading "African American Firsts," it declares he was the "first casualty of the American Revolution." Yet, again, on page 233 the story changes when it reads, "Attucks is believed by many historians to have led a group that converged on a British garrison to help enforce the Townshend Acts. He was the first to fall." It goes on to say that Gray and Caldwell were killed in the same spot and Maverick and Carr died later from injuries sustained there. On page 338, information is repeated from page 9. It reports he was "one of the first men killed in the Revolutionary War." And, finally, on page 357 in the section entitled "Figures From the Past," Attucks is reportedly known as "the first to defy, the first to die." The section also reiterates the earlier information that Attucks attacked a soldier and one soldier panicked, firing into the crowd.

Conclusion

From the conflicting reports and an overview of the literature, I believe Crispus Attucks was one of the first men to die in the Revolutionary War but no account gives evidence that *substantiates* that he was the very first to die. It rather indicates what "some people think," or "some historians believe" . . . In several places in the literature, it refers to the dedication of the Crispus Attucks monument. I believe some of the information may have been gathered 18 years after the event. I found no official, first-hand report that Attucks was the first to die.

Time used in Library: 30 minutes

---

3. **The classic film *Citizen Kane* is based on the life of William Randolph Hearst (stated during a speech on film history).**

On the Internet:

Using keyword *Citizen Kane* and conducting a search of Lycos, Yahoo, Excite, and Infoseek, I found the information after approximately ten minutes of searching.

In the Library:

First, I looked in the reference section where the directories for films are kept. I had to look through several film directories before I found this film because I wasn't sure what date it was released.

I looked in *Bowker's Complete Video Directory* (1997). The film (1941) was summarized as Orson Welles' film, which "explores the dark side of wealth and power recalling the life of William Randolph Hearst."

Conclusion:

The statement is true.

Time used in library: 5 minutes

---

4. **Retired Supreme Court Justice Thurgood Marshall died on January 24, 1993 (an opening statement in an informative presentation on the impact of Marshall on the Supreme Court).**

On the Internet:

Using keyword *Thurgood Marshall* and conducting a search of Lycos, Yahoo, Excite, and Infoseek, I found the information after about ten minutes of searching.

In the Library:

First, I looked in the encyclopedias. In *Collier's Encyclopedia*, under the section about *Thurgood Marshall*, it states his date of death was, in fact, January 24, 1993.

Conclusion:

The statement is true.

Time used in library: 2 minutes

---

5. **Overeating is the leading cause of heart disease (a persuasive appeal to entice individuals to join a diet club). (Gouran, Wiethoff, & Doelgar, 1994).**

On the Internet:

Using keywords *obesity, overeating, heart disease*, and *cardiovascular disease* and conducting a search of Lycos, Yahoo, Excite, and Infoseek, I was unable to substantiate the statement after one hour of searching.

In the Library:

In the encyclopedia under the keyword *heart disease*, there are no leading causes of heart disease listed.

In the Statistical Abstracts, under *heart disease* and *obesity* as keywords, there were no charts or tables for leading causes of heart disease.

In the Health Library, using a search to find related reference books, two books were used to determine the validity of this statement.

In *Cardiovascular Medicine* (1995), Kannel says a "long term relationship between obesity and risk for Cardiovascular Disease is strong for both men and women." On page 1821, the article says, "It is argued that obesity, in the absence of other CV risk factors, is not a risk factor for CVD." Also under the Smoking section (page 1820), the article reads "of the lifestyles that promote CVD, cigarette smoking predominates as the most powerful modifiable risk factor."

In *Heart Disease: A Textbook of Cardiovascular Medicine*, obesity is reported as a contributor with other factors but is not reported as the leading cause.

I also looked at some other journals but found no evidence that obesity is the leading cause of heart disease.

Conclusion:

First of all, semantically, the statement is far from the truth. The speakers report that "overeating" is the leading cause. They do not use correct word choice in relating their message. I immediately envisioned millions of people sitting at the table like King Henry VIII, gorging themselves until they developed heart disease. They probably meant to say that long-term overeating and the accompanying weight gain, or obesity, is the leading cause.

But, they would still be wrong. There was no evidence to substantiate these speakers' claims that obesity is the leading cause of heart disease. There are many factors contributing to the development of heart disease.

It was interesting that the articles and journals I looked at written by nutritionists heavily indicated obesity but the articles and journals I read by medical doctors looked at a variety of causes.

Time used in library: 1 1/2 hours

Submitted by: Pamela Dawes

Answers to Mission: Possible Listening Quiz:

   1. T
   2. T
   3. T
   4. F
   5. T
   6. T
   7. F
   8. T
   9. F
10. F
11. T
12. F
13. F
14. T
15. T

Part Two

Contexts
of
Human
Communication

CHAPTER 5

Perceiving
Ourselves
and Others

> My friend and I used to fight all the time. We'd pick on each other something
> awful. I started avoiding spending time with her because she made me feel so
> bad. One night we ended up at a mutual friend's house, and she asked me why I
> hadn't been around lately. It was the first time we really talked about how we felt
> about each other. That one evening didn't change everything, but at least I got a
> chance to let her know how bad her comments had made me feel.
>
> — Jennie, first-year college student

Jennie's experience illustrates that how we feel about ourselves depends a great deal on how others react to us. Our friends and family shape our self-identity and self-esteem. Understanding who you are, what you believe in, and how you communicate those values must come first before you can improve your relationships with others. *Intrapersonal* communication is the silent talk you frequently have with yourself, sometimes referred to as "self talk." Think of those times you gave yourself a pep talk: the "you can do it" before a big game; the "just keep smiling" when you realize you have to pass your ex-boyfriend or girlfriend walking on the street; and the "calm down, you can handle this" when you were facing a major challenge. All of these are examples of conversations with your inner self, aim at helping you face and cope with life's stressful events. This inner self is influenced by stimuli you receive from others.

The American philosopher William James said, "Only those items which I notice shape my mind." We are bombarded by stimuli every day, and we can't absorb every piece of information sent our way. Therefore, as that famous writer puts it, "Only those things that we notice are the things that shape who we are and what we think." We select the stimuli we will pay attention to, and these in turn shape our perceptions of ourselves. In this chapter we will discuss:

- Self-perceptions.
- Perceptions of others.
- How we share those perceptions and disclose things about ourselves.
- How we can increase the accuracy of our perceptions of the world and those in it.

Perceptions of Self

Perception is the process by which we give meaning to certain stimuli in our environment. As children we are told many things about ourselves by our parents. Some of the things are very positive:

"You're such a good girl."
"You were very brave to do that."

"What a nice job you've done."

Some children, however, receive very negative messages.

"You're so stupid."

"You can't do anything right."

The messages about ourselves that we pay attention to are the ones that shape our self-concept. It is interesting to note that some individuals are able to be successful and happy despite negative messages they have received. They choose not to pay attention to those messages.

Close your eyes for a moment and think of all the adjectives that describe who you are. What words would you write about yourself? Would they have something to do with your physical appearance: height, hair color, clothing, age, gender, race—or would they provide other information such as personality traits or what your major is? There are many ways to describe yourself, but those perceptions that you retain are the things that you most often think apply to you. Whatever characteristics you would identify as your own makeup is your self-concept.

This relatively stable perception or impression that you have of yourself is based on objective feelings you have about yourself, and your self-esteem is the evaluative part of your self-concept. Your self-concept might have to do with physical characteristics; self-esteem is an *evaluation* of those characteristics: I'm too tall, too short, too fat, too thin. Your self-esteem is your feelings of self-worth; it affects everything you do and not only how you think about yourself but how you react to others as well. Your self-esteem and your self-concept are affected by the feedback you get from other people. Therefore, *inter*personal interaction is directly related to your identity. Self-concept and self-esteem are developed early in life and may be dictated by what is called a life script.

Following a life script is similar to playing a part in a play. The script represents what you have been told you should be or how you have been told you should act. Often, children follow a life script laid out for them by their parents or family members. That is why so many children end up going into careers or professions similar to those of their parents. Sometimes this life script is healthy and positive, and sometimes it is negative and defeating. Sons and daughters often find it quite difficult to explain to parents that they can't follow the "script" their parents have written for them. Consider the father who wants the son to enter the family business while the son would rather have a career doing something else. In refusing to follow a life script, children can be made to feel like failures—not because they are not capable of being successful but simply because they haven't done what their parents always hoped they would do. Awareness of our life scripts is essential in examining our self-esteem. We also can create scripts for ourselves that can be damaging. The self-fulfilling prophecy is one of those phenomena.

The self-fulfilling prophecy is a prediction about future behavior that comes true because after the prediction has been made—*you act as if it were true*. For example: students sometimes say, "I'm not good at taking tests." These students come into the exam nervous and upset and keep saying to themselves, "I'm not good at taking exams." They get more nervous and, sure enough, their nervousness causes them to make mistakes. Consequently, they do poorly on the exam. They have confirmed that they "are not good at taking exams." They have lived out their own prophecy and made it true.

In a much more damaging way, some self-fulfilling prophecies affect a person's entire life. A young child who is told, "You're stupid" or "You just can't do anything," and lives out that prophecy is a person who has acted in a way that was predicted when he or she was very young. We observed one little girl, a very articulate and cheerful preschooler, turn into a quiet and sullen child who failed repeatedly at school. One of the reasons this happened was that her classmates started telling her that she wasn't as smart as the rest of them. She was younger than the other students and probably should have been held back a year to begin with. She just needed to catch up with other children in terms of physical and psychological development. But she was in fact held back; children said to her, "You're stupid." Soon we started hearing her say, "I must just be stupid. School is hard for me." She started believing the "prophecy" and sure enough she failed over and over again. This child went from being happy and confident in her abilities to one who was quiet and withdrawn and an underachiever. People tend to live up, or down, to labels that significant others give them. Once labeled, we tend to act in such a way as to confirm the label. All of these scripts clearly affect your self-concept.

The self-concept has a number of aspects, or "faces." There are parts of your self-concept that you share with everyone, for example, what music you like or your choice of career goals. This first aspect of yourself is open to everyone. This is public information that you would rarely hesitate to share with other individuals. Then there is another part of yourself that is known only to you, which includes your secret desires and hopes for the future and things about yourself that you don't want others to know. This is private information that you share only with close friends or family members. There is a third type of information about yourself that is known to others, but you are unaware of their knowledge. The person who dominates conversations and doesn't seem to be aware of it, or the person who tells bad jokes and still thinks they're funny, would be examples of information others have about an individual that is unknown to him. Everyone else knows that the jokes are terrible except the person who is telling them. These three types of knowledge all contribute to your self-concept as well as the perception others have of you.

One of the things you can do to enhance your self-concept and understand better how others see you is to ask for feedback. This would ensure that those parts of yourself that are known only to others, and not to you, become a part of what is known to you as well. You will never find out how others perceive you if you don't ask. We are hesitant to provide feedback to others unless they ask for it. As you will see, however, sometimes feedback should be taken with a few grains of salt.

Improving your self-concept is not simple or easy. What makes it so difficult is that people who know us expect us to behave in certain ways, and when we change that behavior, they notice. They helped us create the self-concept we have and will be surprised when we attempt to make some major change. When you are trying to change your self-concept, it is as if you are saying, "What you helped create is not good enough anymore and I'm different now." One example experienced by many college students is going home from college and noticing that some of your friends who did not go to college have not changed and yet you feel very different. There is stress between the new image

When children told one little girl she was stupid, she started believing it.
She lived up to a self-fulfilling prophecy.

you have of yourself and the frozen image they hold of you as a part of their high school experience.

We know that individuals who are confident in their abilities tend to be more successful. Sometimes just smiling throughout the day will result in increased self-confidence. This seems like an elementary solution to a complex problem, and yet we know that smiling and laughing do have a real impact on your outlook even though you're consciously telling yourself to smile. You actually end up feeling better about yourself. You can be your own cheering section. This means thinking of ways to reward yourself when you have accomplished something you have set out to achieve. Individual celebrations are among the best ways to enhance your own self-image. Don't wait for others to recognize what you've done but be proud of the fact yourself. Finally, try to identify those life scripts that have been laid out for you to follow, and make sure that the course you are following and your own behaviors are qualities that you *want* to emulate, not the negatives that someone else has indicated you must perform. So, while you ask for feedback from others, put it in perspective.

Perception of Others

In addition to perceptions of ourselves, our perceptions of others influence and affect our communication behaviors as well. We have so much information and stimuli coming at us each day that we must select only what is meaningful to us. Selective attention is our ability to process certain stimuli and filter out the rest. This means that we will make some mistakes. We may stereotype others simply because we can't keep track of all the individual stimuli that we are receiving. Since we are exposed to more information than we can possibly manage, the first step in perceiving others is to select from all the data and impressions.

There are several characteristics of stimuli that will increase the chances we will pay attention to it:

- First, stimuli that are intense often catch our attention first (purple hair, extreme height, etc.). We focus on those things in our environment that appear to be out of the ordinary. Students who shave their heads should expect people to stare at them because a bald head on an 18-year-old will attract our attention.

- An abrupt change in stimuli also attracts our attention. For example, we will notice a friend who has always been very talkative and dominant in conversations who suddenly becomes very quiet and withdrawn. This stimulus attracts our attention because it is not what we expect.

- Finally, most of our selection is based on our individual motives and background. If you are motivated to take some particular action you will notice stimuli related to your goal. For example, if you are anxious about being late for a date, you will notice a clock you pass on your way. If you are hungry, you will notice restaurants. And if you are looking for a partner, you will more readily notice all the attractive people around you.

The three characteristics of stimuli mentioned above explain selective attention. There are other variables at work that lead to selective retention—the follow-up to selective attention. Selective retention is selecting stimuli that we will remember. We more actively remember messages that are favorable to our self-image than messages that are unfavorable. In short, we remember the good and forget the bad. An amazing example is people who have lived through terrible crises and who have bonded. Notice what communities say after a tornado or hurricane. They talk about how it brought the town together. Or consider individuals who have suffered some atrocity or horrible experience in their lives and yet have found a way to survive that experience through selectively attending to the wonderful people that have helped them throughout that process. This phenomenon happens every day. These experiences are examples of how we manage to remember those things

Stimuli that are intense often catch our attention first (purple hair, extreme height, etc.)

that are consistent with who we think we are and to discard those ideas that are not.

One of the processes that is ongoing as we attend to other people is using perceptual filters. This is the process of screening out, or filtering, certain information. This filtering process is based on psychological and physiological characteristics and expectations that are a part of our past experiences.

Psychological filters include our motivations, desires, and expectations based on our past experiences. We may have had some personal experience in which a violent act affected us or someone in our family. This experience may make it exceedingly difficult for us to perceive a person who commits a violent crime in any other way other than someone not worthy of our sympathy. In the fall of 1997 a 14-year-old high school student opened fire on a group of students during a prayer meeting in the lobby of their school. Three girls were killed. The gunman claimed to be an atheist. The other high school students attending the prayer meeting know intellectually that all atheists will not be violent. However, their interactions with atheists may forever be affected by this horrible act.

Physiological limits include physical impairment, your body type, age, heredity, and temperament. These physiological characteristics will influence your perception of others in the world. For example, if you have always been thin without dieting, you will probably continue to think that those who are heavy simply overeat, and those who are heavy will continue to believe thin individuals are simply lucky. Because of our own physiological limits, we may interpret the actions of others from a narrow perspective.

Finally, expectations serve as filters for our perceptions of others. We expect people to act in a consistent way, and therefore, when they modify their behavior we may tend to ignore it. We keep seeing the world in the future the way we've seen it in the past. This is called perceptual consistency. We like

Figure 5.1 Which do you see first, the old lady or the young woman?

people and the world to be consistent. The most difficult experience is to deal with individuals who are unpredictable: one day he's pleasant, the next day he's mean. It is easier to cope with a mean-spirited individual who will be like that all the time. Then we can develop coping strategies that help protect us from his attacks.

Another way perceptual filters work is that some stimuli become more prominent than others. This is called the figure and ground phenomenon. Much of the data you receive each day are perceived as being in the background, or the *ground*, while a few things appear to be in the foreground and serve as the *figure*. For example, take a look at the picture in Figure 5.1. Look at it for a long time and you will begin to see two pictures emerge. The first outline or shape that you see is the figure, and all the rest of the coloring in the picture is the ground. Over time a different picture will emerge, and that image becomes the figure; the rest of the drawing and colors become the ground. Those things that are most important to you will serve as the figure among all the stimuli that are presented to you.

One last concept that helps us understand perception is the concept of closure. It is very difficult for us to deal with ambiguous situations. Therefore,

---

SPOTLIGHT ON DIVERSITY

As hate crimes began to increase, President Bill Clinton declared "war" on such violence early in 1997. Four Army enlisted men were accused of killing a black couple in the fall of 1997. The jury heard testimony giving them motive and placing them at the scene of the crime. The motive was hatred for races other than white and membership in a Neo-Nazi organization. The defendants claimed a local chapter of the organization brainwashed them and gave them the weapons that were eventually used in the killings. Based on what you have learned about how perceptions of others are formed, do you believe this is an adequate defense? Are there groups of people you have attributed certain characteristics to? How could you have broadened your perspective?

What do you think?

---

when we have a few facts and we don't have a complete picture of what someone is like, we tend to fill in what is missing. We want to experience closure, or the satisfaction of completeness, in our perception of that other individual. This gets us into difficulty when we take a few examples and then stereotype someone as being a certain way because he or she is a member of a particular group. Stereotypes may be based on physical characteristics, speech, beliefs and attitudes, or even clothing. We have explained that this happens because there are so many stimuli you cannot take them all in. We should be careful that we don't immediately associate a group of characteristics with an individual because of skin color, other physical characteristics, or the part of the country he comes from. Try to see each individual as unique, while attempting to acquire a total picture of that person. We should suspend our views of others until we've collected enough information to make a judgment about the kind of *individual* they are and how they will behave.

Perception Improvement

So, how can we improve the accuracy of our perceptions? First, we can assume a less authoritarian attitude and be less rigid in our expectation of others. Sometimes we develop expectations for others that are impossible for them to live up to. We need to allow others to make mistakes and to make different choices from our choices. For example, if Damon chooses a different career path from the one his parents would have chosen for him, does that mean he has made a mistake or simply made a different choice? Should his parents think less of him?

Second, we should try to increase our objectivity and consider all the factors that contribute to the way another person behaves or acts. When a friend whom we respect cheats, are we able to look at other factors that may have been operating? Was she under a great deal of pressure? Were there others who influenced her? This doesn't mean that individuals shouldn't be held accountable for their actions. It does mean that our perceptions of them ought to be flexible enough to allow them to learn from their mistakes and move on.

Third, we should try to put ourselves in the other person's shoes—to practice being empathetic with the plight of individuals who happen to be "categorized" because he belongs to a certain group. It is impossible ever to understand completely what another person is experiencing but we can be more empathetic if we try to see the situation from that person's perspective.

Finally, we should acknowledge the fact that our perceptions are subjective, that they are influenced by our past experiences and our own self-concept and are therefore always subject to misinterpretation. Just because it is the way I see the world today doesn't mean it's the way I will see it tomorrow, or the way that anyone else sees it today or tomorrow.

Sharing Perceptions

We have discussed how we form perceptions of others. Now, we need to explore how our perceptions of ourselves are shaped and in what ways we are able to share our self-perceptions with others.

Definitions of Self-disclosure

Self-disclosure is information we share with others about ourselves, which determines, to a great extent, the types of relationships we will have and the way in which we are viewed by others. Self-disclosure is what individuals reveal about themselves—their feelings, experiences, and innermost thoughts—to other individuals. Sometimes this information is rather superficial, ranging from public facts all the way to being very private, intimate, and risky. In the beginning stages of a relationship the information received or given is superficial, such as where your hometown is located, where you went to school, what your major is, and what kind of music you like. Riskier self-disclosure includes life events that have had a traumatic impact on your life, your religious beliefs, or your deeply held values. One researcher argues that self-disclosure is not a dichotomous event, meaning you do not need to have *either* disclosed *or* not disclosed. Instead she says:

> Self-disclosure is an ongoing process that is extended in time and is open-ended, not only across the course of an interaction or series of interactions, but also across the lives of the individuals as their identities develop and unfold, and across the life of a relationship as it evolves. (Dindia, 1997, p. 411)

The process of self-disclosure is circular. Self disclosure does not necessarily move from nondisclosure to disclosure in a linear fashion. Full disclosure is not realistic given the inherent risk involved in revealing intimate information. Additionally, total concealment is impossible from a relationship. We are unable to conceal everything about ourselves because the very act of trying to hide our identity is revealing, and while interacting with others we even reveal information nonverbally. The very nature of a relationship demands that a certain amount of information be shared. Who we are as individuals, as well as who we are in relationship to each other, is affected by the amount of self-disclosure present in that relationship.

Is disclosing our accomplishments a successful strategy? Is boasting going too far? What differentiates a "positive" disclosure from a more "boastful" disclosure? How does our previous perception of the individual as well as our own self-confidence affect how we give meaning to what a person says about themselves? We are sure you've heard the old adage, "If you don't talk well about yourself, no one else will." But how far can you go in patting yourself on the back without leaving people with a negative impression because you sound boastful or arrogant?

Does the following statement sound like an assertive individual who is honest about what he or she can accomplish, or a boastful bore?

I've recently been promoted to assistant supervisor in the marketing research department of my company and it's about time! I'm the hardest working and most dedicated employee my company has. On top of that, I get along well with everyone. Although most people are nervous about doing a good job in a new position, I'm not the least bit worried. I've always performed exceptionally well at everything I've done. In fact, I should be promoted to head supervisor before too long.

The authors of one study tried to determine the difference between boasting and positive self-disclosure (Miller, Cooke, Tsang, & Morgan, 1992). The results of their study revealed that "boasts" tend to indicate power and status, involve exaggeration and elaboration, and emphasize being good, best, or even better than others.

> In many ways boasts embody instrumental and competitive emphasis typically associated with masculinity. Perhaps then, it is not surprising that perceivers consistently attribute characteristics such as masculinity, outgoingness, confidence, pride, and success to those who boast. On the other hand, when individuals generate positive statements, compared to boasts, they are more apt to emphasize their own effect, and the responsibilities of the job, express surprise, minimize accomplishments and be more attentive and stress the role of others and how honored one is by others' gestures. (p. 392)

What conclusion can we draw from this research? When individuals want to be liked and viewed as socially sensitive, they should disclose positive information about themselves but stop short of bragging. On the other hand, if they want to be viewed as confident and successful, then they might be better off bragging. It is a thin line between promoting yourself and being assertive about who you are and what your strengths are, and boasting in an unattractive way. Be careful to present yourself in such a way that you will always be able to demonstrate that you can do what you say.

Conditions Needed for Self-disclosure

In order for one person to disclose himself or herself to another person there must be a high degree of trust between the individuals who are in dialogue with each other. This trust will depend on past experience with this individual and the degree to which he held previous confidences in trust. One study looked at characteristics of the person receiving or listening to a message to determine differences between men and women during self-disclosure. The researchers concluded:

> Before women will disclose they find it more important than do men that the receiver be discreet, trustworthy, sincere, liked, respected, a good listener, warm, and open. In addition, women feel more strongly than men that, as a sender of disclosure, it is important that they be accepted, be willing to disclose, be honest, frank, not feel anxious, or be provoked into giving information. Thus, as criteria for disclosing, receiver and sender characteristics apparently are more salient [important] for women than men. (Petronio, Martin, and Littlefield, 1984)

As a consequence, women are more likely than men to assess carefully the personal characteristics of the listener before sharing personal information since they appear more concerned than men that their information will be held in confidence.

Characteristics of self-disclosure include:

- *Amount* (how frequently I share information about myself).
- *Depth* (how detailed my disclosure is).
- *Intimacy* (how personal the information is).
- *Honesty* (was I truthful).
- *Intention* (whether I shared the information by accident or meant for you to know it).

Men and women differ along most of these dimensions. Women disclose more evaluative, in-depth, emotional, and opinionated messages than do men (Wheeless, Zakahi, & Chan, 1988).

Of course, some would argue that this is because men do not self-disclose very often and therefore have nothing to fear. On the contrary, Julia Wood and Christopher Inman (1993) suggest that male closeness is revealed more in joint activities. "Sharing joint activities seems central to how men create and recognize closeness" (p. 289) and regard "practical help, mutual assistance, and companionship as bench marks of caring" (p. 291). Women tend to demonstrate closeness by sharing feelings and secrets. "Men do not value discussion of feelings and problems nearly as much as concrete assistance and/or activities that distract them from their troubles." We would suggest that men and women may disclose differently, but one style of disclosure is not preferred over the other. What is important in male-female relationships is to remember this difference and not assume that if the other person does not disclose in the same way that you do, it does not necessarily follow that he or she feels any less or more closeness or intimacy than you.

Another condition for disclosure that has been identified by researchers is reciprocity, or the amount of disclosure revealed by the person with whom you are talking. This means that Stephanie's self-disclosure to Alice causes Alice to self-disclose to Stephanie and vice versa. One of the early researchers in disclosure, S. Jourard (1971), originated the idea that self-disclosure is reciprocal. He coined the term "dyadic effect" to represent the idea that *"disclosure begot disclosure."* Thus, in relationships self-disclosure increases as the relationship develops and continues.

The degree of reciprocity is affected by the relationship itself. It is not only intimate relationships that generate self-disclosure. Perhaps you have had the experience of meeting a stranger on a plane or in a new place and finding yourself involved in a conversation about life stories. Part of the reason this occurs is you assume you will never see this person again. Imagine your surprise if she should show up at a party and be the best friend of one of your close friends. So another condition of self-disclosure sometimes is *anonymity*. Anonymity allows us to reveal ourselves to someone without fearing the consequences. All of us say things differently in a private setting from the way we would in a more public one.

Disclosure and Locus of Control

Many researchers have studied the amount of self-disclosure across cultures. These researchers have attempted to make a connection between the cultural background of a group of individuals and the degree to which they will disclose with others. One research study by L. R. Wheeless, K. V. Erikson, & J. S. Behrens (1986) examined the interaction between a person's culture and his locus of control and self-disclosure. The researchers studied two broad categories of cultures: American and non-western. Locus of control is the extent to which you are influenced by either your own internal goals and motivations or by rewards provided by others. External locus of control is the degree to which you are influenced by external forces and rewards. Internal locus of control is the degree to which you are influenced by your own values and rewards. For example, does a person work hard because her salary will increase or because it gives her internal satisfaction? These researchers discovered that locus of control did appear to mediate differences in cultural origins. In other words, the way in which an individual is motivated had as much or more impact on his willingness to disclose as his cultural origins. Those persons with external locus of control were more influenced by their particular culture's values since they were more externally motivated and therefore disclosed in a way that seemed appropriate for their culture. Those with internal locus of control, however, appeared to be less influenced by their cultural environment.

We must be careful not to stereotype people as behaving in one way or another because they are from a certain culture. What is your impression of Italians and how they self-disclose as contrasted with people from England? Do we have perceptions about openness based on cultural differences? The authors of this study suggest those cultural differences are mediated by the individual's own internal focus or external focus and this, in combination with cultural differences, affects how much that person will disclose. So we should not necessarily expect an Italian to be more expressive and to disclose more than a Briton.

Interaction Between Self-identity, Perceptions of Others, and Sharing Perceptions

If other people treat us in a way that is consistent with who we believe we are, that is confirmation of our identity. If you believe you are almost always on time and someone compliments you for being punctual, that confirms your perception of your behavior. On the other hand, if others treat us in ways that are inconsistent with our own self-perception, that's rejection. I think I'm usually on time and someone mentions that I've been late recently, I feel they are rejecting my image of myself. Finally, if others respond to us in a neutral way, suggesting that we are irrelevant, this is disconfirmation. Not to be recognized at all is worse than to be rejected.

Our perception of ourselves as well as our perception of others and our ability to share parts of ourselves with others depends on our interactions and our dialogues with other individuals. The way in which they respond to us will either confirm or deny our image. We all have had the experience of passing someone on the street, waving and saying hello, and having the person walk right past us. At the time we may feel hurt and ignored, even if we realize the person may not have seen us; the impact is still present. Each day our ability to withstand negative feedback varies by our mood, our past experiences, and our behaviors on that particular day. Some days negative feedback may not affect us in any great way. Other days, when other things are not going well, one negative statement may be the one additional negative stimulus that makes us feel bad about ourselves.

We will be able to help ourselves cope more effectively with the variety of feedback and remarks we receive on a daily basis if we recognize that our self-concept is critical to our success, and that our reactions to others will change that self-concept. In order to begin the process of improving and understanding how we relate to others, we have to understand ourselves and how we initially react to others. The next chapter will help us look beyond the self and instead identify how we can improve our own communication processes with others.

Summary

Our perception of ourselves (*intra*personal communication) depends a great deal on our interaction with others (*inter*personal communication). Self-concept is the relatively stable impression we have of ourselves; self-esteem is the evaluative part of self-concept, or how you feel about that concept. A self-fulfilling prophecy is a prediction about future behavior that becomes true because you act as if the prediction were already true. Selective attention is our ability to process certain stimuli and filter out the rest. These "filters" may be psychological (our motivations and past experiences) or physiological (lack of hearing, heredity factors, etc.).

Self-disclosure is the amount of information we share with others about ourselves. It is what we reveal about our feelings and innermost thoughts.

Self-disclosure is characterized by the degree of depth, amount, intimacy level, honesty, and intention involved. Finally, our self-perception is influenced by the degree to which others either confirm or disconfirm our identity.

At Your Bookstore

Derlega, V. J., Metts, S., Petronio, S., & Margulis, S. T. (1993). *Self-Disclosure.* Newbury Park, CA: Sage.

Jourard, S. (1995). *The Transparent Self.* New York: Van Nostrand Reinhold.

McKay, M., & Fanning, P. (1992). *Self-esteem.* Oakland, CA: New Harbinger Publications.

Modell, A. H. (1993). *The Private Self.* Cambridge, MA: Harvard University Press.

Pennebaker, J. W. (1997). *Opening Up: The Healing Power of Expressing Emotions.* New York: Guilford Press.

Schultz, W. (1994). *The Human Element: Productivity, Self-esteem, and the Bottom Line.* San Francisco: Jossey-Bass.

CHAPTER 6

Building, Maintaining, and Ending Interpersonal Relationships

The year was 1988 and it was the beautiful sunny month of July. The nerves had kicked in with my friend and me, but we were happy to be going away from home for a week. Not knowing what to expect, we arrived at this unfamiliar place, surrounded by many unfamiliar faces. With only one step in the door, two young girls we'd never seen before approached us, spoke to us, then welcomed us with a hug! Returning the nice gesture, Ashley, my friend, and I glanced at each other, wondering what might be ahead in the few days to come.

It turned out that first simple hug sent me to a week I have never forgotten, a week of communication which probably changed my life. It was the National Youth-to-Youth Drug-Free Conference, a week spent with people from all over the country learning and teaching why drug-free is the best choice to live your life. The reason I remember this week so well is because of the many people that I met and will never forget.

One of the most important times of communication happened when our small "family" groups would join together. These groups consisted of about ten kids led by a group counselor. Our group counselor was a recovered heroin addict whose main purpose was to tell her story and hopefully make a mark on our minds about the danger of drugs. I remember the times that our group sat in tears because of the events that had unfolded in her life and the many people she had lost due to drug use. Her intense way of communicating the dangers of drugs stayed with me. The many people that I met that week and their stories also have stuck in my mind and have given me a memory that I will never forget.

— Laura, third-year college student

Laura's life-altering experience focused on building relationships in a very short period of time. Our lives are made up of *inter*personal relationships— connections established with friends, family, co-workers, and associates. These relationships have a dramatic impact on our lives and our feelings of well-being.

What makes the difference between a mediocre day and a great day? The authors think it's relationships that confirm your positive self-image: a friend who asks you to do something with her just because you're fun to be with, a roommate who tells you he's glad you ended up living together, or a family member who lets you know she thinks you're a terrific person. All of these examples are illustrations of *inter*personal relationships that positively influence your life.

This chapter will discuss:

- The nature of *inter*personal communication.
- The stages of relationship development, including communication during initiation, maintenance, and termination of *inter*personal relationships.
- Repairing relationships with problems, as well as resolving family conflicts.

One person communicating to himself or herself is *intra*personal communication. More than two people can be considered a small group. *Inter-*

personal communication is communication between two persons who are in some way connected. Consequently, in this chapter we are not talking about strangers who meet by chance and share their life story. We're talking about *significant others* in your life: family members, co-workers, friends, roommates, and all others with whom you spend a significant portion of your life.

*Inter*personal relationships experience life cycles in which the participants may move toward, or away from, each other over time. One researcher (Parks, 1997), has identified six factors that affect the life cycle of an *inter*personal relationship:

- *Interdependence* in a relationship means the individuals have separate identities, interests, and activities although at the same time each of the individuals in the relationship has attitudes and beliefs based on the other person. In fact, one person's happiness may depend on the other person's enjoyment. While Jodie and Andrew do many things together, and care deeply about each other's happiness, they also maintain separate interests and, to some extent, separate lives.

- *Variety and breadth of interaction* change during the life span of a relationship. Conversational topics and behaviors vary and include a wide assortment of ways of interacting. Jodie and Andrew began their relationship by talking about more "public" topics like their hometown and general interests. Now that they have been dating for over two years they have covered most topics of mutual interest, and they now know a great deal about each other's lives.

- *Depth, or intimacy, of interaction* refers to the degree of self-disclosure and level of intimacy of the relationship. As the relationship continues, both friends and romantic partners begin to share their innermost thoughts and beliefs. Thus, the quality of the relationship is now "deep." Jodie and Andrew have reached a point in their relationship where they share their private thoughts and attitudes, making their relationship more intimate.

- *Commitment* is the degree to which there is an expectation that the relationship will continue into the future. When Jodie and Andrew decide to get married they are making a permanent commitment to each other and to their relationship.

- *Predictability and understanding* increase the more Jodie and Andrew share their life together. After some time they can predict with high accuracy what the other will think or do. One person's behaviors are both predictable and desirable according to the other person's standards.

- *Communicative code change* occurs once the couple know each other so well that they can finish each other's sentences and understand a unique language known only to them. Special words and phrases come to have meaning for the couple. Because they have shared so many experiences, a form of shorthand language evolves. This "code" affirms the relationship bond and increases the efficiency of their communication.

Each *inter*personal relationship—romantic, friendship, or family—goes through life stages and a growth pattern. An examination of these cycles at the initiation, the maintenance, and finally the termination of a relationship, will organize our discussion.

The Initiation Stage of a Relationship

In the very early stages of a relationship we are just trying to get noticed. "Pick up" lines, used by individuals to begin a conversation, vary from sincere to ridiculous. The following story by one of our students demonstrates where one can go wrong.

> I was heading for my favorite bar; I had been dateless for several weeks so I was looking for someone to meet. As I went in some girl from my economics class recognized me and said hello. This sent my ego through the roof. I searched the crowd and for some reason didn't see anyone that matched my mental picture of what I was looking for. Then out of the corner of my eye I spotted her. I moved toward her, took a deep breath, and said, "Do you hum here coffin?" She gave me a confused look and before she could react I turned and headed for the door. On the way home I repeatedly beat myself against the head and promised myself that I would come up with a better opening line next time.

First impressions are long-lasting and difficult to change. Therefore, we want people to think well of us during those initial encounters. Unfortunately, in our attempts to be clever we sometimes say foolish things. The following is one of our favorite lines we've heard in our class. In fact, this one was awarded first place by a class of 400 students. A young man reported using it but did not report how successful he was with it. "Can I borrow a quarter? I have to call my mother and tell her I just met the girl I'm going to fall in love with."

During the initial stages of a relationship we regularly share public information about ourselves. When the conversation does not proceed past basic introductions, or when we see someone for only a few minutes, our conversation is rather superficial. This is called "phatic communication".

Phatic Communication is a scanning process in which you are attempting to determine whether or not a relationship will develop. Phatic communication is superficial and helps maintain a relationship at the acknowledgment level. However, it serves a very important purpose. Phatic communication acknowledges the other individual and lets him or her know you think that person is important enough to recognize. But most important, without it the other person feels disconfirmed or not acknowledged. Examples are when you greet someone and she does not respond, or, in a meeting, when you make a suggestion and no one comments on it and the discussion continues as if you had never spoken. Disconfirmation may be even more direct, as when some-one says, "Your ideas are foolish." To be ignored is the most negative kind of

Phatic communication acknowledges the other individual and lets him know you think he is important enough to recognize.

feedback one can be given. If you've ever been ignored by someone, you know how bad it makes you feel.

Relationships are regularly initiated because of your proximity to another person. As you learned in Chapter 3's discussion of proxemics, the physical distance you are from someone else is an important factor in communication. College students who live in dorms tend to make friends with the students on their floor. Because you are close to each other in terms of physical space, you tend to associate with each other. Proximity, or physical closeness, has a huge impact on whether or not a relationship will get past the initiation stage. Proximity tends to help us minimize less desirable traits. In other words, the closer we are to someone physically, the more we *want* to like and believe in him or her. Familiarity in and of itself may increase liking.

Couples separated by great a distance must work very hard at maintaining the relationship. In fact, one researcher discovered that couples in long-distance relationships develop some unique patterns of interaction to overcome the distance:

> Although geographically separated couples miss daily intimacy and shared activity, marital partners invest themselves into their relationship when they are together. When geographically separated couples reunite for short visits, they tend to give their relationship a priority and spend less time on unimportant obligations and trivial conflicts. (McPherson, 1996, p. 99)

One couple had a "date" every Friday night to go to the movies—over the telephone! They each rented the same video and watched the film together, talking and laughing throughout. This gave them common experiences to share. With their jobs, they could afford the phone bill, and it was well worth the intangible benefits.

One of our students explained his distant relationship this way:

> When I first left home to go away to school I had a girlfriend I had been dating a while and was pretty serious with. The problem was I was going to be leaving to go away for school and she was staying home to attend school. We were used to seeing each other almost every day and we knew we would not be able to do this any longer. We were going to have to find other ways to communicate with each other that did not include face-to-face. The first option was obvious—talking on the telephone. But this option can tend to get a little too expensive, which we figured out very quickly. So now we were going to have to find other ways of communicating. Writing each other letters and sending little gifts to each other helped us to be able to stay in touch and stay close and not grow apart. Also, something we each learned at school helped us to communicate, and that was using E-mail. This way we could send each other messages very quickly and very easily, avoiding having to use the postal service. Using a good blend of ways to communicate without seeing each other, we were able to stay in touch enough that it made missing each other's physical presence a lot easier. As a result we were able to maintain our relationship while living away from each other.

This student and his friend learned to use technology to stay in touch daily, giving the couple a sense of shared experience. The U.S. Navy uses the same approach to help sailors stay in touch with their families. Sailors may be at sea for months at a time. One Navy official recently reported that more than 5,000 E-mail messages were sent from one ship to the home base each day. This way the individuals in the service, who would normally be out of touch for months, could check in with their families on a daily basis.

Just as being in the same place at the same time as another person may lead to a relationship, so can your network of friends and associates be of assistance. Establishing a friendship or learning about a person you want to meet by asking your friends who know him or her is using networking; others can help you find out if this is a person you want to get to know better. "Everyone is connected indirectly to everyone else. As we know from small world studies, 5 to 10 links are usually all that are needed to connect any two randomly selected persons" (Parks, 1997, p. 351). We use networks as reference points for the new people we meet. If someone we trust tells us another individual is a person we would like, we tend to believe that someone. One of the authors lives in a small community where people immediately try to make connections to every new person they meet, even to the extent of identifying who used to live in the house the newcomer has purchased.

Another variable in the initiation stage that will increase liking is similarity, or the degree to which we hold similar beliefs and values. We want people to be like us. Job interviewers want to hire people they will be comfortable working with. Among the things that affect initial attraction in the initiation stages is perceived reciprocity of liking. That is, if the other person likes you, you tend to like him. It is hard to resist someone when he demonstrates respect and affection for you.

Along with similarity, physical attraction also plays a dominant role. The old saying, "Beauty is in the eye of the beholder," certainly holds true in relationships. Jodie was initially attracted to Andrew because he was tall and had a warm smile. Andrew wanted to meet Jodie because he liked her long dark hair and easy laugh.

In order for the relationship to move to a more permanent status, four requirements must be met (Patton & Griffin, 1981, p. 320):

1. *Self-disclosure* by both participants.
2. *Positive inter*personal perceptions so that each feels positive about the other.
3. Sharing of information about each other's *self-concepts.*
4. Predictions made and fulfilled regarding *desirable responses* to each other. (In other words I feel free to tell you what I want from you.)

The following example demonstrates how these four requirements may be met:

> Suppose you meet someone on the tennis court. You like this person's looks. Your attraction initiates a degree of involvement on your part. You chat a while and you like the sense of personal values implied by the conversation. She expresses regard for friends, appreciation of personal skill and achievement, and an interest in conversing with you. You play tennis for an hour and receive an impression of honesty in keeping the score, determination to do one's best, and fairness in judging out-of-bounds serves. At lunch you are impressed by her courtesy and consideration for others, cleanliness in eating habits, and friendliness in meeting your needs or wishes. During the next half hour you hear of her hopes for graduation, ambition to be a pediatrician, frustration over required courses, and sadness over the recent loss of a grandfather. If over the ensuing days such self-disclosure continues and you can continue to be interested in such personal information, involvement in the relationship will increase. In addition, disclosure of the way she feels about you may lead to even greater involvement. If she shows interest in and respect for your hopes, ambitions, values, and frustrations, your degree of involvement will be heightened, and the relationship will be of greater importance both to you and to her (Patton & Giffin, 1981, p. 320).

As the two individuals described above develop their relationship, they will also identify expectations of each other that may lead to a more permanent relationship. These expectations may be created because of society's norms. For example, expecting the male to ask the female out and being responsible for the expenses of the date may be a norm of society one partner expects the other to live up to. As this norm changes the male may begin to expect the female to cover an equal amount of the costs. One partner may begin to expect that they will always have a date on Saturday night so when he discovers that she has planned to go out with others, he thinks the relationship must be in trouble. The more these expectations are *shared*, the more likely the couple will move to maintaining the relationship.

Maintenance of the Relationship   ❖ ❖ ❖ ❖

A Feeling of Trust

Probably the single most important factor in maintaining relationships is trust. Trusting another person means you feel confident that no harm will come to you if you share information with this individual. Trust is also relying on another person in a risky situation and believing the other person will assist you in reaching your goals. Potential loss, if trust is violated, is greater than the potential gain.

Usually, trust and confidentiality are connected. If I share personal information with you and then discover that you have shared it with others, I will not trust you with such information in the future. As one author put it, "The increased vulnerability which rises with intimacy is tolerable only if accompanied by a belief that the partner will not exploit it" (Hinde, 1981, p. 14).

As we share more information about our hopes, dreams, and fears, we open ourselves up for criticism. We share our private thoughts only with those we think will accept them and not be critical of us because of them. This is being vulnerable. If someone were to exploit our trust in them we would have difficulty rebuilding the relationship. In the cartoon "Peanuts," Charlie Brown continues to trust Lucy to hold the football for him to kick even though she pulls it away at the last second every time. Most of us are not this trusting. In fact, all of us know of individuals who follow the philosophy, "Once bitten, twice shy," meaning if someone breaks a trust once, the individual won't give that person a second chance. These kinds of experiences affect our self-concept, which in turn affects our willingness to trust in the next relationship. If someone has a low self-concept he or she is unlikely to be able to trust others to any great degree.

Support for the Relationship

A second way relationships are maintained is through relationship networks. The way a particular relationship changes over time will be intertwined with what happens in the participants' other relationships. For example, if Jodie's best friend goes out with Andrew's good friend, and one ends up hurting the other's feelings, Jodie and Andrew's relationship is likely to be affected by it. At the same time, individuals often develop close ties to the family members of partners and continue those relationships long after the partnership has dissolved.

The network of relationships in which our relationship is imbedded definitely affects the likelihood that our relationship will continue. "Attraction to members of the partner's networks and attraction to the partner should be related" (Parks, 1997, p. 364). Liking your partner's family and friends should lead to greater liking for the partner. At the same time, if you dislike his or her friends or family, the relationship may be difficult to maintain.

Messages Sent, Messages Received

Confirming messages contribute to the continuation of a relationship. These types of messages confirm our self-concept and give us positive feedback.

Disconfirming messages do not acknowledge our self-concept and actually do damage to our self-esteem. Consider the following:

Disconfirming Messages

1. Ignore what has been said.
2. Make no nonverbal contact, in fact, avoids eye contact and touching of any kind.
3. Engage in a monologue.
4. Ignore the person's request, fail to return calls, do not answer questions or letters.
5. Interrupt and make it difficult when the person wants to express himself or herself.

Confirming Messages

1. Acknowledge what has been said.
2. Maintain eye contact and touch and acknowledge the other person.
3. Engage in dialogue.
4. Acknowledge the other person's efforts.
5. Encourage the other person to express his or her thoughts and feelings.

Obviously the examples of confirming communication are those that will increase and heighten the enjoyment that one receives from an *inter*personal relationship. Here are some examples that would demonstrate confirmation, rejection, and disconfirmation.

Confirmation

Lynn: Guess what? I just got that internship I wanted for the summer.

Sara: Congratulations, I know you were really nervous about getting one; I'm really happy for you.

Rejection

Lynn: Guess what? I just got that internship I wanted for the summer.

Sara: Are you sure that's the one you want to take? I heard that internship doesn't pay much money.

Disconfirmation

Lynn: Guess what? I just got that internship I wanted for the summer.

Sara: Uh huh, I wonder what's for dinner at the dining hall?

Learning how to cope with disconfirming messages will protect your self-esteem. Learning not to use disconfirming messages will make you a more effective communicator. Some of these messages are sent because of different needs we each have. Understanding that our needs may differ in a relationship is critical to being able to accept the other person's needs as different from, but not less important than, our own.

Interpersonal Needs

In the early literature on the sociology of *inter*personal relationships, William Schultz (1958) identified three *inter*personal needs that will determine the extent to which an *inter*personal relationship lasts:

- *Inclusion.*
- *Control.*
- *Affection.* The authors would add behavioral flexibility and realistic expectations to this list.

Inclusion is the extent to which we want to be a part of others' activities. Some individuals like to be a part of everything that is going on, so they have a high need for inclusion. Others enjoy solitude and do not like being in large crowds. They have a low need for inclusion. Neither is the "preferred" way to be, but knowing this about yourself will help you make decisions about future careers and partners. If you would prefer to work alone, then your career should be in a field where you have a good deal of independence and do not have to work through others—for example, as a computer programmer. On the other hand, if you enjoy working with others to accomplish a task and do not get frustrated when fellow workers are not "pulling their weight," then perhaps you are cut out to supervise the activities of others.

The second *inter*personal need is control. All of us want to feel in control of our relationships and our activities, but the level of need to control varies from person to person. Some people like to dominate discussions and be the leaders of whatever groups they are a part of. Others are just as happy to be followers. You may, in fact, be in control of your personal life but not of your professional life, or vice versa. Difficulties arise when both partners in a relationship have an equal need to control or dominate the relationship and decisions the partners make. The opposite would cause problems, too. Sometimes neither partner wants to make decisions!

Finally, the need for affection differs among partners. Your need for affection may depend in large part on your family of origin. If your family demonstrated affection openly, and expected affection to be shared, then you will probably expect it in your relationships. You would be unhappy if your partner never told you he loved you and never demonstrated his love for you in public or in private. On the other hand, you may have been raised in a family where open affection was not acceptable. As a result, you might be uncomfortable with public displays of affection. It is important to understand that neither attitude necessarily demonstrates the depth of affection one actually feels. The difficulty arises when partners have different needs for affection. Thus, a woman might be wondering if her partner really loves her because he

Love is a deep form of affection for another person.

never shows her much affection and is actually embarrassed by her more obvious displays of affection.

What makes some couples stay in love for 40 years while others end in divorce? We must not know the answer to that question since 50 percent of marriages now end in divorce. Chances are very good that one out of every two readers of this book is a child of divorced parents. At the same time, interestingly enough, it is far less likely that your grandparents were divorced. This increase in the divorce rate has occurred almost within one generation. Let's discuss first what holds people together, and then talk about those things that pull them apart.

Love is a deep form of affection for another person. There was a time when to say "I love you" meant a permanent commitment. At least 50 percent of the time, that is not the case today! Couples need to share the same understanding for the words, "I love you." For one person it might mean, "You are so great to be with. I really have a good time when I'm with you." To another it could mean, "I really love you and want to spend the rest of my life exclusively with you." According to some authors (O'Hair et al., 1995, p. 307), love is made up of three components:

- *Intimacy* is the aspect of love that is the most emotional and involves the feelings of support, sharing, and respect. It is the connection that the two parties feel with one another.
- *Passion* is the physical attraction, the desire or sexual excitement.
- *Commitment* is the aspect that develops with the idea that the relationship could possibly be long term. It is made up of the decisions that each individual makes affecting whether or not the relationship will continue.

Thus, "falling in love" may mean one or all of the above attributes. The many components of love need to be understood by both partners so that misunderstandings can be minimized.

Patterns and Expectations in a Relationship

The patterns of interaction in the relationship result in identifying the relationship as complementary, where one person dominates the decision-making process and the other is more submissive, symmetrical, where the two partners are more equal in who makes the decisions, or parallel where the partners alternate in making decisions depending on the topic and their expertise. Healthy relationships tend to move in and out of these forms of interaction. In some cases the relationship is more complementary and in other instances it is more symmetrical. For example, Jodie makes most of the decisions about vacations, where and when it is best for the couple to travel. In this case Andrew complements Jodie's decision-making by being more submissive about vacation plans. On the other hand, Andrew is currently making decisions about their building a new house. While Jodie is involved she would just as soon leave the details of the construction up to Andrew. Now the relationship is once again complementary with Jodie being more submissive in the decision-making process. When it comes to major career changes for either of them they fully participate in the decision-making process since any changes will dramatically affect both of them. In this case they are in a symmetrical relationship.

Most communication specialists agree that the greatest skill individuals need in order to establish successful and fulfilling relationships is behavioral flexibility. This means that individuals are able to adapt their communication style to the needs of a particular situation. We are not suggesting that a person can change his or her basic personality. If you are shy you are unlikely to become outgoing in order to be a successful communicator. If you try to change your style to that extent you will probably be very uncomfortable. But you can slightly modify your interactions with others so that when the other person needs to talk you are quiet, even though you are used to talking. Or

Spotlight on Ethics

The all-male group "Promisekeepers" has been criticized because some people interpret their guidelines as making the male in a heterosexual relationship, the dominant member of the relationship or of the family. Others who are involved claim that the group does more for the equality of women in that men "promise" to be faithful and loving toward their spouses. The reason this group is somewhat controversial is their views on complementary and symmetrical relationships.

Locate the guidelines for this group in your library. Do you think this group is recommending a complementary or symmetrical relationship between husbands and wives? What are the concerns being expressed by both sides of this issue?

when the other person needs for you to tell her you care about her, even if you are shy, you can manage to let the other person know how you feel. Successful communicators attempt to adapt to the communication situation. They are flexible enough in their approach and in their use of various communication strategies that they can adapt to the setting they find themselves in.

Another variable leading to successful relationships involves developing realistic expectations. Earlier we talked about the impact of expectations on the relationship. These expectations can come from society and the media at large which may lead us to believe we must conform to certain behavior patterns, or they can come from our demands on each other. If Jodie marries Andrew because she loves him but doesn't like the fact that he hunts, goes fishing frequently, and is not interested in current events and she thinks that she will be able to change him, she will be in for a big surprise. Our expectations for each other must be realistic, possible, and achievable.

One last concept applied to *inter*personal relationships can explain why some relationships last and others do not. Exchange theory suggests that social interaction is regulated by the individual's desire to get the maximum pleasure and minimum pain from the other person. Individuals are most attracted to a person who provides the highest ratio of rewards for the lowest amount of costs. Relationships generally will not be maintained unless the partners feel rewarded in some way. If the cost in time and energy exceeds the benefits derived from the relationship they are likely to terminate that relationship (Thibout & Kelley, 1959). For example, if a friend asks you to help them study for an exam, it will cost you time taken away from your own studies. Perhaps what you get back will be worth the effort: deepening friendship. However, if you judge the other person to be merely an acquaintance with whom you are unlikely to interact again, then the time it takes is more costly to you.

Termination of Relationships

Popular literature has a lot more to say about how to start relationships than it does about how to successfully end them. In fact, many relationships end leaving both partners feeling that their self-esteem has been severely damaged. There may not be a "good" way to end a relationship. However, there certainly are factors that contribute to ending a relationship, and an understanding of these factors may make us more sensitive to early warning signs so we can either correct the problem or better prepare ourselves for ending the relationship.

A number of factors discussed earlier can lead to the ending of a relationship, for example, the exchange of benefits. Andrew asks Peter, his roommate, to help him study for a test Peter took the previous term. What Andrew really wants is for Peter to try and remember what was asked on the exam. Peter has to decide if this is ethical and if the time and energy he will expend helping his roommate is "worth it." What he may get in return is his roommate's loyalty and help with another subject at some later time. Is that enough of a reward for Peter to continue to help Andrew? Perhaps, if it is the first time, but if Andrew continues to ask for this type of help and does not give Peter any help in return, this relationship may be heading for termination.

The same relationship networks we mentioned above as ways to start relationships can also contribute to their ending. As problems start in the relationship, partners shift interaction from shared to unshared networks of friends. The network of relationships the two people once shared start to shift. Network members withdraw either because of negative judgments of one or both partners in the relationship or fear of adverse impact on their own relationships. When a couple divorces, friends often find themselves in the awkward position of having to choose which partner to continue their friendship with. Divorcees often complain that they lost not only the person with whom they were sharing their life, but also a large part of a network of friends who supported them as well.

As a relationship deteriorates, each partner seeks to keep his or her own identity from being damaged. A well-known researcher, Erving Goffman (1959), called this "facework." Saving face is highly significant in some other cultures. Even in the American culture it is very important to protect your self-esteem. Thus, we engage in behaviors that help us avoid being hurt.

> Avoidant facework includes such practices as steering a conversation away from topics that would be embarrassing to self or other, pretending not to hear a belch or burp, or ignoring a rude comment. It also includes "disclaimers," statements used to preface remarks that could reflect negatively on the speaker, like: "I could be wrong but. . . ." or "Some of my best friends are Catholic, but. . . ." (Metts, 1997, p. 374)

As these face-saving strategies become more dominant, the partners are no longer able to trust each other enough to share how they are really feeling. Instead they use diversionary tactics to deflect possible harm. For example, as Jodie and Andrew's relationship starts to deteriorate, they start "testing" each other to find out the limits of the relationship. Jodie may make a disparaging remark about herself and wait to see if Andrew comes to her defense. Or Andrew may imply that he is no longer interested in some of their joint activities, to see if Jodie tries to persuade him to continue to be as highly involved as he has been in the past. They are both trying to "save face" or avoid a direct confrontation when the other person admits he or she is not as committed to the relationship as they once were.

❖ ❖ ❖ ❖   Divorce

Some relationships actually "terminate," meaning the friends or partners decide to go their separate ways and expect never to see each other again. Other relationships significantly decrease in commitment or interaction but continue in some form. For example, parents who get divorced still must maintain some kind of relationship because they are jointly responsible for, and connected to, their children for the rest of their lives.

One team of researchers found that individuals more often perceived their divorcing parents as deceiving them if they were dissatisfied with the quality of communication with their mothers; deception was not associated with satisfaction with communication between fathers and their children.

> It may be that mother and child establish a very trusting relationship in the formative years, thereby creating more dissatisfaction if the mother is believed to have engaged in deceptive behavior (i.e. greater violation of expectations). Additionally, in this study, as in other reports . . . the mother was typically the parent who broke the news of the divorce. Children may have associated negative feelings with their mothers who were the bearers of bad news, and who may then also have been perceived as deceptive. Hence, children may react more negatively to her than to the partner who was not the initial source of negative information. (Thomas, Booth-Butterfield, & Booth-Butterfield, 1995, p. 239)

Clearly, the negative consequences of how the children are told about the divorce are long-lasting. It is interesting to note that in this study the children lost trust with the mother more frequently. One of our students described the type of communication that went on during his parents' divorce. It was another situation where the mother was the bearer of bad news:

When my parents got a divorce they had not told my brother and me that they were having any troubles at all. One day my mom drove my brother and me to school and out of nowhere she told us that she and my father were going to separate. I could not believe it at all because it came as a total shock. But from that point on she talked to my brother and me about everything that was going on. With this open and honest communication came an understanding about the situation. It made it easier for me to deal with because we communicated about the problem. My father and I, however, did not communicate about the divorce so well. We *never* talked about it and kept everything from one another. This made us grow apart. But after a while we did start to talk about it more and more. This communication allowed us to open up our relationship more and allowed us to get closer than we had been. Due to this experience I found that without communication our relationship could have been destroyed and we could have grown apart from each other.

— Erin, second-year college student

This student learned the hard way that sharing information is critical in a crisis situation. Children worry most about how life will change, and when parents fail to tell them how the divorce will change their daily routine they may imagine a scenario worse than what is really going to happen.

There are many types of post-divorce relationships between the parents and the children. One researcher has examined the forms these post-divorce relationships can take. Elizabeth Graham (1997) has studied post-divorce families as they attempt to redefine themselves. Her subjects identified turning points, or times in the relationship when important events occurred that affected the relationship. These turning points led Graham to identify the following types of post-divorce relationships:

1. Establishment of the *well-functioning binuclear family*, when things begin to settle into a routine.

2. The *dysfunctional former spousal relationship* that involves fighting and conflict with the former spouse.

3. *Life-improving events* such as returning to school or reaching financial stability.

4. *Major life change* like remarriage of either former partner.

5. *Parent-child problems* where conflicts increase between former spouse and children.

6. *Emotional divorce* when the former partners realize there is no future in the relationship, and experience a final sense of "letting go."

7. *Relocation* when one of the parents moves away.

8. *Personal hardship* which might include health, financial, or personal problems.

Surprisingly enough, the most frequently cited turning point was the well-functioning binuclear family. Graham says that maintaining a functional relationship, despite previous differences, is an important accomplishment because it suggests the two former partners are committed to having a successful divorce even if they did not have a successful marriage, particularly if there is a child or children involved. This study indicates that there is a relationship after divorce for parents of children and that it can be a satisfying one.

Some writers have attempted to suggest "repair" work for couples who want to reverse the trend in their relationship that is leading to termination. S. Duck (1997) indicated a relationship is in need of repair when one or more of the following four main factors emerge:

1. A significant inconsistency occurs between the definition of the relationship as perceived by outsiders, and the definition accepted by at least one partner.

2. Obstacles emerge to block a mutually agreed-upon shift from one relationship stage to the next.

3. Relationship partners maintain significantly different definitions of the relationship along with different expectations of each other.

4. A major difference exists between the definition of the relationship and the behaviors exhibited in the relationship.

These may be perceived as "warning signs" that the relationship needs help. Certainly the two partners must have the same understanding about the level of commitment to the relationship. Obstacles may be disagreements about how to spend time together or future plans. We may think we agree but act is if we have two different ideas about our time together.

The following repair tactics are then suggested:

Steps in Repairing Relationships
1. Reduce turbulence in interactions.
2. Improve communication.
3. Bring out the partner's positive side.
4. Focus on the positive aspects of the relationship.
5. Reinterpret the behavior of the partner as positive and well-intentioned.
6. Reduce negativity toward the partner and adopt a more balanced view.
7. Reevaluate the attractiveness and unattractiveness of alternative relationships and alternative partners.
8. Enlist the support of others in order to hold the relationship together.
9. Obtain help to correct matters or to end the relationship.
— O'Hair et. al., 1995, p. 315.

These steps are appropriate only if both parties want to "repair" the relationship. Clearly direct and honest communication is central to any of these approaches. When a couple considers divorce they have to recognize the impact that divorce will have, not only on their own lives, but on an entire family, as well as mutual friends. That includes not only children but grandparents, aunts, uncles, cousins, and in-laws (those people related to the family by marriage). We will close this chapter with a discussion of communication in the family.

Family Communication

What is a family? In today's society a family can be defined many more ways than as the traditional father, mother, and two to three children. A family is a group of people sharing living space and committed to supporting each other psychologically and financially. The shared living space could also include families that actually share two or more living spaces as occurs with stepchildren with two residences or long-distance relationships. This means that a family may be made up of stepparents, stepsisters and stepbrothers, other family relatives like grandparents, two unmarried adults with or without children, a gay couple, or a group of unrelated individuals who decide to live and work together to create a home. The residents of the Blessit House in Chicago consider themselves a family although none of the residents are related. They are bound together by a tragic set of circumstances. All are in the latter stages of AIDS and have no other family to take care of them. So, our definition of family needs to be broad in scope to accommodate all possibilities. Despite the different descriptions, families share the following characteristics:

- Defined roles.
- Commitment to the relationship.
- Responsibilities toward the family.
- A shared history.

❖ ❖ ❖ ❖

Family communication influences us in the way we see the world, especially in terms of "shaping ambition, skill development, moral development, attitudes toward power, and behavioral/leadership styles" (Kelly, 1997, p. 23). The family teaches us how to understand our world, how to behave, and how to adapt our communication in certain situations. For example, girls learn from their mothers the appropriate way to behave. And boys look to their fathers or an older preferred adult to develop their views of masculinity. Unlike relationships we build with other people, where we have the option of moving in or out of the relationship, our relationships with family members are set and exist in a very real and permanent way.

Degree of Shared Attitudes

Conformity orientation is the degree to which a family creates and maintains an environment that stresses a sharing of attitudes, values, and beliefs. This orientation exists on a continuum, with the high end indicating a uniformity of attitudes, values, and beliefs, and the low end indicating a greater difference among family members in regard to attitudes, values, and beliefs (Fitzpatrick, 1997). If a family is high in their uniformity of attitudes, values, and beliefs, there should theoretically be less turmoil and problems in that family. However, if family members differ greatly in their values, problems can result. For example, if the child in a family does not value good grades while the parents consider success in school to be a basic value they hold dear, rebellion could be the result.

Conversation orientation is the degree to which families create and maintain an environment where members are encouraged to state their opinions on many topics (Fitzpatrick, 1997). This orientation exists on a continuum, with families on the high end allowing a great deal of time and freedom for interaction about any topic, and families on the low end of the continuum interacting less frequently and placing limitations on what topics may be discussed with all family members. Examples of prohibited conversations that might lead to communication barriers include, but are not limited to, the inability of family members to ask for help or emotional support, talk about their dreams and ideas, express anger, show their pain, talk about their needs, voice disagreement, show affection, or ask for attention.

Depending on the family's orientation, members may either feel free to talk openly about topics important to them or feel constrained to share their true feelings. "Family talk" plays a significant role in shaping attitudes and beliefs. Some families use the dinner hour as a time to talk about issues that matter to them. However, in today's fast-paced world most families report that they no longer eat together. One child has soccer practice, while another is home. When the soccer player is home the other child is at a scout meeting, while mom and dad juggle family time between evening meetings for their jobs. Managing the conflicts that arise from these different needs and difficult schedules is an important skill.

"Family talk" plays a significant role in the shaping of attitudes and beliefs.

Conflict in Families

Conflict is a natural part of any relationship and in Chapter 11 we discuss in some detail how conflict can actually be helpful to the communication process. Conflict may arise over a wide variety of issues. As mentioned earlier, when one member of the family does not meet the expectations of another concerning intimacy, this may cause conflict. Another cause of conflict in families occurs when intimacies outside the primary relationship are established. Examples of this problem might be extramarital affairs but could also include children who spend a great deal of time with friends outside the family unit. Both examples are threatening to the family if they lead to resentment and insecurity. A third cause of conflict is undefined expectations. These expectations can be over minor details like who will do a chore on a specific night or can be the result of unrealistic expectations of family members for each other. Financial difficulties also contribute to conflict in the family. Money worries, the inability to get ahead financially, working long hours, or struggling to make ends meet can all create a negative environment leading to conflict within the family.

Children learn how to handle conflict by watching the adult role models in the family. C. L. Hale, B. F. Farley-Lucus, and R. W. Tardy (1996) examined the strategies of children from their own perspective in *inter*personal conflict resolution. The conflicts they discussed fell into two categories: (1) verbal (conflict as a product of the spoken word), and (2) nonverbal (conflict as a disapproving look or other nonverbal communication). From discussions with children (second graders to high school students) concerning the aftermath of a conflict with another child, four themes emerged: confronting, seeking involvement from third parties, ignoring, and treating others with kindness. For the children, confronting the other person could be either in a positive or negative way, ranging from apologizing or just trying to get to the source of the problem, to physical confrontations or shouting matches. When third

MISSION: POSSIBLE

How would you describe the communication patterns in your family? If you were to draw a picture of how communication takes places in your family, what would it look like? Each family is unique and sets up its own special patterns of interaction, some of which are destructive. You can't change anyone else's behaviors, but you can control your own behaviors and your reactions to others. Compare your family's pattern of interaction with those of another family you know well. How do the two families show affection? How are conflicts resolved? Who talks the most in the family? How are decisions made? Do either of these families look like any family on television? What are the similarities and differences? What do you like about the way your family communicates? What do you dislike? Which family member would you have the most success with in sharing this information? What is preventing you from sharing it?

parties became involved, the person involving the third party might be viewed as a "tattletale" and this method of resolution had potential for actually creating a larger problem between the students. Avoiding the other person was a frequent approach for the children involved in conflict. And, lastly, acts of kindness (such as complimenting the other person, writing a letter of apology, or doing something nice) were more prevalent in primary grade levels. Surprisingly, the researchers also discovered that the children seemed to learn early and quickly socially gendered conflict behaviors: girls' "talk" and boys' "actions" constituted grounds for conflict and responses to conflict.

Summary

*Inter*personal relationships form and shape our lives. We started this chapter by saying we thought what makes a great day is when someone whose opinion you value tells you what a great person you are. Our self-esteem, and consequently our success in our personal and professional life, depends to a great extent on the opinion others hold of us. Learning how to integrate all those relationships can make the difference between an unhappy and isolated individual and a happy, productive member of a team and a family. In the next chapter we will discuss communication in small groups where others are depending on your contributions.

At Your Bookstore

Alberti, R. E. (1995). *Your Perfect Right: A Guide to Assertive Living* (7th ed.). San Luis Obispo, CA: Impact.

Anderson, K. (1997). *Friendships That Run Deep: 7 Ways to Build Lasting Relationships*. Downer's Grove: IL.: Intervarsity Press.

Canary, D. J., & Stafford, L. (1996). *Communication and Relational Maintenance*. San Diego: Academic Press.

Nardi, P. M. (Ed.), (1992). *Men's Friendships*. Newbury Park, CA: Sage.

CHAPTER 7

Living and Working in Small Groups

❖ ❖ ❖ ❖

Last summer while working as a lifeguard at a waterpark, I was involved in an accident where communication played an extremely important role. I was guarding on a tube ride that consisted of five separate water pools. A woman flipped backwards off her tube, hitting her head on the slide. She was suffering from a serious head and neck injury, so it was important that all of the lifeguards communicated properly and moved quickly.

A whistle was blown indicating to the lifeguards to stop other riders and call the EMT staff to the scene. The lifeguard attending the woman's section immobilized her head until a stretcher came. I was called down to assist in placing the woman on a backboard to transport her from the pool. Communication was extremely important in a situation such as this. All the guards had a specific responsibility that had to be performed correctly and in unity with the other guards so as to keep the victim from further injury.

— David, second-year college student

As David discovered in his summer job, working together as a team can be essential in saving a person's life. What would have happened if the lifeguards had not functioned as a team? More tube riders could have continued down the slide and collided with the woman and the assisting lifeguards. Or valuable minutes could have been lost waiting for someone to assume responsibility and call for emergency medical help. Fortunately for the injured woman, David's team of lifeguards worked together quickly to assess her injuries and transport her from the accident scene.

In this crisis situation, David discovered the importance of communication when working in small groups. David's experience focuses on one very specific life-threatening situation, but some sorts of encounters with small groups occur everyday. The reason is simple. Small groups are a part of everyone's life. In this chapter, we will look at

- The communication that occurs in the small group context, and the types of groups.
- Advantages and disadvantages of working in groups.
- Roles in groups.
- Communication processes that occur in group life such as group culture, cohesion, and leadership.

The Nature of Group Work

Importance of Small Group Communication

From the moment you are born, and throughout the rest of your life, you will be a member of many groups, whether it is the family in which you were raised, a youth group, a clique of friends, or a department you worked in at your summer job. If it isn't already apparent, groups are an unavoidable part of human interaction, not only in interpersonal relationships but also in education, politics, and business.

Historically, small groups have been essential to human survival. For example, our Stone Age ancestors probably traveled together for protection from other tribes or ferocious beasts, hunted in groups to increase the likelihood of making a kill, and lived together for the purpose of companionship. Are we in our contemporary society much different in reliance on groups? Every day, millions of people carpool to a common workplace. The milk we buy at the grocery store comes from a cooperative of dairy farmers who pool their resources to provide a product. The small group remains an integral part of our lives.

Small group communication is a "human communication system composed of three or more individuals, interacting for the achievement of some common purpose(s), who influence and are influenced by one another" (Rothwell, 1995, p. 46). Let us break down this definition. It describes a form of communication set apart from other forms by:

- Size of the group.
- Commonality.
- Mutual influence.

The primary difference between *intra*personal (self-talk) or *inter*personal (dyadic) communication is group size. Group communication occurs among at least *three people*; however, the upper limit of what constitutes a group is debatable. Depending on the maturity, purpose, and unity of the group, a group could contain as many as 20 to 30 people. The one thing we can be sure of is that as each new group member is added, the group becomes inherently more complex. More people mean more avenues for interaction.

Having a common purpose is another important component of our definition of small group communication. Why do groups meet? A family meets to decide where to go on summer vacation. A government commission meets to formulate world policies. A group of employees meets to discuss how to best complete a work task. The common purpose that unites a group is literally the glue that holds it together. Rarely will groups without a solid, identifiable purpose be successful and maintained because the energy and focus needed for working productively as a small group is time-consuming. Few people want to take time out to sit around and stare at five or six other people without having anything to accomplish! Even a social group may have the common purpose of companionship or friendship.

The final part of our definition of small group communication focuses on mutual influence. It is impossible to enter into a group and emerge without having been influenced behaviorally, morally, or psychologically by the other human beings in your company. The groups we belong to impact our lives and the decisions that we make. Perhaps you were raised in a family that encouraged you to do charitable acts for other people. Is it any surprise then that you find yourself being a Good Samaritan later in life? Unfortunately, the influence that groups have on our lives is not always as positive as in the preceding example. Often we are amazed and appalled by stories in the media that detail a horrific murder by a tightly knit cult or the crude hazing rituals of a youth gang. The influence that occurs in that group—to convince a member to commit an act as heinous as murder—demonstrates the immense power of small group communication.

MISSION: POSSIBLE

Think for a moment about all the different groups you currently belong to. First, list these groups on a sheet of paper. Next, indicate how long you have been a member of each group. Why did you join each of these groups, assuming that you had a choice in the matter? For example, your family is a type of small group, although you did not originally have a choice to become a member of that group. How many groups did you list? Most people can list at least 8 to 10 groups that they are a member of at any one time, although your list may include 30 or more groups!

Types of Small Groups

We can examine groups according to four basic types:

- Primary.
- Social.
- Learning.
- Work.

A primary group is the most basic and enduring group that you will belong to in your lifetime. When students list the groups they belong to, one that is frequently overlooked is the family. Why is it that we fail to mention the one group that probably has more influence than any other group in our moral, psychological, and intellectual development? From birth, your family is a primary group. Other examples of a primary group include a close circle of friends that you have had since grade school or a group of co-worker or colleagues that you have worked with for many years.

Closely related to primary groups are social groups. Primary groups are much more long-lasting than social groups; your family is a primary group all you life. Social groups are "weekend friends" or people you are friendly with while in college or other temporary situations. Social groups may not be as long-lasting as primary groups, but they often exist for the same purpose. Social groups exist to provide friendship and companionship. Our need for friendship and identification is mirrored in the media on a daily basis. Popular television shows like *Friends*, *Seinfeld*, and *Melrose Place* demonstrate our society's interest in social groups. Each week, we tune into these shows, often laughing and crying with the characters as they struggle through the complex interpersonal problems that are a part of group life. Although there are times when our friends cause us agony and annoyance, our lives would be empty indeed without them, and counter to our basic human nature.

Learning groups are collectives or groups having some mutual interest that form to educate the members for some purpose, such as a Bible study group, poetry club, or physics study group. One of the authors encountered an interesting learning group years ago when she worked as a features article reporter for a small newspaper in Pennsylvania. The author was sent to write a story about an educational group that was celebrating its 50th anniversary. The Springfield Women's Club was formed half a century ago by women who were primarily stay-at-home mothers and wives, sharing a desire to be intellectually informed. Each time they met, a member presented a report on a

Although you're probably a member of many small groups at this very moment, why not start your own interactive book or television group? Once quite common in the early part of the century, book groups have undergone a dramatic revival of popularity recently, due to celebrity endorsements by the talk show hostess Oprah Winfrey and others. In a book group, members select a book to read for the month and then meet to discuss their opinions and viewpoints of the material. In larger cities, consultants are even hired to organize book groups for people! Your enjoyment of reading and finding others who enjoy the same type of material are the cornerstones of an enriching book group. Set one or two meetings a month to discuss a particular book that everyone has agreed to read. Your group could focus entirely on mystery novels or autobiographies or sports books. If you're a TV buff, you can have a similar experience with a TV viewing group. Whether you and your friends are fans of *ER, Dateline NBC, or Monday Night Football*, you can make plans to meet on certain nights to catch your favorite shows and talk about them afterwards.

geographic location, famous artist, or intriguing poet. The group politely listened and followed the presentation with lively discussions. Even today, in a time when technology has changed the way that knowledge is filtered through society, these women still choose to seek each other out for purposes of education rather than turn to a less socially interactive source such as a book or the Internet.

Another common type of group that you will encounter in your life is the work group. Work groups take on many forms, but are united by a common desire to accomplish a task. It could be an ad hoc committee to solve a small town's parking problem or a group to discuss sexual discrimination in the workplace. Work groups, unlike other groups, are characterized by more task-oriented communication. Because work groups are so focused on a particular task, it is likely that much of the communicative interaction that occurs will be oriented toward this goal. While the group may engage in social chat throughout the meeting, members will likely bring the group back to focus with a comment like, "We're straying from the agenda" or "Let's get back to our problem here instead of talking about what our plans are for the weekend." Phrases or comments such as these are less likely to occur in a primary or social group setting.

Working in Groups

To this point, we've discussed the importance of small groups in different aspects of society and the types of groups that we might belong to sometime during our life, but we haven't looked at what all the fuss is about groups anyway. Why join them? Why use them to solve problems? And, equally important, why do they not work sometimes? From a communication perspective, groups boil down to one common dynamic—*interaction*. When groups are formed and members interact, the potential benefits are many, as are the potential downfalls. In this section, we will look at five common advantages that groups produce, as well as five problems that can occur in group communication.

People working together in a group format may achieve more than each individual working alone.

Five Advantages of Using Groups

Two heads are better than one. A primary reason why people work in groups is to reap the benefits of having more than one brain working on the problem. But what occurs with groups is more than just having a few more hands involved in the project. Groups undergo a synergistic effect. To borrow from the physical sciences, synergism is the phenomenon of working together to have a greater total effect than would the sum of the individual parts. This occurs when certain drugs are combined and have a more powerful effect than any one drug could have individually. The total potential for group interaction is more than that of just the combined individual members.

Another very obvious advantage of group work is division of labor. The Beatles understood this principle well. A famous Beatles song states, "I get by with a little help from my friends." Anyone who has ever had to move into a new apartment, residence hall, or house understands this fact as well. Rather than taking 10 hours for you to move all of your possessions into your new domicile, a few friends helping can accomplish the task in a quarter of the time. When members of a group are given specialized tasks and assignments through division of labor, the job can usually be done more quickly and efficiently. With their efforts coordinated through clear lines of communication, the group can accomplish tasks that are too overwhelming, time-consuming, and complex for any one group member to tackle. Henry Ford built an American legacy on this very same idea, revolutionizing the way in which products around the globe were made with his concept of the assembly line.

Along these same lines, we can understand how work groups can create a better solution to a problem by pooling knowledge and resources. If Saturn Corporation was undertaking the development of a product, whom would they ask for advice? More than likely, executives from all levels of the corporation would be convened, from product design to marketing to sales and customer service. Members of the committee contribute their opinions to the interaction based on their years of experience in the industry. Members can offer the pooled resources of their various departments to complete the design and implementation. By pooling their knowledge and resources, group members can be more productive and efficient.

A fourth advantage of using small groups is what could be called the boomerang effect. The boomerang effect is what occurs when people are discussing and interacting in ways that increase the potential for a pool of ideas. For example, imagine a student committee that is trying to increase the number of commuters who use the university recreation facilities. Celina, Paul, and Ebony, members of the student development committee, could each work individually to develop their solutions and bring them to the university council. However, what can occur if they interact as a group is much more powerful. Let's sit in on one of their discussions:

Ebony: I was thinking that the most effective way to get more commuters to use the recreation center is to offer them a discount on their tuition.

Celina: Well, I guess that's a good idea, but I was thinking more along the lines of reasons why commuters don't use the facility right now. I'm a commuter and I'd spend more time on campus using the facilities, but I'm torn between staying here and rushing home to spend more time with my kids.

Paul: That's a good point. I never would have thought of that, Celina, but it reminds me of a program that I heard of at another university. They offered a child care service at their recreation center for commuters like you so that you could use the facilities.

Celina: Yeh that's a great idea but putting my kids in a day-care facility—even if there were one—still wouldn't solve my problem of how to spend more time with them.

Ebony: Wait. The student group in my recreation services program is always looking for projects to take on for community service. We could put together exercise and recreation programs for kids and parents. The parents could participate and work out with their children if they wanted to. Either way, it might be a solution for commuter students with families.

Paul: Finally, we've come up with an idea worth keeping.

This dialogue demonstrates the boomerang effect. Through communication, Celina, Paul, and Ebony were able to use one another to create not only more, but better ideas and solutions. Like the action of a boomerang, when one member offered an idea or comment, this provided the stimulus for another member to build on what was just said, and so on. The ideas that were generated were propelled by the comments of another group member.

Last, group work has the advantage of increasing commitment on the part of those involved. An assembly line worker is likely to feel more committed to a work project if he or she has been involved in a work decision. The concept of a "quality circle" refers to an organizational group that does just that. Quality circles are used in many companies around the world. They are made up of nonmanagerial workers who make suggestions, solve problems,

Groups can be difficult to work in when certain members dominate the group or are not committed to the task.

and then offer their ideas to management. Workers feel more committed to their organization and their jobs if they feel that their input is taken into consideration.

Five Disadvantages of Using Groups

If we stopped discussing group communication at this point, you might think that working in small groups is always advantageous and preferable to working alone. But, as one student points out, anyone who has been a member of a group knows that it's not always that easy.

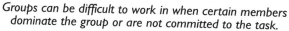

I found out how critical communication is between a small group of people when I was elected to Senior Prom Committee. Eight of us were chosen to represent and serve the junior class. It was a great experience, but at various times the communication was ineffective. It is difficult to get your message out and understood by all. Another problem we encountered was among the group of officers. We all had different viewpoints, desires, and opinions. Not everyone was willing to compromise. In the process of persuading others to agree, more than likely we ended up convincing ourselves instead of others. We had many decisions to make—for example, how much money to spend on the prom, the location, decorations, and party favors. Communication was essential to agreeing and getting along.

— Adriana, third-year college student

> ## Ways You Can Create More Equal Participation in Groups
>
> - In a non-threatening manner ask quiet group members their opinions and if they would like to contribute.
>
> - Use a round-robin technique in which all members share an idea or comment, but always give members the opportunity to pass if they do not want to contribute.
>
> - Steer discussions away from more dominant members in a respectful way by saying, "Raul thank you for presenting so many good ideas. What do others in the group think about the project?"

Group work may have its advantages, but it has many disadvantages as well. Working in groups can be time-consuming, mentally exhausting, and quite challenging.

First, communicating in groups is time-consuming. When you work alone, much of what you do is mentally processed without your having to express it. For example, do you remember taking the Scholastic Aptitude Tests to enter college? On the math section of the test, you worked quickly through the problems, scratching notes here and there, but calculating the problems silently. Now, imagine if you had to explain out loud to someone each problem, how you would solve it, and the answer to the problem. The time it would take to undertake this would be considerable. Working in groups requires the same time commitment. Because few people are mind readers, much of group time is spent discussing ideas, thoughts, and opinions. In other words, group work is different from individual work because each member must communicate, either through oral or written communication, what would normally be processed silently.

This time-consuming process of sharing ideas and opinions in groups does not always apply to all group members. Unfortunately, another disadvantage of small group work is unequal participation in discussions. Because of different styles of communication and levels of comfort, members participate differently—and often unequally—in group discussions. Some members may dominate and overwhelm conversations, while other members' voices may be entirely lost in such discussions. And the most verbally aggressive and dominant person in the group may not have the best ideas. This is one reason why groups fail. The best potential ideas may be buried when introverted or nonassertive people feel uncomfortable communicating because of a few dominant members.

Group work is also problematic when group members feel that there is an unfair workload in the group. Perhaps the most common complaint people have when working on group projects is that they feel they are doing more than their fair share of the work. The whole premise of working in groups is that the task and the labor can be split among many people. When individuals feel they're doing more work than any other group member, frustration, anger, and hostility can occur. A sense of inequity may occur if a few group members feel as if they are "carrying the weight" of other members. Take, for example, the concerns of one student, who shared her thoughts on a project in her small group communication class:

> I always liked working in groups until now. I was really excited about the group project until Lang started to slack off. He wouldn't attend group meetings or call to tell us why he wasn't coming. We didn't even give him that much to do when we split up the work, and he still couldn't pull his own weight in the group. I got totally frustrated because I had to do his work. Even though we were all angry at him when he did come to the next meeting, we just ignored him to show him that we were angry.
>
> — Wendy, second-year college student

Wendy and other members are angry at having to take responsibility for Lang's share of the group project, but they fail to communicate their frustrations with him. Even though this group is angry over the unfair workload of certain members, they're not resolving the problem with Lang constructively.

Sometimes groups may not live up to their potential when they engage in rate busting. Rate busting is a term that originated in early studies of manufacturing. The group phenomenon was noticed particularly among blue-collar workers who were paid a certain rate if they reached their quota, or set number of pieces or products for the day. The quota was set by an engineer who observed several workers and determined an average rate for the group. Often, the group members conspired to produce less than what they were capable of so that all members could keep up with the pace of the work. Members who excelled and produced more than other members were actually teased, chastised, and even pinched and punched for breaking the group's norm. How does this occur in other groups? Group members may feel pressure to lower their abilities or skills to match the rest of the group and create a level of equality. For example, one of the authors had a student who was concerned about the mutual presentation she had to give with her group. An outstanding student and excellent public speaker, this woman explained that she felt intense pressure from her group to give a mediocre speech in the group's presentation. The other group members did not want to be overshadowed by her performance. As this example illustrates, rate busting can have negative effects on individual members, as well as on the group's quality and performance.

The final disadvantage to group work is what has been described as the grouphate phenomenon. For some people, group work is so distasteful they actually avoid group situations. Relying on and sharing control with other people is difficult for some people to cope with. Interestingly, S. Sorenson (1981) found that people who hated group work the most were those who had little skill or training in how to communicate in groups. Individuals who had been trained in effective group communication skills were less likely to exhibit the grouphate phenomenon.

People who aren't skilled communicators may find group work overwhelming and unpleasant because they don't know how to use communication to solve problems in the group, resolve conflict, or express their opinions. Unfortunately, if people never gain those communication skills, it is unlikely that they will overcome their feelings of grouphate. The example given in the box that follows highlights the need for you to continually improve your communication skills.

SPOTLIGHT ON DIVERSITY

For many cultures, the grouphate phenomenon is difficult to understand. In particular, groups are a natural part of life in many South American and Asian cultures. Unlike the United States culture, which promotes individuality and independence, other cultures believe that life revolves around the concept of the group. For example, in Japan every aspect of daily life occurs in a group context, from close family and friend groups to groups in the workplace (Mathews, 1996). Groups in this culture provide stability and structure to life. It is in the context of interacting with others that Japanese develop their own identities. Rather than being seen as a burden, groups determine and influence behaviors, attitudes, values, and beliefs.

Japanese are socialized to be extremely loyal to their groups. This striving for consensus and harmony even determines Japanese communication styles and patterns. Decisions are made within the group and personal recognition is actually avoided or shunned. Consequently, statements that single out the originator of an idea or opinion in Japanese groups are unlikely to emerge. Communication by younger members may also be limited according to deference to older members in the group. In these ways, Japanese learn the forms of group communication appropriate to their culture.

What do you think?

1. *Do you originate from a culture that stresses the group or the individual?*
2. *If your culture privileges individualism, how do you think this has shaped your attitudes about group work?*
3. *Have you ever heard of any negative effects of emphasis on groups in other cultures?*

Interacting in Groups: Role-playing

Now that we have discussed the different types of groups that you might belong to and some advantages and disadvantages of working in those groups, it is important to look at what might happen when group members actually begin to interact. A role can be described as a set of behaviors or characteristics that a member adopts, either consciously or unconsciously, in group interactions (Brilhart & Galanes, 1989). In order for groups to develop, certain types of roles are necessary (adapted from the typology of Benne and Sheats, 1948).

First, groups need members to internalize "It" roles, which are defined as roles that help the group achieve the task at hand. These roles assist the group in discussing what the task is and how it should be accomplished. For example, in order for the group to work toward the task, the group may need someone to say "I have a new idea" (initiator-contributor), "How many people will we need to serve with this plan?" (information seeker) and "Should I take some notes on this?" (recorder). Another important "It" role is the devil's advocate, or someone who responds negatively to group ideas for the sake of argument and to encourage constructive conflict. When a devil's advocate does not emerge in a group, the entire group may be in danger of producing fewer ideas and poorer-quality solutions than other groups.

In addition to "It" roles, group members adopt "We" roles as well. "We" roles are ones that contribute to the group members' emotional satisfaction and social well-being. Few groups are strictly all business, and group members need socio-emotional encouragement in order to continue or exist. It is important to have group members who will contribute to the group by saying, "If you both give a little, this plan will meet all our needs" (compromiser), "That's a really great idea" (encourager), and "Now, let's just try to get along here" (harmonizer). "We" roles such as these promote cohesion and harmony among group members and may contribute to the group's continued existence. How many times have you stayed in a group not because you thought the task was particularly important but because the group members supported one another and created an environment you wanted to be part of?

"It" roles and "We" roles are necessary to group functioning, but that's not to say all group members will engage in communication that benefits the group. "I" roles refer to self-centered roles that members may adopt that detract from group goal achievement and harmony. Unfortunately, few groups are able to escape the emergence of "I" roles to some degree. When members engage in "I" roles, they are placing their individual needs above group needs in destructive ways. For example, you can recognize self-centered behaviors occurring when members say, "We don't really need to work on this project. Let's go get something to eat instead" (playboy/playgirl), "Hey, that was my idea in the first place" (recognition seeker), or "I'll determine how this problem should be solved in this group" (dominator).

Whenever such self-centered roles emerge in a group, other members should try to subvert or channel the behavior in other directions. For example, a dominator's behavior could be controlled by saying, "That's great that you're willing to take such responsibility in this project, but we were brought together in a group format so that we could hear a variety of ideas rather than just one for solving this problem." Using assertive, yet nonthreatening, statements such as these may help to reduce the continuation of "I" roles.

The roles that members in a group adopt are a matter of a variety of factors, including:

- Personality of the member.
- Nature of the group.
- Needs of the group.

For example, you might consider yourself a naturally aggressive and outgoing person who tends to adopt the role of initiator-contributor in group discussions. However, you might tend to be more of an information seeker while working on a task that you know little about. Or, you might see that no one in the group is adopting the role of encourager, so you step forward to provide that type of socio-emotional support for the group. Role-taking in groups is a complex and dynamic process that is everchanging based on the group's members and the group's needs at any particular point in time.

Contemporary Applications of Research

Group Culture and Cohesion

When groups make decisions that contradict societal norms of right and wrong, we speculate how such a decision could have been made. How, we wonder, could a group of fraternity brothers willingly haze a fellow member? How could a group of government officials conspire to destroy evidence or hide materials from the public? The answers can only be found within the group itself. To those of us outside the group, it is difficult to understand a group's decisions and choices. The reason for this difficulty is that we have not shared in the group's culture. Group culture refers to the shared set of values, beliefs, rites, rituals, heroes, and stories that a group holds. For example, a Little League baseball team may have a ritual handshake that the members perform before each game. Or a religious cult may have a set of beliefs that bind the group together. When a group upholds a certain belief, value, or ritual, it tends to be celebrated by the entire group and becomes a part of the group's culture.

Culture creates a sense of cohesion, or a willingness to stay together, among group members. In many groups, having a strong group culture and a sense of cohesion is necessary for survival. Such is the case of a small group at Bonaventure House studied by researchers Mara Adelman and Lawrence Frey (1994). Bonaventure House is a facility opened by a Chicago religious order of monks in 1989 to foster assisted living for AIDS patients.

Approximately 30 residents live at Bonaventure House at any given time in a dormitory atmosphere. Since its opening, 62 percent of the residents have died from this merciless disease. At Bonaventure House, the residents are faced with the effects of their disease as well as the new experience of group living and the conflicts due to personality differences, unmet expectations, and varying commitments to shared living. What ties residents together is a common way of viewing themselves and others that is created through shared communication. Even though their group is continually faced with the prospect of death, the group remains highly cohesive by maintaining a strong group culture. For example, the group has developed a buddy system to help newcomers adjust to life at the facility. Each newcomer is paired with a veteran resident who introduces him or her to other residents and explains the house rules. Because death is a daily part of life at Bonaventure House, communication practices have also been initiated to deal with the loss of group members—while still maintaining cohesiveness. A death of a group member is announced by placing a burning candle set in a small wreath of flowers in the house and keeping it lit for 24 hours. Upon entering the house, each group member immediately understands, through the symbolism of the lit candle, that a fellow member has tragically left the group.

Other group rituals help cement this group together as well. For example, a balloon ceremony is performed whenever a resident passes on. Remaining group members are given a balloon in which they write final messages to the deceased and attach them to the balloons. Prayers or songs are shared and the balloons are released as a means of remembering past members and moving closer to existing members.

❖ ❖ ❖ ❖

Spotlight on Ethics

In January 1997, the nation was shocked by the airing of a homemade video detailing the hazing rituals of Marine paratroopers at Camp LeJune. The video, made in 1993, shows an airplane hangar where several young men are lined up along a wall facing a group of fellow Marines. As part of a traditional initiation process, the younger members were forced to endure the pain of having their paratrooper uniform pins jammed into their chests by senior members. Holding the sharp end outward, the senior members would shove the pins, with brutal force, into the chests of the new initiates. For almost 30 minutes, these initiates were required to tolerate the ritual, although bloody and writhing in pain.

At the end of the ritual, the senior members congratulated their new comrades with handshakes, hugs, and laughter. These new members had been inducted into the group as a means of demonstrating their loyalty, strength, and dedication to the group. Although military officials explained that such behavior was not condoned, the members explained that such rituals were necessary to bind the group together and guarantee the success of the group in dangerous situations. Is this a process of testing group member loyalty or a classic case of groupthink?

What do you think?

1. *Should one of the group members have questioned the practice? Why didn't individuals follow their personal ethics rather than allow the group to make decisions for everyone in this case?*

2. *Is it always easy to be the one person who questions group decisions?*

3. *Why would it be difficult in a group like the one described above to be a devil's advocate?*

Groupthink

As we see at Bonaventure House, strong group ties are necessary to bind the residents together for purposes of social, intellectual, and physical support. However, there are instances when cohesion can inhibit a group's process and progress. Sometimes, a group—particularly one that habitually engages in decision-making—can become so cohesive that groupthink dominates the communication process of the members. Groupthink describes what occurs when a group's desire to maintain cohesiveness and avoid conflict results in a mode of thinking that overlooks contradictory evidence and opinions. The process of groupthink was first observed by Irving Janis in the 1970s as he studied famous governmental decisions revolving around the Bay of Pigs invasion, the Korean War, the Vietnam War, and the Watergate scandal. Janis believed that groups charged with making these decisions were so overly concerned with group unity and cohesion that they failed to examine adequately the problem at hand, resulting in devastating consequences.

Another example regarding groupthink that may be more familiar to you involves the Space Shuttle Challenger disaster. Where were you when the Space Shuttle Challenger exploded on January 28, 1986? Many people can remember exactly where they were when the tragedy occurred. The entire nation was devastated when the Challenger exploded, killing every astronaut

Methods For Preventing Groupthink
• Assign a devil's advocate to test the group's idea. A group could designate a devil's advocate and rotate the position from person to person in each meeting.
• Present the group's ideas and solutions to an outside expert or liaison. Use someone not involved in the group's decision to test the group's ideas and decisions.
• Create a system where all members have a "second chance" to critically evaluate the group's final decision. In other words, encourage each member to openly express concerns and evaluate the pros and cons of the idea before any decision becomes finalized.

aboard, including civilian school teacher Christa McAuliffe. Evidence of groupthink emerged when senior-level NASA officials ignored the warnings of the manufacturer responsible for making the O-ring joint seals. Why would they ignore such warnings? To some degree, NASA officials may have chosen to overlook negative warnings because they were under intense pressure to maintain a successful launch record. With all of the excitement surrounding this special launch, the officials may have chosen to take a risk rather than dampen the group's and the entire nation's enthusiasm for the project.

As this example illustrates, groupthink can have very negative, even deadly, side effects. When you are a member of a group, you should be aware of groupthink symptoms. Interestingly, communication is responsible for both the emergence and prevention of groupthink. For example, you might recognize symptoms of groupthink in your group if you hear communication that elicits agreement on the part of other group members. If Bob says, "We all believe in this plan, don't we?" he's suggesting that every member is in agreement. This may not be the case, but Bob's phrasing has created an atmosphere that may make it difficult for people to disagree. Also, be wary of groups in which little contradictory information is being presented. Groups that exhibit groupthink tendencies tend to have low levels of disagreement in their communication. If all members of your group are nodding their heads in agreement and appearing to give little attention to alternative ideas and opinions, groupthink may be occurring. This group might need to test more ideas and be more critical of its decision-making process.

Leadership in Groups

Political activist James McGregor Burns once said, "Leadership is one of the most observed and least understood phenomena on earth" (1978, p. 2). Decades later, although more research has been done on leadership, it's arguable how much more we know about it. Many people believe that having a good leader is the single most important aspect of an effective decision-making group. What is leadership anyway? Leadership is defined as "communication which modifies the attitudes and behaviors of others in order to meet group goals and needs" (Hackman & Johnson, 1991, p. 11). In group situations, a leader may be appointed or may emerge during the group's interaction. For example, the president of the Student Senate at your college or university is an appointed leader. Emergent leadership is more likely to occur in groups found in class projects and business groups. In these situations, it is assumed that group members will share in leadership responsibilities, or that one person will emerge as the group's leader.

Approaches to Group Leadership

Although we are still puzzled by the concept of leadership in groups, it is not for want of study and research. For decades, scholars have tried to uncover how leadership functions in groups and have developed theories to explain leader behavior.

One theory of leadership argues that leaders possess certain traits that nonleaders don't. The trait approach to leadership is based on this premise. This approach assumes that leaders have specific innate qualities separate from other group members. Perhaps a leader must be physically attractive, tall, and communicate confidently. Although this would certainly describe a leader like President Bill Clinton, it does not adequately describe his former presidential opponent, Ross Perot, a wildly successful and wealthy businessperson kidded for his gangly appearance, protruding ears, and short stature. While Ross did not win either presidential campaign he ran in, he is, nonetheless, a billionaire who has led his companies to great success. As this example points out, the trait approach is problematic because it doesn't account for the Ross Perots in the realm of leadership.

Despite hundreds of studies, the trait approach could not isolate a consistent set of characteristics, so other researchers speculated that successful leaders could be explained by their leadership style. The style approach says that styles, not traits, affect leadership abilities (Lewin et al., 1939). This research assumes that a leader takes on a style of leadership within the group setting. For example, leaders can be categorized as *laissez-faire* (exert little control over group members), *autocratic* (want complete control over the group) or *democratic* (provide guidance and structure for the group, but allow members freedom) styles. Not surprisingly, research shows that democratic styles of leadership tend to be the most successful, producing more effective and satisfied groups.

Other researchers argue that the style approach is too rigid, that it doesn't explain how people change their styles in different conditions. This group believes that leadership can best be defined through a situational approach. P. Hersey and K. Blanchard's (1988) situational theory of leadership states that specific styles will be effective for specific circumstances.

For example, adult leaders of a youth soccer team might adopt a *telling* style of leadership in which they tell the group what to do and how to carry out the task. In other situations, this approach may be ineffective. Imagine how long you would last as a leader in a class project if you spent all of your time bossing around your colleagues and making decisions for them. In a situation such as this, Hersey and Blanchard suggest that you might be a more successful leader if you adopt a *selling* approach by presenting your ideas and using friendly persuasion to convince your fellow group members. While other leadership theories do exist and more studies are underway, the one thing you can be sure of is that leadership is an adaptive process. Whether leadership involves certain traits, styles, or situational approaches, you can be sure group leaders will not survive long if they aren't flexible, adaptable, and willing to change.

Becoming a Group Leader

In order for a group to succeed, ideally its members need to engage in shared leadership and responsibility. The most successful groups are ones in which a member will emerge as a leader when needed, although some members may never care to take on such responsibility. Eric might absolutely hate being in charge of meetings and rules, but he excels at creating harmony in the group and attending to its maintenance needs. Selva, on the other hand, might use her abilities most effectively to coordinate group tasks and assignments. Both Eric and Selva serve very different leadership roles in this example, but they both equally contribute to the greater good of the group. There is, of course, no recipe for becoming a group leader, but it is important to remember that group leaders tend to be communicatively competent. In other words, a group leader is likely to be someone who can interpret and absorb information and decide what needs to be done. Group leaders are flexible because they can behave appropriately with different people and in different situations.

If you're still undaunted by the challenges of being a group leader, there are several strategies that can improve your chances of being accepted as a group leader. First, don't fall into classic pitfalls that separate leaders from nonleaders—failing to participate, talking too much, acting inflexible, and appearing uninformed or uncaring. More specifically, M. Z. Hackman and C. E. Johnson (1991) advise you to:

1. *Participate early and often.* While there is a difference between participating in and dominating a group discussion, your chances of being considered a group leader are increased by frequent participation. Research shows that failing to participate in group discussions will almost surely eliminate you from being considered for a leadership position. Your frequent participation allows group members to form impressions about your leadership potential.

2. *Focus on communication quality as well as quantity.* It's not enough to just open your mouth and hope for the best in group discussions. Becoming a leader, as well as a responsible group member, entails thoughtful consideration of not only the messages you're sending, but the messages that other group members are sending as well. In all your interactions with your group, you should strive for clear, concise communication that moves the group toward its goals through questioning, clarifying, and supporting statements.

3. *Demonstrate your competence.* Every group wants to feel as if its leader or leaders are competent. If you were a member of the Flying Walendas trapeze troupe, would you want to place your safety, security, and well-being in the hands of an incompetent Floyd Walenda? Of course not, and most groups expect their leaders to express their skills and abilities in similar ways. Being dynamic, enthusiastic, and considerate of group members through

Dos and Taboos of Small Group Work

Simply reading a chapter on small group communication does not ensure that you'll be an effective group member. Like riding a bicycle or painting a portrait, being an effective group member takes commitment and practice. In addition to understanding and being on the lookout for the principles described above, you can improve your small group skills in several ways.

1. Do be open-minded. Remember that your opinion is only one among many.

2. Do take mental and written notes. Even if there is an official recorder in the group, making your own notations can help you sort out your own thoughts.

3. Do engage in active listening. Group work demands active listening more than many other communication situations.

4. Do your fair share and a little more to move the group toward its goal.

5. Don't point fingers and blame others when your group makes mistakes. Take responsibility for your actions and the actions of the group and move the group on to the next task.

6. Don't engage in destructive criticism. If someone is not completing a task, openly and constructively discuss the situation rather than complain outside that person's presence.

7. Don't overlook groupthink tendencies. Be willing to assume the role of devil's advocate if no one else in the group is doing so.

8. Do use multiple channels of communication to be more effective. Rather than relying only on face-to-face communication to remind a group member of a meeting date, send a written note or E-mail message as well.

9. Do summarize the group's interactions, ideas, and progress frequently. Because the human memory is so fallible, it is important that all group members retain a "group" memory through frequent summarization.

❖ ❖ ❖ ❖

your verbal and nonverbal communication will increase your ability to provide leadership to your group.

4. *Help build a team.* Perhaps the most important, and yet tricky, part of being a leader is recognizing when the group needs leadership and when group members need to be left alone to accomplish tasks. Successful group leaders continually demonstrate, through word and deed, that they are team players. Recognizing others' contributions and instilling confidence in your group members may set you on your way to becoming an integral leader in your future group interactions.

Summary

Why learn how to communicate in groups? Throughout your life, small groups will be part and parcel of your existence. Small group communication refers to the interaction that occurs among at least three people who share a common purpose and engage in a process of mutual influence. Groups can be studied and understood according to four basic types: primary, social, learning, and work. The type of group has a significant influence on the communication that occurs among members.

Working in groups has its advantages, including the synergistic effect that occurs when several people collaborate and tasks are divided among more people. When members interact in small groups they are also able to pool their knowledge and resources and boomerang their ideas off one another to produce more and better solutions. Lastly, group work is more likely to increase commitment on the part of all members.

On the other hand, working in groups can be time-consuming and result in unequal participation, unfair workloads, and rate-busting. The grouphate phenomenon may occur when people dislike working in groups, due, in part, to their lack of communication skills.

The dynamic processes that occur in groups are a result of communicative interaction. When groups interact, members begin to adopt and take on "It" roles (task-related), "We" roles (relationship-related), and "I" roles (self-centered). However, what is perhaps most interesting about each group is the culture, or shared set of values, beliefs, and rituals, that is formed. This shared set of understandings binds the group together through a process of cohesion. Too much cohesiveness in groups can be detrimental when groups are unwilling to disagree or initiate conflict for fear of disrupting their cohesive ties. Lastly, groups can be defined by the type of leadership that emerges, although it is difficult to describe whether certain traits, different styles, or certain situations make a group member a leader.

At Your Bookstore

McBride, N. F. (1997). *How to Have Great Small Group Meetings: Dozens of Ideas You Can Use Right Now*. Colorado Springs, CO: NavPress Publishing Group.

Neblett, P. (1996). *Circles of Sisterhood: A Book Discussion Group Guide for Women of Color*. New York: Writers & Readers Publishing.

Slezak, E. (1995). *The Book Group Book: A Thoughtful Guide to Forming and Enjoying a Stimulating Book Discussion Group*. Chicago: Chicago Review Press.

CHAPTER 8

Interacting in Organizations

I think I learned the hard way how important communication is in a work environment. For five summers I worked at a residential camp in Kentucky. My last summer there I was promoted to an administration-type position. I was in charge of the junior counselors, the 16- and 17-year-olds who worked for the camp. During the summer, we had meetings on every Sunday night to discuss the plans for the coming week. I would give them their assignments and times off for the week and we would discuss any problems or suggestions they might have.

Halfway through the summer these meetings got a little boring; nothing new was ever said. Our program was running great at that point and we felt there was nothing we could do to improve it, so, we decided not to have the meetings anymore. That was a mistake. The first week that we did not have our weekly meeting, the junior counselors did not show up to work their activities, they were taking more time off than they were supposed to, they were sneaking off doing things that they were not allowed to do, and they started numerous disagreements with each other. I realized then that our meetings were more important than I'd thought. Communication between the group stopped, and therefore our ability to work as a team stopped. I learned the hard way that in order to have a program run smoothly, you need to be able to communicate with one another on a regular basis.

— Jyoti, third-year college student

Jyoti learned an important lesson: managers must have regular, constant, and predictable contact with employees. She also learned that more goes on at work than work. Friendships are formed, careers are made or broken, and work gets accomplished through a complicated patchwork of relationships. This chapter will help you learn how to manage those complex networks in organizations by focusing on:

- The historical development of the field of organizational communication.
- Recent changes in the workplace.
- Work relationships, including friendships and office romances.
- Organizational culture.

In an earlier work one of your authors defined organizational communication as "the study of the flow and impact of messages within a network of interactional relationships" (Tortoriello, Blatt, & DeWine, 1978). The organization is a complex network of relationships in which individuals must make sense of their job tasks. Communication is the process through which that sense-making occurs. Communication in any environment is a process in which persons share meaning verbally and nonverbally. The organizational environment has its own set of complexities that contribute to the success or failure of communication.

The individual known as the "father of organizational communication," W. Charles Redding, identified some of those complexities of organizational life:

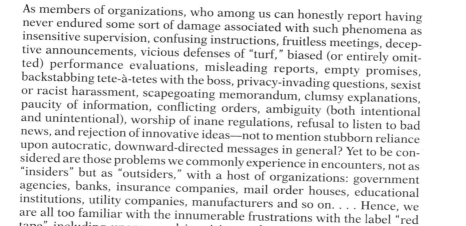

As members of organizations, who among us can honestly report having never endured some sort of damage associated with such phenomena as insensitive supervision, confusing instructions, fruitless meetings, deceptive announcements, vicious defenses of "turf," biased (or entirely omitted) performance evaluations, misleading reports, empty promises, backstabbing tete-à-tetes with the boss, privacy-invading questions, sexist or racist harassment, scapegoating memorandum, clumsy explanations, paucity of information, conflicting orders, ambiguity (both intentional and unintentional), worship of inane regulations, refusal to listen to bad news, and rejection of innovative ideas—not to mention stubborn reliance upon autocratic, downward-directed messages in general? Yet to be considered are those problems we commonly experience in encounters, not as "insiders" but as "outsiders," with a host of organizations: government agencies, banks, insurance companies, mail order houses, educational institutions, utility companies, manufacturers and so on. . . . Hence, we are all too familiar with the innumerable frustrations with the label "red tape" including unanswered inquiries, pedantic adherence to esoteric rules, incomprehensible prose, condescending (even insulting) statements, evasive explanations, refusals to accept responsibility, inconsistent assertions from different sources, violations of common courtesy, and so on. (as quoted in DeWine, 1994, p. xxiii)

In every instance of organizational failure that comes to mind, human communication behavior seems significantly involved. The study of organizational communication attempts to address these issues. Scholars and practitioners who work in the field of organizational communication have diverse areas of research:

- They examine the flow of messages in the organization to determine how information is disseminated.
- They determine which individuals do not receive information, how much information is enough, and which are the most effective channels of communication to distribute that information.
- They study the quality of superior-subordinate relationships and how co-worker relationships affect getting the job done.
- They conduct communication audits, which are similar to financial audits, to determine where the communication problems exist and to make recommendations about how to improve communication in the organization.
- They may distribute surveys, conduct interviews with employees, observe communication on the job, and examine written materials produced by the organization in order to collect data from which to make their recommendations.
- They help corporate executives realize more and more that communication problems can make or "break" a corporation.

Richard Brown, CEO of Wireless & Cable, in London, explains that communication is the basis for the way in which a business functions.

There are many ways to describe a business enterprise; for example, there is a legal description, such as you would find embodied in its articles of incorporation, there are material descriptions that describe the business in terms of its capitalization, its assets, or its sales revenues. There are functional definitions that tell you what the business does, what needs it meets, and what products or services it provides. But if you are looking to understand what a business truly is, and how it really works, I believe the most pertinent starting point is to define it from the human angle. Simply put, before it is anything else, a business is a group of people organized around a common goal. When a business is understood this way, the universal importance of organizational communication becomes clear. It is not only a discipline for specialists, but a core element of leadership. After all, whether you are talking about the CEO or the shop foreman, leadership is at base a matter of influencing people to agree on and pursue a goal. The leader knows that people do the job and that motivation is essential if people are to do it well. (DeWine, 1994, p. xxix)

It has taken managers and CEOs (chief executive officers) some time to learn this lesson. This chapter, it is hoped, will help you understand how important communication is in the organization. You will spend a large percentage of your lifetime working in some kind of organization. Learning how to build relationships and communicate information within that organization will save you hours of time, financial loss, and personal disappointment.

In order to more fully understand the field of organizational communication, we begin with a review of its historical roots. Since texts entirely devoted to the topic of organizational communication will contain a more developed discussion of this history, what we present here is only a brief overview so you can understand where organizational communication fits into our discussion of human communication.

Historical Roots

The focus on human communication problems and organizations came about as a reaction to the bureaucratic model being used at the turn of the century. Max Weber, a university professor in Germany; Fredrick Taylor, an American engineer; and Henri Fayol, in France, all focused their attention on a scientific approach to management. This approach included a belief in the following:

- *Division of labor*—where each person had a unique portion of a larger job assigned to him or her (more likely "him" since women were not a part of the workforce in any numbers at this time).
- *Hierarchical relationships*—with a very clear and strict reporting order so that one only talked to, and reported to, the next person in the chain of command.
- *Authority* without question or challenge.
- *Order* and organizing tasks for efficiency.
- *Time and motion studies*—to determine how a worker could complete a task more quickly by eliminating any wasted movement.

The scientific management approach addressed the issue of efficiency, trying to find the quickest and most efficient way to complete a task. Time and motion studies were examinations of how tasks were completed to see if they were being done in the shortest amount of time with the least amount of effort. This model of organization looked at human beings as machines and attempted to answer the question: "How can we make these men/machines more efficient?" This created industrial consultants called "efficiency experts." These individuals would study human beings doing a task in an attempt to come up with methods to make those tasks simpler and separated into a few easily understood steps (Perrow, 1986; Redding, 1985; and Redding & Tompkins, 1988).

Imagine your manager watching your every movement in order to discover how to help you, like a machine, work faster. There was no consideration of human relationships and the impact they might have on productivity. However, at the time this approach was introduced it was considered "modern" and quite advanced. Human beings were seen as another piece of equipment that had to be "maintained" so they would work at the highest level of efficiency.

In the 1930s two researchers turned managers' attention away from the machine model to a focus on human beings and their attitudes toward work. Chester Barnard's formative book, *The Functions of the Executive*, praised the virtue of worker cooperation and the key importance of communication— "the first function of the executive is communication." While Barnard was an executive at Bell Telephone in New Jersey, a series of famous studies were being conducted by Eton Mayo at the Hawthorne plant of Western Electric in Cicero, Illinois. A second researcher, F. J. Roethlisberger, was also called to study the Hawthorne plant by the local managers. Both of these professors were from Harvard University and were industrial engineers. Initially, their intent was to study the environment and what kind of impact it had on efficiency.

The researchers established a variety of conditions under which they would study worker efficiency, using the machine model as their guide. The first series of studies they conducted had to do with the lighting in the plant. They had a control group whose conditions were not changed at all and an experimental group whose conditions went from normal lighting, to intense lighting, to very weak lighting as low as candlelight. They were amazed to learn that as the lighting intensity increased, productivity also went up. When the lighting intensity decreased, productivity again went up. When lighting was not changed at all, for example, with the control group, productivity increased. In other words, whether they did nothing or made dramatic changes in the lighting, people worked harder. What could be the possible explanation for this? Eventually the researchers concluded it was because they were paying attention to the workers that they worked harder. The workers were unaware of any conditions the researchers were changing; all they knew was that someone was taking an interest in them and in how they were performing. So they tried harder under all conditions.

What emerged from these series of studies was called the human relations management theory. This management approach suggested that if we can improve human relationships among the workers then productivity and work efficiency will also improve.

Thus began an entire field of research and application that looked at the relationship between human communication and management. Researchers discovered that worker productivity had a lot to do with superior/subordinate relationships, more so than with the environment or other physical and technical characteristics. This was the beginning of the field of organizational communication. W. Charles Redding, referred to earlier as the founder of the field of organizational communication, developed the first Ph.D. program in organizational communication (see Redding, 1985). During the time Redding was developing a graduate program at Purdue University, researchers at Ohio University were developing the first undergraduate major in organizational communication (see Boase & Carlson, 1989).

For many years students at these institutions and others studied various aspects of organizational communication including superior/subordinate relationships, information flow, organizational structure, and message analysis. They realized that change in one part of the organization affected change in every other part of the organization. A general systems model of communication emerged, which recognized the complexity of the communication process. One cannot simply look at one unique part of the system without realizing that the process is dynamic, ongoing, and connected to every other part of the system.

More recently, researchers have focused on democracy in the workplace. S. A. Deetz (1992) and G. Cheney (1995) are perhaps two of the best-known scholars to look at the emergence of democracy in the workplace. Deetz has for a long time advanced the position that research in organizations from the employee's perspective will move the field forward, and that organizations in the twenty-first century need to take a more democratic and humane approach to workers. His approach suggests that too much research has been conducted from a management perspective. Workers have not been given a true voice in decisions that affect their lives. Cheney's research focuses not only on U.S. corporations but on Spanish worker-owned companies as well. Some of the models he has examined have served as potential prototypes for the United States. Deetz's and Cheney's work has never been more important than it is today, during a time when organizations are undergoing massive change. Many see these changes as detrimental to the worker. In order to understand what you will be facing in the workforce, an examination of these changes is important.

Changes in the Workplace

In the last decade, organizations have come under increased pressure to downsize (reduce the size of the staff) but produce more. Increased competition from foreign companies, as well as economic conditions in the United States, have forced organizations to get "leaner and meaner." Recently, researchers have begun to study the impact of reductions on the workforce. There are a many names given to this process including downsizing, delayering, resizing, outplacement, layoffs, and the old-fashioned word "firings." Researchers have examined the impact of downsizing on the displaced worker, as well as on the survivors—those who did not lose their jobs and remained in the organization. These survivors are often asked to pick up additional job responsibilities from those whose jobs were eliminated.

One team of researchers discovered that communication between the manager and workers plays a vital role in maintaining the survivors' loyalty to the organization. They found the following conditions lead to reduced loyalty to the organization: the degree to which employees are uncertain about their career future, low satisfaction with work, little supportive communication from their managers, along with the financial reward they are receiving (Johnson, Bernhagen, Miller, and Allen, 1996). Organizations must realize

the negative impact downsizing has on employee loyalty and commitment to   ❖ ❖ ❖ ❖
the organization's goals.

Another researcher discovered that there were various stages that employees experienced as their colleagues were eliminated from the workforce. K. Edgdorf (1996) discovered employees did not express as much emotional reaction to the downsizing during the process itself, but immediately following the elimination of their friends, and co-workers' jobs the "acceptance of inappropriate behaviors could be viewed as the temporary acceptance of emotional and physical displays by organizational members" (p. 162). Organizations need to be sensitive to these rather dramatic changes experienced by employees immediately following a major downsizing effort.

Because of downsizing, employees have to be more flexible so they can adapt to new job descriptions. No longer can a person expect to be employed by the same organization, or even in the same type of career, throughout a lifetime. Jobs change and whole industries change. Employees must acquire skills and experiences that are transferable to a variety of settings and unique job descriptions. Narrowly defined careers may place someone out of the job market.

One other development that goes hand in hand with downsizing is organizational empowerment and total quality management. The trend in organizations today is to fully engage employees in decision-making processes that affect them directly.

Empowerment programs have been implemented to enhance employee commitment and productivity through participation in decision making and self-directed teams. In theory, people will implement decisions to the extent they have participated in developing the solution. This means all employees need training in decision-making techniques.

M. Papa, M. A. Auwal, and A. Singhal have studied the empowerment of women in the Grameen Bank in Bangladesh. Small village committees determine who gets loans among the "poorest of the poor." Participation within this organization offers opportunities for empowerment for the stockholders. This is an elaborate model of empowerment offered to the more than two million bank members (1997, p. 219).

Two researchers have identified two dimensions of empowerment: feelings of competence and feelings of authority or control (Chiles & Zorn, 1995). In order to feel you have been given the power to accomplish tasks, you must first have a high self-concept, or a feeling that you are a competent individual. If you lack this confidence, then the freedom to make decisions will be of little use. At the same time you must feel that you have control over the outcomes of your labor. It is the manager's job to help employees gain the confidence they need and then give them the authority to make the decisions.

These researchers have also discovered that the organizational culture sometimes works against empowerment. For example, one of their subjects said, "Sometimes, in a way, this department is a little stuffy, in that you feel almost hidden, strict guidelines, corporate, so to speak, vs. just go in and do a good job and that's the most important thing" (Chiles & Zorn, 1995, p. 18). In this instance, the worker seemed to be suggesting that the culture itself prevented people from doing what they saw as a good job. This study also pointed to the fact that the personality of the leader has a great effect on the empowerment of employees. For example, one employee suggested how much influence the boss has: "I feel like people, myself and others, have a much higher job satisfaction and work harder on their own because of the person they are working for, it's very effective. I think the new vice president is creating a very loyal organization because of the kind of person he is" (p. 20). G. Fairhurst (1993), a well-known researcher in organizational communication, eloquently expressed this same thought when she said, "Just as an artist works from a palate of colors to paint a picture, the leader who manages meaningfully, works from a vocabulary of words and symbols to paint an image in the mind of an organizational member" (p. 333). It is in the language used that a leader can help establish the organizational culture.

Total Quality Management (TQM) refers to a constant focus on improvement. It is an approach to management that hopes to improve not only the quality of the output but increased customer satisfaction through more efficient use of resources and participation in team decision making. "Attention must be paid to the internal campaign for TQM with the foot soldiers. It's the lower participants in the organization who manage the culture and do the work of the organization" (Fairhurst, 1993, p. 366). Top-level management cannot change a culture simply by ordering change to happen. Successful organizations go to great lengths to involve employees in understanding and supporting the culture of the organization. Unfortunately, some organizations use the language of empowerment and participative decision making without being fully committed to the process. Workers can be told that TQM will increase the productivity of the company, which will insure each job, when actually it may be another way to have fewer individuals do more with less resources.

Another major change in how organizations work is called re-engineering, which means reassessing how work gets done and developing new processes to increase efficiency. Re-engineering attempts to answer these questions: How can people increase their productivity? How can we do more with less? How can we get more production with less manpower? This movement sounds vaguely similar to the early scientific management approach; however, corporate leaders would claim this new approach is more encompassing, dealing with human relations issues as well as the organizational structural changes.

The introduction of technology is another major change in organizations that has greatly influenced and changed the way in which work gets done. One of authors of this text has studied computer-mediated communication (CMC) and how the introduction of such systems has changed the nature of relationships in organizations (Compton, White, & DeWine, 1991). One hundred twenty-three people participated in interviews and completed surveys to identify communication events in their work life that were influenced by computer-mediated communication. While E-mail systems were preferred over playing "telephone tag," sometimes people used E-mail and other technology to retreat from using face-to-face communication.

Technology has increased the efficiency of communication, but at the same time it has sometimes destroyed the relationships that existed prior to its introduction. Organizational managers need to work closely with communication consultants and researchers to discover the best use of technology so it enhances human communication, not destroys it. One example from the Compton, White, and DeWine study that poignantly points this out is the following:

> My director, who lacked personal communication skills, took such a liking to our E-mail system that he would sit in his office all day and never come out. He preferred to send electronic notes to everyone rather that stick his head out the door. We all had desks near his office and it got to be a joke to see who got the most or least notes from him in a day. (Compton, White, & DeWine, 1991, p. 40).

This was a classic case of a man retreating from personal contact and turning instead to the computer. No doubt, there are many individuals like this one who exist in corporations today. In this situation, technology makes poor communication skills even more obvious.

The desire for greater efficiency is acknowledged by participants in an organization, but they also express concerns. For many, computer-mediated communication systems have resulted in poorer communication with supervisors, more supervisory control, anxiety about having to learn new technology communication systems, and even loss of employment.

> As the information age continues to evolve, periods of significant disruption and anxiety among the workforce will probably occur. In an attempt to minimize disruptive influences, business communication professionals need to be sensitive to the concerns expressed by individuals in this study. The process of actively keeping in touch with the workforce and their interpretations of new communication and information technologies may be useful in assuring both a high quality of worklife and the efficiency required to be competitive in the information age. (Compton, White, & DeWine, 1991, p. 40).

In Chapter 15 we continue in greater detail this discussion of the influence of technologies on human communication. At this point it's important to understand that whatever work you enter, the interaction between how human beings relate and their use of communication technology will have a significant impact on your own success as an employee.

All these changes in the work environment—downsizing, re-engineering, empowerment, introduction of total quality management, and technology—have produced increased stress for individual employees. Interpersonal communication skills are essential to cope with this stress and the changing nature of work. For example, to make technology work for you it is necessary that human interaction be clear and direct. The successful manager or leader recognizes how important human communication will be to his or her success. The difference between a manager and a manager who is also a good leader is:

> The leader is always aware that the job is being done by people. Leaders tend to be behavior and people centered, whereas, mere managers can often be mechanistic and thing centered. Leaders appeal to their people for contributions to customers, to the public interest, and to the long-term goals of the corporation, but managers tend to push the team with quantified, short-term objectives. Leaders give energy to an enterprise by defining purpose, and managers steer the energy. Leaders define success in terms of product and service achievement and managers define it by numbers. Leadership becomes essentially a matter of communicating—communicating the goal and communicating the enthusiasm needed to achieve that goal. Certainly this means the most effective leader will be a consummate communicator. (DeWine, 1994, page xxx)

Leaders can help integrate changes into the organization and see to it that they enhance human interaction. Clearly, along with technological changes all organizational members need to be sensitive to how to manage interpersonal relationships at work.

Interpersonal Relationships at Work

At the beginning of this chapter we said a lot more gets done at work than work itself. In fact, for many people, the majority of their interpersonal relationships start as work relationships. This is because a majority of your time is spent at work and it is the most logical place for you to meet and make friends and future life partners. We know how important it is to manage these relationships. For example, the author of *The Changemasters*, Rosabeth Moss Kanter, said, "Any strong attachment to something or someone, other than the task at hand, is likely to pose a threat to the openness, inclusion, collaboration, and trust essential to post-entrepreneurial organization. It limits the flexibility to redeploy people; it is distracting to both those participating in it and those observing." (1983, pp. 284–285). Kanter, as well as others (Naisbitt, 1982; Naisbitt & Aburdene, 1990) have indicated that the hierarchies of organizations are collapsing. Organizations are becoming more flat, with decision-making at the lowest level of the hierarchy. An organization is described as "flat" when there are few hierarchical levels from the top of the organization to the bottom. If there are fewer hierarchical levels, more people at each level are involved in decision-making; consequently, many more meetings among those who must make decisions are necessary. The increase in workers' participation in management has encouraged group interaction as well as stronger interpersonal links between co-workers.

The Nature of Superior/Subordinate Relationships

The relationship that has been studied most frequently in the field of organizational communication is the superior/subordinate relationship. One researcher who has done an extensive amount of research in this area is Fred Jablin. In his review of the research he concluded the following:

- Superiors believe they communicate with subordinates more frequently than they actually do.
- Superiors believe they communicate with subordinates more effectively than they actually do.
- Subordinates believe that superiors are more open to communication than they actually are.
- Subordinates believe they have more persuasiveability than superiors believe they do. (1979, 1985, 1987)

This research suggests superiors and subordinates think they are communicating when, in fact, there are huge differences between their perceptions of how well they are understanding one another. This can lead to disastrous results when employees and superiors do not understand that a gap exists in the information they are sharing, resulting in poor decisions. E. M. Eisenberg

It is important that the superior and subordinate perceive that they are in agreement.

and H. L. Goodall, authors of one of the leading textbooks in organizational communication, reached the following conclusion, "Although shared understanding is critical in some situations—as in high risk operations such as air traffic control—in general, it is more important that the individuals in the relationship perceive themselves as being in relative agreement. From the organization's perspective, low levels of agreement and accuracy can be disastrous, and leave important misunderstandings unrecognized and unaddressed" (1993, p. 227). Not only are superior/subordinate perceptions quite different; when information is shared it is sometimes greatly distorted.

Research tells us that when subordinates communicate with their superiors, information distortion occurs in direct proportion to the trust they have in their superior, the aspirations they hold for their own upward mobility, and whether the information will reflect negatively on them (Daniels, Spiker, & Papa, 1997). For example, the more the individual is interested in being promoted, the less likely she is to pass along negative information. She knows her boss does not want to hear it. Why make her boss unhappy with her for bringing this bad news? Of course the smart boss will realize that this negative information is absolutely critical to making informed decisions and will reward employees for sharing it.

In one corporation a mid-level manager made a mistake that cost the company $500,000. When the CEO (Chief Executive Officer or President of the company) called him to his office, the employee was so sure he was going to be fired he began the conversation with, "I know how serious this is and you can expect my resignation on your desk in the morning," attempting to avoid a negative conversation. The CEO answered, "Are you crazy? Why would I fire you now when I have just invested $500,000 in your education? You are too valuable to let go." This boss's philosophy was: The lessons we learn from our mistakes are quite valuable. One would hope nevertheless that not every employee's education would cost this much or the company would soon be out of business! However, you would also expect the employee had learned some very important lessons, which will help the company save money in the future.

The Use of Persuasion

Researchers (Rubin, Palmgreen, & Sypher, 1994) have also looked at how both subordinates and superiors have used compliance-gaining strategies and compliance-resistance strategies to get the other to do what they want. These persuasive strategies include:

1. *Promise*: If you comply, I will reward you.
2. *Threat*: If you do not comply, I will punish you.
3. *Positive Expertise*: If you comply, you will be rewarded because of "the nature of things." For example, if you do what I ask, you will be successful in your job.
4. *Negative Expertise*: If you do not comply, you will be punished because of "the nature of things."
5. *Liking*: The person doing the persuading is friendly and helpful to get the other person in a good frame of mind so that he or she will comply with the request.
6. *Pregiving*: The persuader rewards the other person before requesting compliance.
7. *Aversive Stimulation*: The actor continuously punishes the target and indicates he will stop the punishment contingent on compliance.
8. *Debt*: You owe me compliance because of past favors.
9. *Moral Appeal*: You are immoral if you do not comply.
10. *Positive Self-feeling*: You will feel better about yourself if you comply.
11. *Negative Self-feeling*: You will feel worse about yourself if you do not comply.
12. *Positive Altercasting*: A person with "good" qualities would comply.
13. *Negative Altercasting*: Only a person with "bad" qualities would not comply.
14. *Altruism*: I need your compliance very badly, so do it for me.
15. *Positive Esteem*: People you value will think better of you if you comply.

16. *Negative Esteem*: People you value will think worse of you if you do not comply.

One researcher identified the strategies people are likely to use in response to the above persuasive tactics. Kim White (1987) surveyed 204 employees of seven different organizations to determine the most frequently used resistance strategies:

- *Citing personal belief* or saying the request goes against your personal feelings about the way "things should be."
- *Postponement* or an indirect refusal to comply immediately and sometimes a promise to consider the request later.
- *Table-turning*, which includes suggesting that the person making the request needs to assume some responsibility for completing the task.
- *Negotiation* when the person does not completely agree but offers alternative actions.
- *Refusal* without an explanation or because the action violates some organizational rule.
- *Citing constraints* of time, money, and resource.
- *Citing conflicting plans*, which justifies your refusal and may be based on family obligations as well.

All of these tactics can be used by both management and workers and will be met with varying success. It is a good idea to think of a variety of persuasive appeals and match the appeal to the person and the situation.

Some of the above strategies clearly are intended to indicate who holds the most power in the relationship. *Power* is the ability to get someone to do something they would not normally do on their own. Too often this power has been studied only from the perspective of a management tool. We know, however, that power can also be held by the employees acting as a group. Unions, for example, can hold a great deal of power to persuade upper management to change some practice or policy or increase wages. In an earlier work, one of the authors (Gibson-Hancox, 1997) studied power and discourse in a blue-collar work community. By interviewing 51 blue-collar workers, observing organizational ceremonials, and probing more than 500 pages of organizational documents, Melissa Gibson-Hancox discovered a form of control exercised by peers at one organization where relatives and friends of established workers were most likely to be hired as new employees. These family ties

> give co-workers license to critique the work behaviors of others because they have "sponsored" that individual into the organization. To maintain the good standing of the sponsor in the organization, new recruits may feel obligated to work hard and demonstrate their worthiness. Workers identify so strongly with organizational ideologies that they are willing to control others in the name of achieving organizational goals. (p. 300)

Persuasive appeals are used by organizational members at all levels of the organization. These various appeals begin in the early stages of entry into the organization, during the assimilation process.

❖ ❖ ❖ ❖   ## Assimilation into the Organization

Another important concept studied in superior/subordinate relationships is assimilation. The assimilation process is one of the most important procedures for superior/subordinate relationships. During assimilation new employees acquire attitudes about work and the way in which people function at work. Researchers argue that assimilation has three stages:

1. Anticipatory socialization which occurs before the new employee enters the organization.
2. Encounter which begins when the person enters the organization and is confronted with how that organization functions.
3. Metamorphosis during which new employees change old behaviors to meet the standards of the new environment in which they find themselves.

T. D. Daniels, B. K. Spiker, and M. J. Papa described part of what goes on during this process. "Just as the organization attempts to influence and mold the new member, the new member may attempt to put his or her own stamp on the organization, create an individual identity within the organization, stake out his or her territory, or in some other way obligate the organization to adapt to the new member's goals, values, and needs" (1997, p. 141). For example, college graduates are eager to put what they have learned to work and to help their new organization benefit from what they have learned in school. Older employees may resent this "newcomer" trying to show them how to do something they have been doing for years. Working out this tension is part of the assimilation process.

The success of the assimilation process may determine how long the individual stays in the organization. If he embraces the values of the organization and learns the norms so as to be an effective employee, then his association with that organization may last for a long time. On the other hand, the organization cannot retain an individual whose values and norms reject the mission of the organization.

Openness

Openness in communication is another major topic in the research field of superior/subordinate communication. According to Fred Jablin, in an open communication relationship, "Both parties perceive the other interactive as a willing and receptive listener and refrain from responses that might be perceived as providing negative relational or discomforting feedback" (1979, p. 1204). Your authors have conducted numerous "communication audits" in organizations. A communication audit is like a financial audit—only instead of checking the accuracy of the financial statements for a company, a communication audit assesses the communication health of the company. It answers such questions as the following: How satisfied are employees with communication throughout the system? Do supervisors communicate effectively with those they supervise? What channels of communication are most effectively used? In all the communication audits that have been conducted by the authors of this textbook, employees over and over again have asked for open channels of communication and sharing more information from the upper levels of the organization. No matter how much information a superior shares with subordinates, and no matter how open the superior feels the relationship is, (for example, maintaining an "open door policy"), subordinates often still feel that they aren't receiving as much support or as much information as they need to do their job. It is rare to find people in any organization who are completely satisfied with the relationship they currently have with their superior. Part of this may be due to the very nature of the relationship, because the superior must evaluate the performance of the subordinate—which changes the relationship from one of equity to one of superiority.

While superior/subordinate relationships are critical to the success of the organization, co-worker communication has become even more dominant given the use of quality teams and cross-function project teams. These co-worker relationships not only help to accomplish tasks but provide a framework for personal friendships that extend beyond the work environment.

Peer Communications

The study of peer, or co-worker, communication has not been as extensive as that of the superior/subordinate relationship, but we know that friendships are formed at work and not only are tasks accomplished but long-term relationships are established. Perhaps this "horizontal" communication is one of the most important keys to an employee's success at work. In one study of emotions expressed at work, V. R. Waldron and K. J. Krone (1991) asked people to identify emotional events. The most typical emotions that people identified were 39 percent insults or complaints, 32 percent protests or defenses, and 15 percent justifications or admissions. The authors concluded that many emotions were suppressed, that "employees who continually withhold emotional messages are likely to experience emotional burnout" (p. 302). Since this is more prevalent in the superior/subordinate relationship than it is in co-worker relationships, friendships become one outlet that employees have to express some of these emotional reactions, and co-worker communication is therefore even more important.

Peers can provide the emotional support needed to resolve problems and handle conflicts in the workplace. A good deal of research has been conducted within group or work-team communication. In Chapter 7, we discussed the team or workgroup and how communication functions in that context. That is probably the best example of co-worker communication that exists in the organization. Communication with co-workers occurs in work teams where not only are tasks accomplished but personal relationships are enhanced or destroyed. Individuals who are under stress to perform often take their frustrations out on those in their immediate environment. When you get angry with a friend, you can stop socializing with that individual for a period of time, or forever. When you get angry with a co-worker, often you must continue to work together to get a task done. You do not have to like everyone you work with, but you do have to figure out how to continue working together if you want to be successful at your job.

Life-long friendships are formed at work.

Cross-functional teams are one of the current examples of communication cutting across all areas and divisions within an organizational context. Previously, organizations were divided into isolated and unique subgroups, each having its role to play in the production of the product or providing the service. Today, top-level teams, as well as mid-level and entry-level teams, cut across functions and units in order to work on a project or see a product through its production from beginning to end. This supports the total quality management movement, where it is thought that employees will be more productive if they understand the product more completely and have a say in how it is actually produced.

At the turn of the century, five-sixths of all new workers in the United States will be women, African-Americans, Hispanics, and immigrants according to W. B. Johnson and A. H. Packer (1984). Researchers and practitioners are therefore being encouraged to incorporate diversity issues into their management programs. The traditional Western management techniques may not be as effective with such a culturally diverse workgroup. For example, values that managers have always felt were held in common by all organizational workers may no longer be common. Getting ahead, being promoted, making more money, and status in the corporation may not be the things that all workers strive for.

How can managers today be prepared for such a diverse workforce? How can managers have a better understanding of what values are important to employees? And finally, what will you do to help increase your sensitivity to the diverse workforce in which you will be working? Successful cooperation among diverse groups of people is critical to the success of organizational teams as well as working friendships.

SPOTLIGHT ON DIVERSITY

John Rowlin owns a mail order company that sends gardening equipment and seeds across the country. He started with 2 employees and now employs 52 individuals including sales force and office workers. Recently he fired one employee, who is now suing him for discrimination. Sandra Griffin claims she was discriminated against when Rowlin found out she was married to an African American. She is suing for damages and back pay. Rowlin claims it is his company and he has the right to hire whom he wants. It is a private company and it does not receive any federal grants or support.

What do you think?

1. *Whose position do you support: Rowlin or Griffin? Why?*

2. *Have you ever been treated unfairly? If so, what did you do about it?*

Friends at Work

As we indicated earlier, not only do co-workers communicate about tasks, but friendships are formed. Many people are concerned that opening up their private life for examination by those whom they supervise, or must be supervised by, will make them too vulnerable, and yet we know that co-workers can provide a great deal of support for one another. In the end, each person must decide individually the extent to which he or she will consent to be vulnerable. In one instance the male boss was perceived to have a very close personal friendship with the office manager. Others perceived that the office manager had access to information that the rest of them did not have. This friendship became a handicap to the boss and made it more difficult for him to supervise the office manager. When the friendship involves a male and a female, others may perceive there is a sexual element in the relationship. The most sensitive type of personal relationship in the organization is a romantic relationship.

Office Romances

A great deal has been written in the popular press about office romance and various coping strategies. The advice has ranged from "dealing with the culprit privately" to "saying no to office romances" to hiring professional consultants to run gender-awareness sessions focusing on sexual tensions. One author suggested breaking up office romances by practicing crisis management instead of reactive damage control. Many authors would suggest that the damaging effects of office romances are far-reaching. Yet recent research indicates that (1) office romances are on the increase since men and women are spending more time at work, and (2) they are less damaging than we might have thought (DeWine, 1994). In our own work, we found that the majority of people accepted the fact of office romances. It did not appear to affect co-worker relationships negatively; people were fairly neutral toward romantic partners. Office affairs do occur. Since it is not likely they can be ruled out, we must figure out how to cope with them and limit their negative impact.

Techniques In Developing Relationships

1. *Develop your closest friendships outside client systems.* Everyone needs someone in whom to confide, but as much as possible those confidences should not affect the work relationships that already exist. Consequently, confidences should be shared with individuals not in the immediate work environment, i.e., spouses or close friends not in the organization. If confidences are shared at work, it is critical that you do not betray the confidentiality entrusted in you. Generally, information shared with friends at work should be more general, and specific individuals should not be named.

2. *Don't start an intimate relationship unless you are prepared to cope with the consequences.* Those consequences may include one of the partners leaving the company if the relationship interferes with their ability to work together. Other consequences, such as a lack of trust by co-workers, perceived favoritism leading to resentment, and breakdown in relationships among co-workers, may not be so obvious.

3. *Recognize that males and females will cope with friendships at work differently.* We know from a number of recent research studies that although males feel just as close to their friends as females, they may not verbalize that closeness or self-disclose in the same way females will.

Here are a few suggestions.

Each of us has a unique approach to developing friendships. One individual will approach the office secretary with friendly overtures, maintaining the relationship first and asking for help second. Others will think first of the work to be done, and only when it is completed will then turn to maintaining the relationship with small talk. Understanding this difference allows us to be more tolerant rather than rejecting one approach or the other.

Dealing with human beings in an organization means dealing with relationships. Many of the problems organizations face today are caused by dysfunctional relationships among those who must make decisions about the organization's future. We live much of our lives at work and we need to be sensitive to all the relationship issues that exist. Not to do so results in ignoring a major portion of our lives and significantly influences our productivity, to say nothing of our general well-being. Making this picture of friendships even more complex is the issue of sexual harassment.

Sexual Harassment

Sexual harassment must be a part of the discussion when we talk about office relationships. Sexual harassment occurs when one individual asks for sexual favors in exchange for work-related favors (i.e., promotions, salary increases, or job security). In addition, if one or more individuals create a "hostile work environment," they can be charged with sexual harassment. What constitutes a "hostile work environment" must be determined by the courts but can include crude remarks and sexual jokes. One author has summarized several surveys in which 70 to 90 percent of working women report having experienced conditions that constitute sexual harassment. According to the Equal

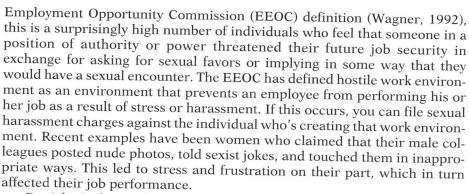

Employment Opportunity Commission (EEOC) definition (Wagner, 1992), this is a surprisingly high number of individuals who feel that someone in a position of authority or power threatened their future job security in exchange for asking for sexual favors or implying in some way that they would have a sexual encounter. The EEOC has defined hostile work environment as an environment that prevents an employee from performing his or her job as a result of stress or harassment. If this occurs, you can file sexual harassment charges against the individual who's creating that work environment. Recent examples have been women who claimed that their male colleagues posted nude photos, told sexist jokes, and touched them in inappropriate ways. This led to stress and frustration on their part, which in turn affected their job performance.

Daniels, Spiker, and Papa pointed out:

> In 1986 the United States Supreme Court adopted the standard of offensiveness to a reasonable person. In recent years the standard has been changed to "reasonable woman" by some lower courts. Women tend to differ from men in their interpretation of harassment situations, and the intent of the "reasonable woman" standard is to privilege the female interpretation over the male interpretation. Thus, the behavior alone does not constitute harassment. Harassment is defined by a combination of behavior, the circumstances under which it occurs, and its effect on women. If the sexualized condition of the workplace is unwelcome, i.e., "neither solicited, nor desired" and a reasonable woman would be offended by it, it probably constitutes a "hostile environment." (p. 87)

One could look at a series of stories told by communication specialists for examples of what some consider sexual harassment in the work place. The editor of these stories (Wood, 1992) selected the following story as an example of an undergraduate student placed in an awkward position by a young professor:

> I was an undergraduate with excellent grades and great enthusiasm for most every course I took. He was a young assistant professor—younger than some of the TAs for courses I was taking. I loved the first course I took from this new, young professor. He focused massive attention on me, made me feel special, and bolstered my confidence. He became my informal advisor, working along with my official advisor who was very special in my life because she was a fine teacher. I had an opportunity to travel to another state for a competition. This was a great honor, and I had won a qualifying competition at my university. Expenses would be paid for both me and an accompanying faculty member who would also serve as a judge for other events in the competition. My young, male professor volunteered for this duty to the department chair and it was all settled.
> We arrived at our destination with my professor gallantly assuring me that he had arranged everything. Our rooms were set and we would have a lovely dinner together. It was very special. I remember feeling nervous about both the competition and going out to dinner with him. When we got to the hotel, I discovered that he had arranged for adjoining rooms. I WAS PETRIFIED! I don't remember much about the dinner, but I do remember what happened after.
> When we returned to our rooms I hoped and hoped that he would just say "good night." But he seemed to slide into my room, expressing concern that I was very tense about the competition that would occur the next day. He said he would rub my neck a little, which would make me feel better.

Before I even knew what was happening, he was behind me, rubbing my neck, unzipping my dress, kissing my neck, moving his hands down my back and around my body. I just wanted him to go away, to leave me alone . . . to be my friend. It was all the worse because I knew he was married and had children. I wondered if he would push me down, if he would threaten me. But I said "no" . . . and was very lucky because he listened, saying something like "Well you need anything or just want to be together, you knock on my door." God, I was lucky! But the incident scared me and it made me very reluctant not only to be around this professor but to be in any situation with a male professor where doors were not open, other people around. And I wondered and worried about what he would do after we returned from the trip. I was in a course of his: would he give me a rough time?

This young woman had a difficult time dealing with the advances of a person in a position of authority, a person she trusted. Certainly it would make being a student in his class very difficult for her. The hearings for Clarence Thomas' admission to the Supreme Court and Anita Hill's charges of sexual harassment against him brought the attention of the entire country to sexual harassment issues. In a collection of studies about the Thomas-Hill hearings, three authors conducted interviews with organizational members about their perceptions of sexual harassment, given the hearings. They concluded: "Most of the research on sexual harassment and subsequent attempts to legislate policy has failed to look deeply into the consequences of not only the behavior itself but also the attempts to take communicative action—to redress wrongs or to enact changes in the company or the institution" (Cooks, Hale, & DeWine, 1996, p. 253). Sexual harassment continues to be a problem with which managers and corporate executives must deal. What will you do if you find yourself in a compromising situation? How will you help others avoid such situations? One way that organizations can help protect employees is by providing adequate information about what steps should be taken. Information flow in the organization becomes a critical step in the process of providing a "safe" environment in which to work.

Information Flow

As relationships are formed and friendships developed, the work of the organization must continue. This work is done primarily through the flow of information up, down, and across the organization. Information that comes from the top of the organization down to the lowest-level employee clearly contains directions about how to get a job or task done, as well as a sense of the values and culture this organization represents. Information about tasks is usually specific and narrowly defined. Cultural information is vague or sometimes implied, yet it is that second kind of information that affects how people are able to assimilate and use the information about tasks. In other words, the values or principles in which the organization believes, and the kind of supportive or nonsupportive environment in which people exist, will have a direct bearing on individuals' ability to understand the task and its importance. Unfortunately, organizations spend less time communicating about their cultures, their mission, and their values than they do explain-

❖ ❖ ❖ ❖

Tips for Surviving the Organization

1. "Organizational empowerment" means every employee will need communication and group problem-solving skills.
2. It is important that the superior and the subordinate perceive they are in relative agreement with one another. Disagreements occur in all relationships but people in effective relationships perceive disagreements as part of a larger state of general agreement.
3. You should share more information, not less. Open access to information will positively influence teamwork.
4. Communication with peers is critical to the success of cross-functional teams.
5. Be careful to separate office romances from sexual harassment.
6. We tend to believe face-to-face communication more than written communication. Follow up memos with face-to-face reinforcement.
7. Pay attention to cues that tell you about your organization's climate and culture.
8. Develop a "paper trail" to document decisions that are made.

ing the details of the task. This leads to misunderstandings about how people are to behave and what priorities to set.

As we indicated earlier, when organizations begin to get flatter (have fewer hierarchical layers) the information flow is easier. In Chapter 2 on verbal communication you learned that as messages are passed from one person to another, a variety of distortions occur: substitution of one idea for another, elimination of detail, generalization of content, and outright sabotage of the message. Therefore, the more hierarchical the organization is, the more likely the message is to be distorted by the time it reaches the employees. Thus, the flatter the organization, the less likely the information will be distorted.

Research about organizational communication began from a management perspective about how information can be clearly communicated from the top to the bottom of the organization. Some of this information focuses on performance appraisal or feedback about how an employee is doing on the job. Traditional organizations spend a great deal of time figuring out how to be precise or exact in those decisions—thus the reason for time and motion studies. However, as we also indicated earlier in this text, the quantity of information shared does not necessarily indicate its quality. We know that employees, no matter how much information may be shared, can still be unsatisfied with their knowledge about the company. It is the kind of information that is shared and the context in which it is shared that makes it meaningful. Often employees feel there is no legitimate way for them to provide feedback about work conditions as well as tasks that they are being asked to do.

Even when organizations try hard to communicate with employees there may still be a lack of understanding. There are a variety of answers to this problem. Often organizational members are given contradictory messages. In writing, superiors may say one thing but mean something entirely different. For example, the manager may say, "I want you to feel free to come to me with any problems you may have," but she doesn't expect an employee to need constant reassurance on a daily basis. Second, employees may be over-burdened with an overload of information, more information than they can process or assimilate. And because employees may not want to take the risk of providing negative feedback—that the information they have received is not complete—superiors often are not aware that their communication isn't getting through. Assumptions are made and decisions carried out that are based on erroneous perceptions.

One of the worst forms of misinformation is the grapevine. When formal communication fails to get through, the grapevine and gossip take over. The chance remarks one hears in the hallways often have far greater impact than the formal inter-office memos that are sent to everyone. We tend to believe more of what we hear face-to-face than what we read in a hard copy. Managers often are trying to track down the source of a new rumor.

One of the major functions of information flow is the reduction of uncertainty. Communication researchers have known for a long time the most difficult situation to respond to is an uncertain one. If a person always ignores you, then you begin to develop coping strategies to handle the feelings of rejection. What really throws you off balance is when that same person all of a sudden starts talking to you in a kind way. You do not have a set of strategies with which to respond. Therefore, the more information we collect about individuals, and the more knowledge we have about the organization and its mission, the more uncertainty is reduced. In the absence of complete information, gossip flourishes.

Karl Weick, a social psychologist, wrote a text that had a significant impact on the thinking of organizational communication scholars. Regarding the concept of uncertainty, Weick asserts that the more equivocal messages (those having multiple interpretations) are, the more we need help from others in understanding them. "Organizations have developed as social systems for resolving equivocality and increasing the certainty of life. Organizations are established to undertake many of the more difficult tasks that human beings face" (Kreps, 1986, p. 111). Therefore, communication strategies help increase certainty.

Three principles that help people cope with uncertainty are the following: (1) when the information presented has little equivocality, organizational members rely heavily on rules to guide their behavior; (2) as uncertainty increases, more communication efforts are required to respond to it, as is often the case in a crisis situation; and (3) all of this happens because equivocality makes rules less useful. For example, universities today are very concerned about campus safety. When parents hear about some incident of crime on the campus of the school their son or daughter is attending, the university must immediately increase its information to parents to reassure them that their child will be safe. Ordinarily, students expect to follow whatever rules have been developed for their safety. However, when a crisis occurs those rules may not be as meaningful as the latest information released by the university. As equivocality increases, we will depend less and less on the pre-established rules of the organization (Daniels, Spiker & Papa, 1997, p. 50–51). The more flexible an individual is, the better he or she is able to respond to an uncertain climate. The climate or culture of the organization will dictate in many respects how we respond to crisis as well as daily tasks.

Organizational Climate and Organizational Culture

For the past several decades organizational scholars have studied the relationship between the "climate" in the organization and how satisfied workers are with their jobs. We are not talking about temperature control here, but rather how comfortable, supported, and welcomed workers feel while they are at work. Organizational climate may include your relationship with your boss and other employees, the flexibility of rules and policies, and generally how work gets done. At Walt Disney World there are strict rules that enforce an environment of "drama." All employees are called "actors," even those who sell soft drinks, and the campus of Disney World is called the "stage." This reinforces for all employees that they are part of the "show," which provides entertainment for visitors.

Organizational culture may include a unique language for that organization, a certain style of dress, rituals performed, and shared values. One of the authors was once a trainer for a consulting division of a major accounting firm. The first clue that this organization had a clearly defined culture was that everyone, males and females, were wearing charcoal gray suits. Next, there was a large display that everyone passed each day depicting, in life size figures, the founding of the organization. New employees were given a book written by the founder and quizzed on its contents. Mottoes about teamwork hung in every meeting room. The culture of this organization was on display for anyone to see.

A variety of popular books have been written on organizational culture including T. E. Deal and A. A. Kennedy's (1982) *Corporate Cultures*, T. J. Peters and R. H. Waterman's (1984) *In Search of Excellence*, and R. M. Kanter's (1989) *When Giants Learn to Dance*. All of these books suggest ways in which corporations can be more effective by paying attention to their own culture and what it communicates to workers about the way in which they should do their work. These authors also point out that not all cultures are positive. Some cultures work against the success of an organization.

For example, a colleague of ours worked with a major automobile company as a consultant, and was asked to evaluate their team leadership program. They wanted all mid-level managers to receive additional training in implementing quality teams. Top-level executives were convinced that a team approach to decision making would make their company more successful. The problem was that these managers were living in a very different culture. The regional managers of the car dealers rewarded productivity by giving individual bonuses for each sale. This incentive program worked in direct opposition to the goals they were trying to implement. Why would one dealer share his or her success and give the whole "team" credit when his or her income was directly tied to individual effort? In this case, the corporate culture worked against the company's desire to be more team orientated.

Organizational climate has been linked to satisfaction and commitment so that the more satisfied employees were with communication, decision making, leadership, motivation, and goal setting the more likely they were to be committed to the organization (Guzley, 1992). Elements leading to a positive climate and a rich culture were also identified by Peters and Waterman:

1. *A bias for action.* Companies that are successful do not react, they are proactive.

2. *Close to the customer.* These companies never forget who their customer is and how much attention those customers need.

3. *Autonomy and entrepreneurship.* The most successful companies are ones in which workers were given more responsibility for decision making, thus encouraging entrepreneurship.

4. *Productivity through people.* Successful companies never forget that their most important investment is in the people working for them.

5. *Hands-on, value-driven.* A common understanding of the core values is essential for these companies to be competitive in the marketplace.

6. *Stick to the knitting.* Or continue to work with the products and services the company knows best. When a company gets so large that it is producing items that are not central to what it knows best, then the company is likely to have a difficult time. A fast food restaurant that goes into the used car business does not make much sense.

7. *Simple form, lean stuff.* This concept refers to the structure of the organization. The successful companies have simple structures with easy access to anyone in the organization.

8. *Simultaneous loose-tight properties.* The top-performing companies are flexible and can adapt to the constantly changing work environment. They use the most appropriate management approach for the particular situation; therefore their structure may be constantly changing.

Often such a culture is maintained through "folk heroes," or those individuals in the organization who are closely identified with the founding principles. Warren Bennis (1986), a leader in organizational development, explains how this vision of the founder or the corporate leader effects the corporate culture:

> I believe that the single most important determinant of corporate culture is the behavior of the chief executive officer. Her or she is the one clearly responsible for shaping the beliefs, motives, commitments, and predispositions of all executives.

In one study the researchers discovered that employees were less satisfied with the company if their views of the culture were significantly different from those expressed by the founders of the company. They concluded that founders not only bring to the company a value system that suggests "how things should be" but "how things should not be" as well (Morley & Shockley-Zalabak, 1991). In essence, these are the "folk heroes" that Deal and Kennedy identified as critical to the development of an organizational culture. Warren Bennis also identified the corporate leader as the most influential factor in developing a strong corporate culture (Bennis, 1986; Bennis & Namus, 1985).

❖ ❖ ❖ ❖

Spotlight on Ethics

Dr. Charles W. Robinson, Jr., a courtly 61-year-old pathologist, is an unlikely government informant. But the San Antonio physician is a leading reason the Justice Dept. won a record $325 million fraud settlement against SmithKline Beecham Clinical Laboratories Inc. on February 24, 1997. Four years ago, Robinson, medical and records director of a SmithKline lab, uncovered a suspicious bill charging Medicare separately for five tests normally sold together at lower cost. After complaining in vain to his employer about a pattern of billing abuses, he quit, filed a private whistle-blower lawsuit against SmithKline, and worked with federal investigators on the case. The law that permitted Robinson to take on SmithKline is the little-known False Claims Act. It encourages employees to take the risk of suing employers who are ripping off federal programs by protecting the employee from dismissal and promising a maximum of 30 percent of the damages arising from any resulting case.

Defenders of the law say

- the False Claims Act has decreased fraud in the defense and health-care industries and had returned more than $1.2 billion to the federal government
- because the cases are brought by private attorneys, the False Claims Act increases the Justice Dept.'s ability to police fraud

Opponents say

- the majority of whistle-blower lawsuits fail, wasting the time of corporate executives, judges, and federal investigators
- disgruntled workers use the law as blackmail against employers
- because of harsh penalties and negative publicity surrounding the suits, employers feel compelled to settle even weak cases.

—"Whistle-Blowers on Trial," *Business Week*, 1997, p.172

Have you ever observed practices by someone you worked for that you thought were unethical? How do you think you would handle such a situation should you encounter it? Do you agree with the opponents or the defenders?

Companies should pay careful attention to how the corporate culture will enhance or obstruct those changes. A corporate culture cannot be "managed" or "changed" just because someone decides a new one is more appropriate. A culture exists through the belief system of the organizational members. Changing the attitudes and value systems of a large group of people is a huge task. People take their cues from leaders. Bill Gates initially kept Microsoft on the sidelines of the boom in activity on the Internet, but later refocused the entire company on the Web. His ability to change course and redirect the attention of an entire company to a new technology has kept him one of the wealthiest people in the United States.

We are suggesting that you behave in an ethical manner; however, you will encounter others who will not deal honestly with you. Therefore, you must also protect yourself from those in the organization who are unethical. We would give you three suggestions (in the box on the following page) if you

Coping With Dishonesty

1. *Develop a "paper trail."* Dishonest people rarely will put in writing what they have promised you. Therefore, you have to have your own written record of events. Write a memo to someone saying, "This is to confirm our conversation last Thursday . . ." and detail what was said. At least this will give you your own written record and if the person does not respond in writing then you have at least identified your understanding of the conversation. You could also keep your own diary of events and paper copies of less permanent communication—i.e., hard copies of E-mail messages.

2. *Have witnesses.* As much as possible have someone else hear the conversation or meeting so that it is not just your memory of what was said but that of another person who can recall the event as well. This is especially important if you feel you may be harassed in some way.

3. *Detach yourself from the "game."* People play political games in the organization through the use of gossip or providing misinformation. Our best advice is to "walk away" from the game physically as well as psychologically. Don't engage in gossip, because you may find yourself the topic of conversation one day. The best approach to inappropriate comments is often simply not to respond. Ignoring a comment is sometimes more effective than responding to it since often people are trying to get some kind of response from you on purpose.

find yourself in a situation in which you feel the other person is behaving in a dishonest way that may be detrimental to you.

Since so much of your life will be spent inside the walls of an organization, learning how to establish good working relationships as well as developing friendships will be critical to your success and happiness. Understanding the culture of your organization will help you perceive what is expected of you and whether your values and the values expressed by the organization are a good fit. Remember, you want to wake up each morning eager to go to work and face the challenges presented to you.

MISSION: POSSIBLE

Think of the last place you worked. It may have been a summer job or it may be a job you currently hold on campus. Was there anyone at work you had difficulty dealing with? Perhaps the person was unfriendly, or even downright impossible to work with. First, imagine that a future employer has somehow received this person's name as someone who could talk about your work habits. What do you think that person would say about you? If you were called for a reference, what would you say about that person's work habits? You never know when someone you've not had a particularly good relationship with will be called upon to describe you to someone else. What could you have done, or could you do now, to at least make this a tolerable working relationship? Remember: you don't have to like everyone you work with, but you do have to work with everyone.

Summary

Whether your first full-time job is a few years away, or you have been in the work world for years, you will want to be in an environment that supports your interests. Everyone wants to work with others in a positive work environment. Because of the many changes in the workplace (downsizing, total quality management, empowerment programs, technology, and re-engineering), it is more and more important that you understand how to work with a variety of people in collaborative efforts. The superior/subordinate working relationship will be an important contributor to your success. You will want to learn how to use compliance-gaining strategies and how to resist those techniques as well. Because of cross-functional teams, peer communication is critical to the team's success. How information is disseminated throughout the organization, the grapevine, and equivocal messages can result in information underload. Organizational communication scholars study the organizational culture to determine how successful communication patterns are in the organization. Finally, you will face many ethical dilemmas on the job and in order to protect yourself you will want to develop a paper trail, have witnesses to conversations where there is a question about follow-up, and detach yourself from any organizational games being played.

At Your Bookstore

DeWine, S. (1994). *The Consultant's Craft: Improving Organizational Communication.* New York, NY: St. Martin's Press.

Goodall, H. L. (1994). *Casing the Promised Land: The Autobiography of an Organizational Detective as Cultural Ethnographer.* Carbondale: Southern Illinois University Press.

Kanter, R. M. (1989). *When Giants Learn to Dance.* New York, NY: Simon & Schuster.

Wood, J. T. (1992). "Telling Our Stories: Sexual Harassment in the Communication Discipline." *Applied Communication Research, 20* (4), 349–362.

CHAPTER 9

Interpreting Messages in Mass Communication

A few years ago, I was watching TV in the afternoon and much to my dismay, the program I was watching was interrupted by the annoying tone of the Emergency Broadcast System. In my experience, 99.9 percent of the time EBS warnings only served to interrupt whatever program I was watching. To my surprise, this tone was followed by my local news station telling people to take cover. Apparently, there was a tornado headed in my direction.

As I looked outside my window, I could see the dark clouds moving in and felt "the calm before the storm." I quickly rushed to find my family, and we all got flashlights and blankets and positioned ourselves in a safe place.

The story would be much more exciting if I could say the tornado struck our house, and we were thrown 200 feet and lived, but that would be embellishing. The tornado never hit my home, but the event make me realize the benefit of the EBS in relaying important messages to a large number of people. The EBS allows a massive audience to become aware of oncoming danger. It allowed me the time to prepare myself and avoid possible injury. I believe it was an effective means of helping me prepare for the worst.

— Valerie, second-year college student

The message that Valerie got from the television certainly had an effect on her. It sent her running around her home, gathering up her family members, and preparing for disaster. As Valerie's experience demonstrates, the mass media have the potential to influence your behavior, as well as the behavior of a great number of people. However, not all the messages broadcast by the mass media are recognized as intentionally persuasive—as was that of the EBS. Some of the messages that are sent are more subtle.

The goal of this chapter is to help you interpret the messages you receive from the mass media. The chapter:

- Defines the mass media.
- Looks at the process of mass communication.
- Studies the power and ethical use of the mass media.
- Examines the issues posed by mass media in society.

Because the media are far-reaching vehicles for persuasive messages, everyone from advertisers to politicians uses them to communicate products and ideas. As a potential receiver of these messages, you will want to be aware of how they attempt to influence you, whether that's getting you off the couch and out of harm's way as in Valerie's case or getting you to buy a particular brand of soap or vote for a particular candidate.

Recognizing the Mass Media

Throughout our daily activities we are bombarded by messages. They clamor for our attention, and many, if not most, came from sources other than the human beings we encounter. The morning edition of the local newspaper you read over breakfast, the voice of Howard Stern on your car radio on your way to work, the Hard Rock Cafe T-shirt on the college student you pass on the way to class, and, indeed, this very textbook are all examples of how the mass media attempt to communicate messages in your life.

From the time Johannes Gutenberg's printing press facilitated the creation of identical texts, people have been creating messages intended for large or mass audiences. Today we have numerous—indeed ever-increasing—channels through which to communicate. At one time, messages had to be delivered directly to the person by a messenger, or, in societies that developed writing, via a handwritten document. As we learned in Chapter 4 on listening, messages typically undergo some change whenever they pass through a source. In fact, part of the fun of playing the game "Telephone" is enjoying how distorted the message gets as it travels from one source to another. A key advantage of messages channeled through the mass media, then, is their ability to reproduce the same content for a large audience with a minimum of distortion.

Everywhere we look or listen in contemporary society we are assailed by these messages. Among the most easily identifiable of these message producers are the news media. If you watch the evening news, subscribe to a national weekly such as *Time* or *Newsweek*, pick up the local newspaper or *USA Today* or listen to a radio broadcast on National Public Radio, you are receiving messages from news organizations. An equally recognizable set of message producers are those found among the entertainment industry. Your favorite situation comedy or soap opera, the last film you saw in a theater or on a video cassette, the trading cards you bought at the local hobby shop, and the novels you browse through at the campus bookstore are additional examples of mediated messages.

The common characteristic in each of these cases is the product-oriented nature of the message. A commodity is something that can be packaged and distributed. Think about the contemporary uses of news, gossip, and fiction, and you will understand that they function like packages from a JC Penny catalog delivered to your front door. Just like that new dress or autographed baseball you ordered by mail, mediated messages are tailored, wrapped up, and shipped to you. Whether they arrive in your mailbox, your radio, or your television, mediated messages are commodities. They are intended for you to consume and for creating in you a desire to consume more.

This culture of consumption is apparent in the news media but downright blatant in the entertainment industry. We pay admission to see the latest Brad Pitt film, budget for cable television in our monthly expenses, and shell out several dollars for a copy of *Cosmopolitan*. We rarely balk at the expense of such goods and services because we feel rewarded by the enjoyment we get from such products. However, part of maintaining an industry is to make sure a consumer's appetite is never completely satisfied. Soap operas and other serial programs are specifically designed to encourage consumers to return to the program time and time again. Who would not be eager to tune in again next time when the program ends with a cliffhanger and invites one back again with a cryptic "To Be Continued . . ."? The mass media encourage us to interact with them—and to return to them.

Figure 9.1 Mass Communication Industries   ❖ ❖ ❖ ❖

Advertising	Computer Software	Newspapers
Books	The Internet	Public Relations
Broadcast Television	Magazines	Radio
Cable Television	Motion Pictures	Recording Industry

Characteristics of Mass Media

Thus far in this chapter, we have talked about some specific examples of mass media in your lives. But individual tastes (not everyone reads the *Wall Street Journal*, even though it is the highest circulating daily newspaper in America) and access to technology (not everyone has access to the World Wide Web) differ. Which mass media play a role in your life? If we define some common characteristics for mass media, you can apply these concepts to particular cases with which you are most familiar. The characteristics you need to identify involve:

- The nature of the source.
- The audience, the channel.
- Feedback.

The sources of most mass-mediated messages are complex organizations. Figure 9.1 lists several of the media these organizations utilize. Although it is possible for a lone pirate operator broadcasting from his cabin to produce mass-medium messages, the majority of mediated messages come from complex organizations composed of numerous individuals. Even though you might associate the *CBS Evening News* with anchor Dan Rather, the program would not make its daily broadcast if not for the numerous producers, reporters, and technicians who help Rather collect, organize, package, and broadcast the news. Given the limited amount of time newscasts have to air (approximately 22 minutes), someone has to make a decision as to what will and will not air on a particular broadcast, or, for that matter, what will fit into a particular issue of a publication, given its space limits. These decision makers are called gatekeepers. As the name implies, gatekeepers can determine what information gets passed along into the public forum—and what information does not.

Just as we, the consumers, do not know the identities of all the people involved in the process of making a mediated message, they, the producers, do not know who will consume it. In other words, in mass media contexts, the audience is anonymous to the source. Even in large public settings like sports stadiums, the source (the announcer) has a better idea of who (the spectators) is receiving the message. But the producer in Hollywood, the reporter in Washington, and the disc jockey in New York, can only guess at precisely who might or might not be receiving their messages.

*Gatekeepers such as producers, reporters, and news anchors
control what topics are and are not broadcast to the public.*

As you might have noted, the channels involved in mass media involve some distance- and time-transcending technology. Obviously, when you go to a film, you recognize that the exotic locations shown on the screen might be halfway around the world, and you realize that the movie was filmed several months, or even years, ago. Marshall McLuhan (1964) defined technology as anything that extends the senses. The discoveries of film, radio waves, and fiber optics have done just that, helping us to encounter stimuli previous generations had not even imagined. As you might guess, we use technology in other contexts as well. Every time you pen a letter to your grandparent or pick up the telephone to call your significant other, you use technology to engage in a distance-transcending two-person context. The difference, of course, is that in a mass media context, the use of technology extends to many, many more people.

Finally, the mass media, unlike a communicator who faces an audience in the context of interpersonal or group communication, does not receive immediate feedback. Thus, the response to a mass-mediated message comes through delayed feedback. If you object to a particular opinion piece in the *New York Times*, the author is not seated next to you for you to express your objection. Instead, you would have to write a letter to the editor, call the managing editor's office, or cancel your subscription. Whatever reaction you choose, you cannot express your feedback to the source immediately. It will take anywhere from a few minutes to a several days for your feedback to get back to the source. Compare this delayed feedback to the immediate reaction your instructor gets when she announces a pop quiz!

Spotlight on Ethics

The funeral of Princess Diana on September 6, 1997, may well have been the most watched television event in history, with an estimated audience of over 2 billion people tuning in. In the wake of the tragic accident that claimed Diana's life, critics blamed the paparazzi, tabloid photographers who stalk celebrities, in part for the tragedy. Eyewitnesses reported that Diana's car was attempting to outrun paparazzi pursuing her on motorcycles when the accident occurred.

Journalists from the more respectable media were quick to question and then condemn exploitative photographs. Diana's picture had always garnered attention, resulting in high sales for the publications in both Great Britain and in America which featured her face. But while investigative news programming and op-ed pieces were joining the paparazzi-bashing bandwagon, a plethora of TV specials and commemorative issues of leading publications dedicated to Diana's memory appeared.

The commodification, or packaging, of Diana's death, burial, and legacy resulted in increased revenues for the media outlets that had turned an occurrence into an event. (In fact, the day after Diana's demise, American television networks had transformed the accident into an event by beginning hour-by-hour coverage that labeled the story with logos such as, "The Death of a Princess.") By cashing in on her demise, it certainly seems that the other media were engaging in the same type of exploitation they were condemning the tabloids for.

The media had certainly covered other events that allowed us to share our collective grief, notably the explosion of the space shuttle Challenger in 1986, but Princess Diana's death calls into question the economic and social functions of the media. Mother Theresa died within one week of Diana, but her death did not merit nearly as much media attention, even though both women were renowned humanitarians. In one notable issue, *People Weekly* devoted 49 pages to Diana and 3 to Mother Theresa.

What do you think?

1. *Were the media reflecting the demands of a consumer culture or were they building a market for their product?*
2. *How do you feel about "media events" built out of tragedy?*

Now that you know what characterizes a mass medium (organizations, anonymous audience, technologically facilitated channels, and delayed feedback), can you identify additional examples of the mass media in your own life? It's important that you do, for as scholars have debated over the last half century, the presence of media in your life can affect the way you think of the world. As we shall see in the next section, a number of theories examine the degree to which the media influence us with their potentially persuasive messages.

Theories of Media Effects

By now you know that a message can be intentionally persuasive, but it cannot be *actually* persuasive until someone chooses to react to it. In other words, an advertisement might tell you one brand of battery outlasts another, but unless it affects your next purchase of batteries (or at least your belief in which battery is superior), it's only so much talk. Obviously, you don't react to every single mass-mediated message that you receive. But since the early twentieth century people have feared the effects that these messages have on people's behavior. Over the last half century, communication scholars have investigated just how persuasive the mass media are, and have tried to determine how much they influence our lives. Research reflects two main points of view: the direct effects perspective and the limited effects perspective.

The Direct Effects Perspective

> When I was about 12 or 13 and attending middle school, I craved television. I was not allowed to watch TV at home because my parents were very religious and believed in limiting the media that I was exposed to. They thought MTV had too much violence and nudity. HBO was really bad because they ran movies rated 'R' which were totally off-limits to me.
>
> I remember one time when everyone at school was talking about the movie *Footloose* and how the preacher's daughter and Kevin Bacon's character were so promiscuous. I felt like I was missing out on the whole world.
>
> — Jeremy, third-year college student

Jeremy's parents probably feared that the morally questionable material on these channels would have a negative impact on their son. The first students of mass communication began with the assumption that the messages of the mass media had direct effects on the audience. This idea of the impact of messages is often discussed using the analogy of the hypodermic needle analogy. As you know from visits to a medical office, a hypodermic needle can be used to pierce the skin and inject substances directly into the bloodstream. In like manner, the direct effects model presumes that the audience is directly influenced by the messages it receives from the mass media (Klapper, 1960). As they were described in the above example, Jeremy's parents are people who probably would ascribe to the direct effects model; they feared that messages of violence and sex would corrupt their son.

The direct effects model received some credibility in the early days of mass communication research, thanks to the widespread reaction to one notable radio program. On October 30, 1938, Orson Welles' Mercury Theatre broadcast a re-enactment of H. G. Wells' imaginative novel *War of the Worlds*. People tuning into the broadcast (oblivious to the disclaimers issued at the start of the broadcast) assumed the presentation about an invasion from Mars to be an actual newscast and panicked. The influence of that performance in particular led some scholars to believe that the media could easily manipulate the masses (Cantrel, 1940).

The problem with the direct effects model is that people are often confronted by two or more conflicting messages, such as when competing candidates broadcast campaign messages. In such a situation, people must be making a decision between messages. Scholars thus proposed a modification to the direct effects model and suggested that another factor played a role in mediated messages (Lazarfeld, Berelson, & Gaudet, 1948). In the message flow model, individuals were found to be influenced by others who had previously consumed mediated messages and had formed opinions on the candidates. These informed individuals were called opinion leaders and they were the more immediate cause of persuasion, even though they themselves were still apparently affected by the direct effects of one or more messages.

Although the major focus of recent scholarship has tended to shy away from any variation of direct effects, George Gerbner and his collaborators (1986) have proposed that the media do set a tone for our perceptions of culture. According to his cultivation theory, the media influence us by establishing in our minds certain expectations about the nature of society. For example, a grandmother who sees repeated acts of violence on television in program after program might become afraid to travel outside her home at night because the mass media have cultivated a perception in her mind that to do so would be dangerous.

Evert Dennis (1988) summed this perspective up best when he said that the media do not tell us so much what to think as they do *what to think about*. According to Dennis, the media engage in agenda-setting, a process by which their selection of topics influences what issues will be focused on. As we suggested earlier, every newscast has only so much time and thus only so many stories can be presented in a given telecast. Some topics, like the president's speech or a downed airplane, are selected for presentation while others, like a dog show or the opening of a new bicycle shop, are not. According to the agenda-setting model, people tend to discuss the president's address more often than the dog show because the media have elevated it in importance through their focus on it.

Certainly, translating a narrative from one medium to another can set a different agenda for the text as different people interpret and represent the story. Two researchers (Cooper & Descutner, 1996) analyzed the movie *Out of Africa* and concluded that the film version set an agenda very different from that of the original book. In fact, they claim the film version diminishes the role of the female lead character and portrays her as "alienated from Africa, dependent on men, uninterested in personal freedom, and indifferent to the moral and political issues of gender and race. Lost as well in the translation is any sense of the voice and vision for which [the book] has been justly celebrated for decades" (p. 248). The film version "also functions to marginalize the injustices of colonialism by deploying narratives that glamorize the Europeans and conveniently obscure any disconfirming aspect of colonialism" (p. 248). Thus, the reinterpretation of a producer and director can reshape the message of an author and reflect a completely different political agenda.

The Limited Effects Perspective

The direct effects, message flow, cultivation, and agenda-setting models paint a fairly deterministic view of the role of media in our lives. However, the audience may have more than a passive role in interacting with the media. Contrasting views of the media's role see them as having more limited effects than previously supposed. For example, although your cable system may carry well over 100 different channels, you can't possible view all of them at the same time. You exercise selective exposure to the media available. That is, you

The earliest mass media were printed publications. Since colonial times people have relied on newspapers to inform them about happenings in distant places.

choose to consume those media products that are most in keeping with your own attitudes. A person's decision to watch the evening news rather than sit-com reruns says something about his priorities and interests. Selective exposure means audience members make a choice about what kinds of messages they receive.

Another way in which the audience takes a more active role while interacting with media is demonstrated in the theory of uses and gratifications. According to this perspective, audiences pick and choose bits of information from the mass media that suit their own needs. Janice Radway (1984) talks

❖ ❖ ❖ ❖

MISSION: POSSIBLE

Now that you are more aware of the potential role the mass media plays in your life, consider what sources you turn to most frequently. Make a list of the five television programs, periodicals, or web sites that you return to on a regular basis.

1.

2.

3.

4.

5.

Now look over your list. Are there commonalties among your selections? Consider what your list says about the types of messages you choose to selectively expose yourself to. A person who lists *Frasier, Friends, The Drew Carey Show, Seinfeld,* and *The Simpsons* is getting a presentation of reality substantially different from that experienced by someone who listed *Cops, Homicide, NYPD Blue, America's Most Wanted,* and *L.A. Law.*

Also consider what kinds of advertisers sponsor these shows. Are you a part of the target audience these advertisers want to reach? If so, do you purchase the products you see advertised in these media?

Monitor your own consumption of mass media in the coming week. Note from which sources you find yourself getting your news, information, and entertainment.

---

about how some women use romance novels to escape the pressures of home life. The women seek out the novels so that they can use them to escape and receive some form of gratification from the pleasure of reading.

Several theorists from a school of thought called cultural studies suggest that the audience is a lot more savvy to the manipulations of the mass media than most previous scholars have given them credit for. Stuart Hall believes that audiences are constantly engaged in the process of decoding the messages of the mass media and constantly rejecting or adapting the messages they receive to fit their own conceptions of reality (White, 1983). Like many modern theorists, Hall is particularly suspicious of the content of mediated messages, believing that the existing power structures in society use them to maintain their privileged positions. However, just because the elite control the production of such messages, it does not necessarily follow that people will unconditionally accept them. Limited effects perspectives of the media acknowledge the role of media in presenting the possibility for change but believe the individual retains free will in making decisions.

Media Issues

Propaganda

One of the most interesting uses to which the mass media can be put is in the service of propaganda. Propaganda is typically associated with the spreading of politically charged messages, but any campaign to further an idea is propaganda. When a campaign committee tries to promote their candidate by distributing buttons that read "I Adore Al Gore" or by phoning potential voters for their support, they are engaging in propaganda, although the committee might be hesitant to call it that. The word *propaganda* certainly has a negative connotation, and typically you will hear one side in a campaign label the other side's efforts as propaganda.

One interesting case involving the effects of a particularly powerful piece of propaganda occurred in Nazi Germany. As part of his campaign to cement the German people's loyalty to him, Adolph Hitler sponsored annual parades of Germany's military might in the city of Nuremberg. Although these were impressive shows for those in Nuremberg, not everyone in Germany could witness the sheer power of these demonstrations. For the 1933 rally, Hitler's administration hired Leni Riefenstahl to film a documentary of the event. The resulting mass-media product, *Triumph of the Will*, became a potent symbol of German solidarity when shown in film theaters across that country. The film consists of numerous images of the German military on the march, of the German people cheering at the rally, and of the Führer himself delivering crowd-pleasing speeches. Moreover, the film became a potent symbol for German power to other countries as well. *Triumph of the Will* showed people outside of Europe just how powerful the Nazi regime had grown and how much they had to fear from the impressive German military.

In light of our discussion of the direct and limited effects models, you can see how each perspective might explain the effect of the film phenomenon. If one were to subscribe to the direct effects claim, one would argue that people who saw the film believed the message that the German military was an unbeatable foe because it was so well documented in *Triumph of the Will*. On the other hand, a limited effects argument would suggest that the film was well received by the German people because following the harsh conditions of the Great Depression they wanted to believe that Germany was great again.

Of course, propaganda isn't merely something of the past. Advertisers still use campaigns today to help us identify with their products. One highly successful campaign over the last decade has been sponsored by Absolut Vodka. In a series of ads published in major magazines, Absolut has taken the now distinctive shape of their bottle and dressed it up in all sorts of imaginative ways to catch the reader's eye and impress her with the company's ingenuity. For example, one ad pictures a mountainside with ski slopes forming the outline of the beverage bottle (see Figure 9.2). The object of the campaign is to get people to identify with the shape of that particular brand of vodka, so that when they are shopping for alcohol they will recognize the shape of the bottle from among its competitors and buy that brand. Would you attribute the resulting behavior to direct or limited effects?

Campaigns such as those begun by Absolut Vodka are all around us. Whether advertisers are telling you it's "Always Coca-Cola" or "Drink Pepsi, Get Stuff," advertising messages are vying for your attention and your devotion. However, as a critical consumer of mediated messages, you know that just because a medium says something does not mean you have to accept it. Recognizing that the mass media bombard us with persuasive messages does not necessarily mean that the mass media control our opinions. However, recognizing their potential to limit our choices and direct our desires should make us all more critical of the roles they play in our lives.

Figure 9.2   Absolut Vodka has sponsored a successful campaign encouraging consumers to identify with the shape of their bottle.

Source: The Absolut Company. Reprinted by permission.

Globalization of Culture

In addition to its ability to promote propaganda, the mass media have been criticized because of their spread throughout the world. For instance, while walking through the streets of Tokyo, Japan, one can see people dressed in the latest styles modeled on *Melrose Place* and sipping Coca-Cola. While this might not seem like such a crime to the culture who produces—and consequently profits from the adoption of—these commodities, critics find it undesirable for media to facilitate the displacement of a native culture for a global culture.

The globalization of culture through the mass media results in domination by an outside culture over an indigenous one. This relationship can be described as "postcolonialism." Colonialism is, of course, a political relationship in which one nation governs another, dictating the governmental policies, religious doctrine, and customs the colony will observe. Military force and economic ties are used to maintain the dependency. The historic colonization of the Americas and Africa by European principalities has no current equal: Few colonial relationships still exist in this traditional sense. Instead, media producers now foster a new kind of dependence by making people around the world reliant on their products. Postcolonialism, then, refers to the condition in which the ideals of one culture are attempting to dominate those of another.

It is true that the mass media hold the ability to influence our perceptions. Because the messages they convey come from some authority, people will follow the advice, adopt the styles, and identify with the concepts introduced by media. But as savvy consumers of mediated messages, you will want to be wary of the unstated influences *behind* the messages you consume. Just because a way of living is presented in a medium does not mean that the way is necessarily the right way. Media critics want those of us who read magazines, watch television, and listen to the radio to continue to doubt that the way a medium depicts the world is the only legitimate way to think, believe, or live. Actively questioning the intentions of the sources behind mediated messages is the one way to understand the degree to which the media influence your own life.

Summary

Persuasive messages pervade our lives, from our interpersonal interactions to the mass media. People are constantly attempting to create change in others, whether it involves convincing someone to carry out mundane tasks or to purchase particular products. The messages of the mass media are themselves commodities, carefully planned and intended for our consumption. Among the common characteristics of the mass media are a source that is a complex organization, an anonymous audience, a technologically mediated channel, and delayed feedback.

Previous communication scholarship labored under two contrasting views of how the mass media affect their audience. According to the direct effects perspective, the media deliver messages that substantially influence a passive audience. According to the limited effects perspective, the audience actively selects, uses, and decodes the information made available by the mass media. Understanding how we interact with mediated messages helps us to be more critical of propaganda and the globalization of culture and makes us better consumers of all the messages that bombard us.

At Your Bookstore

Crowley, D. J., & Heyer, P. (Eds.). (1995). *Communication in History: Technology, Culture, and Society* (2nd ed.). White Plains, NY: Longman.

Lowery, S. A., & DeFleur, M. (1995). *Milestones in Mass Communication Research: Media Effects* (3rd ed.). White Plains, NY: Longman.

McGinniss, J. (1969). *The Selling of the President, 1968*. New York: Penguin Books.

Peppers, D. (1995). *Life's a Pitch: Then You Buy*. New York: Doubleday.

Sproule, J. M. (1997). *Propaganda and Democracy: The American Experience of Media and Mass Persuasion*. New York: Cambridge University Press.

CHAPTER 10

Connecting
Across Cultures

> A few years ago on my first trip out of the country, I realized how important my skills of communication really are. After four years of studying Spanish, I decided to travel to Spain for a week. I always had done well in class, but I feared using what I had learned as my only form of communication. Once in Spain, however, I had to depend on my skills of communication in our hotel, to eat, to shop, to travel, and to find my way around an unfamiliar country. This experience made me realize how important communication was in our world. I found myself becoming more confident of my ability to communicate and eager to use my new-found skills. I learned that communication works two ways. I needed people to understand me, and I needed to be able to understand them.
>
> — Chantal, second-year college student

To say that the world, composed of approximately 5.8 billion people, is shrinking sounds ridiculous. But to some degree this is exactly what is happening. In sheer numbers, human beings take up a greater percentage of the world's geography than at any other time in history while the boundaries and barriers that have kept us apart for so long are rapidly disappearing. We are, as Marshall McLuhan (1964) explains, increasingly becoming a global village. If we could shrink the world to the size of a village of 100 people, keeping the existing ratios, there would be 59 Asians, 15 Europeans, 14 North Americans, and 12 Africans. To say that the "face" of the world is multifaceted and multicolored is an understatement. Across the globe, organizations, schools, and places of worship are becoming more diverse, as people from different cultures encounter each other on a daily basis through technological developments in transportation, economic opportunities, and communication capabilities.

Understanding, as Chantal discovered while traveling in another country, is the basis of all intercultural communication. She needed to understand the people of the culture she was visiting, and she needed them to understand her. It is this common striving for understanding that describes intercultural communication. In this chapter, we will:

- Describe the process of intercultural communication by describing the link between culture and communication.
- Explore the underlying factors that influence intercultural communication.
- Offer some suggestions for becoming a better intercultural communicator.

Defining Intercultural Terms

Let's begin with a definition of culture. Although hundreds of definitions exist, culture quite simply refers to the shared values, beliefs, norms, rituals, and ways of knowing common to a group of people. Traditionally, the realm of culture has been linked with the study of anthropology and sociology. Scien-

MISSION: POSSIBLE

While you may have heard the term "sub-culture" used before, this label implies that the culture is lower or inferior to the dominant culture. It is important to recognize co-cultures as being of equal importance to more dominant cultures. On the side of your notebook, jot down all the cultural affiliations you have. How many co- cultures can you identify with? Perhaps, you are a female, African American college student who plays in the university band. Which of these cultural affiliations influenced you most and which influenced you the least? Recognizing how cultures have contributed to who you are is the first step to understanding and communicating better with others.

tists have long studied cultures of the world and the diversity that exists among the world's peoples. Diversity refers to differences in terms of sex, age, disabilities, race-ethnicity, sexual orientation, and cultural origins.

Within a culture, there exist any number of co-cultures, or groups of people that exist within a dominant culture. For example, in Malaysia, ethnic Malays comprise almost 60 percent of the population, but the remaining demographic population includes at least two co-cultures: ethnic Chinese (30 percent) and Indians (more than 9 percent). Co-cultures can be united by any commonality—race, gender, religion, or physical attributes. For example, a co-culture could refer to people with disabilities, to Mormons, or even to women. Even though women comprise almost 51 percent of the population in the United States, they are still considered a co-culture because white males have traditionally been the dominant group.

Understanding cultures and co-cultures involves active learning and interaction. When we strive to understand and communicate with other cultures, we are trying to reduce our own uncertainty. Anxiety/uncertainty management theory, proposed by William Gudykunst (1995), can help to explain why and how we communicate with other cultures and co-cultures. Gudykunst believes that when we encounter a person from a different culture or co-culture, the anxiety and uncertainty we feel about the person may motivate us to find out more information in an attempt to predict the other person's behavior. For example, when a couple of a different ethnicity moves in next door to you, you may be prompted to learn more about them and their cultural values and beliefs to reduce your own anxiety. You want to know in what ways your new neighbors are similar, or dissimilar, to you. Communication becomes the mechanism for learning about other cultures and co-cultures.

Linking Culture and Communication

Culture Affects Communication

As we have just mentioned, communication is the process by which we come to understand other cultures. But, it's not enough to say that communication is a tool for understanding. In so many ways, culture affects communication in ways that we may never even realize. Culture shapes, influences, and motivates behavior. Many scholars have pointed out that culture is our invisible teacher. Culture and communication are inseparable. For example, a Caucasian child raised in the United States might be socialized or trained through the expectations of his culture to be verbally aggressive, talkative, and outgoing. In fact, he might be praised for being articulate and persuasive through language. On the other hand, Navajo Indian parents might raise their child to be modest, quiet, and nonaggressive. The Caucasian parents might view the Navajo child as being unintelligent and introverted; the Navajo parents might view the Caucasian child as being rude and undisciplined. Our perceptions of the behaviors of people from other cultures, as might be the case of the Caucasian and Navajo parents described above, are expressed through communication. Your verbal and nonverbal communication is intrinsically linked with the culture or co-cultures in which you live. Quite simply, we could argue that everything we say, do, and believe is shaped by the culture that we are a part of.

Culture governs the conditions and circumstances under which you send and interpret messages. Culture influences communication in more ways than perhaps first imaginable. Culture influences whom you communicate with, how you communicate, why you communicate, and what topics you communicate about.

Assimilation vs. Accommodation

In the United States, a popular children's television series, *School House Rock*, taught generations of young children about a variety of topics, including government, language, and culture. One episode featured the concept of assimilation. Assimilation is the *absorbing* of cultural groups into a dominant culture. In assimilation, members give up their individual cultural characteristics for the dominant culture and become something new. In a *School House Rock* episode, assimilation was referred to when the program talked about how America was founded by immigrants from around the world who came to the giant "melting pot" of the United States. The episode featured cartoon characters dressed in their ethnic garbs who jumped into a giant pot and melted into one group called "Americans." Interestingly, in a speech given on July 19, 1918, President Theodore Roosevelt explained this concept: "There can be no 50-50 Americanism in this country. There is room here for only 100 percent Americanism, only for those who are Americans and nothing else." Almost a hundred years after the peak of immigration, it is interesting to ask the questions, What is an American? What does an "American" look like, dress like, act like, or speak like? Does an American live in Texas, wear cowboy boots, and have fair skin and freckles? Or does an American live in New York, wear designer clothes, and have dark skin?

Summing up what the typical American is like may be an impossible task. For the most part, cultural groups don't readily give up their identities when entering a new culture. Although the image of one country/one people is a patriotic one, it is more likely that complete assimilation is neither possible nor desirable. Just as the melting pot metaphor implies, something that goes into a pot and becomes similar isn't even attractive to look at, like cake batter after all the ingredients have been mixed together. When things or people melt together, defining differences and characteristics are lost. Another U.S. President made a very different observation about culture. On October 27,

1976, Jimmy Carter explained, "We become not a melting pot but a beautiful mosaic. Different people, different beliefs, different yearnings, different hopes, different dreams."

Accommodation is the *acceptance* of cultural differences in a dominant culture. In accommodation, members retain their cultural identities. If we imagine it as a tossed salad, all the ingredients retain their individual qualities. The carrots don't become like the lettuce; rather, they exist alongside, more like a mosaic. In many countries, the accommodation model is probably a more realistic theory of how cultures exist. Although the *School House Rock* episode served to educate children about the founding of the United States of America through a melting pot metaphor, it did not go on to talk about the experiences of those immigrants after entering the country. Indeed, in the United States immigrants literally created ethnic pockets throughout the United States. China Town, Little Italy, and German Village are all examples of cultural groups being accommodated by the dominant culture in a number of U.S. cities.

There certainly is a fine line between assimilation and accommodation. In certain situations, it is desirable for one cultural group to assimilate to the dominant culture; in other circumstances it is not. One of the authors explored this issue with a student in a basic communication course. The student remarked, "Why do we need to study intercultural communication anyway? I'm from the United States and everyone wants to be like us. We are the dominant culture of the world. I don't see the need to study about other cultures." What the author found so startling is that the statement came from a young African American man. The author discussed the fact that just because one cultural group is dominant in whatever context does not necessarily make that culture superior.

Clearly, we must be careful of making judgments about what cultural groups should assimilate and which ones should not. Life, as we know it, might be very different if every cultural group assimilated the norms, values, and beliefs of the dominant culture at any given time.

Using this student's story as an example, it is easy to see how our beliefs about assimilation and accommodation are reflected in our communication. Like that young man's, your statements may very well reflect the degree to which you accept and respect a co-culture as is or expect its members to assimilate to the dominant culture. It is wise to monitor your communication when communicating interculturally.

Prejudice and Discrimination

As we have seen, our approach to communicating with other cultures may rest on our attitudes towards assimilation and accommodation. Sometimes communication can go beyond a statement that reflects whether, for example, we believe homosexuals should be allowed to marry, or whether Amish should pay taxes. It is true that our language reflects our perspective of cultural assimilation; it can also communicate what could be considered detriments to intercultural understanding.

Prejudice is the holding of certain beliefs about an idea, concept, or group of people. If your friends ask you to pick where to go on Saturday night for dinner, you might say, "Well, I'm a little prejudiced. My parents own the Taco Shack. Let's go there." As this statement indicates, you are reflecting a pre-formed opinion about the best restaurant in town. Unfortunately, we often think of prejudice in terms more negative or weighty than this. William Carew Hazlitt once said, "Prejudice is the child of ignorance." Prejudice essentially is an internal process, a setting of preformed attitudes in the mind. Ultimately, when some action is taken because of prejudice, discrimination is occurring. Imagine that a male manager in a company makes the comment to a fellow manager, "I think women are lazy." That is an example of *prejudice*. However, if that manager then purposely gives the worst job assignments to the female workers, *discrimination* is occurring.

Discrimination is often viewed as prejudice put into action. In 1997 a controversy arose over gay culture issues and censorship on television. The sitcom *Ellen* featured the television "coming out" of the character played by actress Ellen DeGeneres. In a later episode, Ellen kisses a woman she is romantically interested in. Before the episode aired, a furor arose when it was announced that a programming warning would be issued for that episode. DeGeneres and other gay rights supporters publicly argued that this was dis-crimination, that similar labels were not placed on every other show on tele-vision that featured heterosexual kissing and even more explicit sexual activ-ity. DeGeneres argued that the prejudiced feelings of the network executives and censors about homosexuality resulted in discriminatory actions against her sitcom in the form of a parental warning. In 1998 the sitcom was can-celed, although the network argued that is was not because the show high-lighted gay issues.

Underlying Variables in Intercultural Communication

Values and Beliefs

The culture or co-cultures in which you were raised have had a tremendous impact on who you are, what you stand for, and how you interact with others. What would your life be like in another culture? For most of us this is a ques-tion impossible to answer because we aren't even aware of the impact that our

---

SPOTLIGHT ON DIVERSITY

Even the act of gift giving reveals the underlying values and belief structure of a culture. Gift giving customs vary across the world (Morrison, Conaway & Borden, 1994). In Costa Rica and Japan gift giving is an expected part of international business. But in Belgium, England, and Chile gift giving is not appropriate for business dealings, unless long-time associates are involved. In the United States, there are laws regulating the dollar amount of gifts made to organizations.

Not knowing the norms of gift giving can send very unintended and perhaps negative messages to other people. In Argentina, Brazil, and Bolivia, for example, it is inappropriate to give a pocket knife or sharp object as a gift. The giving of such an object symbolizes the severing of a friendship. In China, older generations may perceive a gift of a clock or handkerchief as symbolic of funerals and mourning, although younger Chinese do not. And even the way you thank a sender of a gift varies from culture to culture. For example, in Egypt it is taboo to accept a gift with your left hand, and in many other cultures it is extremely rude to open a gift in front of the giver. All of these differences in just gift giving alone!

What do you think?

1. *What purpose do gifts serve in a culture? How do they reveal the underlying values of a culture?*
2. *How would you learn what gifts are appropriate for different cultures?*

---

own culture has had on us. Culture pervades our communication at such a deep level. To a large extent, you *are* your culture.

The complicated network of values and beliefs of a culture underlie communication, just as a system of roots supports a tree. What a culture values is represented in language and action. Proverbs and clichés used by a culture are quite revealing. In the United States, many clichés and sayings reflect the value placed on freedom, individuality, and striving for success. Sayings like "Pull yourself up by the boot straps" and "The early bird gets the worm" represent these values. As members of the culture adopt these sayings, they internalize the underlying message. They make the beliefs expressed in the sayings part of themselves, and they thus act them out. Over time, the sayings and behaviors become ingrained in the culture and passed on to others through the process known as socialization.

Individualism vs. Collectivism

What we have been describing above could more formally be categorized as the degree to which the culture displays individualism or collectivism. In Geert Hofstede's (1980) well-known analysis of cultural variations, he explains that there is a fundamental difference in a culture's orientation toward individualism and collectivism. Cultures around the world can be placed on a continuum in this regard. Cultures that highly value collectivism were found by Hofstede in Asia (Hong Kong, Singapore, Thailand, Taiwan), South America (Peru, Colombia, Venezuela, Mexico, Chile), and Africa. Countries that

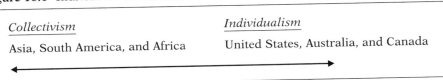

Figure 10.1 Individualism and Collectivism in World Cultures

Collectivism   *Individualism*

Asia, South America, and Africa   United States, Australia, and Canada

Source: Adapted from Hofstede, G. (1980). *Culture's Consequences: International Differences in Work-related Values*. Beverly Hills, CA: Sage.

rank high in individualism include the United States, Australia, Canada, and the Netherlands.

Individualism and collectivism differ because they represent radically different approaches to work, play, and ultimately, communication. To Robert, a young man in the United States, values such as individual initiative, freedom of expression, and self-congratulation are important. On the other hand, Yuya, a young man from Japan, has been socialized to believe in extended families, harmony, and group work; he believes in placing importance on the group's goals above individual goals. These differences are significant, resulting in very different world views. While Robert has learned to value freedom and independence, Yuya places importance on family and group relationships above all else.

Imagine if Yuya and Robert were assigned to a work team in a transnational organization in which they were both employed. Their orientation toward individualism or collectivism would affect when, where, and under what conditions they worked together. In Japan, for example, the highest priority in the culture, and in the workplace as well, is the formation and development of interpersonal relationships between individuals and groups. As E. T. Hall and M. R. Hall (1987) explained, "The loyalty that is felt between members of a work force is strengthened by *amae* [dependency] among the group" (pp. 54–55). A young person like Yuya is taught to seek, rather than avoid, dependency. Consequently, Yuya's communication would likely be focused on maintaining group harmony and dependency. If Yuya were a part of a work group at a Japanese company, rather than saying, "I have devised an effective plan of action for the company," and taking credit for the idea even if it did originate with him, Yuya would be more likely to say, "We have devised an effective plan of action for the company." In so doing, Yuya has maintained harmony within the group. However, Robert, who is from a more individualistic culture, might be more likely to take credit for the idea because he has been socialized to be more independent and less reliant on group relationships.

Collectivism influences family relationships as well as work-group relationships. In many cultures, family relationships are naturally intertwined within an individual's life. For example, K. Witte and K. Morrison (1995) found that even the type of communication that occurs in a doctor-patient context is affected by familial ties. For Filipinos, Koreans, and East Indians, medical visits are a family affair. The patient is accompanied by friends and family members when she goes to the doctor's office. Native Ethiopians and Japanese are not accompanied by family members, but the health-care provider is, in those cultures, expected to provide diagnoses, particularly nega-

As our society becomes more diverse, the importance of learning to communicate with people from other cultures becomes apparent.

tive ones, directly to family members rather than to the patient. Even in these examples, collectivism affects the actions, communications, and beliefs of the individuals involved.

High Context/Low Context

In his preeminent work on language, E. T. Hall (1976) suggests that cultures differ in terms of contexting of communication. Contexting is the message and tone of voice that a person uses to communicate and the circumstances of that communication. High-context cultures are ones in which the form of a communicator's message is based on an assumption that the audience shares his background and values. There is a heavy reliance on unspoken information. High-context cultures use "shortened words, phrases, and sentences and rely on hidden, implicit, contextual cues such as nonverbal behavior, social context, and the nature of interpersonal relationships" (Ferraro, 1990, p. 55). Low-context cultures on the other hand, rely on very explicit message sending and leaves little to assumption.

Cultures can be placed on a continuum of high- and low-context communication. On one end of the continuum, Swiss-German, German, Scandinavian, and North American cultures rely on explicit communication messages. Japanese, Arabic, and Latin American cultures, on the other end, are most likely to use implicit communication techniques. Low-context cultures value honest and direct verbal messages, and high-context cultures place much less faith in the power of words and more in tradition, intuition, and ceremony. For example, in the United States a handshake is a traditional greeting. And although perceptions may be formed about people based on their handshake (i.e., too firm, too weak), not much is actually communicated by a handshake. The Japanese carry much more communicative power in their greeting—the bow. As one student explains:

> The bow is very important in Japanese culture. Most people bow when they meet people. The degree to which you bow has meaning. When we were children in school, we were taught to bend at the waist at a 30-degree angle. In the case of formal ceremony, people usually bow at 60-degrees. The lower the bow, the more respect you have for the person. This culture of greetings has been continuing since ancient times. I think the Japanese bow shows that we want to be together and catch a companion's eye by showing our modesty.
>
> — Masakazu, first-year college student

As Masakazu points out, the bow in his high-context culture has implicit or unspoken meaning that may be lost on someone not from that culture. Each degree of bowing has a significantly different and unspoken message, recognizing the contexting that occurs between communicators. Similarly, in Thailand, when people greet each other, they clasp their hands in a praying position. The height of their clasped hands indicates authority and status. For example, clasping hands above the head is an act reserved for religious figures, while clasping hands at the waist level is used with subordinates and co-workers.

There appears to be a link between contexting and the level of individualism or collectivism. The cultures that are individualistic also tend to engage in low-context communication. Cultures that focus on collectivism tend to be high-context in terms of communication. This seems to make sense. In an Asian culture that values collectivism, people rely on intuition to understand each other. They can do this because they have worked very hard at cultivating interpersonal relationships among their group members. Striving for belonging and maintaining harmony helps communicators anticipate each other's feelings and actions. On the other hand, people in individualistic cultures are taught to be independent and assertive. Communication is a primary way to do this. Communicators in these cultures are taught to express their goals and show their independence through language. For example, a child might be told by a parent, "If you want something, you have to ask. I'm not a mind reader."

Power Distance

The degree to which a person acknowledges or defers to authority also affects communication. Imagine that you are an accountant in a large company. What would you do if you discovered that a superior was blatantly wrong and had miscalculated expenditures for the month? Would you point out the mistake, regardless of how high up in the organization's hierarchy the superior was, or would you keep quiet out of respect for authority? Your answer to this dilemma could rest in your cultural upbringing. For example, if you were from a South American culture, you might choose the latter option. As D. A.

Victor explains, subordinates in these cultures are "more likely to accept the fact that their superiors had greater power than they had and to believe that a superior was correct because that superior outranked them, whether the superior was in fact correct or not" (1992, p. 177).

Cultures vary along lines of power distance, or the way in which unequal power relationships are handled within a culture. According to findings, cultures such as those of Austria, Israel, Denmark, Sweden, and Ireland are perceived as low in power distance: People in these cultures strive for equality and have a low tolerance for authority. In contrast, cultures with the highest-ranking tolerance for unequal power structures include the Philippines, Mexico, Venezuela, India, and Singapore. In high-power-distance cultures, this means significant differences in communication.

Although we generally see power as a negative factor, Marshall Singer (1987) says that "every communication relationship has a power component attached to it" (p. 2). What does he mean by this? In some cultures, as in the United States, there is an assumption of equality in certain relationships, particularly among co-workers, peers, and friends. However, in other cultures, power is an important factor in communication situations. This power can run along lines of race, age, economics, or prestige. As Gary Althen explains, "The fact that a 27 year-old Korean student expects obedience from a 26 year-old Korean student, or that a graduate of a Chinese 'key university' has more influence than a graduate of a lower-ranking institution is easily lost on most Americans" (1994, p. 187).

One of the authors of this text experienced this in a summer class with students from the United States and Japan. The Japanese students were exchange students from an international sister university and were experiencing U.S. culture for the first time. They were taking the class to improve their conversational English and learn more about the topic of communication. An immediate difference noticed by the author was these students' unwillingness to challenge the issues being discussed and engage in critical thinking, a requirement of the class. While the U.S. students challenged, criticized, and asked questions about the topic for the day, the Japanese students sat quietly with their heads bowed. The author was puzzled and the U.S. students became angry that they were the only ones participating in class.

After several weeks, the author asked one of the Japanese students what was wrong. The answer was simple. In their culture, challenging the issue was really a challenge to the power and authority of the teacher. In fact, the Japanese students expressed how embarrassed they were when the U.S. students critiqued the ideas and issues put forth by the instructor. Clearly, these differences in perceptions of power and authority mattered in the communication exhibited by both cultures. For the students who had been born and raised in the United States, critiquing and questioning came naturally, but to the Japanese-born students, this process was threatening to the status of the person in authority. The communication that resulted was very different.

Intergenerational Communication

As previously described, diversity refers to the differences that exist among people. There is a tendency to view diversity along gender and racial-ethnic lines. However, an equally interesting area of intercultural research focuses on diversity along *age* group lines. Researchers have already spent a great deal of time studying the perceptions of the elderly across cultures. As you might guess, the elderly in collectivistic cultures such as those found in Asia, Africa, and South America are viewed with a greater degree of respect and adoration than are those in individualistic cultures (Carmichael, 1991).

A. Williams and H. Giles (1996) have studied the communication that occurs between younger and older generations of people. They studied 129 young adults (median age = 18.5 years) in the United States to discover how they viewed communicating with people of earlier generations. They believe that when people of different generations meet, they follow a communication predicament model (CPM). In other words, when a 13-year-old adolescent meets a 70-year-old, they both begin trying to fit perceptions based on physical characteristics (clothing, hair style) and communication (stuttering, aggressive) on one another. Interaction with that person can either uphold or dismiss those initial perceptions. In the research study by Williams and Giles, they wanted to understand the perceptions that young adults had of older adults.

On the one hand, Williams and Giles found that young adults in the study held many negative perceptions about communication with older adults. For example, the young adults complained that older communicators didn't pay attention to the conversation, had closed minds, and seemed to be out of touch. As one participant explained about an older person, "He appeared to be so close minded and unreceptive to new ideas" (Williams & Giles, 1996, p. 233). In addition, older people were viewed as being difficult to communicate with because of poor hearing (not responding to comments) and mental concentration (rambling).

However, the researchers found that the young adults did have positive communication experiences as well. They spoke of the mutual interests and insight that older communicators provided. As a participant described her communication partner, "Her knowledge of the past, the way things used to be, the prices, wars, rationings she has seen, which seem more vivid, real when I talk with her compared to books or TV" (Williams & Giles, 1996, p. 237). The study of intergenerational communication is both interesting and necessary, particularly as the large number of Baby Boomers and Generation Xer's work, play, and interact with each other more frequently. As society becomes more and more diverse, intergenerational communication is one of the areas that will need further attention in the coming millennium.

Improving Intercultural Communication

Recognizing Ethnocentrism

As the world shrinks more and more, our opportunities to practice communicating with other cultures increase dramatically. Today, it would not be out of the ordinary for a teenager in Brazil and a teenager in Australia to be Internet conversation partners, nor would it be unusual to be sitting in a multicultural classroom in kindergarten, high school, or college. So, learning to communicate across cultures is perhaps more important than at any time in the past. Generations before ours found intercultural communication to be a novelty; younger generations find it a necessity.

❖ ❖ ❖ ❖

MISSION: POSSIBLE

How can you improve your intercultural understanding and communication skills? One way is to become actively involved with people from other cultures thorough community service. In every community or university setting, there are opportunities for you to learn more about others while volunteering your time. For example, if you are a Spanish major hoping to teach Spanish or work as a translator, you could volunteer to read to children at the local chapter of the Hispanic American Council. If you are an international business major, why not volunteer as a "tutor" to your college or university's international student organization. If you are a human services or health communication major, spend volunteer time as a reader for people with visual impairments.

Interpersonal contact is the primary way of improving intercultural communication skills. Spending time with people from other cultures can have great benefits for both you and the people you are volunteering your time to. In the spirit of service learning, many people, including you, benefit from this generous gift of time. Other ways for increasing diversity learning include attending discussion groups, viewing documentaries, reading ethnic and special interest magazines, engaging in travel, and taking college courses.

Perhaps the first step toward improving intercultural communication is to be aware of ethnocentric tendencies. Ethnocentrism is the tendency to view one's own culture as superior to others. It is important to understand that ethnocentrism is neither wholly avoidable nor wholly undesirable. Most of us can't help but look at our own culture positively. And, to some degree, it is important to be proud of your culture, to carry on the values, beliefs, and practices that comprise your heritage. Ethnocentrism becomes a barrier to effective communication when it prevents you from viewing *other* cultures positively or respecting other cultural practices and beliefs. Being able to mentally say, "I understand that I may be shocked by the practice of eating dogs in Malaysia because it is not practiced in my own culture, but it does not make the practice right or wrong" is the first step toward improving intercultural communication.

By recognizing your own ethnocentrism, you can begin to appreciate the diversity of cultural affiliations around you. Respecting people different from you can be difficult, particularly given the environmental, parental, and societal influences that surround you. Being curious about other people and being mindful that differences do exist are important steps to improving your intercultural understanding. Rather than resisting intercultural differences, we, as a society, need to embrace intercultural differences. Perhaps the group No Doubt says it best in their song, "Different People," when they remark, "But the most amazing thing/That I've seen in my time/Are all the different people/And all their different minds."

Avoiding Stereotypes

The second step toward improving intercultural communication is to avoid stereotypes. Stereotyping, or the practice of holding rigid conceptions or categories about a group of people, may be a detriment to intercultural

Spotlight on Ethics

Ethics refers to the study of moral standards in a society. Ethics becomes particularly important when discussing intercultural communication. Even the most competent intercultural communicators may struggle when interacting with people from other cultures whose core values and practices differ greatly from their own. Communication teachers tell students to avoid ethnocentrism and to live by the motto that other cultures are just different, not wrong in their actions and beliefs. This approach is known as cultural relativism. In other words, another culture's values, beliefs, and practices are meaningful and can be judged only in that culture.

However, Henry Bagish (1981), among others, has questioned the concept of cultural relativism. His argument is that some cultural practices violate more universal standards of ethical behavior. For example, is it abusive for the Dani tribe of New Guinea to cut off the fingers of young girls to exorcize ghosts? Are all practices "culturally relative" and free from judgment?

What do you think?

1. *Are there standards of right and wrong that are universal or is everything culturally relative?*
2. *Who, if anyone, should intervene when cultural practices go beyond ethical standards?*

---

communication. Stereotyping is a necessary evil. If we didn't stereotype initial information, we would be too overwhelmed to function on daily basis. What if every person you passed on the street had to be mentally categorized as either a "male" or a "female" through a formal process of deductive thinking. Walking down the street would soon become a nightmare! Instead, we tend to "stereotype" gender according to physical characteristics, such as facial features, physical attributes (i.e., breasts), and vocal patterns. Sometimes, however, after further investigation, our initial stereotypes are proven wrong.

Stereotyping is an attempt to lump all people of a certain culture or group together under a common set of characteristics. While we tend to think of stereotyping as a negative practice, it can actually be positive in nature. Think about the following statements. Asians are intelligent. African Americans are superior athletes. Even positive attributions could be problematic to intercultural communication. Simply applying these statements to the "all" test proves the point. Are *all* Asians intelligent? Are *all* African Americans superior athletes? The answer is obviously no. Whenever you hear yourself saying, "All men act like . . ." or "All Muslims are . . .", be wary about what you are about to communicate.

Ultimately, it is important to realize that as the world shrinks, so too should the perception that isolation is neither possible nor desirable in our contemporary society. With increases in technology, transportation, and economic opportunities, improving intercultural communication skills is not something that you *should* do, but something that you *must* do in order to be a productive citizen of an increasingly complex world. Avoiding ethnocentric tendencies and stereotyping seems like a simple two-step recipe for improving your skills, but rarely is intercultural communication that easy. Communicating across cultures is difficult, challenging, and certainly worthwhile.

Coping Strategies in Intercultural Encounters

❖ ❖ ❖ ❖

What are some practical tips for intercultural communication? Young Yun Kim and Sheryl Paulk (1994) asked Japanese and American employees who worked together what strategies they could offer for communicating with each other. Although these strategies differed slightly according to nationality, the employees' suggestions are ones that you can use in your everyday encounters:

1. *Learn cultural differences.* It is important to gain as much information about other cultures as possible through books, the Internet, and conversations with others who are familiar with the culture—including travelers, teachers, and businesspeople.

2. *Be patient.* Communicating with a person from another culture can be time-consuming and frustrating. Don't let your impatience get in the way of communication.

3. *Be open-minded.* Remember that the values, beliefs, and practices of a culture affect the communication process. Be mindful of your ethnocentrism and seek understanding rather than judgment.

4. *Forget previous bad experiences.* If you have had an encounter with someone from another culture that was not pleasant or productive, have a "short-term memory." Don't base new encounters solely on past ones that were negative.

5. *Listen attentively.* Language, perception, clothing, and behavior may all intrude on intercultural understanding. Listening closely and focusing on what the other person is saying are crucial.

6. *Be persistent.* When people from different cultures run into difficulties, the natural response might be to quit trying to communicate and chalk it up to cultural barriers. However, persistence is a common quality of competent intercultural communicators. Even when things appear hopeless, be persistent in your communication efforts.

7. *Speak clearly and enunciate.* Asking for a "pitcher" of water and a "picture" are two very different things. Speaking clearly and enunciating properly can help clarify your message.

8. *Use simple words and avoid slang.* One of the greatest hindrances to intercultural understanding is slang. Be careful of slang usages and use simple words and sentences.

9. *Use multiple communication channels.* If a verbal message does not seem to be understood by your cultural partner, try nonverbal messages instead and vice versa. Increasing channels of communication—verbal or nonverbal, written or spoken—can increase chances of understanding.

10. *Keep a sense of humor.* Miscommunication is bound to occur in intercultural encounters. Humor may very well be the universal communicator. Keeping a sense of humor in intercultural communication will help you and your intercultural partner stay on the right track!

Summary

Learning to communicate across cultures is perhaps more important than ever before. Culture—the shared values, beliefs, norms, rituals, and ways of knowing common to a group of people—shapes who we are and how we communicate. Co-cultures are groups of people that exist within a dominant culture. The co-cultures to which we belong also have a profound influence on our being. When we encounter someone from another cultural affiliation, our curiosity and anxiety cause us to want to know how this person is similar to or different from us. To some degree, anxiety/uncertainty management theory can explain our motivation to communicate across cultures.

Culture affects communication at the most fundamental levels. We are not born knowing how to talk, what to wear, how to interact with others, or how to express emotions. These are all things taught to us by people in our cultural groups. Our behavior, through language and action, is the direct result of our cultural upbringing. Whether we expect other cultural groups to assimilate into our own culture or whether we accommodate cultural differences is also expressed through communication. Prejudice refers to attitudes or beliefs held about a group of people. When prejudice is transformed from thought to action, discrimination against a cultural group or member occurs.

There are several underlying factors in intercultural communication that were identified in this chapter. Cultures or co-cultures differ in the underlying value and belief systems that create an intricate network for referencing behavior. These values and beliefs may be exhibited in the degree to which the culture is individualistic or collectivistic. Communication also may be affected by whether a culture is high or low context. High-context cultures rely on unspoken relationships and intuitions, whereas low-context cultures rely on explicit verbal and nonverbal messages. Communication also may be influenced by the power relationships between the message sender and the receiver.

As the world becomes increasingly diverse in terms of race, ethnicity, gender, physical ability, and a host of other factors, communicating across cultures is a necessity. You can improve your intercultural communication skills in two important ways. First, recognize your own ethnocentric tendencies, or the belief in the superiority of your own culture. Second, be aware of how your communication with others is affected by the stereotypes that you hold. Like other things, being competent in intercultural communication takes practice, an open mind, and a willingness to learn about others.

At Your Bookstore

Axtell, R. E. (1993). *Dos and Taboos Around the World.* New York: John Wiley & Sons.

Kochman, T. (1984). *Black and White Styles in Conflict.* Chicago: University of Chicago Press.

Kabagarama, D. (1997). *Breaking the ICE: A Guide to Understand People From Other Cultures* (2nd ed.). Englewood Cliffs, NJ: Prentice Hall.

Yamada, H. (1997). *Different Game, Different Rules: Why Americans and Japanese Misunderstand Each Other.* Oxford, England: Oxford University Press.

Part Three

Applications
of
Human
Communication

CHAPTER 11

Managing
Conflict Through
Communication

From about my sophomore to my senior year in high school my parents and I seemed to be in a constant fight. They thought I was too wild, and I thought that they were way too strict. When we fought, everything escalated until we ended up screaming and slamming doors in each other's faces. Our disagreements would always start about one thing, then take a total U-turn and conclude with a completely unrelated topic. These blowups became so frequent that I ended up rarely talking to my parents unless it was to tell them where I'd be, and they only spoke to me when they had to.

We later realized that much of our problem had to do with the way we communicated. Every weekend I knew I was going out, and they knew I was going to ask if I could. However, I would always wait until I was ready to walk out the door to let them in on my plans, and every week they waited until the last possible moment to ask. With so little time to discuss things, it was really difficult to reach any kind of middle ground. Sometimes compromise takes time, and we needed to allow for that. Once we began to set a specific time to discuss weekend plans, we found that this kind of planning relieved a lot of tension between us and we began to talk to each other again.

— Tamika, fourth-year college student

For Tamika, the growing pains she experienced during adolescence were characterized by her frequent disagreements with her parents over social privileges. She felt her parents were too strict with how she spent her free time; her parents thought she was too reckless and disrespectful by not asking for permission to go out ahead of time. When they refused to allow her to go because of their own hurt feelings, Tamika became angry, feeling as if they didn't care about her need to socialize with friends. Constant fighting caused a rift between Tamika and her parents that was finally resolved through only one means: improved conflict management.

Often, when we hear the word *conflict* we begin to feel queasy. Why? Because conflict tends to conjure up images of a battle, a fight, or a disagreement with friends, family members, acquaintances, or even complete strangers. For most people, conflict rarely has a positive connotation. Not surprisingly, it's impossible to turn on the television or radio without hearing about a conflict that has erupted between police and a youth gang or a conflict between opposing political groups in another country. Conflict is truly a fact of life.

This chapter is designed to introduce you to the topic of conflict and the skills necessary to manage conflict through communication. We will:

- Define what conflict is and why it occurs in the interactions that we have with others.
- Discuss the role that communication plays in managing conflict.
- Look at five styles of approaching conflict to help you assess how you generally approach conflict situations.

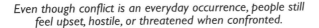
Even though conflict is an everyday occurrence, people still feel upset, hostile, or threatened when confronted.

- Examine different roles that you might play in managing conflict in your own life by acting as a mediator or arbitrator in various interpersonal, group, and organizational situations.

Examining Conflict and Communication

In the amusing popular book *Live and Learn and Pass It On* an anonymous 55-year-old person remarked, "I've learned that it's a lot easier to react than it is to think." Why is that? Perhaps it is because we are still "fight or flight" animals by our very nature. As C. D. Mortensen explains, "The historical record shows that conflict is universal, pervasive, and widespread throughout the animal kingdom" (1991, p. 275). The human instinct to fight or run away when a threat is issued is an innate reaction that we have carried over from our earliest prehistoric ancestry. When our Stone Age ancestors were faced by a snarling saber tooth tiger, they had two options: fight or run for it. And even today, our immediate reaction to a friend who says, "Why did you ruin the sweater you borrowed from me?" might be to yell back or walk away angry, with our adrenaline pumping.

Even though conflict is an everyday occurrence, most of us probably don't take the time to think about what conflict actually is. Conflict can be defined as "an expressed struggle between two interdependent parties who

Figure 11.1 Positive *v.* Negative Conflict

Positive conflict can:	*Negative conflict can:*
• open up issues for discussion • lead to better solutions and ideas • lead to increased understanding • help people see themselves in different ways	• divert energy from people and tasks • create barriers to understanding • decrease productivity • destroy morale.

perceive incompatible goals, scarce rewards, and interference from the other party in achieving their goals" (Hocker & Wilmot, 1991, p. 12). Imagine that a friend of yours starts dating your ex-boyfriend/husband or girlfriend/wife. If you no longer have special feelings for that person and don't care about your friend's new love interest, then you can move on because conflict isn't occurring. But what if you still have even a particle of interest in your ex and might even like to reunite in the future? Suddenly, your friend has gone from that person you go the movies with every Sunday afternoon to being a genuine rival.

Conflict is occurring in this scenario for several reasons. Conflict is imminent because you and your best friend are interdependent. In other words, you are dependent on that person for something, be it friendship, employment, or a host of other factors. Although your exchange of wild hand signs and unpleasant words at a driver who has cut in front of you might seem like a conflict situation, it probably isn't—unless the person in the car turns out to be your new neighbor or your current boss. If you are not interdependent with the driver in the other car for some reason, this situation will have little bearing on your future health and well-being. Conflict is an issue when it involves interdependent people, people we will see or interact with again and again. Your incident with the belligerent car driver can be forgotten if the person is a stranger (and assuming the person doesn't chase you to the next exit), but the one with your best friend can't be if you're roommates.

How else is a situation indicative of conflict? Conflict is expressed either through words or actions. If you harbor ill feelings toward your best friend because of the relationship with your ex but never express your feelings or do anything nasty to sabotage their union, then conflict is probably not occurring in the true sense of the word. If, on the other hand, you call up your friend and demand that she break up with your ex, conflict is occurring. By picking up the telephone and issuing a verbal command to your friend you have expressed your perceived incompatible goals. You view your friend as an interference to reuniting with your ex, and your friend, in turn, sees you as an interference to a blossoming new relationship.

Generally, we tend to view conflict as a negative, destructive force. However, conflict can be a beneficial force that results in increased understanding and communication. (See Figure 11.1.) How we cope with conflict determines whether the process will benefit or harm our relationship with another person or group. Imagine what life would be like without conflict. Everything would become stale and stagnant. If no one ever disagreed, we can only shudder to think what would still exist in terms of public policy, ethics, and technology. In fact, we saw in the chapter on small group communication that the phenomenon "groupthink" occurs, with disastrous results, when members are unwilling to express conflict. Disastrous consequences related to national decisions regarding the Gulf War, the Whitewater Incident, and the Space Shuttle Challenger occurred, in large part, due to a lack of conflict.

Levels of Conflict

Now that we know what conflict is, let's look at the various forms it takes. Researchers suggest that the setting of the situation determines the kind of conflict that will occur. We will focus first on the types of conflict that occur in interpersonal and group settings.

Communication and Conflict

Communication plays an important role in the conflict process. First, communication serves to move conflict from the private to the public arena. In other words, conflict emerges within our minds as we perceive someone interfering with our wants, needs, and goals. The expression of that perception moves from our minds to the public arena through communication. Whether through a passive remark (verbal communication) or an outward punch in the nose (nonverbal), we are communicating this perceived interference to the other party.

Second, communication can either help or hinder the conflict process, as we saw with Tamika's story at the beginning of the chapter. Tamika wanted to go out with friends on the weekends, but she habitually waited until she was walking out the door to ask her parents if she could go. Her parents perceived this as a sign of disrespect and forbade her to leave the house. She, in turn, probably perceived this as an invitation to battle and the whole negative cycle continued. Harsh words were exchanged until the entire process turned negative. It wasn't until Tamika and her parents set a time well in advance to discuss where she was going that they resolved their ongoing conflict. As Tamika discovered, communication can either help or hinder the resolution of a conflict situation.

Communication also changes the conflict process. Think about a time in which you knew you had to confront a friend or loved one about something. You probably carefully rehearsed what you were going to say over and over again in front of the mirror, driving in your car, or while lying in bed. However, your meticulous plan may have gone right out the window the minute the other person responded. The response we think the other person will have in a conflict situation is a guess at best. We can never be quite sure what is going to occur in the ensuing interaction that we have with others. Consequently, once the interaction begins, our response may be quite different from what we had anticipated. Perhaps you can recall a conflict situation in which you entered entirely calm and collected, only to find yourself, just a few minutes later, angry, frustrated, and having said a few things that you wished you had not said. Because communication is transactional, you can never fully know what will occur before it actually does.

How can you tell when a conflict is getting worse or working toward being resolved? You can probably tell that conflict is escalating when individuals begin using name-calling, threats, or sarcastic remarks when discussing the problem. In addition, nonverbal cues such as trembling, invading the other person's personal space, avoiding eye contact, or engaging in hostile gazing could indicate that conflict is escalating.

You can do your own assessment of conflict escalation just by watching your favorite television drama or soap opera. Mentally note what communication cues occurred when conflict seemed to be escalating. What verbal cues indicated that conflict was increasing? What nonverbal cues indicated that conflict was increasing? By learning to recognize communication cues of conflict escalation, you can take an important step toward becoming a better conflict resolver in your own life.

Interpersonal Conflict

According to H. B. Braiker and H. H. Kelley (1979), there are three types of conflict that occur in interpersonal relationships—particularly marital or romantic relationships.

The first type of conflict is behavioral conflict. Behavioral conflict is specific behaviors that a spouse or romantic partner might have that differ from ones that you have and that are somehow interfering with the relationship. For example, conflict may arise over your partner's preferences in music, sexual behavior, or discussion topics. If you're horrified when your partner begins discussing very intimate details of your relationship when out to dinner with friends, you may be experiencing a behavioral conflict with your significant other.

The second type is Normative conflict, which evolves when you and your romantic partner disagree over the norms and rules of the relationship. One common cause of normative conflict in an intimate living situation involves household chores. Working women are most likely to offer this complaint. Even though millions of women work outside the home, they are still responsible for nearly 70 percent of the household chores. The inequity felt by women in this situation can emerge as conflict with their partner—as this student discovered:

My wife and I have a great relationship except when it comes to working around the house. When we argue, it tends to be about who did the dishes last, who vacuumed the floor, or whose turn it was to do the grocery shopping. I'm taking classes full-time and she's working to get us through, so we both have busy schedules. Sometimes I'm just too tired or have to study, so I don't get a chance to work around the house or help out with the kids. I know she's just as tired when she gets home from work. I'd have to say that our conflicts over maintaining a household are the biggest problem in our relationship.

— Tyler, fourth-year college student

As Tyler discovered, normative conflicts, ones that revolve around the norms of a relationship, can be among the most difficult to resolve.

Lastly, personal conflicts may emerge between you and your partner regarding each other's characteristics, attitudes, and level of selfishness. For example, personal conflicts can arise when one person in the relationship believes the other partner has sexist, racist, or other discriminatory attitudes toward others. You might become angry over the sexual jokes that your partner makes at parties, or the racist comments he or she makes about others.

Group Conflict

Slightly different areas of conflict emerge in a group setting; here the relationships are less intimate than those we saw above. Although groups can become very cohesive in nature, they differ—in terms of conflict—from interpersonal conflicts. The majority of conflicts that occur in group situations are directly related to group goals. Usually this occurs in the form of a problem, project, or objective that the *group* has been formed to tackle.

The different types of conflict that occur in groups include:

- Task.
- Procedural.
- Interpersonal.

According to Larry Barker, Kathy Wahlers, and Kittie Watson (1995), if a group is faced with disagreement over the nature of the project or the facts related to the issues, the group is experiencing task conflict. Task conflict is necessary for groups to devise quality solutions and ideas, but there can come a point where the group's wrangling over tasks can be unproductive. Groups can spend too much time arguing about every aspect of the problem and waste valuable time in finding a solution.

Similarly, if a group cannot agree on how to accomplish the goal, for example, whether to use an agenda or what decision-making process to use, the group is experiencing procedural conflict. Lastly, personality clashes, or relational problems that emerge within a group are considered interpersonal conflicts. Just as we discovered in the proceeding discussion of interpersonal conflict, it is possible for group members to have conflict over norms, behaviors, attitudes, and characteristics of others in the group.

A contemporary example will help us look at these levels of group conflict. In the late 1990s, the United States was littered with incidences of school violence—in Paducah, Kentucky; Edinboro, Pennsylvania; Jonesboro, Arkansas; and Littleton, Colorado, to name just a few. Schools and communities nationwide were suddenly forming committees to prevent future violence against students and teachers.

Imagine that a school board has formed a committee to prevent workplace violence. Unfortunately, at the end of the semester, the committee has achieved nothing. One-half of the members think that the school should shoulder the greatest responsibility for school violence and take preventive measures including installing metal detectors and hiring security guards. The other members on the committee believe that the responsibility should be left to parents to monitor their children. The committee is losing valuable work-

---

SPOTLIGHT ON DIVERSITY

Affirmative Action laws and globalization have changed the composition of the United States workplace. According to the U.S. Department of Labor, by the year 2005, women will account for nearly 48 percent of the American labor force, and African Americans, Hispanics, and Asians will also constitute a significant portion of the future work world. This change from a predominantly white male workplace to a more diverse workplace is not occurring without conflict. Diversity training and sensitivity workshops have just begun to scratch the surface of creating a work environment that is more inclusive for everyone.

But in practice, changing the attitudes and behaviors of people is difficult and controversial. For example, in 1993 Jerold McKenzie, an employee of Miller Brewing Company, was fired for describing an episode of *Seinfeld* to a female co-worker, Patricia Best. In the episode, Jerry Seinfeld is discussing a recent date he had, but he can only remember that the woman's name (Dolores) rhymes with a part of the female anatomy. McKenzie photocopied the term from a dictionary and showed it to Best. Several days later, she reported the incident to the Personnel Department and McKenzie was asked to leave the company. In the 1997 suit, McKenzie was seeking damages for lost wages and benefits, citing that he had applied for more than 70 positions in different companies but had been denied employment because he was considered a "pervert" by those who had heard of the firing. On July 15, 1997, the jury awarded McKenzie $26.6 million from Miller Brewing, Co., Best, and another supervisor.

What do you think?

1. *Should this employee have lost his job for the sexual joke he told, or could the company have taken other measures to educate the worker?*

2. *What, if any, future conflicts might occur in this company because of the employee's firing and subsequent lawsuit?*

3. *The jury in this case seemed to be saying that claims of sexual harassment can go "too far" in the workplace. Do you agree?*

---

ing time arguing over the task at hand. When members cannot agree on the most basic issues around which the group was formed, they can never proceed to devising solutions. This is an example of task conflict.

What if the group *did* agree that the school needed to take action and use preventive measures in the school. Now, they must decide whether to install metal detectors at all of the building entrances and exits. In facing an important vote on the metal detectors, the anti-violence committee could experience procedural conflict if some of the members wanted the vote to be unanimous and other members wanted it to be a majority vote. These two decision-making processes have two very different procedures and outcomes. If the committee cannot decide on which decision-making process to use, conflict over procedure is occurring.

Lastly, imagine that the principal of the school was assigned to head up the anti-violence committee. His hidden agenda, however, is to shift any blame from the school administration in terms of past violence. Throughout the meeting, he continually disrupts other members and points out that this problem "begins at home" and that he shouldn't have to deal with such problems in the first place. Because other members of the committee see their purpose as providing a safe school for everyone, they quickly become annoyed at this member and argue with him at every opportunity. Clearly, interpersonal conflict has erupted in this group.

Organizational Conflict

As you might imagine, organizations can also be sites of conflict. Because we spend so much time of every day working in organizations, opportunities for conflict naturally emerge. Conflict in organizations can occur between individual employees (interpersonal) and among departments or teams (group). However, conflict can also occur at the *intra*organizational and *inter*organizational levels.

*Intra*organizational conflict is conflict that occurs within an organization, among departments or levels of employees. Ruth Smith and Eric Eisenberg (1987) uncovered *intra*organizational conflict in their research on Disney. Throughout the company's history, deceased founder, Walt Disney, had tried to foster a climate that made all employees feel like family. This metaphor of the family became a part of life for Disney employees, that is, until a labor-management strike occurred in 1984. When management began to freeze wages and eliminate benefits, the employees no longer felt like part of a big happy family and went out on a 22-day strike—an *intra*organizational conflict at the United States' best-loved theme park.

*Inter*organizational conflict may occur when different organizations are competing for scarce resources or rewards, or debating differences in values and goals. Sometimes, when two organizations merge, *inter*organizational conflict can arise. For example, imagine the conflict that might occur when two large hospitals, which had formerly competed against each other for patients and local resources, decide to merge. One hospital had always advertised its high quality of patient care; the other one had prided itself on efficiency and speed of delivery. Now, the newly formed organization must somehow reconcile these apparently contradictory values.

Styles of Conflict Management

Preferences for Conflict Management

You may think that the way you respond in a conflict situation is unpredictable, but that's not entirely true. Instead, research suggests that people have preferred communication styles for managing conflict. They are based on:

- Personal preference.
- Attitude.
- Setting.

When the group Tragically Hip wrote the song, "Fight," they could have had this in mind. As a few lyrics of the song explain, "Do you think I bow out cause/ I think you're right/Or cause I don't want to fight?"

Do you give in when faced with conflict or do you enjoy a good fight? Whether you realize it or not, over the years you probably have developed your own pattern or style for communicating in conflict situations. If, as a child, you learned that the only way to get a favorite toy from a younger sibling was to compromise, you might be likely to employ the same strategy in your relationships later in life. Or perhaps you were the younger sibling who felt picked on by your older brothers and sisters and tried to avoid conflicts at all costs. This pattern of avoiding conflict may very well have carried over into your future communication habits. As early as the 1960s communication researchers became interested in the way that people communicate in conflict situations. Although it would be a mistake to assume that you behave in the same way in every conflict event, you probably have a preferred style for coping with conflict that emerges. According to Robert Blake and Jane Mouton (1964), basic styles of conflict management include:

- Avoiding.
- Accommodating.
- Competing.
- Compromising.
- Collaborating.

To look at these styles, let's first imagine a scenario. You've recently volunteered for the special events committee of your local United Way. A fundraising dinner is being held next weekend, and you and another volunteer, Pat, are in charge of the event. Literally hundreds of invitations need to be hand-signed, folded, addressed, and mailed by Tuesday. The chairperson of the committee informs you and Pat that you will need to stay into the late hours of the evening and all day tomorrow working on the invitations. If the invitations do not go out on time, the entire dinner could be a disaster. Pat told you yesterday about a prior family commitment that was scheduled for tonight. You don't have any immediate plans, but you don't want to have to stay after hours either. So, what would you do to resolve this dilemma?

One possible solution to this conflict would be to avoid the matter completely. Perhaps you feel very uncomfortable with the entire situation. You know of Pat's plans and you would rather not make her choose between the social obligation and the task at hand. The thought of approaching Pat to discuss the matter makes your palms sweat, so you opt not to approach Pat and just stay after to do the work yourself, thus avoiding the conflict situation entirely. An *avoiding* style like this is often characteristic of a person who views conflict as negative, destructive, and gut-wrenching. The person may even have a fear of resolving conflict, taking a "flight" rather than "fight" approach. While avoiding conflict usually is not productive, there may be other times (according to Conrad & Poole, 1998), when an avoiding style is actually beneficial to the situation:

1. When you need time to think about the conflict.
2. When you don't have much to lose or the issue is trivial.
3. When you gain by stalling the other person.
4. When the problem will go away on its own.
5. When people lack the skills necessary to manage the conflict.

A couple of problems exist with the avoiding style nonetheless. Several negative consequences include continually unresolved issues, decisions made by default, self-doubt, and the prevention of creative input and ideas.

Another possible solution to this scenario would be for you to tell Pat that you will stay after today to finish the invitations. You know that Pat has some type of engagement, and you don't want to ruin Pat's plans. You agree to do the work so that Pat can go home on time. If this sounds like the way you might approach this conflict, you would be likely to use an *accommodating* style of conflict resolution. If you use this style, you tend to be more concerned with maintaining harmony within the relationship than you are with the task at hand. Even if the invitations take the entire evening to complete, you're willing to do them so that Pat can keep her family commitments. Although you might feel a bit resentful, you don't want to jeopardize the friendship you have with Pat. Other times the accommodating style is useful include:

1. When you don't have much to lose.
2. When you want to maintain the relationship.
3. When you want to save time in certain situations.
4. When you're wrong.

Be aware that the accommodating style may result in decreased respect or recognition from others and your own frustration at not having your own needs met.

Maybe avoiding or accommodating isn't your style at all. You feel that Pat should do as much of the work as you—perhaps more. You can't help that family plans were made ahead of time. In fact, you stayed late the last time there was a crisis situation and you feel it's Pat's turn to handle this emergency situation. You insist that Pat stay and work late tonight if she wants to maintain her position on the special events committee. If you would handle the conflict in this manner, you would be adopting a *competing* style of conflict management. Sometimes it is necessary, and even desirable, to adopt a competing style. You should employ the competing style:

1. When you know that you are right.
2. When the relationship doesn't matter.
3. When you have much to lose.
4. When you need or want to show your status.

Be wary of the negative consequences of competing however. Competing styles often lead to reduced communication, damage to the relationship, and lack of commitment from the other person.

Perhaps you would be more likely to want to *compromise* with Pat. You realize that you will have to work with Pat on other committees well into the future and you don't want your relationship to be damaged; however, you don't want to always feel like a doormat that people step on; they shouldn't, you feel, leave you to to do all the work. You go to Pat and suggest that both of you stay after and split the work completely. Perhaps, as you explain to Pat, you both will get the job done early and you both can go home sooner than if one had to stay and work solo. If you prefer this style, you are consistently

MISSION: POSSIBLE

Recall the last two conflicts in which you were involved. Was the conflict located at an interpersonal, group, or organizational level? How did you manage each conflict event? Did you compete, collaborate, accommodate, avoid, or compromise in each situation? What underlying factors influenced the way in which you managed the conflict? Lastly, how, if at all, would you manage the conflict differently if you had the chance to do it over again?

concerned with finding a position that allows both sides to win a little. Compromise is appropriate:

1. When you need to keep the relationship strong.
2. When there's a chance you may be wrong.
3. When a decision must be made for the sake of time.
4. When both parties have mutually exclusive goals.

Compromising is not without its downfalls. Often compromise is a short-lived solution with which no one is entirely satisfied.

The last style of conflict management builds on the basic principle of compromise in which both sides get something. Perhaps you and Pat could pool your ideas and resources to *collaborate* on a solution. Although it might take time to reach a solution that both of you agree on, it may be worth it because you would both walk away feeling as if you have effectively resolved the conflict. Maybe you and Pat agree to come in several hours early and work through your lunch to finish the invitations. That way, neither of you will have to stay after work. Or maybe you and Pat plan to pool all your friends who have offered to help you with charity work in the past and give the invitations to them to complete. Collaboration can often let both parties get what they want and maybe more. Other times when collaboration is helpful are:

1. When ensuring future good relationships with that person.
2. When there is time to collaborate.
3. When both people have the same skill level.
4. When you want to attack a common problem.

Like the four other styles, collaboration has potential unpleasant consequences, including spending too much time on an insignificant issue and dealing with people who are unfamiliar with the situation.

While the styles approach to conflict has been helpful to researchers in examining how people solve conflict, it's important to recall the interactive nature of communication. The styles outlined above are simply snapshots of people's preferences for managing conflict. What makes conflict so unpredictable and perhaps unsettling is that these styles may change during interaction with others. For example, in an episode of the television show *Murphy Brown*, Murphy and Frank are arguing over a new show they both want to anchor. First, they adopt a competing style with each other, with Murphy arguing that she should anchor the show and Frank asserting that he is the better candidate. Later, they both fawn over their boss, who is technically assigned to resolve the conflict but who tells them to work it out between the two of them. Immediately, they begin to compromise—although not completely honestly. Each says that the other is more qualified for the job, hoping that the guilt will lead the other to give up. As we can see, their styles of resolving conflict changed dramatically when they were interacting with each other as well as during and after their conversations with the boss.

Steps for Resolving Conflict

So far, we have talked about preferences and style for managing conflict. Now it is important to present some key steps in conflict resolution. However, many times it is neither possible nor desirable to resolve conflict because of moral principles. For example, if you were serving on a jury, you might find that the other members of the jury were voting to find the individual guilty and you thought the person was innocent. In this situation, you couldn't really compromise with the other members to find him only "half guilty" or give in and vote guilty if you thought he was innocent. You would have to stand firm even though the conflict between you and the other jurors would still exist. In a situation such as this, you might find that conflict resolution is not in the best interests of those involved.

1. If you believe it is necessary to resolve the conflict, a good first step is to try to *remove yourself from the conflict* in some way if possible. Remember the advice of mom and dad when you were a child. "Count to ten whenever you get angry." Well, it turns out that is a very practical piece of advice. When a conflict situation escalates, the first step to resolving the situation is to remove yourself in some way. Take a deep breath. Count to ten. Get a glass of water. Go to lunch. Do something that will allow you time to think a moment before you react to the situation so that you're less likely to say something that you don't really mean. This doesn't mean that you are avoiding the conflict necessarily but that you need some time to think through your choices intelligently. Think about what the other person is saying and what his or her position is in this situation.

2. Next, you should *empathize with the person*. Often, conflict emerges when people don't feel as if they are being heard or understood. In Chapter 4 on listening, we discussed the process of empathizing, or trying to understand the other person's feelings, attitudes, or beliefs. Many times a conflict situation can be diminished in the early stages if you empathize with the person.

   For example, what if a co-worker exploded with angry words when you asked if the paperwork was completed on a new contract? He shouts angrily about the deadlines that he's been under to complete two contracts in a short amount of time. Saying something like, "Well, that's too bad, but I need this contract now," would probably just negatively increase the conflict. Instead, try to empathize and understand what the person is experiencing by saying, "I'm sorry, I've never been in your position of negotiating two contracts at once, but I imagine that it's quite stressful." With this statement, you have taken the situation to a new plane by avoiding judgment of the person and demonstrating to the person that you understand what he or she is going through in this problem.

3. The third step to resolving conflict is to *ask questions* about the facts, issues, feelings, and thoughts surrounding the conflict. Use this time to explore the other side of the story. Often, this is the most difficult step in the entire process. It is so much easier to get defensive and caught up in our own position, rather than taking the time to listen to what our "opponent" is experiencing. Ask questions about how the situation occurred ("How did you get involved to this degree?") or what has lead up to this point ("What lead to our relationship falling apart?"). Ask how the person feels about this situation ("How does this situation make you feel"?). Perhaps, the conflict will be resolved at this point because you both uncover information that you didn't know previously.

4. After asking about the conflict at hand by gathering information, you should then *reveal how the conflict affects you*. Explain your point of view and how the conflict is affecting your feelings, job performance, or well-being. It is particularly important at this point in the process to use "I" language, a term popular to counseling and psychotherapy. Rather than using language that places blame on others ("You never listen to me!"), it is more helpful to resolving the conflict if you use language that does not directly attack the person or place blame ("I get upset when I feel as if people don't listen to me"). Once you have revealed how the situation affects you, you might offer a suggestion to the problem ("Maybe we could try harder to listen to each other in our relationship").

Is this a sure-fire recipe for resolving conflict in every situation?

No, because conflict is a product of human behavior and does not always neatly fit into a recipe for resolution. When working as organizational consultants, the authors often come across workplace situations in which all of the "right" steps have been tried to resolve the conflict, but to no avail. Sometimes we will encounter individuals in an organization who instigate destructive conflict, make threats, or fail to complete job tasks. Even after we coach the co-workers in conflict resolution strategies, the individual in question continues the behavior. How can you deal with a difficult person like this? If traditional conflict resolution strategies don't work, sometimes you just have to accept that this person is too emotionally draining to be around. Instead of dwelling on the situation and making your own life miserable by complaining about this person, you may need to restructure your work environment to minimize your interactions with that person.

Factors Affecting Conflict Management

Cultural Differences

The process described above for resolving conflict is based on an American perspective. While stereotypic American behavior is to confront disagreements and get everything out in the open, other cultures would not approach conflict in the same way. For example, many people from Thailand avoid confrontations at all costs. They will never say no, but will instead make excuses or pretend that they don't understand English. They may even tell you that they must check with someone at a higher level, when such a person doesn't exist. Likewise, they find it difficult to accept a direct negative answer (Morrison, Conaway, & Borden, 1994, p. 384).

The conflict resolution process described earlier would be difficult in a culture with a high aversion for conflict. Cultures that have a high regard for face-saving, or the "act of preserving one's prestige or outward dignity" are good examples (Victor, 1992, p. 159). In such cultures, any conflict that could damage someone's "face" in front of others could result in both personal and professional shame. Asian, Arab, and Latin American cultures rank high in face-saving, as compared to the German, Scandinavian, and North American cultures which rank low. In such high face-saving cultures, conflict can affect the culture's preference for harmony and respect for others. Consequently, conflict must be dealt with in very different ways.

In many cultures, conflict is dealt with in ways more indirect or private than outright confrontation. In high face-saving cultures, people engage in the practice known as the politeness strategy in order to resolve tensions (Tirkkonen-Condit, 1988). The politeness strategy, which involves indirect and implicit discussion of conflict issues, is used because direct argumentation or confrontation is inherently face-threatening. Conflict is particularly harmful, for example, in Japan or China, if "explicitly negative messages publicly single out and shame someone" (O'Hara-Devereaux & Johansen, 1994). Consequently, the resolution of conflicts is unlikely to occur in public settings, if it is addressed at all. In high face-saving cultures, conflict is characterized by an "avoidance-at-all-costs" approach. In Malaysia even business meetings are polite and friendly events. People do not argue or discuss issues intensely in Malaysia. Similarly, in Japan open confrontation is contrary to traditional values of organizational protocol. Not only do they avoid open discussion of organizational problems, the Japanese (and other Asian cultures) avoid public disagreement at all costs. Resolving conflict through communication in certain cultures can be very different from the way it is in the United States.

Gender Differences

Like culture, gender also appears to play an important role in how conflict is resolved. Not surprisingly, popular books like *Men Are from Mars, Women Are from Venus* have reached best-seller status as men and women throughout the world try to understand and resolve conflicts with one another. Do men and women really differ in preferences for resolving conflict? Think about your own relationships. If your partner is of the opposite sex, does he or she react differently from you when conflict occurs?

In intimate relationships, how conflict is addressed may very well differ according to gender. Research suggests that woman often want to talk about conflict issues with their opposite-sex mates. They want to discuss and describe their feelings. Unfortunately, a strange interaction occurs. The more women want to discuss the conflict, the less men do, perhaps fueling the stereotypical belief that women "nag" their loved ones. Men often need opportu-

❖ ❖ ❖ ❖

Research suggests that men and women resolve conflict differently.

nities to walk away from the conflict rather than engage in it. Listen to the description of this in the relationship of one student:

> It's funny that we should talk about conflict in class today, because my wife and I got into a bad one last night. We were arguing over going to her parents' house this weekend. I told her I had too much work to do. I did want to go, but the more she kept arguing, the madder I got. I turned to walk away and she said, "If you love me, you won't leave." Well, I hate ultimatums like that, but I knew it would just get worse if I stayed there and fought about it, so I left. I cooled down and we smoothed things over later.
>
> — José, first-year college student

What José describes could be a difference in conflict resolution based on gender. Women may be more relationally oriented in such situations, wanting to express their feelings with their mate in order to resolve the conflict. Men, on the other hand, may want to resolve the conflict but on their own terms. However, when a man wants to disengage, the woman may take this as a sign of rejection, resulting in more hurt feelings and conflict situations. It is not yet fully known how gender affects conflict interactions among same-sex couples.

Another interesting gender difference among men and women exists in terms of conflict style preference. If you're a man, do you tend to want to compete in conflict situations? If you're a woman, are you more likely to want to find a compromise to the problem? Research suggests that men and women do tend to use these styles of conflict management, most likely based on socialization during childhood and adolescence (Berryman-Fink & Brunner, 1987). In the workplace, women must often adopt competing styles of conflict resolution in order to survive, particularly in male-dominated organizations (Burrell, Buzzanell, & McMillan, 1992). Even though they prefer not to use a competing style, women employees often perceive conflict situations as "going to war" with others.

Summary

Fight. War. Battle. Unfortunately, there is a natural tendency to view conflict as a destructive force. However, conflict is an inherent part of human communication. Conflict emerges when two interdependent people or groups engage in an expressed struggle over goals, resources, or rewards. Communication moves conflict from the private (in your mind) to the public (to the awareness of the other person or group). Different levels of conflict exist based on the communication context. At the interpersonal level, conflict may be behavioral, normative, or personal in nature. In groups, conflict may arise over disagreements about tasks and procedures or over personality clashes among group members. Lastly, conflict can emerge within an organization among departments or levels of employees (*intra*organizational), or outside an organization as it struggles to achieve goals or obtain resources (*inter*organizational) in competition with other organizations.

Conflict can be managed in a variety of ways, although both culture and gender differences exist. Although the situation tends to determine the way in which we resolve conflict, we tend to fall into a common pattern of conflict resolution. A person who would rather take "flight" than "fight" uses an avoiding approach to conflict. A person who is more concerned with maintaining harmony within a relationship than with tackling the problem is using an accommodating style of resolution. Those people who are continually concerned about maintaining their own needs and concerns may compete in conflict situations. Finding a position that allows both sides of the issue to win a little is representative of a compromising style. The last style of conflict management builds on the idea of a compromise, working more toward resolving the conflict through devising a solution to the problem collaboratively.

You can work towards conflict management by removing yourself from the situation, if possible, to think through your choices, empathizing with the other person, asking questions to discover more about the problem, and finally revealing how the problem affects you. Learning to resolve conflict constructively can mean the difference between healthy and unhealthy relationships with others.

At Your Bookstore

Bishop, S. (1996). *Develop Your Assertiveness*. Dover, NH: Kogan Page Ltd.

Hall, L. M. (1987). *Speak Up/Speak Clear/Speak Kind: Assertive Communication Skills*. Grand Junction, CO: Empowerment Tech.

Robinson, J. (1997). *Communication Miracles for Couples: Easy & Effective Tools to Create More Love and Less Conflicts*. Berkeley, CA: Conari Press.

Stevinin, T. J. (1997). *Win/Win Solutions: Resolving Conflict on the Job*. Chicago: Moody Press.

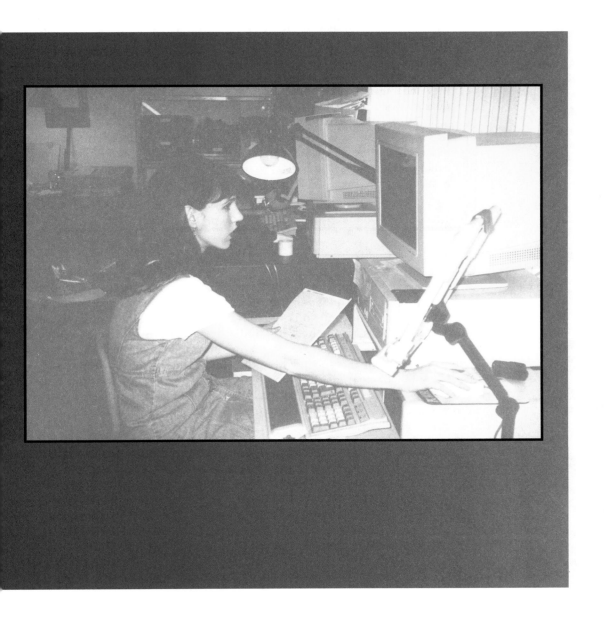

CHAPTER 12

Applying Research to Presentations and Reports

❖ ❖ ❖ ❖

I was president of my senior class in high school. Good communication skills played a prominent role in accomplishing the goals that I had set to achieve. It was necessary to work well with my peers and essential to listen to their opinions and ideas. Not only was it imperative to maintain clear and open communication lines with my peers, but it was necessary to have the same relationship with the faculty and administration. Without their support and approval, many activities would not have been successful.

When various activities were planned for the class, information needed to be dispersed objectively and coherently to the students. It was essential that they understood what was occurring within the school. If other students had questions or suggestions, I tried to welcome their comments without bias.

On one specific occasion, a rumor started stating that the senior trip to Orlando, Florida, was canceled due to insufficient funds. Of course, this misconception needed to be corrected before things got out of hand. The other class officers and I quickly arranged a class meeting to clear the misunderstanding.

— Carina, first-year college student

Having been in a position of authority, Carina understands the importance of communication in a leadership role. Listening to others is certainly a crucial part of that, but then so is speaking. Carina's administration countered the flow of rumors among her classmates by presenting information in a public fashion. As in Carina's case, speaking out publicly is especially important when you have the facts. But where did she get her facts? Carina was in contact with her class treasurer, faculty advisers, and school administrators to get the information she needed to set everyone straight on the class trip. In short, she did her homework. She did research.

Previous chapters in this book have covered topics ranging from how people talk to loved ones to how people talk to unseen mass audiences. You've read about how nonverbal leakage can betray a liar, and you've studied the flow of information in organizations. Some of the information you have read probably seems self-evident. (Before ever having read Chapter 3, for example, you already knew how to spot a liar just by the way one acted.) Some of the information you have read probably jibes with your experience. (Maybe you work in an organization where all the information flows downward; now after reading Chapter 8, you can recognize the power relationships such a flow of information maintains.) Some of the information you have read might even be a total revelation to you. (Perhaps you were surprised to read in Chapter 5 that listening and hearing were not the same thing.) Whether you are finding the information in this book to be familiar, complementary, or all new, it is all the product of *research*, research that has grown out of a tradition of both academic and public inquiry. As you read in Chapter 1, this process has been going on for well over 2,500 years, and the project of learning more about the ways in which human beings communicate is continued by researchers in schools, government, and industry. You may choose to have an active part in that process. This chapter offers:

- An overview of the kind of research being done in the field of human communication.
- An explanation of the tools available to you, as a researcher.

❖ ❖ ❖ ❖

The Nature of Human Communication Research

Human communication studies is a member of the family of academic disciplines called the social sciences. That family includes the related disciplines of psychology, sociology, and anthropology. These disciplines are united by an interest in exploring how human beings function in the social world. If you have already had introductory courses in any of these other disciplines, you know that they, like human communication studies, devote a lot of time to exploring how humans interact. The two approaches to research in human communication studies are quantitative and qualitative analysis.

Quantitative Studies

Most of the members of the social science family developed from a model of scientific inquiry begun in the natural sciences, namely biology, chemistry, and physics. In this scientific method of research, one poses a hypothetical question such as "How many licks does it take to get to the Tootsie Roll center of a Tootsie Pop?" and then sets up an experiment to discover an answer. You have probably worked through such a procedure in your high school science classes. The same rigor is found among social scientists—only instead of focusing on subjects such as the erosion of substances, they measure phenomena such as the amount of time communicators spend in leave-taking behavior.

When social scientists focus on measuring some aspect of human interaction, inquiries of this nature are termed quantitative studies. In quantitative research, some variable is selected for analysis and then is measured against some constant. Typically, the relationship between the variable and the constant is expressed mathematically. Thus, variables are discussed as quantities. A social scientist sets out to explain some *regularity* of human communication. The researcher does this through the mathematical relationship of the variables. However, unlike hard science hypotheses, which typically state—in linear fashion—if A and B . . . , then C . . . , social science experiments begin with the null hypothesis—that is, the idea is expressed as though there were no correlation between variables. The social scientist then asks, "Can I reject the null hypothesis?" If the null hypothesis can be rejected, then the relationship between variables is likely to exist. Here's an example: A social scientist might start out with the null hypothesis "There is no relationship between the amount of time a student spends talking in class and that student's overall performance in the class" in order to find out if students who talk in class do better than those who do not.

There are three factors commonly associated with quantitative research:

- First, social scientists strive for *objectivity* in their work. This means that the quantitative experiment assumes there is an external, observable reality existing separate from individual perceptions.

- Second, the experiments should be easily *replicated*. The experiment conducted by one researcher in New York should, if the directions are followed exactly, produce similar results for another researcher in Los Angeles.
- Third, the researcher establishes the categories for research at the onset of measuring the variable and sticks to those categories throughout the experiment.

Because the variables under analysis are quantified, social scientists rely upon the methods of statistics to analyze their data. Statistics is the study of probability. The question at the heart of statistical analysis is: "Can the relationship between the variables be attributed to chance?" If they cannot, if the probability of the results being accurate is high, then we can say that an analysis is valid. Statistical analysis provides us with an easy way to express and talk about relationships between human actors and their actions.

Qualitative Studies

However, not all human communication research relies upon the quantitative model for discovering knowledge about human interaction. Researchers are not limited to statistical analysis to make knowledge claims about human communication. Quantitative methods rest on one end of a continuum or range that stretches into what is known as qualitative methods. Qualitative studies seek to explicate, or qualify, human communication experiences without necessarily measuring them by quantity. Typically, such research is more concerned with how reality is experienced by individuals than in generating regularities of communication. For example, Dan Modaff (1997) conducted a series of interviews with aging World War II veterans in order to understand better what they experienced in living during a turbulent era in American history. These veterans were interviewed one by one, and each shared details about his tour of military service that differed from those of his comrades, giving the researcher a great deal more information to process in his report.

Qualitative studies differ from quantitative studies in several key ways:

- First, qualitative studies do not necessarily aim at objectivity. You may often find the first-person pronouns "I" and "we" used in qualitative reports, reflecting the author's de-emphasis on impartial distance from the experience at hand. What qualitative studies are aiming for is explaining the common themes that emerge from an individual's, or a group of individuals', explanation of a communication phenomenon.

- Second, because qualitative analysis focuses on the individual experience more than the universal, the results are not replicable. Someone who experiences a communication phenomenon in New York may not experience it in the same way as someone in Los Angeles.

- Third, qualitative researchers do not operate from predetermined categories in their studies. Instead, they approach their research with some general questions that are answered and to some extent modified by the research participants.

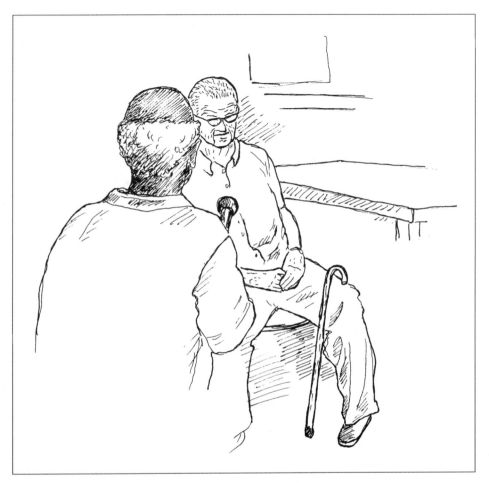

*One way in which scholars learn more about communication
is through interviewing people about their experiences.*

Between quantitative studies and qualitative studies are numerous variations, depending on where a particular method or system used in conducting research is situated. For now, we want you to be aware that different ways of studying human communication are indicative of the different ways in which one can conceive of reality. From one extreme, reality is something out there, existing independent of our beliefs in it. From the other, reality is something constructed by us, shaped by our beliefs and practices. The degree to which one identifies with one perspective over another influences how one approaches the study of human communication.

Reading Human Communication Research

If you continue to study human communication in college, you will undoubtedly read many more textbooks like this one, which are informed by the research results of other scholars. However, you will also find that instructors will introduce you to a number of original research findings, some of which appear as books but most of which are published as articles in academic journals. An academic journal is a periodical like a magazine, but it specializes in the publication of research findings, book reviews, and scholarly debates. Academic journals contribute to the continued growth of the human communication discipline because they help scholars and students keep up with the latest developments and critical issues in the field.

The National Communication Association, the largest professional organization for human communication scholars, publishes six journals that further our knowledge of communication phenomena: *Quarterly Journal of Speech, Communication Monographs, Communication Education, Critical Studies in Mass Communication, Text and Performance Quarterly,* and *Journal of Applied Communication Research.* Other distinguished scholarly organizations also publish journals that affect the study of human communication. The International Communication Association publishes *Human Communication Research, Journal of Communication,* and *Communication Theory.* Several smaller, regionally based associations also sponsor journals, including *Communication Quarterly, Western Journal of Communication, Southern Speech Communication Journal,* and *Communication Studies.* These would be among the best sources to check for the latest research within the discipline.

Although the organization of articles within such journals can vary, most of those of a *quantitative* nature follow a similar pattern. Knowing the features of each of the sections can help you read these articles.

The abstract is a concise summary of the article. Abstracts, which are about 250 words in length, appear at the beginning of articles so that you can read them first. Well-written abstracts can help you determine whether the information contained in the article would be helpful to you and worth your time in reading.

The introduction introduces the topic the article will consider and provides some rationale for its exploration. In other words, the introduction answers the question: Why would anyone study this particular phenomenon? The introduction may also introduce the hypothesis/hypotheses that guided the study and the conclusions reached.

The literature review recounts what previous scholarship has had to say about the phenomenon under study. It serves as a "research paper" in which the author collects and interprets previously published articles or conference presentations. The author uses the literature review to establish an argument for the new study. It might explain, for example, how this latest study differs from or coincides with previous work on the topic.

The methodology section details how the study was conducted. It explains what hypotheses were formulated before the experiment, how subjects were chosen, what research tool was used (a survey, for example), and how analytical procedures were followed (what statistical formulas were used, for instance).

The discussion section allows for researchers to reflect upon the findings of their study. In what ways were the hypotheses upheld? In what ways did they fail? What can we learn about human communication as a result of this experiment? The discussion section is often the most interesting section of an article because it is where the findings can be fully explained.

The references section lists all the works the author used in constructing the article. Everything listed in the literature review should appear in the ref-

erences. Using the references as a bibliography, you can read about other ❖ ❖ ❖ ❖
articles that analyze the same phenomenon.

Articles that tend to fall more to the *qualitative* side of the continuum will
have a less rigid structure to them. Most qualitative articles still provide some
rationale for the work, even though they do not propose hypotheses as such.
They also have a distinct literature review in them and discuss methodology
but in typically longer, more self-descriptive language. For example, researchers often acknowledge their own involvement in the process of conducting the research. The content of qualitative articles focuses on discussion
of one sort or another. The articles also have a reference list for any previous
research that informed the present study. Recognizing these differences can
help you understand and discuss the articles you will read with greater
clarity.

The Beginning Researcher and the Library

If you have written a "research paper" in the past, chances are you are familiar with the "research process" that your 12th grade English teacher ham-
mered into your head. Do you remember having to produce 50 notecards,
each with a different citation, for her viewing pleasure? What's that? 100! If
for no other reason than the sheer number of cards you had to create, you may
have found research to be dull. However, it does not necessarily have to be
that way.

The key to enjoying research is to research something you enjoy. In
human communication studies, that might take you anywhere from how people manage to ask others out on dates to how employers buffer the message
that they are about to lay off a worker. Whatever it is that you are interested in
learning more about, an integral part of that learning process involves conducting research. Though you will find upper-level communication courses
that allow you the opportunity to conduct the types of experimental research
that you often read about, we would like to concentrate here on the type of
research that you can conduct in the library now.

Although libraries seem an unlikely place to learn about human interaction, the vast amount of research that has been conducted over the last 2,500
years—particularly during the last century—represents countless hours of
careful study by those scholars who came before us. Because there is so much
information written on human communication, we need to apply a systematic process to our search for answers. The key to isolating information about
particular topics is realizing that information is contained in a number of
resources. Your library probably has a combination of resources, some of
which are in traditional books, others of which are in periodicals like magazines, newspapers, and journals, and still more of which are found on CD-
ROM databases, via online Internet connections, and in other media like
video tapes, recordings, and artifacts. Because of the variety of places where
you might find information about communication phenomena, you need to
familiarize yourself with your school's library and some basic strategies for
conducting research there.

Approaching the large and complexly organized stacks of the library without a search strategy can be an anxiety producing experience.

The only way to learn how to use a library is to enter one. No amount of prompting from a textbook can prepare you to deal with the unique features you will encounter in your institution's library. Because every library in the world operates under its own rules, possesses its own layout, organizes materials in its own fashion, and offers its own services, it would be pointless for us to guess what you will find in your institution's library. We suggest that if you have not already done so, you schedule a tour of your school library so that you can learn what it has to offer you as you begin your academic career. Knowing what is there will make your educational experience that much easier.

Although we are not going to speculate on what you will find in your library, we would like to suggest some simple strategies that will make using the library for your own research less painful and time-consuming. If you will be writing a paper or giving a speech for this course, you will probably need to inform your arguments with some research. But before you can write that paper or deliver that speech, you need to get started in the library. That's why we make a visit to the library the first of our tips for effective research.

Steps to Productive Research

Time-saver Tip #1: Make time for the library.

One of the best things you could do for your own sanity is to allow yourself enough time to do the work you will need to do in the library. Too often students wait until the day before a report is due to even enter the library, figuring that by pulling an all-nighter, they can still finish their project in time. Unfortunately, such fantasies are often erased when the student discovers that the library itself is crowded, and access to technology is limited by long lines, or that needed materials have been already checked out by other students. Thus, the library should be the first step, and not the last, in drafting any kind of scholastic project. We suggest that you visit the library as soon as your instructor makes you aware of an assignment. Begin nosing around in your library's collection to see if there are materials that you will need to recall from other patrons or order through interlibrary loan.

Time-saver Tip #2: Know your topic before you go (or shortly after arriving).

Sometimes instructors are very pointed in what they want you to research: "Sam, give us a five-minute in-class report introducing us to general systems theory." When you know what it is that you have to research, you can head right to the library and begin tracking down resources that can inform your presentation. However, when instructors allow you more freedom with your topic selection, you will have to take the initiative to determine what it is you will research. Given the assignment to "Deliver a five-minute informative speech," you might be frustrated by exactly what topic you should speak on.

In situations such as this you can adopt a two-part strategy. The first part is to review your own interests. Try using a technique called brainstorming, a process in which you write down every topic that comes to mind without evaluating or judging any of the ideas as they come. You simply keep writing down ideas until you have thought of everything you can. When you have done that, then you review your list, examining it for those items that would best suit an assignment such as an informative speech. For example, let us say your interest in protecting natural resources surfaced as an item in your brainstorming. You could select this as a possible topic and go to the library with the idea that you want to speak about some type of conservation.

The second part of this strategy, then, takes place once you arrive in the library. Here you begin to use the general references available in your library to narrow your topic. You could look up "Conservation" in the online catalog, card catalog, databases, print indexes, or reference books to see what is available to you. More than likely, you will discover that "Conservation" is a broad topic, too broad to cover in a five-minute speech presentation. Reading through your library's catalog of books (online or card), you have noticed that there are a number of books on "Water Conservation." You might select this as a narrower topic and look up one of the books in your library to see if this is still too broad for your purposes and time constraints. Be careful: You may have to narrow a topic a number of times before it is suited to the situation you will be using it for.

If you must select your own topic—and everyone will at some point in a college career—you should not put off narrowing it down. The library is filled with many, many interesting topics, most of which are worth your time and energy to learn more about. However, you will have to discipline yourself to make a commitment to one topic or another early in your research process. The more time you are willing to give to researching a topic, the more you will learn about. Consequently, the quality of your report will reflect this time well spent.

Time-saver Tip #3: Ask a librarian for help.

The way that information is arranged in your library probably makes a lot of sense to the librarian. To the uninitiated, however, libraries can be appear to have complicated layouts. For instance, some books may be in a large collection called the general stacks, some may be shelved away from regular circulation in the reserve room or reference room, and still others may be housed in other library facilities. Even if you have a book's "call number," a type of shorthand that identifies where a book is arranged in the library's collection, you still might be unaware of exactly where the book is located. You might even have difficulty finding where in the library you can begin your search. This is why you need to be willing to ask the librarian for assistance. Most librarians, and even their student assistants, have a good deal of training in helping people conduct searches and they most certainly have a familiarity with the library. Asking for help rather than wandering the library aimlessly searching for a book on your own is a great time-saver.

Time-saver Tip #4: Find more resources than you need.

As you read through reference guides, such as the library's catalog, you will probably note a number of materials the library has on a given topic. Although you may need only three resources for your informative speech, you should not assume that by writing down the titles of the first three books listed in the catalog that your work will soon be complete. One or more of those three books may be checked out or missing from the library's collection. Another, you may discover upon browsing through the book, might be too general for your purposes. As you make a list of resources to track down in the library, you should make a list much larger than you expect to use. This will save you the time and trouble of having to return to the catalog or database for more listings later.

Time-saver Tip #5: Record citation information carefully.

As you read through the list of materials your library has available, you will have to determine which resources you want to check out. The title of the article is typically a good indicator of how useful a resource might be to your particular topic. For instance, a periodical article titled "Conserve water: 10 easy steps to saving a natural resource" seems as if it would be more helpful than one titled "Conservation seminar canceled," especially if you have found a lot of resources and do not have time to read through them all. When you choose the resources you want to read, you will need to record some information about them on notecards. Notecards are such a good library aid because they are easy to carry (even in your pocket), easy to organize and rearrange as you need them, and easy to note information on for each specific resource you want to track down. For periodical resources, you should record the following information:

1. Name of the author (Lappako, David)
2. Date of publication (1997)
3. Article title ("Three Cheers for Language")
4. Publication title (*Communication Education*)
5. Volume and number (volume 46, number 1)
6. Pagination (pp. 63–67)
7. Call number (PN4071 .S74)

For books and other resources, you should record the following information:

1. Name of the author (Herrick, James A.)
2. Date of publication (1997)
3. Publication title (*The History and Theory of Rhetoric: An Introduction*)
4. Place of publication (Scottsdale, Arizona)
5. Publisher (Gorsuch Scarisbrick)
6. Call number (808.009 H566h)

As you will read later in this chapter, having this information handy will make it easier for you to create a bibliography for your written reports. Failing to note this information will cause you wasted time later in trying to track it down. You may even be unable to find it again.

Incorporating Research Into Your Written or Spoken Presentations

One of the temptations you will face when setting out to incorporate your research findings into your presentations is to include everything you've found. However, this is probably an impractical goal, given the page length or the time constraints your instructor has you operating under. Moreover, if all you did was quote other people, something very important would be lost in the process: your contribution. Although your instructors and classmates want you to get the information correct, they are also interested in what you have to say about the topic. Your original contributions and insights are a valuable part of any research project.

Instructors typically ask you to consult more than one piece of literature when you are conducting research in preparation for a term paper or a presentation. While you can learn a lot from a single source, you will get a biased view of the topic from reading only one author or piece. Reading from a variety of sources can help you to envision the larger picture of a given topic. The various writers on a given topic do not necessarily agree with one another. As a researcher, you'll want to be informed about different views on a given topic. By assigning you the task of reading a number of sources, your instructor wants to challenge you to engage in the process of synthesis.

A synthesis is the product of a combination. Every time you read a new batch of material, you synthesize it, that is, you combine it in ways that no one is likely to have done before. You can grasp different points in the literature, comparing and contrasting features of each, until a new understanding of the relationship among the ideas is formed. You already synthesize information every time you notice connections and distinctions among the events in your daily life. Noting the similarity between a professor's style of dress and that of a television character is an example of synthesis, of recognizing the relationship between two previously unrelated concepts. As a student, you are asked to recognize and express relationships among ideas. While expressing your original synthesis, however, you need to acknowledge properly those who introduced the *first* set of ideas.

Attribution of References

Whatever resources you choose to include in your own works, you must give the original researchers proper credit. Ideas, like objects, can belong to other people. Although no one can physically own an idea, scholars have agreed to recognize that original contributions to the never-ending human conversation constitute intellectual property. Have you ever been in a situation at school or work where you came up with the solution to a problem, shared it with a colleague, and then watched in amazement as that colleague received praise for presenting your idea to a teacher or superior? If so, then you can understand the frustration of not being given the proper credit for your contribution.

Using the intellectual property of others without giving them credit is plagiarism. Sometimes plagiarism can be a stark crime, such as one student copying an upper classman's report and submitting it as his own. However, sometimes plagiarism is committed without the intent to deceive. Consider a student who takes poor notes during a library search, neglecting to write down the original researcher's name while recording some statistical findings. Instead of returning to get the name of the source, the student chooses to include the claim without crediting the author simply to save time. In either scenario, copying another's paper or not citing a source, the students have committed plagiarism. In order to maintain your own academic integrity, cite the authors of a piece of information in each of the following circumstances:

1. Whenever you use a direct quotation.
2. Whenever you use statistical information.
3. Whenever you discuss a particular study.
4. Whenever you introduce another person's original ideas.

If you are ever in doubt as to whether or not to cite a particular reference, you can always consult your instructor for clarification. Attribution, the process of giving others credit, is not something we are born with, but, like all our other manners, it is something we must learn.

Knowing that you should give credit to others is one thing, knowing *how* to give them credit is quite another. In general, there are three concepts you need to be familiar with in order to go about the proper procedure for attribution:

- Parenthetical citations.
- Bibliographic citations.
- Oral citations.

Forms of Citations in Written Papers

When you have written research papers in the past, you probably used one or more of the standardized citation systems for documentation. The two systems commonly used in human communication studies are those established by the American Psychological Association (APA) and the Modern Language Association (MLA). While these systems feature many similarities, they are different in a number of key points. Both associations issue style manuals that cover all the finer points of their systems, but because the majority of research in human communication is cited in APA style, we will illustrate our points following their guidelines.

Parenthetical citations, a form of in-text documentation like footnotes and endnotes, are demonstrated throughout this text. You probably noticed that some of our sentences end with parentheses ( ) that typically contain a name, a year, and sometimes a page abbreviation and number, all separated by commas. Parenthetical citations are a type of shorthand that tells the reader where to find the original source of the attributed information. Take a look at the following example:

> A primary goal of interpretive research on organizations is to articulate the taken-for-granted rules, assumptions, values, and beliefs that constitute organizational members' world views (Smith & Eisenberg, 1987, p. 367).

After the quotation you see the now familiar parentheses. Within the parentheses you can identify the names of the authors of this quote, the year the quote was published, and the page on which it appears. This is useful information for someone who wants to confirm a quote or return to a piece of literature to read the context from which that quote was taken. However, how does a reader know where to find this quote? What publication did it appear in? What is the title of the article? As we noted above, parenthetical citations are a type of shorthand. In order to find more information about the source of this quote, one would need to turn to the bibliography at the end of the paper. In the case of this textbook, all our references are listed at the end of the book.

But before we turn our attention there, let's make sure you understand that not all parenthetical citations look alike. Many of the ones in this book lack the page number and have only a name and date: (Hancox, 1997). Does this mean the writer was sloppy and forgot to record the page number? No, the lack of a page number merely indicates that the information preceding the parentheses was not a direct quotation, that is, a word for word recording of what the original authors had to say. Such citations are paraphrases, or the ideas of another rephrased in the writer's own words. Even though the words may be the writer's, that person respects the intellectual property of the originators and credits them for their idea.

Some other parenthetical citations, as you may have noticed, lack either pagination or a name depending upon how the writer has constructed the sentence. When the authors' names are a part of the syntax, or word order, of the sentence, only the date appears in the parentheses:

> On the other hand, Smith & Eisenberg (1987) referred to this methodology as "root-metaphor analysis" (p. 367).

Note in this example and others that the names and the date are always closely connected with one another. Moreover, in this example there is a direct quote from the authors and this is indicated by the information in the second set of parentheses. When you are creating your own parenthetical citations, do not assume that the parenthetical information necessarily goes at the end of the sentence. Typically, parenthetical information needs to appear as soon after what it modifies as it can.

What goes at the end of the paper, however, is consistent. Each paper that contains research should have a bibliography, which is a list of books (or other resources) on a topic, all of which have been cited in the paper. In **APA** style, we label such a list as "references". Each item referenced within the list provides the necessary information that will equip someone to find the original source if he or she so chooses. For example, if I looked at the reference list in the paper that dealt with the above examples, I would find the following citation:

Smith, R. C., & Eisenberg, E. M. (1987). "Conflict at Disneyland: A root-metaphor analysis." *Communication Monographs, 54*, pp. 367-380.

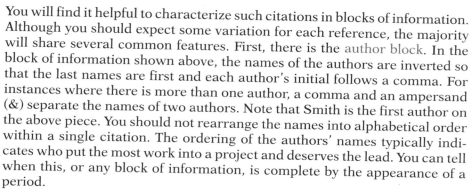

You will find it helpful to characterize such citations in blocks of information. Although you should expect some variation for each reference, the majority will share several common features. First, there is the author block. In the block of information shown above, the names of the authors are inverted so that the last names are first and each author's initial follows a comma. For instances where there is more than one author, a comma and an ampersand (&) separate the names of two authors. Note that Smith is the first author on the above piece. You should not rearrange the names into alphabetical order within a single citation. The ordering of the authors' names typically indicates who put the most work into a project and deserves the lead. You can tell when this, or any block of information, is complete by the appearance of a period.

The next block of information is the date block. For journals and books, a year suffices to identify the time the piece was published. However, periodicals which appear more frequently such as newspapers and magazines should be identified by their month and, if applicable, date: (1998, November 8).

Citations of Articles

The next block of information in a periodical citation is the article title block. Note that regardless of the capitalization used in the publication, APA suggests a uniform style of capitalizing only the first words in the title and subtitle and then any proper nouns (such as Disneyland, the proper name of a place).

Finally, you will find the publication title block. All the significant words in a publication's title are capitalized, with the exception of prepositions (e.g., of, on) and articles (e.g., a, an, the) that appear in the middle of the title. Thus, *The Journal of the American Medical Association* begins with an article that is capitalized but contains one that is not capitalized. This is separated by a comma from the volume of the journal. Both the title and the volume number are underlined or italicized. Another comma separates the volume number from the page numbers on which the article is found. The abbreviate "pp." indicates that the article is multiple pages and the numbers which follow are those pages. A one-page article would only use the abbreviate "p." and a single number.

Citations of Books

Books that appear in an APA reference list are slightly different, as you can tell by comparing the following example with the previous one.

Griffin, E. (1997). *A first look at communication theory* (3rd ed.). New York, NY: McGraw-Hill.

What elements look different to you? What elements have been deleted? What elements are new? Note that the author and date blocks are similar to the journal example above. Since we are citing a whole book in this case, we proceed right to the publication title block. Unlike the titles of journals and other periodicals, a book's title does not use capital letters, as in the case of an article's title (unless of course a proper noun appears in it). This particular example also notes that this book is in its third edition. If a book is still in its first edition, there is no need to note that. But if it is in any subsequent edition, you should note the number of the edition using a combination of the number and its ordinal (2nd, 3rd, 4th, 5th, etc.).

Another difference is that citations of books require a publisher's block. First you list the city and state abbreviation where the book was published (typically found on the title page of most modern books), a colon, and the name of the publisher. In some situations, you will also need to include information on the editors, titles of sections, and pages. For a complete breakdown on how to create both in-text and bibliographic citations using APA style, consult the following:

Publication Manual of the American Psychological Association (4th ed.). (1994). Washington, DC: American Psychological Association.

It will also provide guidance in citing sources other than articles and books. Your school library should have a copy of this text in the reference section, or you can find information on using the APA style in a number of writing reference manuals.

Giving Citations in Speeches

Unlike either the parenthetical or bibliographic citations, oral citations do not follow a set form. There is no standardized method for attributing a source in a speech, but there are some clear goals and guidelines you should have in mind as you construct your own oral citations.

One of the key differences between writing and speaking has to do with the *temporality* of the two media (Ong, 1982). A written composition can be consumed at the reader's own pace. If she wants to know what the title of Smith and Eisenberg's article is, a reader can choose to flip to the reference page and get that information. Likewise, if a reader skips over a section of the composition, all she has to do is reread that section of the paper to discover what the author had to say. Oral compositions, on the other hand, happen in a given time frame. Unless you are watching somebody speak on a video tape, you have more limits on what you get to reconsume. Once the speaker has moved on to another section, the only way a listener can go back to a section of material is to stop the speaker and ask him to go over the material again. In certain social situations, take a university graduation ceremony for instance,

that is highly impractical to do. Because an audience listening to a speech
does not have the luxury to flip back and forth as an audience reading a text
does, good speakers try to be as clear as possible for their audiences. One way
in which they try to be clear is to provide the audience with oral citations.

Actually, you are probably already more familiar with oral citations than
you might expect. If at any time you have shared a story with one friend that
you heard from another, you have probably attributed that information with
an oral citation: "Tafi just told me that Jill is having a party tomorrow night."
When it comes to the more formal context of a public speech, it is just as
important to provide the audience with a clear indication of where your information comes from.

Oral citations are more like parenthetical than bibliographic citations in
their relative brevity. You do not need to give the audience a complete bibliographic citation with author, publication date, article title, and publication
title. Frankly, that is just more information than most of your audience wants
to hear. The goals of an oral citation are twofold. First, oral citations, like the
other forms of attribution, demonstrate you are honest with others' intellectual property. Second, oral citations testify to the quality of your research
efforts. Consider the following two statements:

> According to Dr. Ralph Blazer in the *World Weekly News*, 1 in 50 Ameri-
> cans is more Neanderthal than human.

> The *CBS Evening News* of January 22 reported that more than 250 home-
> less Peruvian youths constitute this roving gang.

Both of these quotations are good examples of someone using oral citations to
inform the audience. Note that they both state some statistical information
and the source that generated it. However, tabloids like *World Weekly News*
often lack the credibility that more conservative media like CBS News have.
Being up-front with your audience about the source of your information helps
them to make an educated evaluation about your message. Consequently,
speakers who use highly respected sources tend to invoke greater believabil-
ity in their audience than those who use more unfamiliar or dubious sources.

Phrasing oral citations is not as regulated a practice as the other two
forms of attribution. In fact, because we rarely say the same thing exactly the
same way twice, the oral citations in a given presentation may sound quite
different from one another. In order to meet the primary goal of informing the
audience, you want to be clear about what the resource is, whether it is a
newspaper article, a personal interview, or an episode from a television
series. The difficult part is doing this without making it sound artificial or
stilted. For instance, a less effective oral citation might sound something like
this:

> The state of Ohio takes its name from the Iroquois word for "fine or good
> river." I found that in the *Encyclopedia Britannica*.

While this example does tell us the source (and a reputable one at that), the
phrasing lacks a smoothness that is easily corrected with practice. Some
alternatives would include the following:

> The *Encyclopedia Britannica* reports that the state of Ohio takes its name
> from the Iroquois word for "fine or good river."

> The state of Ohio, the *Encyclopedia Britannica* records, takes its name from the Iroquois word for "fine or good river."

> The state of Ohio takes its name from the Iroquois word for "fine or good river," according to the *Encyclopedia Britannica*

Although oral citations are intentionally brief, so the audience will not be overwhelmed with unnecessary information, you should have complete citations with you whenever you do speak. If a question-and-answer session were to follow your presentation, inquisitive members of your audience might want to read a resource for themselves and ask you to share the bibliographic information with them. Be prepared by knowing your references or by carrying your reference list with you.

Summary

The study of human communication follows methods of inquiry similar to those used in related disciplines. Both quantitative methods, those measuring human interaction through the use of statistical analysis, and qualitative methods, those explicating individual experience, produce research articles that inform our understanding of how people communicate. Academic journals publish the results of these research efforts. Reading these articles can be easier if one knows what to expect to find in each of the following sections: abstract, introduction, literature review, methodology, discussion, and references.

You need to approach the study of previous scholarship in a systematic way as you begin your own research. You can save a lot of time by following some simple time-saving tips, including making sufficient time to visit the library, knowing a topic before going there, asking a librarian for help, finding more than the minimum number of resources, and recording citation information carefully. Attributing sources accurately is an especially important task. This means using parenthetical citations in the body of your paper, using a bibliographic citation in your reference list, and using oral citations in your speech. Most communication research follows the citation system outlined by the American Psychological Association (APA).

At Your Bookstore

Hacker, D. (1999). *A Writer's Reference* (4th ed.). Boston: Bedford Books of St. Martin's Press.

Lamm, K. (1995). *10,000 Ideas for Term Papers, Projects, Reports and Speeches* (4th ed.). New York: ARCO.

Rubin, R. B., Rubin, A. M., & Piele, L. J. (1996). *Communication Research: Strategies and Sources* (4th ed.). Belmont, CA: Wadsworth.

Spencer, C., & Arbon, B. (1996). *Foundations of Writing: Developing Research and Academic Writing Skills*. Lincolnwood, IL: National Textbook Company.

CHAPTER 13

Preparing for Public Presentations

Communication plays a very important role in my life because I'm a professional motivational speaker. I remember some time ago when I spoke to 25 youths on the importance of goal-setting, leadership, self-esteem, and going after their dreams in life. After the speech was over, a young lady approached me and asked if she could have a minute of my time. She then expressed to me that she was a foster child in the inner city of Cleveland and had no positive role models to look up to. All her life people told her that she would never amount to anything because she was black, had a child, and lived in a poor part of town where there were drugs and violence.

 She then told me that my speech had really touched her and made her realize that life is what you make it. She said that she was going to go to college and study criminal investigation so she could become a police officer in Cleveland. That proves to me that communication is a powerful tool.

— Marcus, fourth-year college student

Public communication can indeed be a powerful tool. As Marcus discovered, public speech events can have profound influence upon individuals, encouraging them to believe in themselves, to move to action, or to choose one course over another. But public communication also plays a crucial role in the operation of society. Consider the last presidential election. The candidates' job is to deliver the message of their respective parties to the public so that people will vote for one over the other. In the 1996 election, more American voters responded to President Bill Clinton's message of "building a bridge to the 21st century" than to either Senator Bob Dole's "15 percent tax cut" or Ross Perot's "It's your government." Because it plays such a crucial role in deciding the future of both individuals and society, public communication is an important topic for skillful communicators to study and understand.

 If you review both Marcus' example and the one about the presidential race, you will note that public communication has two parts: a speaker and an audience. A speaker, either Marcus or President Clinton, is the person presenting the message. The people to whom the message is addressed, like the young lady from Cleveland or the American voters, form the audience. Not everyone a speaker tries to reach hears or accepts the speaker's message; had they in 1996, every American voter would have voted for Clinton and no one would have turned out for either Dole or Perot. Obviously, the relationship between speaker and audience is not as simple as one person talking and a group of people hearing. Because there are many differences among the individuals in a potential audience, one of the most important steps for any speaker to take in the preparation of a public communication event is to understand the audience.

 This chapter and the next look at the process of communicating in a public setting. Almost everyone will be called upon to deliver some sort of public address at some point: toasting your best friend at his wedding, presenting a business proposal to potential clients, or reading before your congregation. The skills of public communication can be applied to a number of circumstances in your life, from having the confidence to ask your boss for a raise to having the ability to present your ideas to your fellow workers in an organized fashion.

This chapter will:

- Dismiss some myths about public communication: that you have to be born with the ability, that the product is more important than the process, and that longer presentations are more impressive.
- Work through the steps of building a public communication event through preparation and practice.

Preparation for a public communication event includes conducting an audience analysis, organizing materials in an outline, framing the presentation with an introduction and a conclusion, and building source credibility. Practicing for the event involves choosing a method of delivery, applying peer criticism, and confronting anxiety. When you finish reading this chapter, you should have the process and confidence you need to make an effective public presentation.

Myths About Public Communication

Many people report that speaking in public is the thing that they fear most. Perhaps this is because a number of myths have begun to surround the whole idea of public communication. But you do not have to buy into them. This section takes aim at three myths about public communication that you should dismiss before you begin to create your own presentations. In short, you should be aware that:

- Effective speaking skills can be learned.
- Practice is more important for a novice speaker than product.
- The quality of the message *is* more important than the quantity.

Myth #1: You have to be born with it.

One widely accepted myth in our culture is that public speaking requires a unique talent. People often believe that the ability to speak well in a public setting is something one has to be born with rather than something that can be learned. While some individuals do possess a tendency toward performing well, that does not mean that the skills they possess cannot be learned by others. Even those who do well naturally may not become *effective* speakers without practice and polish.

Developing effective public speaking skills is like developing any other skill, such as riding a bicycle. Do you recall your own trials with learning to ride a bike? Did you use training wheels? Did you fall off your bike once or twice? Three times? Did your big sister hop on her bike, wobble just a little, and then ride off down your street with no problem? Although a lot of people seem to ride bicycles and give speeches with ease, most often their grace is the product of experience rather than effortlessness. The more you practice developing a skill, the better you become at performing it.

Myth #2: The important thing is product, not process.

Graduation ceremonies are good places to see public speaking in action. Yet as you listen to the valedictorian deliver the graduation address, all you see is the polished product of that individual's efforts. Quite often, good presentations result from hours of preparation and practice that an audience is unaware of. Novice public speakers assume that effective public speakers just stand up and give great speeches with little or no preparation.

That is why it is important to understand, especially if you have not spoken in public before, that it is more important to study the process of preparing for a speech than lament lack of polished product. Although you should certainly aspire to deliver speeches every bit as memorable and moving as Dr. Martin Luther King's "I Have a Dream," you should realize Dr. King's product was the result of years of going through the process of preparing, practicing, and delivering a speech.

Myth #3: More is better.

If you walk into a fast food restaurant and order a combination meal, the server is likely to ask you if you would like to "super-size" your order. For a bit more money you can have a larger drink and a bigger order of fries. "Supersizing" is a common phenomenon in American culture. People flock to see the world's biggest nacho; a television series is rated a success if it has the largest audience; and many individuals determine success by the amount of money they make. Everywhere you look, someone is suggesting yet a third myth, that bigger is better.

But this is not so with public communication. A wise individual once noted three keys to effective presentations: "Be heard, be brief, and be gone." Just think back to your own experiences as a member of an audience. Have you ever lost the speaker's point simply because that person went on for too long? Sure, we all have. Most effective speeches, those whose main points we remember, are often brief and to the point, not long, or full of over-inflated language. They demonstrate the speaker's consideration of the audience more than the extent of her knowledge.

Among the speakers whose communications were quite brief but memorable was Abraham Lincoln. Historians believe that Lincoln wrote at least part of his famous "Gettysburg Address" during the journey to dedicate the graveyard in Gettysburg, Pennsylvania (Library of Congress, 1996). However, before Lincoln delivered his speech, Edward Everett, the most celebrated speaker of his day, gave a two-hour presentation. A century and a half later, people are still studying Lincoln and his four-minute presentation while Everett and his inflated oration have faded into obscurity. More important than the length of a presentation, then, is the quality of thought that goes into it.

Preparing

You probably grew up watching a lot of public presentations—from teachers explaining times tables in your fourth-grade class to religious officials leading your congregation in worship. However, those experiences did not demonstrate the process of *preparing* presentations for you. And although you may have witnessed numerous exhibitions of public speaking, you may not as yet have had the opportunity to present a speech yourself. Speaking in public for the first time can be an unnerving experience, even though experienced speakers make public speaking seem easy enough.

With any new skill you've had to master, you have probably found it to be a less stressful task if you have had some instruction in doing it. Of course, public speaking may at first make you feel anxious. With experience, it does indeed become an easier task to perform. Certain preparatory steps are useful in getting you past your anxiety and ready to speak. By analyzing the audience you will address, by organizing your materials into an outline form, and by taking steps that build source credibility, you will find that you can approach each public communication event with confidence.

Conducting an Audience Analysis

Perhaps the most important step in preparing to deliver any speech is considering who the audience will be. On a larger scale this means choosing to speak on a topic that will be of interest to the audience you will be addressing. For instance, a civic organization would be more interested in hearing about ways to reduce crime in the community than in how to make a grilled cheese sandwich using an iron. Considering your audience means choosing appropriate language for your audience. You would want to find ways of rephrasing accountant jargon when explaining how to file an income tax return to a group of middle school adolescents.

Of course, you may be asking yourself: How do I find out about my audience? In many situations, the speaker is asked to deliver a presentation on a particular subject:

> "Would you be able to tell my cooking club how it is you make your Szechuan chicken, Mr. Sing?"

> "Could you say a few words about how you got this award?"

> "Suzanne, we want you to present the annual report to the shareholders this year."

In these situations, gaining information about your audience is a relatively straightforward process of asking questions of the person inviting you to speak. For example, you might ask your boss how many shareholders will be attending, what kinds of graphics he wants you to use, and how long he expects the presentation to last.

There are, of course, situations in which you will not necessarily be invited to speak but will be compelled to contribute your voice. Perhaps you will address your local board of education in order to urge them not to abandon arts-related extracurricular activities such as band and chorus. Even though you do not necessarily have a contact person in such situations, you can make educated guesses about the composition and disposition of your potential audience by reviewing their demographics.

Demographics refers to the specific characteristics of an audience. They allow us to categorize people and thus analyze a large audience. As you might guess, one of the most obvious demographics has to do with gender. Preparing to speak to an organization such as the local chapter of the National Organization for Women, you would feel safe in concluding that your audience is comprised of females. However, assuming that the local gardening club consists solely of women could prove to be erroneous, especially since many men enjoy gardening. The difficulty in dealing with demographics, then, is that they offer you guidance rather than absolutes. Some of the demographics you might want to consider when approaching an audience include:

- Gender
- Race
- Age
- Religion
- Economic status
- Career
- Organizational affiliation
- Marital status/sexual orientation
- Geographic origin
- Political affiliation

Not every demographic carries equal weight in every speaking situation. If you are asked to speak about your job as director of marketing to a group of new employees, their marital status has less to do with your presentation to them than their career motivations or goals.

Please note that there is a difference between analyzing the demographics of a potential audience and stereotyping, a term that carries with it a negative connotation. Stereotyping is commonly defined as assuming that *all* members of a group possess the same qualities based upon your interaction with a *limited* number of individuals from that group. For instance, assuming that all police officers are rude on the basis of meeting one particularly gruff officer is an example of stereotyping. This differs from a demographic analysis in which you determine that an audience of police officers might consist of individuals who are career-oriented, community-involved, and politically conservative. Though not all of these determinations may prove to be correct, they can help guide your message as you plan to speak to the audience.

In addition to demographics, another way to analyze your audience has to do with their psychological characteristics, including their attitudes, beliefs, and values. An attitude is the loosely committed perspective an audience member takes on a given topic. You might adopt the attitude that one fast food chain serves tastier food than another, but one bad experience at the preferred restaurant could cause you to reconsider that attitude. A greater degree of personal commitment is involved in one's beliefs, or the collection of things one considers to be true. Your confidence that your hard work in this class will result in good grades reflects a belief. A value is the most difficult psychological characteristic to change. Values are the underlying principles that guide the formation of a person's personality. People's values help shape their beliefs and attitudes. Many people share the value that violence is wrong, and guided by that value, few of them would consider intentionally harming another person. As public speakers it is important for you to know the disposition of your audience. Knowing what your audience values, what it

MISSION: POSSIBLE

❖ ❖ ❖ ❖

In many communication courses, you have the freedom to select topics for your presentations. However, some students find it difficult to identify a topic to speak about. In considering what your audience might like to hear about, consider what you are already an expert at. If you are among those who struggle to come up with a topic for a presentation, list as many items about yourself as you can in response to the following:

- Extracurricular activities you participate in.
- Organizations you belong to.
- Places you have lived or visited.
- Causes you support.
- The funniest moments in your life.
- Unusual purchases you have made.

Among the items you listed, you are sure to find one or more topics that would be interesting for your audience.

believes, and what its attitudes are on a particular subject helps you adapt your message to them.

Of course, it is impossible to know everything about every member of your audience. The challenge of audience analysis is to attempt to get as close to as many people within that audience with your message as you possibly can. While we encourage you to incorporate audience analysis as an important part of your preparation, do not forget that you can adapt to your audience while you are speaking. Be alert for feedback. It is an important part of the communication process. In the event that members of your audience fail to recognize the vocabulary you are using, a good way for you to adapt your message would be to insert definitions or explanations for them. In short, the process of audience analysis is the process of being a good host. You make plans for your guests to feel welcome in your home or speech before they get there, and if you see that they are not comfortable at any point, you try to make things easier for them while the event is occurring.

Drafting an Outline

Once you have a reasonably good idea about whom you will be talking to, then consider what it is that you will be talking about. As we discussed in Chapter 12, accurately researched information is a crucial part of an effective speech. Using the methods discussed in that chapter, you should be able to locate and evaluate good-quality information for your presentation. However, many beginners find so much information on a given topic that they are unsure of what to include and what to leave out in their presentations. Some err on the side of copiousness, incorporating so much information that the audience cannot possibly recall all the facts and figures being hurled at them. Part of the process of determining what outside information is relevant and what is not involves:

Organizing your thoughts in a written outline is a key component in planning a presentation.

- Determining what it is that you wish to communicate.
- Finding what you already know.

To begin, then, write down your basic message for this presentation. This goal statement should establish the boundaries within which you will construct your speech. Too often, novice speakers try to tackle a subject that is just too broad for the time they have to speak. For example, automotive repair is too broad a topic for a speech, considering that you could cover all sorts of problems—everything from the tires to the transmission. Narrowing your scope to a speech on winterizing your car would produce a more manageable topic. The resulting goals statement might read something like: "My goal is to provide my audience with some preventive maintenance advice on how to prepare their automobile for winter."

The next step is to write down what you already know about the topic. Did your fuel line freeze up last winter? Your experience with not winterizing your car could serve as a good reference point to begin your research. Did you work in a garage for a few years? You may already possess most of the practical knowledge you need to make this presentation, though checking up on the latest advances would help you make it current. The task of writing down everything you know about a topic, or brainstorming, helps you determine what it is you need to learn through additional research.

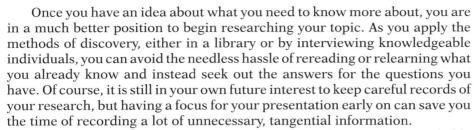

Once you have an idea about what you need to know more about, you are in a much better position to begin researching your topic. As you apply the methods of discovery, either in a library or by interviewing knowledgeable individuals, you can avoid the needless hassle of rereading or relearning what you already know and instead seek out the answers for the questions you have. Of course, it is still in your own future interest to keep careful records of your research, but having a focus for your presentation early on can save you the time of recording a lot of unnecessary, tangential information.

If you have made a careful review of the existing literature, you probably have quite a bit of information to sort through. Reread your goals statement and decide: Will the information you have collected help you achieve your goal? Set aside the information that is irrelevant to your stated goals. Next, reread what it is you already know and what it is you have collected. Note themes that seem to emerge from the information. Do some of your sources note a number of fluids that should be changed before winter starts? Perhaps this will become one of your main points, while the particular fluids will each serve as a subpoint. As you note some general categories your information seems to fit *into*, you are beginning the project of outlining your speech. *Outlining* is the task of giving organization to your presentation.

Depending on the topic and time limitations, most speakers communicate their main goal with the support of two or three main points. Although it is not unheard of to have five or more, you should keep in mind that the more points one includes in a speech, the more difficult it is for the audience to remember them all. Imagine that you have found three main points to support your speech on winterizing your car: change your fluids, adjust your tire pressure, and carry a winter emergency kit. You choose to arrange these points in the chronological order in which these steps should be taken. Someone else may have come up with an entirely different arrangement based on the location of each of these points on the car or based on the order in which they were presented by a respected mechanic. However, this is your speech and you have arranged it in the following manner:

I. Change your automobile's fluids before winter begins.

II. Adjust your tires' pressure to compensate for the difference in temperature at the beginning of the season and throughout the winter.

III. Prepare and carry a winter emergency kit in your automobile.

Under each of your main points, then, you put the details that explain or add support to it. Perhaps under your first main point, changing fluids, you will suggest three projects for your audience: replacing the automobile's oil, flushing and refilling the antifreeze, and topping off the windshield wiper fluid reservoir. You may also support each of these subpoints with further details in such a way that part of your outline would look like this:

I. Change your automobile's fluids before winter begins.
   A. Replace the automobile's oil.
      1. Choose a lighter-weight oil for the winter months, such as a SW30.
      2. Replace your oil filter at the same time for better performance.

B. Flush and refill the antifreeze through one of two options.
   1. Purchase a kit to do this at home.
   2. Have a qualified mechanic perform this task for you.
C. Top off the windshield wiper fluid reservoir.
   1. Do not dilute your wiper fluid with water in the winter months.
   2. Checking this often will keep you from running out when traveling on slushy roads.

As you look at the above example, there are some regular conventions that go into the process of drafting an outline. First, outlines follow a particular pattern of organization, with standard alphabetical and numerical markers and indentation used to show which ideas are coordinating and which are subordinated under others. As you can see, main points are typically labeled with Roman numerals (I., II., III.), the next level of points with capitalized Arabic letters (A., B., C.), and the next subordinate level with Arabic numbers (1., 2., 3.). If necessary, you could further subordinate the information under the Arabic numbers into lower case Arabic letters (a., b., c.) and those in turn into lower-case Roman numerals (i., ii., iii.).

Second, note that if an idea is divided, it should be divided into at least two parts. In the above example, there is no "A." point without its coordinating "B." point and no "1." point without a "2." Think of each level as a sort of pie. Once you take a knife to it, you cannot divide pie "A" into any less than two parts; otherwise, you will have pie "A" and no subpoints. Thus, subpoints, if they come, always come in pairs, threes, fours, and so on. Finally, outlines strive for parallelism, or similarities in grammatical form and substance. In the above example, note how each point is made up of a sentence that begins with a verb. This technique of using the imperative voice will make this presentation come out like a series of instructions to help the audience actually do the work necessary to winterize their automobiles. Of course, there are other methods of making your outline parallel, such as asking a series of questions, but whatever form you choose, you will want to maintain consistency throughout your outline. A poor example of maintaining parallelism follows:

1. Your winter emergency kit should have a flashlight first of all.
2. Carry an empty coffee can and a candle as an emergency heat source.
3. What would you do without sand for traction?

Obviously, this combination of sentences is grammatically unparallel with one another. The first is a simple declarative sentence, the second an imperative command, and the third an interrogative or questioning sentence. Using any one of these grammatical forms is acceptable; however, you want to use them consistently. If we were to revise this using imperative sentences, it might look like this:

1. Equip your kit with a flashlight for any night time emergencies.
2. Carry an empty coffee can and a candle as an emergency heat source.
3. Maintain a supply of sand for gaining traction over icy patches.

❖ ❖ ❖ ❖

Outlining is an especially useful tool for novice speakers to use. If you are giving a speech in this class, your instructor may even require that you submit an outline with your presentation so that you can receive feedback on your abilities to organize information effectively. Even if you are not required to submit a formal outline for evaluation, you will find that practicing the concepts of organization, subordination, and parallelism will make for a more effective public communication event.

Designing an Introduction, Body, and Conclusion

Mostly what you will be outlining will form the main part, or body, of your presentation. However, like a story, a standard speech has a beginning, a middle, and an end. In communication studies, we call these sections the introduction, the body, and the conclusion. Since we've already introduced a good deal of what you need to know about the body of a presentation above, we'll concentrate on the introduction and conclusion here (see Figure 13.1).

An *introduction* is the first part of a presentation and it should include five elements:

- An opening that gains the audience's attention.
- A clear thesis.
- A statement about your relation to the topic.
- A connection to the audience.
- A preview of the main points to follow.

Gaining attention is important because people decide whether or not they will be interested in a speech in the first few seconds. Stating an unusual or startling fact, quoting an expert source, or introducing an eye-catching visual are just a few examples of how you can gain people's attention. A thesis statement declares the topic in a clear declarative sentence. "I will introduce to you three of the best computer accessories on the market today" is one rather simple, but clear, thesis. We'll talk more about building source credibility in the next section, but it is important to state your credentials for speaking about a specific topic early on in the presentation so that people understand how you came to be interested or qualified on the subject. Not only do you need to express your relationship to the topic, but you should make it clear to the audience how the topic you have chosen to speak on relates to them. Finally, you need to preview the points you are about to convey in the body. This helps your audience listen for and attend to your major points.

Once you have delivered all the information in your speech's body, your job still is not finished. The final part of your speech, the *conclusion*, should provide your audience with a sense of closure. Incorporating three components can help you construct your conclusion:

- The summary.
- The reinforced thesis.
- The close with impact.

Because they do not have a written document that lets them flip back and check your major points, your audience needs you to summarize your major

Figure 13.1 Elements for Effective Introductions and Conclusions

Components of an Introduction	Components of a Conclusion
Attention gainer	Summary
Thesis statement	Reinforced thesis
Credibility statement	Close with impact
Connection to the audience	
Preview	

points. You will also want to show them how you've met the objectives of your thesis by restating it. Finally, you will want to leave your audience with a memorable ending. Simply saying, "I'm finished" doesn't leave as lasting an impression as a humorous anecdote, another quotation, an expression of urgency, a final tip, or a reflection. Building a complete introduction and conclusion around the body of your speech demonstrates to an audience that you have not only prepared the content of your presentation well but also that you have carefully considered how to frame that content for them.

In addition, you should incorporate smooth transition statements between each point you make. Considering that the audience in most public speaking scenarios does not have an outline before them, they rely on you to tell them when you shift from one major point to the next. Examples of how these components function in a presentation can be found in the sample outlines in Chapter 14.

Building Source Credibility

When you cannot find something in your local supermarket, you turn to someone wearing a smock and a name tag and ask for assistance. You recognize the knowledge that person has in that particular situation. However, when a speaker walks into a room, you do not always know what qualifications she brings with her unless there are external cues like those worn by supermarket employees. That is why speakers need to work at establishing their credibility—that is, their authority on the subject.

The two aspects of source credibility that an audience will expect a speaker to demonstrate are competence and trustworthiness. Audiences want to know whether you know what you are talking about and whether you mean them well.

Competence is the speaker's familiarity on the subject. If you are speaking about a given subject, people will expect you to demonstrate knowledge of that subject. Of course, you should always describe your competence on a given subject up front, especially if you have not been properly introduced as an expert on the topic. Telling people about your background, years of familiarity, or personal association with the topic lends you greater credibility.

Likewise, you need to establish your trustworthiness, or your honesty, with your audience. Some people can be suspicious of speakers, especially those trying to sell something. A lot of gifted salesmen portraying themselves as trustworthy wind up disappointing their audiences. You need to build up your credibility by dealing with your audience in a fair and honest manner and by letting them know you are doing so by demonstrating honesty in your presentation.

Of course, the best kind of credibility is the kind you bring with you. Your reputation for competence and trustworthiness affects the way people receive you as a speaker and the willingness with which they will listen to your message. Credibility is a factor in public presentations that is largely determined by the audience, but you can play a role in its formation and maintenance. By approaching public presentations prepared to speak and treating audiences with respect, you can help audiences form a positive impression of you as a public communicator.

Practicing

Have you ever been a part of a stage production? Whether you were an actor, a stage manager, or a musician, you know all too well that a performance of *Fiddler on the Roof* does not take shape on opening night. Instead numerous weeks of practice are devoted to polishing a production that only lasts a matter of hours. Actors have to study their lines, stage managers have to learn their cues, and musicians have to learn the songs well enough to play in harmony with one another and with the rest of the cast. Without sufficient practice almost any production would come off as amateurish and uninteresting.

Giving a speech is like putting on your own one-person show. You have to:

- Know your lines.
- Remember your cues.
- Pull together your words, actions, and visual aids in a harmonious fashion.

With all that goes on in even a five-minute speech, isn't it curious that some people choose not practice even once before delivering a speech? One of the best pieces of advice this or any textbook dealing with public speaking can give you is to practice. Speakers who practice just once feel more confident in their presentation than those who decide to "wing it."

Two common situations demonstrate that familiarity with a topic can make you more confident. First, imagine your new best friend has asked you for directions to your home. With great ease you explain which highway to get on, which exit to get off, which street to turn onto, and what color your home is. You have probably given directions to your home a number of times in your life, so that even though you did not rehearse them right before you were asked for the directions, previous practice made you confident in your presentation. On the other hand, you might walk into your next class and have your instructor ask you to give a synopsis of the chapter you were to read last night. If you did not read the chapter, you are in big trouble to start with. However, even if you did study the material, you might not be able to recount every major point in the chapter if you were not prepared beforehand to deliver such a review.

Practicing for a speech, then, is an important step in creating an effective presentation. In this section, we discuss three aspects of practicing for a presentation:

1. You should decide how you will deliver your speech and build a practice regimen suited to that method.

Your attention shifts with each mode of delivery: the impromptu, memorized, and manuscript modes each have the potential to direct the speaker's attention away from the audience. The extemporaneous mode helps focus the speaker on the audience.

2. You should seek out peers who will act as audience and critic for your presentation.
3. You should be aware that communication anxiety is perfectly natural, but that there are steps you can take to confront its potentially debilitating effects.

Choosing a Method of Delivery

Even as you begin planning your speech, you should be considering *how* you will deliver it. But by the time you are practicing your presentation, you really need to know which of the four methods of delivery—impromptu, memorized, manuscript, or extemporaneous—you will be using so that you can begin practicing accordingly. Each of these methods has benefits and shortcomings, and you will need to weigh each of these as you approach each situation.

Speakers who are given little or no time to prepare for a speech engage in impromptu delivery. You may find yourself at your first meeting of a student organization when the president asks you to introduce yourself to the rest of the group. Without rehearsal or preparation, you have to compose and deliver a message at the same time. Really, impromptu speaking is not as scary as it might sound. The vast majority of our everyday conversations are impromptu in nature. The difference, of course, is that you will be the only one speaking in this situation. Impromptu is not the method we recommend for individuals giving extended public presentations. Even though impromptu presentations can appear to be more conversational and spontaneous than any other, they rarely achieve the level of organization and quality of information that the other methods of delivery can.

At the other extreme of speech preparation is memorized delivery. Using this method, speakers first write out their entire speech and then memorize it word for word. As you can imagine, this is the most time-consuming method for an individual to undertake. Memorizing a speech might make you more confident when you give your presentation, simply because you have already created every word you will utter. However, because memorizing a whole speech is a time-consuming—and unnecessary—task, we do not recommend it either. Moreover, individuals who memorize a speech and then lose their place at some point during the presentation have difficulty finding it and appear less polished than they set out to be. They are also less likely to adapt their message to their audience since they are operating from a preset script.

Working from manuscript is yet a third method of delivery. In this method, a speaker writes out a speech word for word and then reads from the manuscript at the presentation. Like the memorized speech, a manuscript gives you the confidence of knowing exactly what it is that you will be saying. Unlike the case with memorized speeches, you are much less likely to lose your place in a manuscript. There are circumstances in which manuscript delivery may be the preferred method, especially in situations that call for you to relate a lot of technical information. However, a common error with manuscript delivery is that speakers often fail to look up from their manuscript in the course of their presentation. If speakers fail to make much eye contact with the audience or if they read in a monotonous voice, they too may appear less polished than they want to be perceived.

Perhaps the best way to approach the public communication event is through extemporaneous delivery. Extemporaneous speakers come to their presentations well prepared, being quite familiar with the material—but not so much that they have memorized every word they plan to use in the speech. Typically, they rely on some form of outline, usually printed on notecards, to help guide them through the presentation. They try to deliver the speech as though they were having a conversation with the people in the audience. In short, extemporaneous delivery tries to combine the best of the other three methods. As in impromptu, the speaker tries to be spontaneous; as in memorized, the speaker knows the main points; and as in manuscript, the speaker has a written guide to maintain organization. One key to keep in mind with practicing extemporaneous delivery is that it will sound a little different every time because of the spontaneous nature of your delivery. Of course, extemporaneous delivery can have its shortcomings, too. Individuals who have not practiced enough may find themselves overly dependent on their notecards and as inattentive to the audience as the manuscript reader can be. However, with sufficient practice, we believe this method provides a presentation style that allows you to appear conversational while being well prepared.

Applying Peer Criticism

Practicing your presentation in the privacy of your own room is one way to grow comfortable with your speech, but it cannot prepare you for interacting with an audience. And even though you may be highly critical of your own performance, you cannot tell how good your eye contact, volume, speed, and other nonverbal cues are without testing them before another individual or two. We highly recommend that you practice your speech a number of times before you deliver it and that on at least one of those occasions you practice it before a peer. Ideally, you should be able to find someone in your class or in your department who understands exactly what it is that you are trying to do. However, significant others, parents, children, neighbors, and other friends can help as well, so long as you explain to them what it is that you are attempting to do. The goal is to find a person or a small group of persons who are willing to listen and, more important, to offer constructive criticism on your presentation. Though practicing in front of any audience will help make you more comfortable with public speaking, performing in front of a critical audience can make your presentation even better.

If you are practicing for a speech in this class, then find a classmate who is willing to work with you on this. Make a commitment to hear each other's speeches well in advance of their delivery dates so that any criticism you might offer one another can be acted upon in time to make improvements for the class presentation.

When You Are the Speaker

In order to get the kind of comments that will help you perform better, you need to let your trial audience know that it is all right for them to be critical of both the content of your message and the quality of your delivery. Explain to them that their honesty with your performance now will help you get a better grade or a promotion. Describe the situation you will be speaking in. Your neighbor may not be familiar with the group you will be addressing, so you will need to explain to him what that audience will be expecting of you. Encourage your audience to identify both things they think you need to do better and things they think you are doing well.

Once you have established the situation for your audience, you need to step into the hypothetical situation. In other words, imagine you are in the moment of delivering the speech. If you lose your place or composure, do not stop and start over. Calm yourself and act as you would if the same thing would happen in the actual presentation. Try to create as accurate a portrayal as you can in your delivery, even if that means looking at other, imaginary people in the room to simulate the experience of a larger audience.

When you have finished, ask your trial audience for honest comments. If, on the one hand, they have only good things to say about your presentation, try to dig a little deeper with questions about the areas of the speech you might have been uncertain of to begin with. Asking "Did you notice how many main points I had?" and "How fast was I speaking?" may lead a flattering listener to make few critical suggestions. On the other hand, you may have a listener filled with critical suggestions. If so, you need to recall that the criticism is of the performance and not of you as an individual. Also remember that you have the right to disagree with any comment your listener offers you. Even if he or she advises you to remove an expletive from your speech for fear of offending others, you have the right to keep that word in your presentation if you feel it is necessary in making your point. Opening yourself up to criticism is a difficult thing for most of us to do; however, being able to listen to and evaluate the merits of criticism is a mark of personal maturity.

When You Are the Critic

Knowing that they themselves are in the same situation, many people are reticent to offer much criticism to a classmate of colleague. However, without your warnings and constructive comments early on, that person's grade or

❖ ❖ ❖ ❖

job performance could suffer later. The key to offering criticism is to offer it with tact. Telling a colleague that "That topic stinks" is obviously in poor taste. A more tactful response would be to express your objection and justify it, "I think you should reconsider this topic. I believe the teacher will have difficulty with your bringing a firearm into class because it violates university policy." With this approach, you are trying to help your classmate avoid offending a portion of his audience, but you are doing it in as direct and nonthreatening a fashion as possible.

In this example, the person offering criticism uses "I" language. In "I" language, the critic offers an opinion from his or her point of view and phrases that comment beginning with the word "I." For example, "James, I don't think I understand how a candle and a coffee can might keep you warm in a car. Could you explain that with some more detail?" is one way to phrase an "I" language comment. Compare this with the comment, "What's with the coffee can? Skip that." By explaining your comments through "I" language, your peer should be hearing that there is simply a problem with communication here, one that can be corrected, and not that he has done anything categorically wrong. Whenever possible, try to offer your suggestions to correct the deficiencies you find in the presentation. Although your classmate is not bound to follow your advice, he or she may take some direction from what you suggest.

Confronting Apprehension

Even after all your careful planning and consistent practice, you may still feel anxious about delivering your speech in front of your class, your fellow employees, your clients, or a room of strangers. This apprehension may arise from the belief that you will not meet your audience's expectations of you (Ayers, 1986). However, what you need to know is that in most situations, the audience wants you to do well, not poorly. In situations in which you find yourself addressing strangers, you should know that they probably have lower expectations than you might imagine, so when you do a good job you please them as well as yourself. In this brief section, we would like to suggest a few ways you can confront and overcome communication apprehension.

Communication apprehension, commonly known as stage fright, begins as a psychological process, which then has physical expressions, such as trembling, nausea, and faintness. Therefore, the first step in confronting it is to deal with it in your mind. When utilizing a process called visualization, you mentally picture yourself giving a great presentation. Although this may sound ridiculously simple, experience shows that it does affect speakers' attitudes toward themselves and their presentation. Just as the self-fulfilling prophecy discussed in earlier chapters can lead a person to a dead end, visualization can lead a person to an open field. Visualization involves creating a positive attitude about yourself and the presentation before the speech and sustaining that attitude throughout the presentation. Moreover, research indicates that students who engage in visualization report decreased communication apprehension (Ayers & Hopf, 1989).

If you are successfully visualizing yourself giving a great presentation, then you will have no need to apologize as you begin to speak. Too often speakers begin their speeches with an apology for their skill, preparation, or

If you suffer from a high degree of communication apprehension, the prospect of having to stand in front of a group of people and make a presentation can be intimidating. One way to lessen the degree of communication apprehension you experience each time you speak is to expose yourself to "doses" of public speaking. This process, called systematic desensitization, suggests that the more exposure you have to that which you fear, the less you will fear it.

You can start by volunteering to speak in settings in which you are already comfortable. Ask a question in your large lecture class. Offer to read the lessons in your congregation. Make a short presentation at your sorority or fraternity meeting. Brief but positive experiences in these familiar settings will encourage greater confidence in your communication abilities and help prepare you to be bolder in less familiar circumstances.

nervousness: "I didn't have time to put this together the way I wanted to, so it might be a bit rough around the edges." Though you may be trying to release a little pressure with this confession, why sabotage yourself with this unnecessary comment? Instead of voicing your insecurities, make a strong, confident beginning, and allow your audience to judge the quality of your presentation without your sowing a seed of doubt in them.

Finally, you can confront anxiety by being at your best physically before a presentation. This means you should get a normal night's rest and not stay up to all hours polishing the speech (or doing other class work). It means you eat normal meals and stick to your normal schedule that day. It also means you take the time to groom yourself in such a way that makes you feel confident. With most presentations, this means you will want to look your professional best. Although the process of preparing and practicing for a speech ought to be largely mental, you still need to meet your physical needs so they are not a distraction to you.

Public speaking is not the easiest thing you will ever have to do in life, but then it's not the hardest thing either. As this chapter has suggested, learning to make effective public presentations is the product of careful forethought and serious practice. No one becomes an accomplished speaker overnight, but then no one becomes an accomplished speaker without making a first speech. By putting your fears and doubts into perspective and dedicating yourself to a systematic approach to the preparation of any presentation, you will find that the task is not insurmountable, as it might first appear to be.

Summary

Making effective public presentations is an important skill for leaders to possess. However, some people believe the myths that speaking ability is innate, that a finished product comes without practice, and that a longer speech is of better quality. These myths are not necessarily true since one can be taught to make effective presentations through practice of the presentation-making process and by focusing on the message rather than its length.

In preparing to make a public presentation, a speaker must conduct an analysis of his audience. Each audience's unique demographics dictates what

❖ ❖ ❖ ❖

topics and language would be appropriate for a given situation. Then, building on the research he has done on the topic, the speaker should focus on the key message of his presentation and develop a goals statement to help him draft an outline of all the ideas to be expressed in the presentation.

Most presentations contain an average of three main points, each with appropriate support details garnered from your research. Following the guidelines for outlining, including order, division, and parallelism, will help you maintain relationships among the ideas expressed in the outline. While outlining helps you identify the body of your presentation, you need to consider the audience and frame your presentation with an introduction and conclusion.

In addition to communicating content in your presentation, you also need to communicate trustworthiness. If your audience is not already familiar with your source credibility, you need to establish it early on in your presentation.

Practicing for a presentation is crucial to making it appear polished. From among the four methods of delivering a presentation—impromptu, memorized, manuscript, and extemporaneous—the authors recommend the last one for its conversational quality. Getting honest feedback from friends and colleagues helps you to refine your message so that you can better communicate your ideas to a larger audience. Moreover, recognizing and compensating for communication anxiety can make you overcome another potential stumbling block. A commitment to working through this process a number of times will show improvement in your presenting abilities.

At Your Bookstore

Gaulke, S. (1997). *101 Ways to Captivate a Business Audience.* New York: American Management Association.

Hoff, R. (1992). *I Can See You Naked: A New Revised Edition of the National Bestseller on Making Fearless Presentations.* Kansas City, KS: Andrews and McNeel.

Library of Congress Web Site. (1996). Abraham Lincoln's Gettysburg Address. Available: http://lcweb.loc.gov/exhibits/gadd/

McKenzie, E. C. (1990). *14,000 Quips and Quotes: For Speakers, Writers, Editors, Preachers, and Teachers.* Grand Rapids, MI: Baker Book House.

Newstrom, J., & Secunnell, E. E. (1997). *The Big Book of Presentation Games: Wake-em-up Tricks, Icebreakers, and Other Fun Stuff.* New York: McGraw-Hill.

CHAPTER 14

Presenting Informative and Persuasive Messages

Seven years ago I was visiting my grandparents in Big Rapids, Michigan. Don't be fooled by the name of the town. Being small, it has a population of around 4,000. The day my family and I arrived, my brother and I decided to go to the local gym and play some basketball. After a couple of hours, we got tired and decided we wanted to go back to my grandparents' house. I got on the pay phone and called my grandmother, who said she would be delighted to pick us up, but she didn't know where the gym was. So she told us to walk to Walgreens, a local drugstore, and wait for her.

My brother and I packed all our gear and headed out to Walgreens, thanks to the handy instructions from the clerk behind the desk in the gym. It took us six minutes to walk there. My brother and I waited, and waited, and waited for my grandmother to come, but there was no sign of her. Then it started to rain. We started to get suspicious after standing in the rain for about 40 minutes. (The store was closed because it was Sunday.) My brother called home again and spoke with my grandfather, who, with a chuckle, explained to us that there were two Walgreens in Big Rapids. He explained that he and my grandmother usually went shopping at the Walgreens closer to their house. The store we were waiting at was on the other side of town. Why such a small town needed *two* Walgreens was beyond me. My grandfather drove over to pick us up 5 minutes later. We then drove to the other store and there was my grandmother, waiting patiently in the car for us.

— Michael, third-year college student

The miscommunication that affected Michael could have been avoided with just a little more information. Had his grandmother or the clerk who gave him and his brother directions considered that Michael was not as familiar with the town of Big Rapids as residents were, either person might have been able to point out that in order to rendezvous successfully with their ride, Michael and his brother needed a bit more information. In this case, the seemingly insignificant fact there were two stores of the same name in walking distance of one another didn't appear to be that important to the sources of information. However, that oversight had some uncomfortable implications for the two brothers, who ended up all wet as a result.

Every day we, as communicators, have opportunities to share our knowledge of the world with others. Although we cannot possibly share everything, one of the surest ways to avoid confusing others is to consider what they don't know when presenting them with information. As public speakers, you will have a distinct advantage over your audience in that you often know much more about a given subject than they do. Consequently, you have the added responsibility to deliver those messages in a way that helps your audience understand the information you are presenting. Certainly, one of the best ways to do this is to put yourself in their position and consider that what you might take for granted, they probably don't already know.

From every classroom you've attended in school, to every training session you've experienced at work, you are already aware that informative speaking is an important part of your everyday communication. More important, as you enter the professions, you will find yourself in positions where *you* are the

MISSION: POSSIBLE

Write out a complete set of directions from your classroom to your home. Now read over those directions to see if they are clear.

Before passing these directions on to a potential visitor, consider what details you might have neglected that someone coming from another town would find necessary. Would that person be able to recognize the route numbers, street names, and landmarks you wrote? Remember that an important part of informative speaking is considering what the audience does not already know.

one delivering the messages. This chapter builds on the information we presented to you in Chapter 13. There we talked about how you could analyze your audience, prepare your presentation, and practice for your performance. In this chapter, we consider how two types of messages, those that are informative and those that are persuasive, help shape a public presentation. We conclude with some specific tips on how to improve your delivery by controlling your energy, utilizing nonverbal signals and any presentation aids.

Informative Messages

Whatever background you bring with you, whether you came to college directly from high school or after years at another career, you are likely to possess expertise in a number of areas. People often turn to you for information. Has a friend or relative ever asked you what your major was and then looked puzzled, asking, "What's that?" You probably responded by defining the field of study, listing some course titles in the major, and projecting what you plan on doing with your degree. Even if you're only a first-year student, you hold a degree of expertise about what you have already learned. This qualifies you to talk about many subjects. Most likely, this is not the only experience you have with sharing information you were qualified to express. Such opportunities will only increase for you. Whenever you are called upon to provide information, you will want to express yourself in as organized and clear a fashion as possible.

Constructing informative messages is a process of providing information to others without necessarily attempting to cause some change in their attitudes, beliefs, or values. You are likely to find that presenting informative messages is especially important in your future career, no matter what field you are presently considering entering. You could find yourself training a subordinate, answering a client's question, or reporting results to your superior. Whenever you find yourself giving someone information he or she did not already have, you will want to construct your informative messages carefully. Therefore, we suggest you incorporate the following three skills in your informative messages:

- Do your homework.
- Organize your information.
- Equip your audience to learn.

In Chapter 12 we talked about the procedures for conducting basic research, and here we want to emphasize the importance of getting your information accurate. The best way to make sure the information you are sharing with another is accurate is to corroborate any one source with other sources. Even information from highly credible sources like U.S. government agencies can be backed up with confirmation from nonprofit groups, businesses, the media, and watchdog groups.

You will then want to be sure that the body of your information is easily understood by your audience so you will want to organize your presentation using a pattern such as spatial, chronological, or topical. Spatial organization presents information in relation to physical placement of items. Teaching a fellow hygienist the position of a dentist's instruments would require a spatial pattern. Chronological organization presents information through time. Explaining the history of the Grateful Dead from its inception through its last concert requires a chronological pattern. Topical organization presents information through a series of logically related categories. Describing dietary requirements as four food groups is topical organization.

You also want to meet your goal of informing your audiences. Think back to the most effective teachers you have encountered as a student. What tools did those individuals use in the classroom that helped you to remember information? Did those instructors use vivid examples, humorous stories, or imaginative exercises to get the point across? Perhaps you recall learning the order of notes in the musical scale as "Every Good Boy Does Fine" and "Fat Albert Can't Eat." This technique is called a mnemonic device because it is an aid to memory. The judicious use of mnemonics can help someone recall an assembly procedure or the rank order of U.S. presidents. Adapting some of the very tools with which you learned best into your own presentation of material could help others to comprehend your message. However, keep in mind that not everyone learns in the same fashion. A mix of teaching tools helps different people learn from the same presentation.

In order to help you conceptualize how an informative message might take shape, we have included a sample outline of a successful informative speech. However, you should not assume this template is the only legitimate method for constructing an informative presentation.

Listen to Me
by Sarah Gregor

Introduction

Impact statement: Huh? What? What is that you say? I didn't quite hear you. Can you repeat that? These are phrases or expressions that you expect to hear from your grandparents, but if you are not careful you too might be uttering these words.

Thesis statement: Even though noise-induced hearing loss can be prevented easily, it is the number one cause of deafness in people of all ages.

Source credibility statement: Like many of you, I enjoy interacting with people and love music. I appreciate the gift of hearing and have dedicated myself to a career in audiology.

Preview statement: I will cover the factors involving noise-induced hearing loss. First, I will describe the two major ways it occurs. Second, I will

❖ ❖ ❖ ❖   show you how the decibel scale works, and finally, I will give you some advice on how to protect yourself from noise-induced hearing loss.

Body

I. Noise-induced hearing loss can be experienced in two different ways.
   A. The first type of noise-induced hearing loss is called temporary threshold shift (TTS).
      1. This is caused by listening to a moderate level noise for a short period of time.
      2. The two main symptoms of TTS include ringing in the ears and misperception of sound (Bahadori & Bohne, 1993).
      3. This type of noise-induced hearing loss can be reversible if it is detected in time.
   B. The second type of noise-induced hearing loss is a permanent threshold shift (PTS).
      1. This is caused by exposure to loud sounds for either a long or short period of time.
      2. Acoustic trauma is a very brief exposure to a loud noise and is a common cause of PTS.
      3. There is a slim chance of regaining normal hearing range from this type of loss (Bahadori & Bohne, 1993).

Transition: Now that I have defined two types of noise-induced hearing loss, let's look at how sound is measured using the decibel scale.

I. The causes of noise-induced hearing loss can be explained in terms of the decibel scale.
   A. The decibel scale is a measure of intensity.
      1. Intensity is defined as how loud a sound is.
      2. The increments on the scale are in logarithmic steps with a range from 0-130 (Borden, Harris, & Raphael, 1994).
      3. Any sound that measures over 85 decibels is dangerous to hearing (Kalb, 1997).
   B. Using the decibel scale helps us understand the intensity of some common sounds.
      1. A rock concert measures 120 db, and 130 db is classified as painful (Kalb, 1997).
      2. Something so common as a lawn-mower measures 90 db (Kalb, 1997).

Transition: Understanding the relative intensity of some sounds should help you to see the importance of protecting yourself against noise-induced hearing loss.

II. Noise-induced hearing loss can be prevent with some simple precautions.
   A. Wear ear plugs if the sound is unavoidable.
      1. Ear plugs are inexpensive.
      2. Ear plugs can decrease the decibel level by 25 db (Bahadori & Bohne, 1993).

B. Educate yourself further.
   1. Learn to recognize the warning signs of noise-induced hearing loss.
   2. Be aware of the different decibel levels of equipment you use.

❖ ❖ ❖ ❖

Conclusion

Summary: The three main points to keep in mind with noise-induced hearing loss are the ways of exposure, the intensity of sound as measured by the decibel scale, and use of precautions.

Reinforce thesis: Because noise-induced hearing loss is the leading cause of deafness, you want to be aware of the dangers to your hearing.

Close with impact: So the next time you're jamming at a concert, please remember to take along your ear plugs! After all, you don't want the next concert you hear to be the last one you hear.

Resources

Bahadori, R. S., & Bohne, B. A. (1993, April). "Adverse Effects of Noise on Hearing." *American Family Physician*, 47, pp. 121-126.

Borden, G., Harris, K., & Raphael, L. (1994). *Speech Science Primer*. Baltimore: Williams and Wilkins.

Kalb, C. (1997, August). "Our Battered Ears." *Newsweek*, pp. 75–76.

As you can see, Sarah did her homework in preparing for her speech. Her list of resources indicates that she used information from a variety of sources, including a scholarly journal, a book, and a newsmagazine. In the body of her speech, you can see how she incorporates this information throughout, always citing the contributions of specific sources. Moreover, she demonstrated her qualifications for presenting this information by announcing her major and personal interest in music. Sarah also carefully organized the information she was presenting. The material within the body of her outline is organized according to a topical pattern, which she clearly introduces and summarizes as types, decibel scale, and prevention.

Sarah also takes steps to educate her audience. For instance, when discussing the decibel scale, she uses specific examples such as a lawn mower so that her audience can relate the familiar sound it makes to the concept of the scale that she is introducing. In addition, Sarah also repeats her main points in the preview, throughout the body, and in the conclusion. Again, this helps the audience to remember what they are to have learned from the presentation. Although there are a number of things Sarah could still do to make this an even more informative presentation, this outline shows skill in doing one's homework, organizing information, and educating an audience.

Persuasive Messages

In making the transition from informative to persuasive messages, let us examine one student's experiences with persuasive communication.

As do many students, last winter I got the blues, except these blues were bad. I got really, really homesick, desperately missed my boyfriend at home, and somehow decided that I had had enough of this university. Within one week I decided that, although I was only a year away from graduation, I was going to transfer to another school. I started calling other universities near my home town for enrollment information. My parents took the news well. They supported whatever decision I made.

However, my friends here thought I was crazy. They refused to let me make such a drastic decision without thoroughly thinking this out. Therefore, I decided to go talk to a few officials at the university, who urged me—with wonderful reasons—to stay. I called my older brothers and talked it out with them. I spent several hours on the phone with my boyfriend who, although he would have loved to have me at home, convinced me I would regret such a move more than anything else.

Well, he was right! Staying here was the best decision I ever made. And if it hadn't been for the communication I had with so many people, I wouldn't be here to graduate this spring!

— Jill, fourth-year college student

As Jill's experience demonstrates, persuasive messages definitely affect our lives.

Every day in many ways you too are confronted by persuasive messages. When your roommate asks you to go with her to the dining hall at a particular time, when your rivals argue a call in an intramural volleyball game, or when a telemarketer tries to convince you to sign up for yet another credit card, people are trying to persuade you. You can easily recognize that not everyone sees the world in the same way you do. Jill, for one, thought that leaving the university would cure her blues, but the people close to her just didn't see it the same way. By supporting their opposition to Jill's move with good reasons, they managed to convince her to stay and finish her degree, a decision that Jill now acknowledges was a better course for her life. Her friends, counselors, and boyfriend literally changed her life with their persuasive messages. Persuasion, then, is the process of creating change in others. It is our sensitivity to persuasion and our capability of persuading others that allow us to negotiate meanings with the world around us.

Some scholars of rhetoric have argued that all messages are inherently persuasive. Clearly, asking someone on a date or arguing a case before a jury are situations in which persuasive messages are exchanged. We can easily see how messages in these situations are attempting to create change. But is a simple statement like "I'm hungry" persuasive? What change could a person possibly seek with communication that appears to be more expressive than persuasive? Richard Weaver (1963) suggests that even in simple declarative statements such as this one, a communicator is attempting to persuade the receiver to see the world as she sees it. The intentional expression of hunger is an attempt to be understood. In being moved to understand the condition of another person, the receiver may thus be persuaded to change. In this case, that change might manifest itself as offering to drive the hungry communicator to the nearest fast food establishment, which is, in itself, yet another persuasive message.

The testimonial of a friend could persuade you to try a new restaurant.

MISSION: POSSIBLE

The distinction between informative and persuasive messages can be somewhat arbitrary. Your own experience has taught you that providing information can persuade you to change your mind, and arguing persuasively requires the use of helpful information. We draw a distinction in this textbook because we want to help you conceptualize the intent behind messages. Informative messages are intended to provide information without purposely swaying the audience one way or another. Persuasive messages are intended to move the audience to adopt some new position or to take some action.

To illustrate this difference, pick an object in your room or in your book bag. List three informative characteristics of this object. Without naming it, how would you describe this object to a friend?

Next write down three arguments to sell the object, as though it were appearing in a commercial. What would you have to say in order to convince someone to purchase this object?

Informative Details	*Persuasive Details*
1.	1.
2.	2.
3.	3.

The distinction in these items illustrates how intent distinguishes informative sharing from persuasive arguing.

Identifying Arguments

When those who study communication talk about persuasion, they are talk-ing about the ways people use symbols—spoken or written—to move one another to a course of action or a change in belief. Being aware of the persua-sive tactics advertisers, authorities, and even our friends are employing can help you determine how others are subtly shifting your perceptions. People use arguments, or persuasive statements backed with reasons, to change oth-ers. Aristotle noted that a communicator's arguments are based on three dimensions: *ethos, pathos,* and *logos.* Today we call these dimensions source credibility, emotional appeals, and logical appeals. Source credibility is based on the audience's *perceptions* of the source of the message. Emotional appeals are raised whenever the source attempts to appeal to the audience's feelings of fear, love, patriotism, anger, insecurities, etc. Logical appeals are raised whenever the source attempts to use factual information and system-atic reasoning. Utilizing any one or more of these dimensions in a given com-munication act results in an argument.

If an instructor suggests that you should study for his tests because he makes them challenging, his argument is based on his credibility. Do you believe him? If your instructor suggests you should study because you are in danger of failing the course, his argument is based on emotional appeal. Are you afraid of such a consequence? If your instructor suggests you study because this course is a prerequisite for another required course, his argu-ment is based on a logical appeal. Isn't it logical that one course follows another? In reality, communicators use a combination of their credibility, emotion, and logic to persuade their audiences. But not all the arguments persuaders use have the same merit.

One manifestation of source credibility we frequently encounter is in the form of the testimonial. A testimonial is an expert opinion. When a new res-taurant opens in town and you are among the first to try it, acquaintances ask you to offer your expert opinion about the establishment. Testimonials should be believed only to the extent that the expertness of the communicator can be established. Although we would be likely to accept supermodel Cindy Crawford's expertness on fashion, we would be less likely to accept her expertness on nuclear physics. Moreover, receivers should be wary of the bandwagon appeal offered in many testimonials. A bandwagon appeal argues that you should adopt a position because it is popular. Advertisements that plead with you to "join in the fun" of a particular event are trying to encourage your participation based on the involvement of others. The authors' advice here is the same as what parents have been offering for decades: "Just because everyone else is jumping off a bridge, doesn't mean you should!"

Arguments that attempt to appeal to our emotions, including our feelings of pity, anger, obligation, and happiness, are common. When Sally Struthers asks us to help her feed starving children, when we attend a neighborhood watch meeting, or when we are convinced to try a new product because it tastes good, we are being shaped by emotional appeals. Such appeals can be suspect, especially when they are framed within a coercive statement. Coer-cion implies the threat of deprivation or violence if the speaker's demands are not met. Coercive statements make an appeal to fear, whether that be the fear of losing another's affections, going to bed without supper, or suffering injury from a mugger. Terrorism is a form of coercion. When militant groups take hostages and demand change, they are engaging in coercive strategy. Of course, coercion is not always so blatant, but it exists in any situation where people threaten to deprive you of material goods or social rights or to do you personal violence if they do not get their way.

A logical appeal you are most certainly familiar with is the example. An example is presented as one of many cases. This textbook uses examples frequently to help you grasp concepts in communication. The example of terrorism used above attempts to argue that because one case of coercion exists, you can expect many cases to exist. Logical appeals use examples in either a deductive or an inductive fashion. In deductive reasoning, a generalization is stated and then supported by a number of examples. If a medical researcher on National Public Radio states that a particular drug is too dangerous and then cites a number of cases in which administering the drug proved fatal to patients, he is using deductive reasoning.

In just the opposite manner, one can create a logical argument through inductive reasoning, that is, by stating a number of examples that lead to a generalization. If a social worker on television lists the names of 20 children on a waiting list and then states that more people need to volunteer for a Big Brothers or Big Sisters program, she is using inductive reasoning. As you may suspect, logical arguments are not foolproof. In either deductive or inductive arguments, one can have too few examples to merit the claims of the generalization. When too few examples are used to argue a point, this is called a hasty generalization. An editorial writer who claims city government is corrupt on the basis of an affair between two employees commits a hasty generalization.

As the frequent receiver of persuasive arguments, you need to be aware of how such messages can mislead you by making use of faulty arguments such as bandwagon appeals, coercive statements, or hasty generalizations. As producers of persuasive messages, you need to realize that carefully constructed arguments avoid making such errors. Because we are all both receivers and senders of persuasive messages, you should recognize that persuasive communication, like all other forms of communication, involves a relationship between communicators.

Example of Persuasive Argument

Here again, we would like to provide you with an example of one student's approach to the assignment of creating a persuasive message to illustrate how sound arguments help construct such a message.

Volunteers Needed!
by Sheila McCombs

Introduction

Impact statement: Ghandi once said, "I shall pass through this world but once. Any good therefore I can do or any kindness that I can show to any human being, let me do it now. Let me not defer or neglect it, for I shall not pass through this way again." As college students trying to cope with the daily stresses of life, we often think we're too busy to volunteer our time or improve our community. Term papers, exams, and deadlines seem to run our lives. But we need to realize that there is a world outside our middle-class suburban haven struggling for survival, and it's happening right here in our community.

Thesis statement: It is the responsibility of all of us to take action now and help fix the problems of our community.

Source credibility statement: I have been involved in volunteering for several years, and I have seen the needs of children in poverty and despair. I volunteered at a summer camp for underprivileged children, and through my experiences I realized that no small gesture of kindness to others goes unnoticed. I also realized that each one of us must take an active role in our community.

Preview statement: Although we all live busy lives, I encourage you to take time out of your busy schedule to improve our community. One way you can become involved is through National Volunteer Week, coming up April 19–25. In the next few minutes I'll give you a brief history behind the week, reasons why you should become involved, and what you can do to participate.

Body

I. First, I want to tell you a brief background of National Volunteer Week.
   A. National Volunteer Week began in 1974.
      1. President Nixon signed an executive order establishing the week.
      2. Its purpose is to celebrate volunteerism by promoting volunteerism on a national, state, and local level (*Trends in Volunteering*, 1997).
   B. Last year, President Clinton joined former presidents and General Colin Powell for the President's Summit for America's Future.
      1. This 3-day event gathered 4,500 people who pledged a commitment to utilizing volunteer service as a way to improve the lives of America's youth.
      2. General Colin Powell said it best, "It is this glorious cycle of giving, receiving, and giving back that we want to pass along to the next generation of Americans. We want them to believe in America, and we want them to know that America believes in them" (*Quotes on Volunteerism*, 1997).

Transition: Since we've looked at a brief history of National Volunteer Week, let's now look at the reasons why you should become involved.

II. Volunteering allows you to make a contribution.
   A. Volunteering increases your awareness of the surrounding community.
      1. According to a 1994 survey by the Search Institute, 74 percent of youth in service-learning will change what they do to protect the environment (*Trends in Volunteering*, 1997).
      2. Eighty-five percent of those now doing volunteer work are doing so on one or more serious social issues, including homelessness, illiteracy, or child abuse (*Trends*, 1997).

   3. Increasing awareness of problems in our community is the
      first step to solving such issues.
   B. Volunteer participation is increasing and you don't want to
      miss out!
      1. Ninety-three million Americans over the age of 18 volun-
         teered in 1995 (*Trends*, 1997).
      2. This represents an increase of 4 million over the 89 million
         adults who volunteered in 1993.
      3. By volunteering, not only will you gain a tremendous sense
         of satisfaction, but you will meet people from many walks
         of life and make lasting friendships.
   C. Many people in our community need your help.
      1. According to the 1997 U.S. Census Bureau, 20 percent of
         U. S. children under the age of 18 were from families that
         lived below the poverty level in 1995 ("America's Promise
         Alliance for Youth," 1997).
      2. Only 52 percent of low-income urban youth said that clubs
         and organizations were available to them ("America's
         Promise Alliance for Youth," 1997).
      3. It is the responsibility of each one of us to care for the chil-
         dren of the world, because they are our future.
      4. Former President Jimmy Carter said, "The well-being of
         our children must be the national priority and the responsi-
         bility of every individual" (*Quotes*, 1997).

Transition: In recognizing the potential contribution you can make as a volunteer, I encourage you to get involved.

 III. You can see that there is a call for us to take a stand and reach out
      to those in need.
   A. Choose to involve yourself in activities planned for National
      Volunteer Week.
      1. First, check out the calendar of events that will be posted all
         over campus.
      2. This will highlight many organizations' volunteer opportu-
         nities for the week.
   B. Along with the volunteer opportunities throughout the week,
      there will be a few events to celebrate as well.
      1. The Center for Community Service is hosting a Volunteer
         Recognition Reception on Tuesday at 7 p.m. in the Student
         Center.
      2. Along with the Recognition Reception, Habitat for Human-
         ity is hosting a benefit concert at the Cantina on Thursday
         at 9 p.m.
   C. Even if you don't volunteer formally by working at a sched-
      uled event, I urge you to become more aware of the need for
      service and do something to improve someone else's life.
      1. Improving someone's life is simple and takes only minutes.
         These contributions are called Random Acts of Kindness.
      2. Helping a friend study calculus, holding the door for some-
         one, or just smiling to a stranger on the street can improve
         another person's life and make you feel better also.

❖ ❖ ❖ ❖

Conclusion

Summary: Since we've learned a little more about National Volunteer Week, the need for volunteers, and what you can do to help, I encourage you to act now, and begin to change our community. We can't do everything, but each of us can do something.

Reinforce thesis: We all lead busy lives, but we need to stop and take a look around us and realize that it is our duty to reach out and help those around us.

Close with impact: "How wonderful is it that nobody needs to wait a single moment before starting to improve the world." Anne Frank said this at a time in her life when her world was crumbling around her. This simple statement demonstrates that even those who have it bad can see the powerful possibilities in helping someone else. Now it is our turn to put aside our problems and make a difference in someone's life today.

Resources

Points of Light Foundation. (1997). *Quotes on Volunteerism* [Pamphlet]. Washington, D. C.: Author.

Points of Light Foundation. (1997). *Trends in Volunteering* [Pamphlet]. Washington, D. C.: Author.

Search Institute. (1997). *America's Promise Alliance for Youth* [Pamphlet]. No place: Author.

Among the many things that Sheila does well in this outline is the fact that she backs up her assertions with reasons. For example, under the second major point in the body of her speech, she not only states that volunteering increases awareness, she supports that declaration by quoting statistical evidence that demonstrates the benefits of what she is arguing. Another strength is found in the timeliness of Sheila's presentation. She delivered this speech just weeks before National Volunteer Week, meaning that her call for change was something her audience could choose to comply with relatively soon. Moreover, if her classmates were to see signs for the events she describes around campus in the coming weeks, her message would be reinforced with each flyer. The ancient Greeks called this the quality of kairos—saying the appropriate thing at the appropriate time—and it is something persuasive speakers should aim to achieve.

Sprinkled throughout Sheila's presentation are examples of the three types of persuasive appeals we talked about earlier. Early in her introduction, she talks about her own experiences with volunteering at a summer camp for underprivileged children and thus establishes her source credibility. Towards the end of the body of her speech, she notes that helping friends or merely smiling not only helps others but makes you, the volunteer, feel good. This is an emotional appeal, emphasizing the positive rewards one gets when choosing to follow the speaker's advice. Finally, she uses logical appeals in a number of instances, notably in the middle of her outline when supporting the claim that many people need your help with statistics demonstrating that 20 percent of children live in poverty and 52 percent of youths have no organizations available to them. Moreover, as you can see from this sample outline, everything we suggested about informative speaking, from doing your homework to organizing your information, to equipping your audience to learn, is equally important in constructing a persuasive message.

Although Sheila provides us with a fairly good example of a first-year student's attempt at persuasive speaking, you should have recognized a number of ways she could improve this for presentation. Certainly, she could corroborate the statistics she used from more than one source. Moreover, if you recognized her assertion "Volunteer participation is increasing and you don't want to miss out!" as a bandwagon appeal, move to the head of the class. Despite these and some other suggestions you might have for improvement, "Volunteers Needed!" demonstrates how a persuasive outline might be constructed as one prepares to deliver the message.

Delivery

Whether the intent of your message is informative or persuasive, you will want to deliver that message in as clear and confident a style as possible. As you read in the previous chapter, by this point in the presentation process you've analyzed your audience, thoroughly researched your topic, meticulously outlined your points, practiced your presentation, considered peer criticism, and anticipated ways to confront your anxiety. You are in front of your audience and ready to speak. What more do you need to consider at this point? Now that you have prepared mentally for this moment, you need to be conscious of the nonverbal elements of your presentation, including dynamic presence, body language, and the use of presentational aids.

Dynamic Presence

If you're not excited about delivering your speech, you can bet no one in the audience will be excited about hearing it. Dynamic presence refers to the energy you bring to a public presentation. Without much dynamic presence, your presentations can seem dull and lifeless. With dynamic presence, you project your voice and you seem interested in the topic and in sharing the topic with the audience. The quality of dynamic presence is not the same as faking enthusiasm. If you are delivering a speech on the serious risks of contracting HIV, it would probably be inappropriate to smile continuously and appear too perky and light. Applying the appropriate dynamics to a given topic means applying the appropriate tone but doing so with an intensity that demonstrates to the audience your interest in the topic.

Body Language

As you know, nonverbal leakage cues can contradict a verbal message and betray a nervous speaker. Unfortunately, those unnecessary nonverbals can distract an audience from your intended message. One of the hardest things for novice speakers to control is what their bodies are doing while they are speaking. Some fiddle with their hands, others play with their hair, and still others dance in place, nervously shifting their weight from one side to another. Of course, you may not even be aware of these leaks. This is another

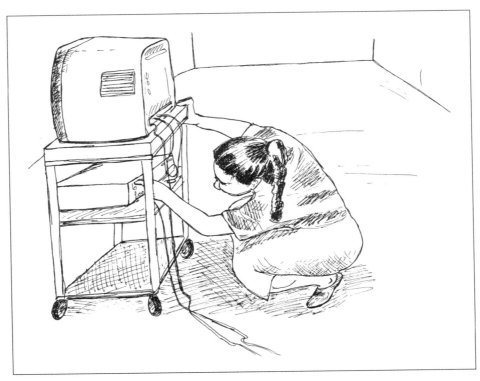

In order to avoid frustration during your presentation, always check on the preparedness of any audiovisual aids you might be using.

reason why it is a good idea for you to practice your presentations before a practice audience before you speak publicly. Peer critics can point out leaks to you so that you are aware of them and can try to monitor them during a presentation.

Ideally, you would appear to be as comfortable in front of an audience as you would talking one-on-one with your best friend. However, try to control unnecessary movements like those leaks described above. As you become more and more comfortable with public speaking, you will find yourself freer to use movement in your presentations. Moving around the room, gesturing, and showing facial expressions can all be used to enhance your message— when done appropriately and deliberately.

Of all the nonverbals under your control, none is more important than maintaining good eye contact with your audience. Eye contact lets your audience know that the message you are delivering is intended for them, not the concrete wall behind them or the floorboards beneath them. Looking into the eyes of several audience members in the course of a presentation helps maintain an audience's interaction with you, the speaker.

Presentational Aids

Another strategy to keep your audience focused on your message (and not your dancing feet) is to use presentational aids. Many people's first encounter

❖ ❖ ❖ ❖

> ### MISSION: POSSIBLE
>
> Using technology as an aid to your public presentations can certainly impress your audience—if you can use it competently. Showing a clip from a situation comedy, playing the lyrics to a familiar song, or listing your main points on a computer monitor can emphasize a point more clearly than merely uttering these materials. Before using any technology, whether it is a video cassette player, a compact disk player, or a computer software program, you should familiarize yourself with the aid thoroughly. You do not want to cause your audience to doubt your credibility just because you cannot find the "Play" button on the VCR. Practice using your aid and just prior to speaking, check to make sure the equipment you are about to use works. Some simple precautions will help you avoid embarrassment and impress your audience with your expertise.

with public speaking is in elementary school with "Show and Tell." The concept represented in that ritual applies to your presentations as an adult, too: people learn from both seeing and hearing. Presentational aids can help your audience envision a place they've never been, examine statistical relationships among quantities, and see the product firsthand.

Although there are countless presentational aids at your disposal, including photographs, charts, and objects, you should be guided in your selection of possible presentational aids by the following:

1. Make sure everyone in the audience has access to it. Do not leave any audience members out of the chance to see and experience the presentational aid.

2. Make sure it illustrates your point. Do not have a presentational aid for the sake of having a presentational aid.

3. Make sure it works. Test any equipment you need to operate during the presentation before you begin speaking.

Finally, do not limit your imagination to visual aids. Stimulating the other senses can have just as much, if not more, of a memorable effect on the audience as showing them something can. Playing a recording, offering a sample of a food, or passing around an object for your audience to hold are just some possible strategies to enhance your presentation. One of the authors had a student pass out small cups filled with sand to a class. The student instructed everyone in the class to place a finger in the cup of sand, close their eyes, and imagine being on the beach. Given such an effective tactile stimulation, everyone in the class was then hooked on hearing what the speaker had to say next.

Controlling these elements of delivery help you construct an effective presentation. Given the hard work you are likely to invest in preparing for a high-quality presentation, you will want the finished product to reflect that investment. Be mindful of the energy you bring to your public address and the non-verbal messages you are sending. The presentational aids you are using put the final polish on your presentation.

Summary

Given that you are bound to be making informative presentations throughout your life, you will want to make them more effectively. Beginning with the presumptions that you are the expert and must anticipate what the audience does not know, we suggest that you do your homework by corroborating sources; organizing information in a spatial, chronological, or topical pattern; and helping your audience to learn by using effective teaching techniques.

The distinction between informative and persuasive messages is best understood as the intent behind each. Informative messages seek to provide information without bias as to the content. Persuasion seeks to cause change in others. In presentations, people are often urged to change through arguments, statements supported with reasons. Speakers build on source credibility, emotional appeals, and logical appeals, both deductive and inductive, in constructing these arguments. As mindful consumers and producers of these messages, you will want to avoid the pitfalls caused by bandwagon appeals, coercion, and hasty generalizations.

If you have invested sufficient time and effort preparing and practicing, then you have only a few more things to concentrate on while you are delivering these messages. The most important of these items is to project genuine interest in speaking, or dynamic presence, to the audience. Be aware of any nonverbal leakage that might prove distracting to your audience and work with presentational aids in such a manner that they punctuate your message.

At Your Bookstore

Cialdinin, R. B. (1993). *Influence: The Psychology of Persuasion.* New York: Morrow.

Silberman, M. (1996). *Active Learning: 101 Strategies to Teach Any Subject.* Boston: Allyn & Bacon.

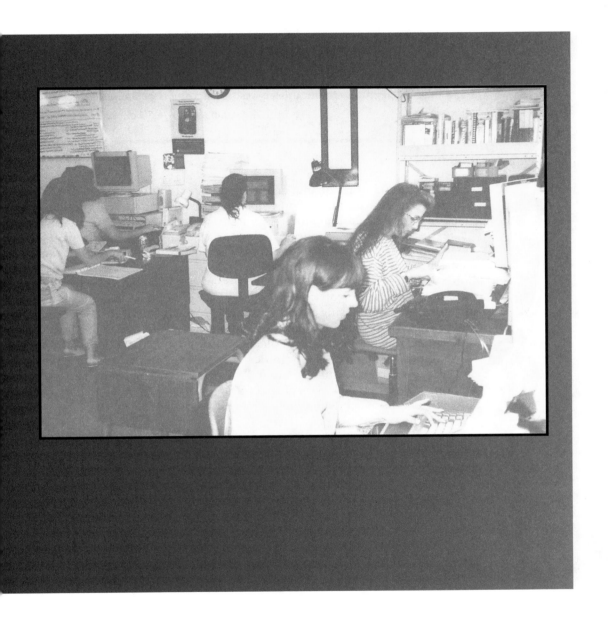

CHAPTER 15

Communicating via New Technologies

> My boyfriend and I e-mail each other daily and usually talk on the phone twice a week. Last week being the first week back in school, I was busy moving into the apartment and only talked to him about 10 minutes.
>
> My e-mail message from him concerned our short conversation. I sent him a message agreeing and said we would talk soon. (I didn't want to talk about the problem via the Internet!) Obviously, I didn't explain because he quickly sent a sarcastic message, upset that I spent one line discussing the problem.
>
> To make a long story short—when we finally talked on the phone we were mad at each other. The situation probably could have been avoided if I called (or if he called) initially, without using e-mail to discuss a problem.
>
> — Jasmine, third-year college student

The frustrating situation that arose between Jasmine and her boyfriend had a lot more to do with the *way* in which they were communicating than with *what* they were communicating. As communication technologies continue to make the distances that separate us appear to shrink, they don't always guarantee that the nature of the communication experience will be the same in each environment. More and more often, we are finding that our communication, and indeed many of our relationships, are being mediated by technology.

Like Jasmine, do you maintain long-distance relationships with friends or significant others using e-mail? Instead of trekking home last weekend, did you telephone your parents instead? Rather than wait to see your instructor during her office hours, did you place a note on her office door? All of these are instances of mediated communication you are already familiar with, and as our technology continues to expand the possibilities for human interaction without regard to boundaries of space and time, you will need to understand how you can use such technologies more effectively.

This chapter:

- Explains the concept of mediated communication.
- Discusses the effects of media on culture.
- Introduces new formats for communicating.
- Reviews research into how people communicate in these formats.

Mediated Communication

As Jasmine's story demonstrates, our communication is increasingly mediated. What does it mean to have communication mediated? Basically, anything that intercedes or intervenes in the communication process constitutes a mediation. For example, the telephone is one technological device that intercedes in the communication process. Another way to think about a medium is as "anything that in some way extends the reach or increases the efficiency of man's physical or nervous system" (Ehninger, 1969). Thus, the telephone actually extends a portion of your nervous system—your hearing— making it possible for you to hear (and be heard) at tremendous distances.

However, what you hear on the telephone isn't the sound of someone's voice but the electronic reproduction of that voice. Have you ever noticed how some people just don't sound the same on the telephone as they do in person? That's because even as technology extends communication it also alters communication in the process.

Another communication technology, electronic mail (e-mail), alters many of the characteristics of communication that we take for granted, including the elements of space, time, and nonverbal cues. When you access your e-mail account, you may find a message from your friend in Nova Scotia (space), sent earlier this morning (time), telling you a joke he just heard (text). Now consider that your friend met you face-to-face with the same joke. Would the communication act have been the same? Your friend's physical presence, accompanied by nonverbal cues like facial expressions and tone of voice, would have provided you with substantially more information. You probably would have interpreted the message differently. As you might guess, each medium, be it sight, sound, written, broadcast, or electronic, affects the quality of messages in different ways. Each medium stimulates one or more of our senses, helping to shape how we get information.

Marshall McLuhan (1964), an influential theorist, once said, "The medium is the message." This phrase, reproduced numerous times by those who study communication technology, points to an inescapable element of modern civilization: Our communication with others is increasingly influenced by the media through which we communicate.

Consider your own interactions with various media. Do you react to each medium the same way? For instance, when you meet a friend face-to-face, you probably give that person your undivided attention. Another friend might happen along and say hello, or the roar of a passing motorcycle might distract you, but basically you are focusing your attention on each other. Now contrast the behavior you exhibit when facing your friend to that which you exhibit when on the telephone with him or her. You probably listen intently and respond where appropriate, but do you find yourself distracted by other things in your immediate environment? Some people mute the television when receiving a telephone call but continue to watch the images on the set while engaged in the conversation—something that would be considered rude in person. Have you ever been caught not paying close enough attention to a friend because you were doing something else while on the telephone?

Part of McLuhan's message includes the idea that different media stimulate the human senses differently. Media that require focus on a single sense he dubbed hot media. Radio, because it focuses exclusively on our sense of hearing, is a hot medium. Media that appeal to more than one sense he dubbed cool. Television, because it stimulates both sight and hearing, is considered a cool medium. McLuhan wasn't trying to assign relative temperatures to the various media, but instead he was noting how much perceptual participation was needed on the part of a receiver to understand a message. Some media provide us with a great deal of information, requiring relatively little work on our part to decode it. However, some media require that we fill in the gaps of meaning and thus we must do more work in interpreting the message. The less sensory information provided, the more the person must contribute to the completion of the message.

In short, McLuhan is suggesting that the essential characteristics of any medium shape the messages that pass through it. There are some obvious differences in the way we interact in person and on the telephone. The way we interpret messages presented on television differs from what we do with messages delivered by radio. (After all, while you will drive a car and listen to the radio, you can't drive and watch television at the same time. At least you shouldn't!) We live in a culture that provides information in many contexts: face-to-face, print, radio, film, television, e-mail, the World Wide Web, CD-ROMs. We need to consider how the information we get through each is affected by its medium.

Media and Culture

Walter Ong (1982) emphasizes not only that media shape our individual experiences, but also that the introduction of a new medium has profound effects upon a whole culture. Among the most significant media inventions in history were writing, movable type, and the telegraph. The significance of writing to the progress of civilization is difficult to understate. The invention of writing allowed people to do an incredible thing: to free up memory. With the ability to record economic transactions, genealogies, and narratives, humans were able to focus more of their mental energy on creative endeavors rather than just memorization.

Writing itself profoundly changed in the fifteenth century, when Johannes Gutenberg introduced movable type in the form of the printing press. Metal letters could be arranged and rearranged to form pages of text with relative speed, meaning that more books were available to more people. Up until that point, everything that was written was written by hand. This meant that books were rare and extremely valuable. The vast majority of people never even had access to a book. Moreover, most people, being illiterate, probably found books irrelevant. The increase in literacy among the masses had a direct influence on historical events such as the development of modern democratic forms of government.

One of the most far-reaching effects of the development of print in the West was the development of individuality (Ong, 1982). Prior to the widespread use of books, people tended to place the needs of the community before the needs of the individuals, in part because the communication of ideas for the majority of the population took place collectively rather than individually. News, when it arrived, came by word of mouth, not from a newspaper or broadcast. The printing press allowed for more books to reach more people. Now ideas could be received in a way that took the community out of the transmission of the message. People could learn just as much (if not more) from reading alone in a room as they once learned in a public forum.

Moreover, with the rise of the idea that certain books were better than others came the notion that certain individuals were better writers than others. Now the gifted writer became the object of respect and becoming a gifted writer became the aim of learned people. Books not only isolated people from the community, they validated the accomplishments of the individual.

Despite the sweeping social changes brought about by the growth of print media, even newspapers were limited by the time it took to deliver one from the press to a newsstand. Samuel Morse eliminated the problem of time in communication with the invention of the telegraph. The telegraph is basically an electrical wire stretched between two points that can transmit pulses from one point to another where they are interpreted as letters. The telegraph

Johannes Gutenberg's fifteenth-century introduction of the printing press was a significant development in communication technology.

allowed for nearly instantaneous communication between points and signaled the birth of the electronic media.

The electronic media have countered the trend toward individualization. The transmission of information around the world has led to a state where we can no longer imagine ourselves as alone. Instantaneous coverage of events in the Middle East for a family in Iowa has reduced the sense that we can be isolated, separate from the events in the world around us. Our sense of what affects us is no longer limited to where we can go or people we can meet. Consider the images and sounds telecast in the wake of the 1995 Oklahoma City bombing. Even though the majority of us do not live in Oklahoma City or even know any of the victims, the tragedy touched us all because of the presence of television in our lives.

Ong suggested that what we are experiencing is a shift toward secondary orality. Secondary orality describes the communal interpretations of mediated, rather than immediate, messages. In cultures without printed books, all people knew of the world was in relationship to their tribe. Such communities are said to demonstrate primary orality because all their culture, from the news of the day to the stories passed down from one generation to the next, was communicated interpersonally. Writing, and to a greater extent, print, decreased a sense of community even as it increased a sense of individuality. However, the introduction of mass media has reintroduced the notion that culture, from the news of the day to the stories that entertain us, is transmitted communally. Television now serves as a metaphorical bonfire around which we all gather to share our daily lives in our global village. Although we have not abandoned our sense of individuality or burned all the books, there is a growing sense that we are more bound together than we are separated. The skills involved with interpreting these community-oriented messages are what Ong calls secondary orality.

Of course, the familiar medium of print is by no means becoming extinct. Novels, newspapers, magazines, and, yes, textbooks will still be a part of our experience for the foreseeable future. However, that doesn't mean that our conception of how to read won't change. Even as people have distinguished the ways in which they interpret a television broadcast from the ways they interpret one from radio, so too might the way we read texts drastically change in the coming years.

New Formats for Media

Hypertext

Think about the way in which you have been taught to read: you are supposed to start at the beginning and read straight through to the end of a document. Have you ever begun a murder mystery only to skip to the last page to see "whodunit"? In that case you violated the rules of reading. If, in the course of reading a textbook, you have stopped reading the text to read a footnote or have paused to consider one of the "Spotlights" in this book, then you've already experimented with the elementary principles behind a form of communication called hypertext. Hypertext refers to nonsequential writing. George P. Landow (1992) suggested that electronic media will allow for a way of reading that depends more on the active participation of the reader than the conventions of the printed page.

A lot of the ways in which we read have been determined by the medium of print. The conventions we take for granted now—like spaces between words, paragraphing, punctuation, and capitalization—did not always exist. Imaginehowhardthatmadereadingespeciallywhenthetextwasevenlongertha ninthisexample.

But just because we've been trained to read a particular way doesn't mean that is the only way to read. Hypertext differs from traditional writing in several important ways, including:

- Reconceptions regarding the order of reading.
- The centrality of a given text.
- The hierarchical power possessed by the author over the reader.

Linearity

First, traditional reading requires that you read in a predetermined order, typically established by the author through the systematic ordering of pages. With this chapter, for example, you are supposed to read the first page first, the second page second, and so on through the systematic process of linearity. In hypertext, however, the reader can choose the order to follow. If this book were in a hypertext format, we could provide you with a link to another part of this book that talks about writing, say the language chapter. You, as the reader could then decide whether to follow up on the link by going to that chapter or to continue reading on in the more traditional order. In books following a conventional format—this text included—cross-references and an index allow the reader *some* degree of interaction.

Centrality

Second, given the ability to link to material outside itself illustrates a second difference between traditional writing and hypertext. Traditional texts assume that they stand alone, that is, they are central to the moment of reading. Hypertexts, because they are typically associated with materials around them that provide a context for the material, no longer hold a central position. In other words, a hypertext more readily acknowledges its position among other texts of equal value. For example, when your instructor assigns you a particular book to read, you know that it is the central text for instruction and evaluation. In a hypertextual environment, the links to outside texts would lead you back and forth from one text to another, lessening the central position of any one text.

Hierarchy

Third, while traditional texts establish a hierarchy of knowledge, with the individual author at the top giving you information, hypertext undermines the power of the writer and redistributes it to the reader. Thus, hypertext invites you to be a more active reader of the text, for in the very process of controlling where it will go next, you are participating in the making of its meaning. In the future, we may talk about the *developers* of text rather than the *authors*. Some scholarly materials have already been produced via hypertext. Certainly the World Wide Web (WWW), which you will read more about shortly, is an excellent example of everything Landow predicts. Hypertext, however, will only catch on if, as Landow notes, it either allows us to do new things or allows us to do old things more easily. If the popularity of the WWW is any indication, then we will all be learning how to read hypertext before too long.

The Internet as a Medium

Internet History

During the last decade, we have witnessed the emergence of a popular new medium for communication in our lives. Chances are that if you are a student at a college or university in the United States you already have access to the resources of the Internet, which include e-mail, discussion groups, and the World Wide Web. The promise of faster and more widespread communication and research that Internet technologies offer stands ready to reshape the way in which we view our world and, as some futurists are predicting, to bring about changes at least as significant as those begun by the printing press.

Although people talk about the Internet frequently, they rarely discuss what it is and where it came from. The Internet is formed through a series of networked computers across the country and around the world. Each of these computer systems, called a node, contributes memory space and processing capabilities to the Internet. Unlike the familiar towers of your local radio and television stations, the whole Internet is not transmitted from a central location. Thus, the Internet is a decentered medium.

The idea for a decentered medium actually began with the U.S. military but was developed by academic institutions (Giese, 1996). The military, as you know, is a hierarchical organization: a general gives commands to a colonel, who gives commands to a captain, and so on down the line. The problem with hierarchies is that they, like a chain, depend upon every link being in place. In the 1960s the military began to worry that a nuclear strike could lead to a breakdown in this communication hierarchy. They turned to computer scientists to build a nonhierarchical and geographically dispersed communication system.

In 1969 the Advanced Research Projects Agency network, or ARPAnet, was launched with a mere four nodes, but these swelled into the hundreds within the next decade. Although the system was designed *for* the military, it was designed *by* research scientists and housed in computers located on university campuses. These scientists began to use the network for their own purposes, as they exchanged ideas for projects and shared resources electronically. In 1979 they launched a similar system called *Usenet News* for the free exchange of information.

Today's Message Center

One of the primary uses of these systems was to transmit electronic mail messages, e-mail. An e-mail system allows a user at one institution to compose a message on a computer and direct it through the network to another user's address located somewhere else in the world's interconnected computer system, whether that is within the same institution or in another country. Some of the addresses on the Internet are not for specific individuals but for discussion groups. Members of these so-called listserves post messages on the Internet as you would post a notice on a bulletin board. A posted message may then be read, and subsequently replied to, by anyone who is a member of the discussion group.

E-mail functions in a primarily asynchronous manner; that is, messages are not exchanged in real time, as they might be on a telephone. A user can open his e-mail account and find messages sent days or minutes before he arrived, just as you might open your mailbox to find letters postmarked on different dates. Asynchronous communication like e-mail gives the user the free-

❖ ❖ ❖ ❖

MISSION: POSSIBLE

If there's anything frustrating about E-mail, it's just that there's so much of it that it can be a daunting task for a professional who has been away from the computer for a few days to sort through all of it. Two ways you can help make sure your messages are read and are remembered are to use concrete language in your subject lines and to keep the body of your messages short and to the point.

We know some people who do not even bother to open messages from their inboxes if they are not intrigued by the subject line. Try your best to get the reader's attention with an original subject line that addresses the matter at hand. Stating "Request for recommendation" is better than a nondescript "Hey!" on your subject line.

Even more important, keep in mind that E-mail messages are more like memos than letters. In other words, they should be brief. After reading the first sentence in your message, a reader should know exactly what your memo is about. Here again, "I would like to ask you to write a recommendation for a scholarship." is superior to "Do you remember me? I was in your fundamentals class last year." In the former example, the reader knows immediately why you are writing rather than having to wade through a lot of unnecessary introductory material. Try to incorporate these simple writing tips into your E-mail correspondence and see how much more people appreciate your efficiency with words.

dom to choose when to respond. Many fans of e-mail cite this as a strength of the medium in that they can deliberate upon their responses longer than in a synchronous medium.

Of course, the Internet allows for synchronous, or real-time, communication as well. Obviously, to have synchronous communication, two or more users must be logged onto the system at the same time. Some of this interaction takes place in chat rooms, locations typically devoted to any number of topics, from gardening to *Star Trek*. Some of it takes place in multi-user domains (MUDs), which are specialized programs that allow participants to enter into fantasy worlds where text is used to describe their surroundings, actions, and dialogues in an interactive role-play. Even though it is highly imaginative, all this interaction is text based. People shape their reactions and interactions solely on the basis of symbols generated on a computer screen: There are no sounds and few images.

Multimedia, in the form of cooperating text, images, and sound, have found a home on the Internet, though. Introduced in 1991, the World Wide Web is a component of the Internet that facilitates the inclusion of images and sound. Thanks to the use of specialized programs called browsers, computers can translate the Hypertext Mark-up Language (HTML) used on the Web. The Web can accommodate e-mail, discussion groups, and chat rooms, plus provide information on a variety of topics, from personal biographies to specialized electronic magazines—all in full color and with sound.

The privatization of the Internet has been facilitated by the U.S. government, which proposed a plan for a National Information Infrastructure (NII) in 1993. The NII plan promotes the expansion of the Internet through commercial and private efforts. Now hardly recognizable as a military communication system, the so-called Information Superhighway promises to bring our world closer together.

❖ ❖ ❖ ❖   ## Cyberspace

One of the ways in which we make sense of a new sensation is to use metaphors to describe our experiences. Often when you ask someone to describe a new sensation, you ask him or her to describe it in terms you are already familiar with. When you ask someone about a new flavor of ice cream, you ask "What does it taste like?" hoping that the person will describe it in terms of flavors you already know. The same holds true for the new media experience we encounter on the Internet: We try to explain the experience in terms of what we have already encountered. Here the most common metaphor deals with a sense of place. Just look at the introduction to the Internet above. We often use metaphors of space—in terms of location—to talk about e-mail: You need to know someone's address before you can write to him or her. The Web, too, is characterized by addresses, including the home page. By using references that suggest locations, we define the Internet in relationship to space.

Thus, scholars and users have come to refer to the imaginary places of the Internet as cyberspace. The term was first coined by William Gibson (1984) in his novel *Neuromancer*:

> Cyberspace. A consensus hallucination experienced daily by billions of legitimate operators, in every nation. . . . A graphic representation of data abstracted from the banks of every computer in the human system. Unthinkable complexity. Lines of light ranged in the nonspace of the mind, clusters and constellations of data. (p. 51)

The key to Gibson's definition is "consensual hallucination" for in that phrase we can best describe how we interpret the arrangements of lighted dots on our computer screens. Cyberspace, like language, is a product of the human mind; it is socially produced and shared among many users. It exists because we choose to interpret the electronic impulses flashing on a computer screen as having meaning, much as we interpret the strokes of a pen to represent letters which form words.

Cyber as a prefix has been applied to numerous Internet associations. Users now talk about the cybernaut navigating cyberia, seeking cybertalk, or perhaps even cybersex. The navigation metaphor here is also apparent, for *cyber* derives from the Greek word for "to steer." Thus, conceptualizing the flow of information available on the Internet as a sea on which one uses a program like Netscape Navigator, or Microsoft Explorer to surf the Net helps us to process the complexity of this new technology.

Research in Computer-mediated Communication

The opportunities for communication opened by the Internet have caught the attention of scholars interested in the ways in which people construct themselves and their relationships using this technology. This broad area of research is referred to as computer-mediated communication (CMC). John December (1997), editor of the online *CMC Magazine*, defines CMC as "a process of human communication via computers, involving people, situated in contexts, engaging in processes to shape media for a variety of purposes." CMC, then, is not the study of telecommunication systems or computer pro-

❖ ❖ ❖ ❖

The self-concepts people present online tend to be more idealized than realistic.

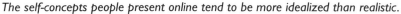

gramming but a study of the way people interact with computer technology. At the center of this definition is the human aspect. Focusing on this aspect has led scholars to ask questions like:

- How is identity constructed online?
- How do people initiate and maintain relationships without physical presence?
- How does the medium affect the quality of human interaction?

CMC continues to grow as a fascinating new avenue for understanding the human condition. Let's look at some questions scholars have investigated involving online identity and the virtual community.

Online Identity

Unlike other forms of communication, such as public speaking, where the kind of clothes you wear or the inflection of your voice tells something about your gender, socioeconomic class, national origin, race, or any other personal characteristics, the new electronic media allow your identity to be much more of a conscious invention. This means that people entering into cyberspace can, to a large degree, create their own identities. For instance, a shy bookworm can present himself as a popular wit or a teenager can emphasize her maturity.

Have you or someone you know initiated a romantic relationship over the Internet? Given the lack of a physical presence, what was it about the person on the other end of the modem connection that made him or her so attractive?

The freedom that such invention allows presents an opportunity for better communication among some participants. Joe Walther (1996) suggests that computer-mediated communication allows users to engage in selective self-presentation, a process of creating one's own identity that often emphasizes the most attractive (real or imagined) characteristics of the user. If the user finds this invented identity accepted or praised among those in virtual space, then he or she may feel more confident and communicate more freely than in a face-to-face (FtF) situation. Walther calls this hyperpersonal communication. He notes that because CMC has fewer channels for communicating with others, one can better manage one's presentation of self.

In essence, the change in medium allows some individuals to feel freer in expressing themselves. Critics don't all agree that CMC is as potentially liberating as Walther believes. For those who consider that the best communication comes from contexts in which the communicators have as much information as possible about one another, the lack of nonverbal cues in CMC makes it pale in comparison next to richer contexts like face-to-face interaction. Perhaps the use of CMC is not so much an issue of it being a better medium to explore one's identity, as it is simply a different medium.

The effects of participating in CMC contexts can, however, be therapeutic for users. Sherry Turkle (1996) explains that users can create everything that exists in cyberspace, from objects used in a role-playing game to an individual's physical characteristics. As we noted, a character in a role-playing game is only known through the self-description that the user provides. This allows the user the opportunity to try on a variety of identities, many of which one would never consider experimenting with in reality, such as gender-switching. This escape into another identity or to join another society allows people to work through problems in ways they could not in reality. However, some people can seek this escape too much. Howard Rheingold (1993) cites examples of individuals who retreated into cyberspace for more than 80 hours a week, which jeopardized their academic life, their employment, their health, and their relationships with people in real life. Cyberspace, then, holds the potential for both interaction and isolation.

Virtual Communities

Kenneth Gergen (1991) suggests that people are becoming more involved in symbolic communities than with their geographic communities. A symbolic community emerges whenever people with common interests acknowledge their interrelationship. Your communication instructor is probably a member of a symbolic community. The National Communication Association is composed of communication scholars and instructors from across the United States and Canada. With more than 5,000 members spread across the conti-

Spotlight on Ethics . . . What Counts?

A number of instructors, alarmed that their students are submitting papers filled with references from the World Wide Web and nothing else, have begun to limit the number of Internet sources one can include in a given paper. Why? After all, it is certainly easier to navigate the Web for information than to wander the library from floor to floor, and aren't all sources of information the same? Unfortunately, new media have a hard time achieving legitimate recognition in the academy, and given that almost anyone anywhere can publish on the Web, it is difficult to say how authoritative some of the sources are.

In doing your research on the Internet, be suspect of sources that lack some collaborative effort. Authority on the Web is a *product of association*. That's not to say that some individuals haven't published some great ideas. However, if you want to increase the chances that someone has read over and checked an article before it's been published, look to see where the information came from and who it is linked to. For example, any of the electronic journals that are part of the MUSE project out of John Hopkins University have undergone a process of peer review prior to publication. This means that scholars within the field have confirmed the accuracy of the information in a given article. Use your own critical thinking skills to weigh the value of any argument you see posted on the Web, but especially those lacking authoritative backing.

What do you think makes a source reliable?

What kinds of sources would you not use in a presentation?

nent, this is a community formed by mutual accord rather than geographic proximity.

The National Communication Association is a highly formal symbolic community. It has a charter, centralized officers, and numerous publications. Yet symbolic communities need not have so rigid a structure. Rheingold argues that symbolic communities emerge in mediated communication as well. He calls these virtual communities and defines them as "social aggregations that emerge from the [Internet] when enough people carry on those public discussions long enough, with sufficient human feeling, to form webs of personal relationships in cyberspace" (p. 5). The Internet has many virtual communities. As a type of symbolic community, a virtual community is not bound by the limits of geography; indeed some virtual communities host participants from around the globe.

This is especially the case when it comes to the activities of fandom on the WWW. Equipped with distance-transcending technology, fans can post fan-oriented publications, or "fanzines," online and carry on conversations about their favorite music groups, television programs, or science fiction franchises. Roger Aden, Christina Beck, and Matthew Smith (1996) examined how fans of the television series *Lois & Clark: The New Adventures of Superman* built and maintained a community online. According to these researchers, fans used the network of relationships to help themselves negotiate their individual identities. Thus, fans can discover people who will confirm their interests and their personalities in these virtual communities whereas they may be unable to locate such people in their geographic communities.

Figure 15.1 Some Commonly Used Emoticons in Online Communication

:-)	;-)	:-(
smile	wink	frown
:-D	:-O	0 :-)
laughing	surprise	angel

Netiquette

Virtual communities, like other communities, have established standards for the regulation of human behavior. Among users the conventions of Internet etiquette, condensed to Netiquette, are communicated to newcomers, or "newbies," in order to socialize them so that their interactions with their fellow users will be more productive and respectful. Victor J. Vitanza (1996) suggests five guiding principles to netiquette.

1. Read some of the exchanges within a particular community before logging on with your first message. Although established contributors to discussion groups often dislike the presence of lurkers, it may be prudent for you to test the waters before jumping into a discussion. Lurkers are people whose presence within a virtual community is undetectable. Even though they receive all the messages posted in a particular discussion, they rarely if ever contribute. In essence, although it is poor netiquette to lurk, prudence is essential before you join a discussion.

2. Avoid flaming. A flame is defined as an online attack of someone. Just as in face-to-face communication, one nasty comment can lead to another and another until an entire conflict, or in this case a flame war, has begun. Common sense dictates that although it is acceptable to criticize ideas, it is socially unacceptable to attack people in public forums. Sometimes, people flame without even realizing it. Because mediated communication filters out a lot of the cues that help us establish tone, what you might consider a witty, humorous remark may be misinterpreted as sarcastic or offensive by the reader. Don't hesitate to apologize to someone if you inadvertently offend him or her.

3. In order to increase the amount of tone you are able to communicate, learn the conventions of your virtual community. One of the ways in which tone can be compensated for textually is through non-alphanumerical symbols called emoticons. Emoticons take advantage of the features on the computer keyboard in order to create sideways pictograms that convey emotional meaning. Thus the combination of a semicolon, hyphen, and a parenthesis gives the appearance of a winking face ;-), which is used to convey a sense of acknowledged humor, sarcasm, or ambiguity. Figure 15.1 illustrates several other emoticons, some of which are merely

---

Figure 15.2 Common Abbreviations Used in Online Communication

AFK	BTW	FAQ
Away From Keyboard	By The Way	Frequently Asked Questions
FWIW	**IMHO**	**LOL**
For What It's Worth	In My Humble Opinion	Laugh Out Loud
RTFM	**RSN**	**WRT**
Read The Freaking Manual	Real Soon Now	With Respect To

---

clever, not necessarily used in great frequency. In addition to emoticons, standards such as using all capital letters to express anger or shouting have emerged. Before you begin typing a message, make sure the caps lock key is not on; otherwise, PEOPLE WILL THINK YOU ARE SHOUTING AT THEM.

4. Be careful of what you disclose on the Internet. Even though we would like to think that what we say to one person will remain between the two of us, there is a chance that your message may be printed out, forwarded, or even hacked into by an outside reader. If you give someone your phone number or reveal a secret you would not want to be made public, you might be surprised to find that an unintended audience has read your message. In short, never say anything on the Internet that you wouldn't want everyone in the network to know.

5. As Shakespeare so succinctly put it, "Brevity is the soul of wit." In other words, keep your messages as short as possible. Convention suggests that users want to read and reply to their messages quickly. One rule of thumb suggests that a message should be no longer than the length of the computer screen. FYI (for your information) you can shorten your messages by using some common abbreviations, which BTW you will find in Figure 15.2.

Future Considerations

Computer-mediated communication (CMC) research continues to explore issues involving the development of personal identity and the role of virtual communities, but the field is open to exploring a number of issues, some of which are limited to the context of computer-mediation and some of which are issues we deal with throughout society. The new technology raises questions about our individual rights to privacy and how free the free flow of information should be. Age-old concerns like gender equality and freedom of expression are concerns that re-present themselves in virtual reality just as they do in physical reality. In addition, CMC raises new questions about how people behave in organizations and how people seek dating relationships in cyberspace. In short, the introduction of CMC has made us look in new ways at how humans interact with one another.

Jim Clark, the president of Netscape, the company that producers a popular program that allows computers to interpret the Web, notes that new media are characterized by three phenomena:

- They have unforeseen consequences.
- They take longer to mature than originally thought.
- They are attacked as something dangerous at first. (Doyle 1996)

Looking at the development of media as diverse as film, television, comic books, and now the Internet, we can see that media grow in ways we never expected, that they reach greatest potential later in their development, and that they are often criticized for their influence on culture. Few people in 1990 thought the Internet would have as profound an impact as it has had on education and business; the majority of people hadn't even heard of it at that time. Likewise, critics have labeled it dangerous and filthy, as vile a medium as has ever been introduced into our society. Of course, we won't know what the potential for the Internet will be yet. However, it helps to track the progress of that growing potential by knowing what research has to say about computers in our lives and being aware of the computer's, and indeed any medium's, influence in our lives.

Mark Poster (1990) suggested that the growth of electronic media is moving our culture from a mode of production to a mode of information. Instead of trading labor for goods—as capitalist societies have for the last several centuries—our economy is shifting so that the mode of exchange is now information. The more information a person has to trade with, the more power and influence that individual possesses. For evidence of Poster's theory just look at the career opportunities available today. Fewer and fewer jobs are involved in production and more and more are involved in controlling the flow of information. There are fewer farmers and steel workers and more accountants and publicists. In fact, blue-collar jobs have declined from 62.5 percent to 43 percent of the U.S. job market (Dutka, 1994). Information seems to be the exchange medium of the future, and students of communication, because they study the concepts that guide the flow of information, are in a particularly strong position as they enter the job market.

Summary

More and more of our interpersonal interactions are being mediated by technology. Of course, media differ in the type of senses they stimulate and thus help shape the messages that pass through them. Communication technologies can be traced back to the invention of writing, an invention that along with the printing press contributed to the Western notion of individuality. Electronic media tend to counter the isolation of individuality, uniting people in common experiences. The emergence of hypertext, or nonsequential writing, has challenged other presuppositions of Western thought, namely linearity, centrality, and hierarchy.

The medium in which many of these reconceptions are being challenged is the Internet. Begun as a communication system for national defense, the Net has expanded into a vast communication network allowing for asynchronous and synchronous electronic mail and the storage and retrieval of data. Scholars have come to refer to the imagined space created by the Internet as cyberspace.

Computer-mediated communication (CMC) studies look at how people are interacting in this new environment. The ability to shape online identities and the emergence of virtual communities are of particular interest to researchers. Virtual communities, like any other we have studied, establish norms for their participants, and the rules of netiquette govern proper behavior in cyberspace. As information becomes a more and more valued commodity, mediated environments for its exchange of information will continue to expand in volume and value and play integral parts in the occupations of the future.

At Your Bookstore

Hauben, M., & Hauben, R. (1997). *Netizens: On the History and Impact of the Usenet and the Internet*. Los Alamitos, CA: IEEE Computer Society Press.

Ludlow, P. (Ed.). (1996). *High Noon on the Electronic Frontier: Conceptual Issues in Cyberspace*. Cambridge, MA: MIT Press.

Marshall, E. L. (1996). *A Student's Guide to the Internet: Exploring the World Wide Web, Gopherspace, Electronic Mail, and More!* Brookfield, CT: Millbrook.

Rodrigues, D. (1997). *The Research Paper and the World Wide Web: A Writer's Guide*. Upper Saddle River, NJ: Prentice Hall.

Turkle, S. (1996). "Parallel Lives: Working on Identity in Virtual Space." In D. Grodin & T. R. Lindlof (Eds.), *Constructing the Self in a Mediated World* (pp. 156-175). Thousand Oaks, CA: Sage.

CHAPTER 16

Understanding
Legal
Communication

> I guess I never even thought about the role that communication plays in the courtroom until the O. J. Simpson trial. Suddenly everyone in the world was glued to the television to see what would happen each day in court. It was like a soap opera that people would tune in to see. As I watched it on television, I wondered how the lawyers for both sides knew what to argue and how to speak in court. I also wondered what the jurors were thinking when all this evidence was given to them. What convinced them to find O. J. not guilty? How did they come to their decision? It was then that I thought it might be interesting to understand how communication is used in the courtroom.
>
> — Danika, second-year college student

The "trial of the century" is how legal analysts, attorneys, and media critics described the 1995 O. J. Simpson criminal trial. As Danika explained, the Simpson trial caught the attention of the world when the former athlete and movie star was charged with the brutal slayings of his estranged wife, Nicole Brown Simpson, and her friend Ronald Goldman. Day after day, the world tuned in to gaze at the judicial melee, which included the likes of prosecutor Marcia Clark, veteran defense attorney F. Lee Bailey, a cast of witnesses, and an array of physical evidence presented to 12 weary jury members. And when it was all over and the verdict was read, more than 150 million Americans—almost 60 percent of the entire population—waited breathlessly for the answer to whether O. J. was guilty of double murder.

Unquestionably, the O. J. Simpson trial attracted public attention unlike that seen in any other trial in recent history. However, while the Simpson trial was a critical incident in judicial history, the public's interest in the law has increased steadily in the past decade. It is impossible to walk into a bookstore today without seeing a number of titles on the bestseller rack written by attorneys, victims, or even jurors of recent trials. Twenty-four hours a day, *Court TV* details trials with in-courtroom cameras and expert commentary. Television shows such as *L.A. Law, Homicide: Life on the Street, High Incident,* and *Law and Order* appear weekly on television. Riveting trials such as those involving Rodney King, Lyle and Erik Menendez, O. J. Simpson, and Timothy McVeigh have catapulted courtroom proceedings into our living rooms. And even the judge's decision to reduce the charges in the 1997 child murder case of British au pair Louise Woodward was first posted on the Internet!

Moving courtroom trials from the private to the public sphere has resulted in an increased interest in courtroom dynamics. Communication is at the heart of what occurs in the courtroom; consequently, the study of legal communication has become increasingly popular. Because of the invasion of legal processes and trials into people's everyday lives, the authors thought it was important to introduce you to some of the principles of communication in the courtroom so that you could be a better consumer of information that is presented to you about contemporary trials. As S. Macaulay points out, "The familiar images shown again and again on film and television . . . teach and reinforce what most people know about things legal. And these ideas and attitudes matter" (1986, p. 31).

In this chapter, we will look at why communication is an important part of the trial process using concepts that you're already familiar with from other chapters.

- We begin by looking at the historical foundations of legal communication from the ancient Greeks and Romans through more modern applications of the law.
- Then we will discuss the formation of impressions, language, and storytelling to give you a better understanding of legal communication and its applications.

The Foundations of Legal Communication

From the Ancients to *L.A. Law*

As we explained in previous chapters, the earliest study of communication began in ancient Greek and Roman societies. It is here that the foundations of studying communication and law began as well. As members of an oral society by nature, the Greeks believed it was necessary to be a good speaker, not only for purposes of entertainment and ceremony but also to protect yourself if you were called to defend your innocence in court. Imagine if you were accused of a crime. Could you defend yourself in today's court system? Most of us would never even consider defending ourselves in court and would immediately find a lawyer to represent us. If you had lived in ancient Greece, that would not be the case. In Athens, importance was placed on forensic rhetoric, or speaking in the courts of law to defend yourself against accusations by others. For example, the earliest written text on Western rhetoric was created in the early fifth century B.C. by Corax, a Greek philosopher. So what was the topic of this earliest written work? Quite simply, it was a guide for speaking in court, designed to help people plead their cases in a court of law.

Other Greek philosophers stressed the importance of being able to persuade others, to argue your innocence in court. For example, Aristotle outlined the canons of rhetoric that would serve as the origins of forensic speaking. These canons focused on building good arguments, using language persuasively, delivering the argument effectively, and understanding the composition of the audience. In his work *The Rhetoric*, considered one of the most significant and influential books in the history of Western thought, Aristotle spends a great deal of time explaining the use of forensic rhetoric in the courts.

Although their Greek counterparts may have developed forensic rhetoric, the Roman philosophers Cicero and Quintilian perfected it. Cicero, in particular, adapted forensic rhetoric into legal advocacy and allowed himself to be hired to plead as an advocate in court. According to legal communication researcher Ronald Matlon (1993), an advocate is "someone who espouses a cause through argument" (p. 1). Cicero's adaptation of Quintilian's principles allowed him to become a masterful advocate in the courts. Indeed, Cicero was known as a particularly skilled speaker who could use emotional appeals to move a jury to tears. Often he was called upon to close the trial because of his reputation for using emotion. According to Cicero, it wasn't enough merely to instruct a jury, the speaker or advocate had to inflame them!

❖ ❖ ❖ ❖

MISSION: POSSIBLE

The role of "advocate" is one that has become quite common in our society, and the concept has extended beyond courtroom use. Think of an instance in which you had to be an advocate for some issue, event, or principle. What were you advocating? For example, did you lobby your college or university Board of Trustees for more technology in classrooms? Did you talk to high school students to convince them to avoid drinking during the prom? Or did you lead a campaign to create more job opportunities for inner city youth? Once you have identified a time when you were in the advocate role, think about the means you used to persuade or argue your case. Were you arguing from emotion, like Cicero, or sticking only to the facts? How successful were you as an advocate and what would you do differently next time?

The legal process can seem intimidating to people
who are unfamiliar with the language of the law.

While interest in and study of forensic rhetoric continued to be important into the twentieth century, it wasn't until the 1960s that researchers from the sociology, psychology, and communication fields began to look more closely at courtroom dynamics. They began talking about and researching issues of courtroom procedures, jury deliberation, attorney performance, and legal reasoning. In many high-publicity cases, experts in these areas were hired to consult on everything from preparing a winning case strategy to interrogating witnesses. In particular, communication consultants were hired to assist attorneys and clients in using more effective communication in the courtroom. To meet this demand, the American Society of Trial Consultants (ASTC) was formed in 1983. ASTC is made up of hundreds of individual consultants and consulting firms from around the United States, many of whom

---

MISSION: POSSIBLE

It's likely that you will sign dozens of "contracts" in your life. These contracts, whether to rent an apartment or secure a student loan, bind you to certain actions or commitments. Take, for example, the paragraph from a standard leasing contract for an apartment:

> All alterations, additions, or improvements upon the demised premises, made by either party shall become the property of this Rental Agreement. Any mechanic's lien filed against the demised premises, or the building, of which the same form a part, for work claimed to have been done for, or materials claimed to have been furnished to the tenant shall be discharged by the tenant within 10 days thereafter at the tenant's expense, by filing the bond required by law.

> *After reading this passage, try to summarize the important part of this section of the contract in one sentence. The legal definition of "demised" and "lien" may be found in the dictionary. Also, if you were signing a leasing contract like the one above, whom could you turn to for legal advice in your community? Investigate any free legal services for students or community mediation centers that could be helpful to you in the future.*

---

specialize in the study of legal communication and have worked in such recent high-profile cases as the Menendez and the Simpson trials.

For the majority of people, however, the legal process is still a relatively confusing and mysterious part of life. You might think that understanding the legal process is unnecessary as long as you stay out of trouble. But the legal process is part of your life whether you are arrested for protesting the cutting of trees in a National Forest, are sued by a neighbor, or have signed a contract for buying a house. Not understanding basic principles of the law and not seeking appropriate legal advice can be devastating in whatever situation you are in. Taking a class in legal communication, law, or political science can help you become more knowledgeable about the legal process.

A primary reason that being arrested, arguing over a contract, or being called to testify as a witness are such nerve-wracking experiences is that the legal system is filled with jargon that the average person doesn't easily understand. In his song, "Jump Up," singer Elton John expresses frustration with not understanding a divorce proceeding, saying, "I do not speak their language/And they hold all the cards." As this song indicates, attorneys and judges are seen as speaking an entirely different language from the rest of us. However, television, radio, newspapers, and magazines have gone a long way in helping people understand more about the legal process. In the following sections, we decipher some of the terms and procedures common in communication and the law.

Modern Trial Procedures

The effect thinkers in the ancient world had on the trial process is evident in our contemporary courtrooms. Cicero was particularly influential in how trials were conducted centuries ago and today we still follow his basic pattern of trial procedure:

- *Exordium.*
- *Narratio.*

- *Confirmatio.*
- *Refutatio.*
- *Peroration.*

First, Cicero argued that a trial must first have an opening section (*exordium*), which would introduce to the jury the issues and participants in the trial. In the exordium, the jury is assigned to the case through a jury selection process called *voir dire*, meaning to speak or say the truth. In *voir dire*, the attorneys try to gauge the attitudes, values, and beliefs of each potential juror through a question-and-answer period. This is the only time when attorneys engage in a personal conversation with the jurors. *Voir dire* is a process of selecting jurors by exclusion. Attorneys do not decide who is on the jury; rather they challenge who should *not* be on the jury because a bias or prejudice might prevent those potential jurors from overseeing the case fairly. Although attorneys do not actually determine who will be on the jury, they do hope to seat a jury that will be favorable to their client.

There are three communication goals involved in the *voir dire* process. Since *voir dire* is the only time the attorneys can interpersonally interact with the jurors, this is a time for very strategic communication. First, *voir dire* is a time for establishing rapport with the jurors. Attorneys who can establish rapport may be viewed as more likable and trustworthy by potential jurors. Studies show that humor is often used by attorneys to communicate a willingness to get to know jurors, thereby relaxing them and creating a favorable impression. Second, in establishing this rapport, the attorney can also use this time for previewing the case. Nothing prevents attorneys from presenting bits of strategic information about the case and the client during the *voir dire* process.

The third communication goal of *voir dire* involves obtaining commitments. A great deal of research suggests if people verbally make commitments in public, they are more likely to keep those commitments. Imagine an attorney engaging in the following discussion with a potential juror:

> Attorney: "You stated earlier that you thought the judicial system should be fair to everyone. Is that correct?"
>
> Potential juror: "Yes, that's true."
>
> Attorney: "You understand that the victim in this case is a child who was burned while wearing pajamas manufactured by my client's company."
>
> Potential juror: "Yes, I've been told that."
>
> Attorney: "Now, this trial will involve a great deal of evidence and expert testimony from both sides in the case. Do you think you can suspend making any judgments about my client until all the information has been presented?"
>
> Potential juror: "I think I can do that."
>
> Attorney: "So, you can agree to hear the evidence without making an unfair judgment against my client just because the person involved here is a young person?"
>
> Potential juror: "Yes, I can."
>
> Attorney: "Thank you for this commitment to upholding justice, and I expect that you'll hold to that promise throughout the trial."

Juries are considered one of the most important small groups in society because of the decisions they must make regarding criminal and civil matters.

By securing the juror's belief in fairness, the defense attorney in this case has gained a public commitment that the juror may feel it difficult to break later on. Communicating statements in public increases the likelihood that a juror will remain open-minded throughout the trial. That juror may even be the one juror who argues for the defense during jury deliberation.

Also important to the trial process is the statement of the case (*narratio*), also known as the opening statement. Although the opening statement will be described in more depth later in this chapter, it is the first real attempt by the attorneys to present the outlines of their cases. The importance of the opening statement cannot be overlooked by attorneys or trial watchers. Cicero believed that being unclear in telling this opening story could cast a negative shadow over the entire case.

In its simplest form, a trial is a setting where a group of people or a judge is asked to decide between two advocates presenting differing stories.

Based on Cicero's pattern, contemporary trials move next to a process where the prosecution and defense advocate their cases (*confirmatio* and *refutatio*). In *confirmatio*, the prosecution presents evidence, witnesses, and material against the accused. The *refutatio* is the defense's response to those arguments and the defense's own counter-arguments to the prosecution. Together the *confirmatio* and *refutatio* make up the bulk of the trial process because each side must present witnesses, evidence, and experts to support the story that was told in the opening statement. In the Simpson trial, both stages were exceptionally complex and drawn out over a period of months. For example, the Simpson defense team compiled a potential witness list of 59 witnesses for their *refutatio*, from DNA experts to a flight attendant who served Simpson on a flight to Chicago immediately after the murders. Given the prosecution's extensive list, combined with that of the defense, it's no wonder the "trial of the century" took what seemed like a century to complete.

The last communication efforts made by both the prosecution and defense occur during the peroration of the trial. What are the last words the jury will hear before going to the jury room? Whatever words the jury members hear, they should work to support the story presented in the opening statement. Many consider the closing argument to be the last great attempt to persuade the jury, to turn them to one side or the other. Research studies show that jurors believe the closing argument is more important and persuasive than other parts of the trial, including the opening statement (Tarter-Hilgendorf, 1986). Not only is the closing argument the last words the jury hears, it is the attorneys' last chance to tie together all the loose strings of the story, to draw to a close all the arguments that have been presented. In particularly complex and lengthy cases like the Simpson trial, the closing argument is the final opportunity to highlight what is important for the jurors to remember and what isn't.

Forming Impressions in the Courtroom

Perception in Action

In Chapter 5, we discussed the concept of perception and how communication affects what we perceive. For example, if you and your friend witness a car wreck, even from the same geographic location, it is likely that you both will have a slightly different story of how the wreck occurred. You might describe the wreck as a miscalculation: one driver forgot to signal for a left turn, and then left the scene, not realizing that an accident had occurred. Your friend might explain the very same accident as a horrible hit-and-run collision caused by an obviously drunken driver. Clearly, the witnesses have painted two very different pictures of the intent of the car driver. How could two people witnessing the same accident describe it so differently? Because of perception, we see the world in slightly different ways, based on our attitudes, values, beliefs, life experiences, and communication skills. These variations of human perception can also be expected in the courtroom.

In the courtroom, attorneys and communication consultants work together as a team to understand the link between perception and communication. Most important, they try to understand how jurors might perceive information that is presented to them. Jurors' perceptions differ from person to person. Attorneys and consultants can't assume that all people will respond the same way to the same person or the same piece of information. For this reason, researchers Lawrence Smith and Loretta Malandro (1985) explain that the attorney/consultant team must ask the following questions regarding each and every case:

1. What is already in the minds of the jurors and judge?
2. What will the opposing counsel put in their minds?
3. What perceptions do you want the jurors and judge to have?

Without answering these questions, the attorney and consulting team cannot begin to prepare how to argue a case. The team must first translate the case into the jurors' mind. How do they do this? During *voir dire*, the jurors communicate what they already believe and feel through discussions with the attorneys. The consulting team can also expect the opposing attorney to use communication to present facts and arguments against the team's client. And communication is the primary way in which the team can create desired perceptions in the jurors and judge during the trial. In this way, communication is important in influencing perceptions in every part of the trial process.

The perceptions that jurors have before even entering the courtroom can have dramatic effects on the trial process. For example, attorneys in every case are placed under a spotlight. This spotlight, however, does not always cast a positive shadow. Just think of all the "lawyer" jokes that you've ever heard or the disparaging comments that you've heard your parents or friends make about lawyers. Even centuries ago, Shakespeare wrote the line "The first thing we do, let's kill all the lawyers" into his play *Henry VI*. Not surprisingly, this long history of lawyer-bashing has resulted in the average person viewing attorneys with distrust and contempt. The mass media have certainly contributed to this perception. Research has shown that because of dramas such as *L.A. Law* and movies such as *The Firm*, we tend to perceive attorneys as power-hungry, greedy, and selfish—we rate them less favorably than any other profession, except stockbrokers and politicians. You can see how attorneys must work against the preexisting perceptions that jurors have about them even before the case begins.

It is also necessary for each counsel to think about what the other counsel will introduce to the jurors. What perceptions will the opposing counsel try to instill in their minds? When attorneys do not anticipate the messages that the opposing counsel will send to jurors, the impact on their case can be devastating. Even in what seem like open-and-shut cases, the perceptions that jurors form in the courtroom may be unexpected and dramatic. For example, the 1992 trial of four Los Angeles police officers accused of brutal treatment of motorist Rodney King demonstrates how communication affects perception. The four officers were brought up on assault charges for delivering 60 blows with metal batons to the body of King, whom they were attempting to arrest on the side of the road.

A citizen armed with a Sony Handycam filmed 81 seconds of the Rodney King incident. This piece of footage proved to have significant impact on the perceptions of jurors, but not in the way that most people thought it should. Strategically, the defense shifted the meaning of the videotape by encouraging the jurors to view the tape in a way that exonerated the officers. The defense attorneys broke down the video frame by frame in slow motion, and they used expert testimony to explain and justify the actions the officers took that day. In slow motion, the beating didn't seem quite so violent and the emotional content of the video was reduced. As you may remember, the jury announced a not-guilty verdict and Los Angeles erupted in such antagonistic riots that 10,000 buildings were destroyed, one billion dollars in damages accrued, 10,000 people were arrested, and 50 people were killed (Gerland, 1994). Did the perceptions that the defense counsel cultivated influence the jurors in this case? Obviously they did.

Forming Impressions Through Communication Cues

The impact that perception has in the courtroom and in the minds of jurors is evident in this dramatic example. The attorneys and witnesses in the Rodney King case were able to use verbal and nonverbal cues to put forth impressions

❖ ❖ ❖ ❖

Figure 16.1 Examples of Powerless Language

Type	Language Examples	
Hedges	"I think"	"I guess"
Hesitations	"Uh"	"Well"
Overpoliteness	"Yes, ma'am"	"Please, sir"
Tag lines	"Okay?"	"All right?"

that would benefit the defense. Verbal and nonverbal cues can impact the trial process in other ways as well. Imagine again that you are that juror in the courtroom. The verbal and nonverbal cues that the attorneys, defendant, witnesses, and judge display have communicative potential for you. You arrange, understand, and make sense of the case based on the verbal and nonverbal cues that you receive from these players in the trial game.

For example, you may form impressions about an attorney, witness, or defendant based on whether that individual uses powerless language or powerful language. In Chapter 2, we introduced the concept of power in language. Because of socialization experiences, powerless language—indirect and humble in tone—is most likely to be used by women and the poor (see Figure 16.1). The use of powerful language by courtroom participants can have a great impact on the impression that you form of those individuals. In several research studies, straightforward, powerful language resulted in jurors perceiving the speaker as being more credible, more persuasive, and more likable than a person who used powerless language in speaking.

If you were a juror, you might also form impressions about courtroom participants based on the vividness of their language. People use vivid language to create a desired picture of an event, idea, or incident. Vivid language is that which is concrete, image provoking, emotionally interesting, and personally relevant. What is the difference between a car involved in a "fender-bender" and a car involved in a "collision which ripped apart pieces of the vehicle"? There may not be an actual difference if we were to view the two vehicles, but the language used to describe these accidents paints very different portraits of the event. Descriptive language creates a desired impression in your mind if you are a juror. This is particularly true if you are listening to witnesses' testimony. We tend to believe witnesses who use vivid language, this tendency is based on the belief (although this is questionable) that the more someone is able to describe the details of an event or person, the more likely it is that the witness is accurate.

Just as verbal cues can influence the formation of an impression in the courtroom, so too do nonverbal cues. As discussed in an earlier chapter, nonverbal communication can be more powerful and more believed than verbal cues. If you, as a juror, are confused by the verbal message that an attorney or witness is sending, you may rely on nonverbal cues to interpret the information.

Attorney F. Lee Bailey, who served on the O. J. Simpson defense team, was very aware of the impact of clothing on impression formation when he defended Patty Hearst, the granddaughter of the newspaper tycoon William Randolph Hearst in the 1970s. Patty Hearst was kidnapped in 1974 by a militant group named the Symbionese Liberation Army. Although the kidnappers beat and tortured Hearst while awaiting ransom, a few weeks after her kidnapping she renounced her family, joined the group, and even participated in a bank robbery with them.

When she was brought to trial for the burglary, Bailey consciously controlled the nonverbal cues that the jurors would see by portraying Hearst as a victim who was "brainwashed" by her captors. What does a victim look like? When Hearst entered the courtroom, reporters explained that she was dressed in a coat two sizes too big and an oversized dress that hung off her rail-thin body. Her long hair hung in strings, appearing almost deliberately dirty and unkempt. This example provides a poignant example of how nonverbal communication, such as clothing, can affect impression formation.

Contemporary Applications of Research: Storytelling in the Courtroom

Storytelling, or narrative, is one of the most basic modes of communication that human beings have. Our Stone Age ancestors probably progressed from scratching out stories of everyday life on cave walls through pictures to expressing the actions in story form. According to W. R. Fisher (1985), all human communication is accomplished through the use of stories constructed and performed with others. Nowhere is this more evident than in the

---

Spotlight on Ethics

In the minds of many trial consultants and attorneys, clothing or dress has great communicative potential. Our clothes, jewelry, and possessions speak volumes about us. Clothing is strategically used by trial participants to create a desired image. For example, in the 1994 murder trial of Lyle and Erik Menendez, image consultants helped dress the defendants in clothing that would create an impression that they were gentle young men who had killed their parents because of some past abuse. Throughout the trial, the brothers often appeared in court dressed in stylish pastel yellow or pink sweaters, no doubt to soften their image as brutal killers. Does using clothing to project a certain impression in the courtroom ever become unethical?

What do you think?

1. *Is this unethical or just strategic in acknowledging the effect that impressions have on jurors by the attorney?*
2. *How was clothing used to create a certain impression in other trials you know of?*

---

courtroom. As R. D. Rieke and R. K. Stutman (1990) remark, "After all, what is a trial? It is two parties, each telling its story and asking society to endorse its version of reality" (p. 48). The use of storytelling as a communication event reduces language and argument to the level of the average juror.

Stories help jurors understand the case at hand but do not necessarily help them make just decisions. Research suggests that jurors often overlook rules and evidence in the courtroom in favor of a good story. As A. B. Pettus remarks, "The clear and well-told story is considered effective evidence, whereas the unclear, nonsensical story is considered ineffective evidence" (1990, p. 92). Such findings suggest that a "good" story with poor evidence is superior to a "poor" story with good evidence.

Bennett's Model

In the 1970s, W. Lance Bennett tried to understand better how storytelling was used in the courtroom. After studying more than 100 trials, he found that story structures were an important part of criminal trials. Why, asked Bennett, are jurors able to process weeks and weeks of disjointed and often contradictory information during a trial? Since childhood, you have been encouraged to explain situations in the form of a story, or your "side" of the event. If your parent interrupted a fight between you and your sibling, the first question would probably be, "Tell me what's going on here." Then, each of you would launch into your "sides" of what happened, complete with a beginning, a middle, and a conclusion, filled with enough details to represent your side of the story. Because jurors use stories to communicate in their own lives, storytelling in the courtroom helps jurors process information and make complex judgments.

Although storytelling is important for communicating information in all phases of the trial, perhaps it is most necessary in the summation, or closing argument. This is particularly true in very lengthy trials that involve months and months of expert testimony and dozens of witnesses. Both the prosecution and defense must use storytelling to create a concise picture in the jury's eyes.

M. K. Gibson (1994) studied the use of storytelling in the case of an officer charged with police brutality. On November 5, 1992, police officers Walter Budzyn, Larry Nevers, and Robert Lessnau were on their regular beat in a Detroit, Michigan, neighborhood known for drug dealing. Budzyn and Nevers approached a car driven by Malice Green with a passenger, Ralph Fletcher, outside a suspected crack house. Budzyn and Nevers asked Green to produce his driver's license. Green refused and bent over the seat with his fist clenched. Fearing that the suspect was concealing weapons or drugs, the officers struggled with Green and used their two-pound flashlights to beat him on the face, head, and legs to subdue him. At least 14 blows were directed to Green's head. After the struggle, Green was rushed to a local hospital, where he died. The item he concealed in his hand was a set of keys. Green was found to have significant levels of alcohol and cocaine in his system at the time of death. While Officer Lessnau was charged with assault, Officers Budzyn and Nevers were charged with the second-degree murder of Malice Green.

Let's look at how Gibson saw storytelling used in the closing argument of the defense's side of this case. Attorney John Goldpaugh was challenged with presenting a story of the events that acquitted Officer Larry Nevers of criminal wrongdoing. Intertwining testimony that the blows inflicted on Green were severe enough to sever parts of the victim's scalp, the prosecution had presented their closing argument story by describing how the death of Malice Green was the result of a vicious, power-hungry cop. Goldpaugh had to reconcile the prosecution's "story" of the death by persuading jurors that the actions taken by Nevers were "just," given the situation, that they didn't arise from a willingness to injure Green.

According to Bennett's model, storytelling functions by identifying the central action of the event. For example, Goldpaugh developed the central action of the case by setting up the struggle as one of self-defense on the part of the officers involved. Goldpaugh remarked, "And I suggest to you that because Officer Nevers tells us, as do other witnesses, that there is a struggle, that in Officer Nevers' mind, in Officer Nevers' heart, there is a life-and-death struggle. The man had his hand on Officer Nevers' gun." Here, Goldpaugh argued that the death of Malice Green was the result of Officer Nevers defending himself in a life-and-death struggle.

After the central action of the story has been identified, Bennett suggests that jurors go through a process of interpreting the central action by drawing inferences around the action. One storytelling strategy that Goldpaugh used was to appeal to the common sense of the jurors, hoping that they would infer that the officers had been just in their actions. Goldpaugh attacked the intentions of Green in keeping his fist clenched, arguing that common sense suggests that if Green did not have a weapon or drugs in his possession, why wasn't he just opening his hand? Appealing to the jurors' reliance on logic and experience, Goldpaugh directed the story to the jurors by saying, "You know there was something there. If nothing else, why wasn't Mr. Green opening his hand? I'm not blaming Mr. Green, but when you get back to common sense, you're hearing these people say this. Why wasn't he at least opening his hand?" In this way, the attorney encouraged the listeners to interpret the actions of Officer Nevers in relation to the questionable actions of Green.

　Bennett's final function of the storytelling model occurs when jurors start evaluating the interpretation of the case by testing the completeness and consistency of the story. In the Malice Green case, the defense attorney encouraged the jurors to test the completeness of the opposing story. In the closing argument, attorney Goldpaugh examined a string of contradictory testimony offered by the prosecution's witnesses. Then Goldpaugh remarked, "Whole lot of different versions there, aren't there? Got to raise some doubt in your mind, doesn't it? Sure raises a lot of doubts in my mind, members of the jury, regarding the credibility of those witnesses, all of them." In this manner, Goldpaugh encouraged the jurors to question the consistency of the prosecution's story and find for the defense account of the event. Unfortunately, attorney Goldpaugh's account wasn't enough to convince the jurors. Officer Nevers was convicted of second-degree murder and sentenced to a 12- to 25-year sentence although he issued a number of ongoing appeals in the years following the original trial.

　As this case suggests, storytelling is a primary way of communicating in the courtroom. Both the prosecution and defense use stories to communicate at the most fundamental level of understanding for jurors. Witnesses, too, use stories to explain their side. Think about a live trial that you've seen on *Court TV* or one depicted on a television show or movie. When an attorney asks a witness to explain what happened, the witness is expected to tell his or her story from beginning to end, complete with necessary details. Stories that seem incomplete or inconsistent are held up for evaluation by the jury. As you can see, communication in the courtroom depends on crafting a good story of the events.

Summary

As the legal system becomes more and more familiar to us, in part by invading our lives through the mass media, it is necessary to understand the trial process and how communication functions in this process. From signing a contract to serving on a jury, understanding the legal process is important in an increasingly litigious society where legal suits are readily brought. This chapter has served to introduce you, as a reader, to a few important concepts and issues in legal communication.

The foundations of our contemporary judicial system lie with the ancient Greeks and Romans. To them, being able to defend oneself, or to be one's own advocate in a court of law, was of the utmost importance. Today, it would be hard to imagine defending yourself in such situations, but you probably act as an advocate to some issue, principle, or idea on a daily basis. Just as it was thousands of years ago, contemporary trials follow a similar pattern of procedure: *exordium*, *narratio*, *confirmatio*, *refutatio*, and *peroration*. In each stage, communication functions in very different ways. For example, the *exordium*, or *voir dire* stage is a time for an attorney to establish rapport, preview the case, and obtain commitments from the jurors, whereas the *peroration*, or closing argument, is a time for weaving a concise story of the case.

Understanding the dynamics of legal communication entails having a working knowledge of impression formation, storytelling, and decision-making processes. Impressions are formed in the courtroom through communication, including the degree to which the language of trial participants is (1) vivid and (2) powerful or powerless. Storytelling is perhaps the basis of all communication in trial proceedings. Bennett's model of storytelling demonstrates how jurors search for a central action in the trial, interpret the action based on inferences, and evaluate that interpretation for completeness and consistency.

At Your Bookstore

Abramson, J. (1994). *We, the Jury. The Jury System and the Ideal of Democracy.* New York: BasicBooks.

Adler, S. J. (1994). *The Jury: Trial and Error in the American Courtroom.* New York: Times Books.

Knox, M., & Walker, M. (1995). *The Private Diary of an O. J. Juror: Behind the Scenes of the Trial of the Century.* Beverly Hills, CA: Dove Audio.

Thornton, H. (1995). *Hung Jury: The Diary of a Menendez Juror.* Philadelphia, PA: Temple University Press.

CHAPTER 17

Using Communication Principles on the Job

In order to get a job in a day-care center for the summer, I had to go through an interviewing process. The center I applied to was very selective in hiring new employees because they thought it was extremely important for the person to know how to handle different situations. The interviewing process took only about a half hour with questions like, "What would you do in this situation?" I had to be very prepared and answer the questions thoroughly. I must have gotten my points across because she called me the next day with the news that I had been hired. Throughout the summer I found that I really enjoyed working with children, and I would like a career in the field of education. If I hadn't prepared for the interview and hadn't gotten my points across to the director, I still would be undecided about my future. Communication helped me get the job that helped me decide what I was going to do with the rest of my life.

— Jennifer, first-year college student

As Jennifer learned, communication plays a critical role in getting a job. Other examples in this chapter will illustrate how important communication is to keeping the job and being successful at it. Open up any major newspaper and look carefully at the help wanted ads. The job titles are as varied as the companies in which they exist. In fact, you often cannot tell exactly what the job will be like from reading the job title. You have to read the ad carefully to uncover the skills necessary to do the job. More frequently than not, the ad will say something like the following:

- "Must have strong interpersonal communication skills."
- "Writing and oral skills are a must."
- "Must be able to interact with customers effectively."
- "Good communications skills are needed."

These ads are not talking about technical communication skills, such as knowing how to install phone systems or network computers. They are talking about *human* communication skills, the kinds of skills you have been learning about in this book.

Whatever your career choice, your job will require that you give and receive instructions and that those instructions are understood so that tasks can be accomplished. Whatever work you do, you will form new friendships and collegial relationships among your peers, while maintaining a complicated network of relationships in your personal life that includes family members, friends, neighbors, and acquaintances. Your success at work, like your satisfaction with your personal life, will depend on your interpersonal communication skills. Let's talk about:

- The skills we have covered in this book
- How those skills would be used in situations in which you may find yourself.

Communication Skills on the Job

Your boss tells you one morning that she needs you to work overtime on Saturday because she's shorthanded on that day. You have already made plans with friends to be out of town. Take a look at the various conflict management techniques discussed in Chapter 11. You could use a *competing* style of conflict resolution in which you feel your needs or goals should be met at all costs: You refuse to work on Saturday. Or you could *avoid* the conflict by simply changing your plans. Or you could try one of the other types of conflict resolution strategies discussed in Chapter 11 such as *compromise, collaborating,* or *accommodating.* Then reflect further on what we said in that chapter about steps to resolving conflict, including *disengaging, empathizing,* and *depersonalizing* and see if any of these steps help you come up with a reasonable solution.

Your best friend says, "Why don't you ever listen to me? I'm really in trouble and I need your help." Refer back to Chapter 4 on listening. Look again at the steps of active listening: getting ready physically and psychologically, attending to feelings first and then to content, using a listening vocabulary, listening with intensity, and suggesting follow up. If you apply these steps in order to help your friend, you will find that you are a much better friend.

You are asked to chair a committee to bring in a band for the annual spring bash. What was suggested in Chapter 7 about the phases of group development that will help you know what to expect when working with this group? You will know that the group is likely to go through a conflict stage before they really begin to solve problems. You might try using a brainstorming session to help get them started.

The concepts discussed in each one of the chapters in this book can be applied to daily problems and communication events. The authors hope you will return to these suggestions and tips not only when you are on the job but in your daily interactions with others.

Communication-related Careers

Four major areas for jobs in the twenty-first century are in the following areas:

- Technology.
- Information distribution.
- General management.
- Salesmanship.

In each of these broad categories, competent communicators will find a welcome home.

Technology and Communication

The introduction of high technology into the workplace has profoundly changed the way people communicate on a daily basis. Instead of playing phone tag, individuals now leave voice mail messages to be listened to at the receiver's leisure. E-mail messages have replaced memos, and computers have become substitutes for personal interactions with secretaries. So, doesn't this just make us more efficient? Sometimes it has also made us less effective communicators. There is a need for communication specialists to help organizations understand and respond to the negative consequences of the introduction of high technology into human communication systems.

Careers that focus on the interface between technologies and human interaction are ideal for communication specialists. You don't have to be a computer programmer to understand how technology changes the content and impact of the message. Our intentions may be quite different from the impact of our words or method of communicating. If we don't understand the difference between intent and impact we will be less effective communicators, and perhaps cause great frustration and damage to relationships. An employee who understands what subtle messages are sent nonverbally, who fully appreciates the importance of trust to relationships, and who is sensitive to the messages we send by our choice of channel, can help organizational members integrate technology in a way that will enhance the communication environment, not destroy it.

Currently, recruiters are looking for employees who have applied computer skills as well as strong human communication skills. The combination of these two fields will make college graduates quite marketable.

The Information Age and Communication Skills

For the past 25 years, we have been experiencing a new shift from a mass production society to an information society. Much more work is associated with the distribution of information than ever before. Careers that focus on information management will be in the forefront of business and industry in the years to come. These careers go beyond what you might typically think of as public relations and include providing information to both the public and employees about corporate mergers, employee benefits, corporate change, and enhancing overall corporate structure. Individuals who can successfully manage information in a way that allows employees to understand up-to-the-minute data about the direction their corporation is heading will become very valuable members of the leadership in that corporation.

A sensitivity to interpersonal relationships is critical to understanding why some employees understand information and follow directions, and others do not. Doctors, for example, have wondered for years why patients don't comply with their instructions. Much of it has to do with the trust patients have in their doctors and how comfortable they feel with that physician and the directions that he or she has given them. Factors such as trust affect the amount of information understood and followed in all careers.

Management and Communication

The higher in the organization you find yourself, the more time you are likely to spend managing others rather than performing the tasks of the organization. Communication skills are essential to management. Getting the job done through the work of others requires coordinating people and tasks and making a good match between the person, the skill level, and the task that needs to be done.

Communication specialists make excellent managers. They understand the decision-making process, the basis for interpersonal trust, how to interpret verbal and nonverbal cues, and they practice good listening habits. All of these are characteristics that employees say they want in their supervisors.

Salesmanship and Communication

"I didn't go to college to be a salesman!" The fact is, no matter what students study in college, 60 to 70 percent of them will end up in sales positions as entry-level jobs. You don't start out as a mid-level manager. You don't begin by being the head of a human resource department. Most organizations want their new employees to understand their product or service from the ground up. They believe people make better managers if they thoroughly understand what the people they are supervising are doing. No matter how much education someone may have, beginning with the product is a must.

What skills do people in sales need? A knowledge of persuasive techniques, how to build rapport with the customer, good listening habits, and being articulate about the product and the company are all critical to successful selling and are communication skills.

So, are you wondering about the type of job titles communication majors might have? The following table (17.1) contains a list of actual job titles held by alumni from a program in organizational communication. These titles represent alumni who have graduated in the last 5 to 20 years. The list is divided into jobs held by graduates who have been out 5, 10, and 15-plus years so you can see what types of jobs recent graduates have acquired compared to those who have been out for some time and have advanced in the organization in which they work. After you take a look at where you might be heading, we'll take the first step toward it—the interview process.

Table 17.1 Jobs Held by Communication Majors

5 years out	*10 years out*	*15+ years out*
Marketing Coordinator for World Bank	Housing Rehab Specialist Gallia/Meigs Community Action Agency	Professor of Communications St. Cloud University
Government Relations Representative, National Utility Contractor Assn.	Sales Associate (Spell) Battel Corporation	President/Owner Hamilton Communications Consulting
Assistant Director of Corporate Communications International Murex	Assistant Director of Admissions Thomas Moore College	Project Director Financial Data Applications Georgia Tech University
Income Maintenance Caseworker Dept of Social Services	Assistant Director of Communication Loyola College	Employee Assistance Counselor & Consultant MedCo Behavioralist Health Center

(continued)

Table 17.1 *Continued*

5 years out	10 years out	15+ years out
Marketing Coordinator Unicom Thermal	Conference Manager Banister & Associates	Personnel Consultant Marvel Consultants, Inc.
Technologies Assistant Deputy of GSA State of Ohio	Attorney—Martin, Purgman & Browning	President Florinex Group North America
Manager of Human Resources GE Capital Financial Services	Personnel Coordinator Charles County Association Handicapped and Retarded Citizens	Vice President Ameritech
Special Events Manager Georgia Lottery Corporation	Management Candidate Peoples Banking Trust Co.	Sales, Regional Manager Metabo Corporation
Graduate Student College Student Personnel	Office Manager Dr. John Strauss	Marketing Consultant Marketing & Public Relations
Manager Elder-Bierman Stores	Assistant Manager Rack's Corporation	Speaker and Trainer Image Plus
Assistant Director Grad School of Management Kent State University	Legislative Aide Ohio House of Rep.	Attorney Gardner, Carlton & Douglas
Academic Adviser University of South Carolina	Assistant Vice President Southeast Bank	Associate Dean Western Carolina University
	Sales Representative Johnson & Johnson	Regional Vice President Campbell & Company
		Journalist Baylor College of Medicine
		Program Specialist Texas Dept. of Public Safety
		Executive Director United Way
		Marketing Representative PYA-Monarch

The Job Interview

Your palms are damp, you feel hot, you've suddenly forgotten everything you learned about this organization, and the person ahead of you sounds as if he's having a great time laughing with the interviewer. You are about to have your first job interview.

"So, why are you interested in our company?" (You're thinking: I just want a job!) These are the typical reactions of people entering their first job interview. Instead, you must focus on how to demonstrate during the interview the skills you have acquired.

How do communication specialists reveal their special skills during the job interview? After all, anyone can say she is a good listener who "likes to work with people." You reveal your skill in the *way* in which you answer the questions. Instead of giving vague, general answers, you supply specific examples of your communication skills in action. Compare these two answers to a job interview question and see which one you find more direct and responsive to the question:

Interviewer: "Tell me about your previous job experience."

Poor Response: "Well, I've had some summer jobs and picked up a few hours during the school year doing odd jobs around campus. These were mostly waiting on tables and answering phones and doing sort of office work."

Better response: "I have paid for 50 percent of my college expenses by working each summer between school years and holding a part-time work-study job on campus during the school year. Being a waitress and office worker has taught me skills like how to handle customers who have complaints by being clear and firm and acting immediately on what they asked. My work-study job taught me how to deal with people in an office when they are short of time and need something done immediately. These are often stressful situations and I found that if I remained calm and continued to provide information to the person who was stressed, I was much more successful."

The second response not only tells the interviewer what the jobs were but in addition describes some of the skills acquired as a result of holding each job. This is really what the interviewer wants to know: What did you learn from these previous jobs that you will be able to apply to a new situation. The person who gets the job is the one who can identify specific examples of the "value added" he or she can bring to that company. This means identifying the experiences that will make you successful in the job for which you are applying. These are not general statements about what you believe to be your strengths but rather are stories about your experiences that demonstrate that you have those strengths. The second example obviously details what the person learned from whatever job was held. In order to prepare yourself for those interviews, you need to think about steps taken prior to the interview, behaviors during the interview, and how you should close the interview.

Pre-Interview

The pre-interview is all the work that goes into getting ready for the interview. The first step during the pre-interview stage is to identify your values and skills. You will be revealing your own set of values during this interview and the interviewer will be deciding if those values fit with the culture of the organization. For example, which of the following factors are most important to you in a job:

- Working independently vs. working through others.
- Lots of autonomy vs. guidance and direction.

- High starting salary with heavy work load vs. lots of financial rewards "down the road" and slow increase in time commitment.

- Immediate challenges vs. starting with tasks well known to you.

- Stability vs. innovation and constant change.

- Spending a lot of time outdoors vs. spending a lot of time indoors.

- Great amount of travel vs. little to no travel.

These are just a few of the values that will shape the type of job and work environment in which you would be most comfortable. For example, your answer to the first set of values ("working independently vs. working through others") indicates whether you would be more comfortable being a manager who must get things done through the efforts of others, or if you would be better as a project director who is responsible only for your own work. If you get frustrated working in groups because you would rather do it yourself, you probably would make a frustrated manager! Knowing how much time you are willing to "spend on the road" will help you avoid jobs that will make you miserable. Do you want the excitement of a company that is constantly changing or would you feel more comfortable in a more stable and established environment? In order to make good choices about the jobs you are applying for, you need to take the next step: researching the company.

Prior to going to that first interview, research the company as thoroughly as possible and prepare questions that indicate you have some knowledge of the activities of the company so you can put your best foot forward in the interview itself. You can find information about the company from a book titled *Standard and Poor's Register* or in your career-counseling center at your university. Every major corporation has annual reports on file and these should be available to you in the library. If you know anyone who has ever worked for the company, a phone call to that person to give you a feel for what life is like inside the corporation will help you a great deal.

Some of the kinds of questions you should be asking, as you do your research prior to the interview, include the following:

- What is the history of this organization and what are its products?

- What kind of financial record has the organization had in the past five years?

- Who are the company's major competitors and who are its "clients"?

- What kind of career path is available in this organization and what kind of training for new employees is required or available?

- What are the duties and responsibilities for this particular job?

- Where would I need to relocate and how flexible would I need to be with regard to travel?

These questions will help you determine if the work environment is one in which you would feel comfortable and one that will meet your individual needs. Without knowing this you might end up in an environment and a job that demands a lifestyle you are ill equipped to accept.

Another part of the pre-interview process is your written work, which you submit ahead of the interview: cover letter and resumé. There are many books written about how to construct a resumé. Most will say: Keep it simple and direct. Be specific about your work experience and your accomplishments in school and indicate outcomes of your activities. For example, don't just list that you were a member of a club; instead, list what you did for that club. Concentrate on presenting an image of yourself that distinguishes you from others who might be applying. What are the unique skills and experiences you bring to the position that others might not have?

For example, one student was a member of a fund-raising committee that staged a talent show to raise money for their local charity. The organizational skills needed to plan and direct that talent show will be quite useful to the company that student enters. She talked about the persuasive tactics she used to get sponsors for the show and to build the acts.

Check out your placement office for assistance in writing your resumé. There may be classes that you will take in communication on interviewing that will also give you the same kind of assistance. Keep in mind that your resumé and cover letter should be like a speech: they have to get the audience's attention, make a few main points, summarize, and wrap it up before the audience becomes bored.

The Body of the Interview

The young man got lost on his way to the interview and parked with only five minutes to spare. To top off his frustration, it was raining and he had forgotten to bring an umbrella. He dashed to the door of the office only to find he had left the office number in the car. Several minutes of checking with the receptionist to find the right office number and then riding in an elevator that stopped on almost every floor made him anxious as he arrived. And worst of all, he was wearing new shoes that hurt his feet!

In order to avoid the problems described above, always be early for the interview. Be prepared for the unexpected. Since you don't know what the norms are in this organization, it is best to assume that they want professional attire unless they tell you differently. This means no jeans or t-shirts and clothes your grandmother would approve of! Even the smallest detail may distract from focusing on your abilities. For example, interviewers have told us that they are distracted by the following: green or blue fingernail polish; hair styles that have hair in front of a person's eyes or that require constantly pushing hair behind the ears; dirty shoes; a lot of jewelry; and limp handshakes. Pay attention to the details before the interview so that nothing distracts the person's attention from what you are saying about yourself.

During the course of the interview you should be prepared for a variety of questions that might be asked. There are two major types of questions:

- Open-ended questions are asked when an interviewer wants to get a sense of what you know and how you present yourself. A question like "Tell me about yourself" is often used as an opening question, which allows an interviewer to sit back and listen to what facts you pick out to present about yourself.

Spotlight on Ethics

One of our students asked us for advice about constructing her resumé. One of the questions I asked her was, "Have you ever served on a school paper or newsletter?" "Yes," she said, "I did help produce the departmental newsletter." "Well, that's an excellent skill to list on your resumé." Under "career-related experience" she listed "Departmental Newsletter—Design and production." When she was asked about it in an interview, she talked generally about the newsletter itself. She was hired and among her job duties was developing and producing an internal newsletter for a corporation. Three months later, she called in a panic. "I still have not produced the first newsletter. I don't really know how to go about it." "Didn't you put together that department newsletter you talked about?" I asked. "Not really. All I actually did was write several short editorials for it." This student was in trouble. She had claimed to do more than she could.

How far should you go in elaborating on your job experiences in order to get the job?

What's wrong with exaggerating a little and learning on the job?

What advice would you give this student?

- A closed-ended question would be a yes or no question such as, "Are you willing to relocate?" Here the interviewer needs direct information and wants a simple and direct answer. The worst thing you can do is give a long detailed answer when the interviewer is asking for a simple short one.

There may be times when your interviewer will ask you an illegal question. Illegal questions are questions about your personal life (e.g., age, religion, membership in groups, nationality, etc.) when those items have nothing to do with the job. But how do you handle answering those questions? Do you simply refuse to answer and risk the chance of offending the interviewer? It is much better to sidestep the question by determining what the underlying issue is. For example, the interviewer asks you if you have a family or intend to have a family and how you will manage having children and working. What he or she is really getting at is, "Will you be committed to the job and will you stick with it?" So that's the question you answer. Instead of saying, "I have children and I'll get a baby-sitter," you should say, "I will take care of my personal life and make sure it doesn't interfere with my job. I'm very dedicated to my work and you'll find that I'm a very committed employee." This allows you to answer the interviewer's concerns without responding to a question that is none of the interviewer's business.

You should also know that EEOC (Equal Employment Opportunities Commission) is the clearinghouse for complaints about illegal job requirements. You can report an individual or a company to the EEOC if you feel you have been discriminated against during the employment process.

Many texts on interviewing will give you examples of the kinds of questions you might be asked, but certainly you should always be prepared to talk

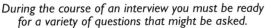

*During the course of an interview you must be ready
for a variety of questions that might be asked.*

about your specific strengths and weaknesses and what you are doing to overcome the weaknesses. Don't ever say, "I just can't think of any weakness."
Rather, think of a weakness that can be controlled and that you are working
on. Every interviewer expects you to have some weakness.

Barbara Walters once said, "The most consistently enduring human trait
is warmth, everyone responds to the person who radiates friendliness from a
serene core." Interviewers like to hire people they are comfortable with. They
like to hire people they think they would enjoy working with. This means part
of the interview process is to be friendly, responsive, and to engage in some
small talk, but let the interviewer know what things you have in common and
what things you don't like. Try to establish common ground with the interviewer throughout the interview by discussing current events or company
news. Remember, some of these interviewers will be just as nervous as you
are. They may be new to this job.

Throughout the interview listen carefully to what you've been told about
the job, and then paraphrase back part of what you've heard in order to confirm your understanding. Many interviewees fail to listen to the question.
They annoy the interviewer by answering a question that wasn't asked or by
giving much more information than the interviewer ever wanted to hear. Be
brief and to the point, answer only the question you have been asked.

Here are some typical questions asked by interviewers:

- "Tell me about yourself."
- "What are your career plans for the next five years?"
- "What did you like or dislike in your last job?"
- "Describe a situation in which you had to convince someone to do
  something. What approaches were successful?"
- "What have you learned from jobs you have held in your life?"

- "Why do you want to work here?"
- "What are your greatest strengths and weaknesses?"

In summary, in the body of the interview you should:

1. Summarize your answers.
2. Support your answers with specific answers or illustrations.
3. Be concise and answer only the questions you were asked.
4. Support your claims with outcome measures of the activities in which you've engaged.
5. Summarize the major points you want to get across.

The Closing

At the end of the interview, you want to leave the interviewer with the most important facts about yourself. Therefore, go over in your mind the main points you want to leave with this person. These may be the things he or she remembers most. End on a friendly, upbeat note. If there's any chance to follow up, offer to make the call or make another trip if the person wants to interview you somewhere else.

Following the interview you still have work to do. Always send a business note to the interviewer thanking him for taking time to talk with you. If you have additional information to share, send that along. And don't hesitate to call one or two weeks later to ask if the person is still in the interviewing process. If you do this in a polite way, the recruiter will not feel you are nagging her. In fact, in many cases it lets her know you are still interested and available. In one case the person who followed up for four weeks, not giving up just because he had not heard from the company, was the person who was hired. The person who waited patiently to hear from the company never did hear from them again.

The Interviewer's Perspective

One student who had a summer job as an interviewer explained the process from the interviewer's perspective:

Over the summer I interned in the human resource department at a hospital near my home town. For a portion of the summer I worked on employment. I conducted close to 60 interviews from radiology technology to housekeeping, nurse's assistants, and dietary positions. At first it was difficult and I needed to use a sheet with questions to ask. I would run into language barriers, and I would have difficulty understanding them or they couldn't grasp what I was saying. Some people, because of their education level, were difficult to carry on a conversation with; their answers were very brief. The other extreme was the lady who would tell you her personal life history and you basically had to cut her off. This job was a very positive experience for me. I gained a good deal of experience and increased my interpersonal skills. I had to be aware of the body language I used, so that I didn't make them feel uncomfortable. At the beginning of the interview I tried to make them feel relaxed by telling them the order I would go in. I made sure to greet them with a smile, a firm handshake, and ask them how their day was going. I tried to give them as much information as I could and left communication lines open by telling them to give me a call if they had any questions.

— Tryka, third-year college student

❖ ❖ ❖ ❖

Tryka used some very positive techniques in the opening of her interviews during her summer job. It's critical to help the interviewee relax and feel comfortable about the interview. Often, interviewers don't do that and instead put the interviewee on edge from the very first question.

First, just as the interviewee must do research on the job and the company, it is the interviewer's responsibility to be very familiar with the requirements of the job and the details of the company so that questions about the position and the corporate culture can be answered. The interviewer's job is first to make the interviewee feel positive about the company. You want each person to go away thinking this would be an excellent company to work for, regardless of whether you think the person will ultimately get the job or not. The job interview is a great opportunity for the company to spread good will among the general public. You can be sure that each interviewee will tell stories about how well or how badly the interview went with "X" company.

Second, it is the interviewer's responsibility to have carefully read each applicant's file so that the questions asked are not simply a repetition of what is already included in the file. The interviewer's job is to extend what is available in the files and get a better sense of how this person would work within the environment and the demands of the job.

Third, the interviewer also must structure the interview in such a way that it achieves systematic coverage of work history, education, and skills so that all the applicants can be fairly compared. It is not appropriate to have a unique set of questions for each applicant. You must be able to compare their answers when all the interviewing has been completed.

Finally, it is the interviewer's job to signal the end of the interview. The interviewee will be waiting for some sign that the interview is over and will be reluctant to bring up the issue himself. Usually, the interviewer will signal the end by saying what steps will be taken next. For example, "We will be interviewing for this position for the rest of this week and hope to make a decision by the middle of next week. You will be notified immediately either that you are no longer being considered or that a second interview will be scheduled. Please do not hesitate to call if you have any questions during this time. It's been a pleasure meeting you."

Summary

All the skills you use during an interview are exactly the skills you will need to be successful on the job. Being a good listener, articulate and to the point, precise about what it is you need, and responding to others' needs will make you successful in your career. Communication skills are needed by everyone, not just by communication specialists; therefore, no matter what your career choice, communication skills will be critical to your success. We hope this text has given you a start on your quest to improve your communication skills. We also hope that you look forward to each day and the communication challenges that will be presented to you! Good luck!

At Your Bookstore

Beatty, R. H. (1992). *The New Complete Job Search*. New York: John Wiley & Sons.

Bolles, R. N. (1997). *What Color Is Your Parachute? A Practical Manual for Job Hunters*. Berkeley, CA: Ten Speed Press.

Clawson, J. G. (1992). *Self-assessment and Career Development*. Englewood Cliffs, NJ: Prentice Hall.

Dawson, K. M. (1996). *Job Search: The Total System*. New York: John Wiley & Sons.

Sullivan, R. (1997). *Climbing Your Way to the Bottom: Changing the Way You Approach Your Job Search*. Chicago, IL: Pure Play Publishing.

Glossary

abstract section of a scholarly article summarizing the contents

abstraction an idea, concept, or statement removed from concrete, specific reality

accommodation the process of accepting cultural differences in a dominant culture and allowing co-cultural groups to retain their own cultural identities

adaptors nonverbal movements that reflect internal states but may be socially inappropriate

advocate a person who speaks or writes for a certain cause through argumentation

affect displays nonverbal movements that reflect and show emotion, usually through facial expressions

agenda-setting theory that the media establish what issues we should pay attention to

analogy comparison of one thing to another for clarity

anticipatory socialization assimilation process that occurs before a new employee enters the organization

anxiety/uncertainty management theory the theory that we seek information about someone from a different culture in order to predict behavior and thus lessen our anxiety

argument persuasive statement backed with reason and evidence

article title block in a bibliographic citation, the name of the specific essay cited

assimilation process of absorbing co-cultural groups into a dominant culture

asynchronous not happening in real or actual time, as in a message being read a while after it has been sent

attitudes loosely committed perspectives audiences have on a given topic; mental or emotional states regarding facts, statements, or circumstances

attribution process of giving others credit for their ideas

audience analysis gathering and interpreting information—such as demographics, attitudes, and values—about a specific group of receivers of a message in order to deliver an appropriate and effective message

author block in a bibliographic citation, the portion providing the name of the author of a reference, in proper form

bandwagon appeal a persuasive technique that argues you should adopt a position because it is popular

behavioral conflict specific behavior or action viewed by one partner in a relationship as interference in the success of the relationship

behavioral flexibility ability of individuals to adapt their communication styles to the needs of a specific situation

bibliography a list of sources (books, articles, interviews, etc.) consulted in researching a topic

boomerang effect increase in potential for a pool of ideas when people interact effectively during discussion

brainstorming process of writing down every topic coming to mind without evaluating or judging their worth

broadcast the delivery of a message to a widely dispersed audience, as through the mass media

browser program allowing access to segments of the Internet

centrality the presumption of stand-alone texts that they occupy a privileged space in the reader's experience

channel means or path by which a message is transmitted; includes written memos, face-to-face conversation, e-mail, television, bulletin board postings, etc.

chronological organization method of organizing material for a speech or other presentation by following the history of the subject matter

climate in communication, the feelings attached by the audience to the message and to the communicators

closed-ended questions questions which can be answered with "yes" or "no"; used when an interviewer wants specific information

co-culture group of people with common characteristics existing within a dominant culture

code-switching changing one's language use from one linguistic community to another

coercion the use of threats to have one's demands met

cohesion the willingness, or bond, which group members possess in order to stay together

collective a group having some mutual interest

collectivism the tendency in a culture to value group decisions and group goals

communication audit study of the quality and effectiveness of communication within an organization

communication predicament model (CPM) a situation where perceptions of another, including that person's ability to communicate, influences the communication itself

competence the speaker's familiarity with the subject

complementary relationship relationship in which one person dominates the decision-making process

computer-mediated communication(CMC) human communication that is influenced by computer technology (such as e-mail, chat rooms, and websites)

confirmatio the stage of a trial where the prosecution presents evidence, witnesses, and material against the accused

confirming messages messages contributing to the continuation of a relationship; these support our self-concept and provide positive feedback

conflict an expressed struggle between two interdependent parties who perceive incompatible goals, scarce rewards, and interference from the other party in achieving their goals

conformity orientation the degree to which families create and maintain an environment that stresses a sharing of attitudes, values, and beliefs

connotation meaning that is suggested by or associated with a word rather than coming from a commonly acknowledged definition

context in communication, the setting—from a private conversation between two people to a public speech sent via mass media

contexting the way a person communicates and the circumstances of that communication referring to either high-context or low-context cultures

convention a procedure or behavior agreed upon by the general group or culture

conversation orientation the degree to which families create and maintain an environment where members of that family are encouraged to state their opinions on many topics

cool media media which stimulate multiple senses, requiring less participation in the construction of meaning by the audience

copiousness the quality of including a large amount of information in a speech

"cough index" an indicator of inattentiveness among members of an audience, especially at a public speech; listeners not engaged in rapt attention tend to cough and fidget

credibility the audience's perception that the speaker is competent and trustworthy

critical listening listening characterized by suspicion and challenge to the message

cross-functional teams groups in an organization that are cut across functions and established units to work on a project or see a product through from beginning to end of production

cultivation theory a direct-effects theory that holds that media establish expectations about the nature of society

cultural relativism an approach that argues that a culture's values, beliefs, and practices are meaningful and comparable only to that culture

cultural sensitivity respect for the worth of another people's identity and heritage

culture the shared values, beliefs, norms, rituals, and ways of knowing common to a group of people

cyberspace the conceptual space formed by human interpretation of the information available on the Internet

date block in a bibliographic citation, the date of a publication, speech, etc.

decentered media media not needing a central sender of the message (such as a television station) but using a series of communicators (such as the Internet)

declamation formal public speaking

decoding translating the signal into some meaningful message for the receiver

deductive reasoning method of arriving at a logical appeal based on a generalized statement leading to a specific example (i.e., "Communication instructors are personable, and so my communication instructor must be personable.")

demographics specific characteristics of an audience

denotation widely acknowledged, dictionary-type meaning

descriptive feedback response that simply describes a behavior without judging or analyzing the person or the behavior

descriptive language language rich with details and specifics

dialect variation of a given language spoken by a group of people

direct effects theory a theory that media influence and shape human reaction in a cause-and-effect relationship

direct quotation word-for-word recording of what the original author stated

disconfirming messages messages that do not acknowledge a person's self-concept and actually does damage to self-esteem

discrimination action taken against an individual or group that occurs as a result of prejudice; attitude stemming from preconceived ideas of difference or inferiority

discussion in a scholarly article, the section in which the author reflects on the findings of a study

diversity differences among people (such as sex, age, race/ethnic background, disabilities, cultural origins, or sexual orientation)

dyad two individuals communicating

dynamic presence the energy and vitality a speaker projects in a presentation

dysfunctional relationship a relationship that is impaired and does not consist of normal interaction

electronic media pathways for messages that are instantaneous, such as television and the Internet

elocution the art and technique of clear, effective public speaking

emblems nonverbal body movements that substitute for words *emoticons* symbols used to express emotion in E-mail messages without using words

emotional appeal technique used by a speaker to play on the audience's feelings such as fear, love, patriotism, etc.

empathetic listening seeing something from the speaker's point of view

empowerment especially in an organization, programs designed to enhance employee commitment and productivity through participation in decision making and self-directed teams

encoding changing the message from a thought or idea into some recognized symbol system

encounter in organizational communication, the assimilation process that begins when the person enters the organization and is confronted with how that organization functions

equivocal messages messages having multiple interpretations

ethics system of moral values setting forth what is good and bad

ethnocentrism the tendency to view one's own culture as superior to others

euphemism a word or phrase substituted for another, potentially offensive, one

evaluative feedback response that provides information about what the listener finds right or wrong about a behavior or message

example the presentation of one specific case that is indicative of many similar cases

exchange theory a theory that suggests that social interaction is regulated by an individual's desire to get the maximum pleasure and the minimum pain from another person

exordium the opening part of a trial, when the issues and participants in the trial are introduced to the jury

expectations the hopes one has that an event will occur in a certain way or that an individual will behave in a certain way; the way one sees the world of the future

extemporaneous delivery a style of delivering a speech that appears unrehearsed but that has actually been carefully prepared

external locus of control the degree to which a person is influenced by external forces and rewards

face-saving the act of preserving personal prestige or outward dignity

factual distractions presentation of facts that do not agree with what the listener knows to be true

family in the best sense, a group of people who are committed to supporting one another psychologically and financially; usually a sharing of space is involved at least for some length of time

feedback information sent in response to a message; sometimes invited by a speaker

figure and ground phenomenon the situation when some stimuli are more obvious (these are referred to as figure) than other stimuli (ground) that recede into the background

filter anything that comes between the sender and receiver of a message to modify it

flame a statement that insults someone

forensic rhetoric a type of speechmaking used to defend oneself in a court of law

gatekeepers decision makers who determine what information is passed along in a public forum and what information is not

general systems model of communication an approach that states that each part of the communication system is related to the system in a dynamic, ongoing process

goal statement in planning a public speech, a statement of the basic message that establishes the boundaries within which the speech is constructed

group communication communication involving at least three people

group culture the shared set of values, beliefs, rites, rituals, heroes, and stories that a group holds

grouphate the tendency of people, especially from individualistic cultures, to dislike group work and interaction

groupthink a phenomenon occurring when a group's desire to maintain cohesiveness results in a primarily negative mode of thinking that overlooks contradictory opinions and ideas

hasty generalization in persuasion, using too few examples to argue a point

hearing the process of receiving sound; a physiological activity, compared with listening, which is a psychological activity

hierarchy the ordering of elements from superior to subordinate

high-context cultures cultures in which communication is implicit and understood through relational familiarity

hot media media with more limited sensory stimulation, requiring greater participation in the construction of meaning on the part of the audience; contrasted to cool media

human communication shared meaning between two or more individuals using a symbol system

hyperpersonal communication a freer, more confident form of communication experienced by some who interact with others in computer-mediated environments

hypertext nonsequential writing, as used in electronic media, that is, nonlinear, decentered, and nonhierarchical

hypodermic needle analogy using an analogy to medical technology, theory to explain the idea that audiences are directly influenced by the messages the mass media send

"I" language personal comments or criticisms that begin with the word "I" to indicate the opinionated nature of the statement

"I" roles self-centered roles that group members adopt and that detract from the group's achievement and harmony

icon image or symbol having religious significance or commanding unquestioned devotion

idiom phrase whose meaning cannot be understood by the meanings of the separate words it contains

illustrators nonverbal movements that help reinforce verbal messages

implicit meaning meaning contained in a communication without being expressed

impromptu delivery a type of speechmaking whereby the speaker has had no time to prepare or rehearse

individualism a culture's emphasis on independence and freedom of the individual, contrasted to collectivism

inductive reasoning method of arriving at a logical appeal based on an example leading to a generalized statement (i.e., "I had cramps the last three times I've eaten sea food. I think I may be allergic to it.")

information superhighway the complex computer-mediated channel for communication

informational listening listening with the purpose of retaining information and learning

informative messages communication with the goal of presenting information, not necessarily persuading

intellectual property a person's original ideas; may be protected by copyright or other law

interference anything—from a physical condition to an attitude—which prevents the message from being received as the sender intended

internal locus of control the degree to which you are motivated by your own values and other personal forces

internalization taking in communicated values or principles and making them your own

interorganizational conflict conflict that occurs when two or more organizations compete for scarce resources or have differing values

interpersonal communication communication between two or more individuals

interpersonal conflict a type of group conflict occurring when members question the values, behaviors, or characteristics of other members

interpretive feedback response that attempts to explain observed behavior and places the speaker in the position of being an analyst

intimate space the closest contact between communicators, usually 0–18 inches

intraorganizational conflict conflict occurring among departments or groups of employees in an organization

intrapersonal communication the silent talk you have with yourself, sometimes referred to as "self talk"

introduction section of a scholarly article that introduces the topic and provides the rationale for the study

irreversible or unerasable communication messages that will "color" all future interactions and cannot be erased or forgotten

"it" role a type of group role that helps the group achieve its goals and tasks

jargon language or specialized vocabulary used within a group (such as doctors) and often foreign to those outside that group or profession

kairos (from the Greek), saying the appropriate thing at the appropriate time

kinesics a form of nonverbal communication that refers to posture, movement, gestures, and facial expressions

language a collection of words and the accompanying ways in which they are interrelated through conventions

leadership communication that modifies attitudes and behaviors in others in order to meet group goals and needs

leakage *see* Nonverbal leakage

learning group collective or group having as its goal the education of its members in a specific area

life script a perceived plan for the living of your life, similar to playing a part in a play, a useful tool in examining self-esteem

limited effects theory an approach to media influence that believes media's ability to persuade is restricted

linear-thinking culture a culture that is print-oriented, used to reading in a sequential manner, and tending to be more individually focused

linearity the process of moving through something sequentially; typically associated with the traditional method of reading a document one page at a time

linguistic community any distinct group of language users

listening a psychological activity; compared with hearing, which is a physiological activity; this is a combination of hearing sound and giving meaning to the speaker's message

listserves on the Internet, address lists of members of a discussion group

literature review section of a scholarly article reviewing what previous scholars have written on the same subject

loaded terms language with either explicit or connotative meaning that demeans human dignity

locus of control. *see* internal locus of control *and* external locus of control

logical appeal in persuasive public communication, an argument supported by facts

low-context cultures cultures where communication via message sending is very explicit and understood

lurker someone whose presence within a virtual community is undetectable

manuscript delivery a mode of public speaking in which the speaker writes out a speech word for word and then reads from the manuscript at the presentation

mass communication communication in which the channel or medium has the potential to reach large numbers of people simultaneously; once restricted to newspapers, radio, and television, now expanded by the new electronic media

mass media media such as newspapers and TV capable of reaching large audiences; can also be designed to reach only small, niche audiences, such as specialized publications and "narrowcast" channels

mediated messages messages that are not face-to-face but transmitted by and often shaped by a certain medium, especially channels such as writing, the telephone, and the Internet

medium the means of transmitting a message; anything that extends a person's ability to communicate

memorized delivery a mode of public speaking in which the speaker writes out and rehearses a speech to the point that it is memorized

message a signal sent, either verbal or nonverbal

message flow model theory of mass communication that suggests that some people are indirectly influenced by the media through contact with people who have had contact with the media

metamorphosis in organizational communication, the assimilation process during which a new employee changes old behaviors to meet the standards of the new environment

method a system for conducting research

methodology section of a scholarly article detailing how research was conducted

mnemonic device any technique or "trick" created to assist the speaker or listener to remember something (for example, setting the words of the preamble to the U.S. Constitution to music)

multimedia any forum for the presentation of messages combining more than one channel

narratio the opening statement, or story, presented by the defense and by the prosecution in a trial

netiquette internet etiquette

networking communicating with connections to assist achievement of a goal, such as finding a job

node computer system that contributes to the construction of the Internet

nonverbal communication all messages transmitted from person to person without the use of words

nonverbal leakage gestures, facial expressions, and other nonverbal messages that reveal true feelings or intent

normative conflict disagreements that relational partners have regarding the norms and rules of a relationship

null hypothesis in a quantitative study, a statement that no correlation exists between variables

objectics nonverbal communication that refers to how clothing, ornaments, jewelry, and other artifacts communicate messages

open-ended questions questions with no specific answer; used by an interviewer when he or she wants to get a sense of what you know and how you present yourself; contrasted to closed-ended questions

opinion leaders individuals influenced by the media who in turn help shape the views of others

oral citation the practice of acknowledging the source of an original idea during a presentation

organizational communication the special form of group communication that occurs within an organization such as a corporation

organizational empowerment employee participation in decision making to enhance employee commitment and productivity

parallel relationship a relationship in which partners take turns as to who is in charge of making decisions, depending on the topic and their expertise

parallelism the quality of making elements in a set, such as an outline, similar in terms of grammatical form or substance(i.e., *consider* and *request*, not *consider* and *requesting*)

paraphrase repeating what an individual has said in your own words

parenthetical citation a form of in-text documentation of resources used in a written report

perception the process by which we give meaning to certain stimuli in our environment

perceptual consistency seeing the world in the future the way we have seen it in the past

perceptual filters the process of screening out or filtering certain information

peroration closing arguments presented by the defense and by the prosecution in a trial

personal conflicts the perceptions that partners in a relationship have about each other's characteristics, attitudes, and level of selfishness

personal space the territory or turf one needs, in a physical and psychological way, to maintain individuality and privacy; the distance used for conversation and nonintimate communication (18 inches–4 feet)

persuasion the process of creating change in others through communication

phatic communication a screening process used to help determine whether or not a relationship will develop

phonology the study of the pronunciation of words and how this has changed over time

physical interference loud distracting noises or visual distractions that prevent the listener from clearly receiving the message *physiological limits* anything that prevents a person from participating in the full range of activity, including receiving messages (as due to limited hearing but also including temperament and heredity)

pictogram emoticon; use of computer keyboard characters and features to punctuate emotional meaning in an electronic message

plagiarism use of another person's original ideas without giving credit

politeness strategy a communication practice in which conflict is dealt with indirectly rather than through direct confrontation

politically correct language communication that reflects respect for the identity and worth of others

postcolonialism a condition in which the ideals of one culture are attempting to dominate those of another

power distance the way in which unequal power relationships are viewed within a culture

powerless language communication that is characterized by hedges and overpoliteness

pre-interview the preparation for a job interview, consisting of several steps beginning with identifying your skills

prejudice the holding of certain beliefs about an idea, concept, or group of people without just grounds

primary group the most basic, enduring, and essential of the various types of groups to which an individual belongs, such as the family

procedural conflict conflict occurring when the group is uncertain about how to accomplish the goal or task

propaganda a persuasive message that is essentially political, or related to power

proxemics the study of how people use space and distance to communicate nonverbally

psychological characteristics the attitudes, beliefs, and values of an audience one should consider when constructing a message

psychological filters motivations, desires, and expectations based on past experiences

psychological interference thoughts, such as worries, that prevent the listener from focusing on the message

public distance the space (over 12 feet) that is maintained in larger communication contexts

public speech communication aimed at a large, often unrestricted audience, as contrasted to interpersonal communication

publication title block in a bibliographic citation, the name of the journal or other publication

publisher's block in a bibliographic citation, the name of the publisher of the book or journal

qualitative studies research inclined to use the tools of language to explain phenomena

"quality circle" in a business organization, a group of nonmanagerial workers who make suggestions, solve problems, and then offer ideas to management

quantitative studies research inclined to use the tools of mathematics to explain phenomena

rate busting a phenomenon that occurs when group members conspire to produce below their potential

receiver the listener (or reader) in the communication process

reciprocal communication the stimulation of a reaction from one person when another talks

reciprocity the amount of disclosure revealed by the person with whom you are talking

recursive-thinking culture an oral-based culture tending toward circular rather than linear thinking

re-engineering reassessing how work gets done and developing new processes to increase efficiency

references the section of a scholarly article listing all the works the author used in constructing the article

referent the object a word symbolizes

refutatio the defense's counter-arguments to the prosecution's arguments

regulators nonverbal movements that control communication

relationship networks the interconnection between people's relationships; the way a particular relationship changes over time intertwined with what happens in other relationships

rhetoric the art of communicating effectively

roles the behaviors that individuals exhibit while working in groups

Sapir-Whorf hypothesis that theory that suggests that cultures develop language in ways which prioritize relevant experiences to them

secondary orality the communal interpretations of mediated, rather than immediate, messages

selective attention the ability to process certain stimuli and filter out the rest

selective exposure the choice to consume those media products that are most in keeping with your own attitudes

selective retention the selection of stimuli that you remember

selective self-presentation the process of creating your own identity, which often emphasizes the most attractive (real or imagined) characteristics

self-concept the relatively stable perception or impression you have of yourself

self-disclosure what you reveal about yourself to others: your feelings, experiences, and innermost thoughts

self-esteem the evaluation of your self-concept

self-fulfilling prophecy a prediction about how you will behave, which comes true because after the prediction has been made, you act as if it were true

self-talk intrapersonal communication, inner talk rather than interpersonal exchange

semantic distractions portions of a general communication that prevent focus on the totality

semantics the study of the way words convey meaning

sender the originator of a message—spoken, written, or nonverbal

sexist language language that perpetuates stereotypes about gender differences

situational approach to leadership a theory that suggests it is the situation that determines success as a leader

slang informal language usually enjoying short-lived popularity

small group communication communication among three or more individuals interacting for the achievement of some common purpose through a process of mutual influence

social group not as enduring as a primary group, often existing for a similar purpose: to provide friendship and companionship

social sciences the study of the forms and functions of human society

social space the 4-12 foot personal space you maintain with strangers or people you interact with formally

socialization the training of human responses for participation in society

Sophists itinerant teachers of communication who lived in ancient Greece

source in the communication process, the originator of the message

source credibility the audience's perception that the speaker is trustworthy and competent

spatial organization a mode of organizing a presentation according to the relationships of items in physical space

Standard American English the English language characterized by those practices considered to be the most acceptable to educated people in the United States

statistics the study of probability

stereotyping assuming that all members of a group possess the same qualities based on interaction with a limited number of individuals from that group

stimuli all the events, messages, and other agents of change that prompt a response by the receiver

style approach to leadership theory that the communications from a leader provide evidence of a particular style

support all the facts, references, testimony, etc. that help make the point of a communication, especially public speaking

symbol anything that stands for something else

❖ ❖ ❖ ❖   *symbolic community* a community that evolves because people share common interests rather than geographic proximity

symmetrical relationship relationship in which two partners are fairly equal regarding who makes the decisions

synchronous occurring in real time

synergistic effect increased effectiveness through the interaction of two or more separate elements

syntax the arrangement of words into statements

synthesis the product of a combination of things

systematic desensitization exposing yourself to something feared, such as public speaking, in small doses to diminish and conquer that fear

tactile communication sending or receiving a message through the sense of touch

task conflict a type of conflict that a group engages in when it is uncertain about the nature of the problem or project

territoriality tendency for human beings to claim space that they believe is their own

testimonial source credibility derived from expert opinion

testimony as in a trial, sworn statement of fact or firsthand observation used as evidence

text any collection of symbols, including documents, films, events, and places

therapeutic listening *see* Empathetic listening

thesis statement the declaration of a speech's topic in a clear concise statement

topical organization the organization of information through a series of logically related categories

total quality management (TQM) an approach to management that hopes to improve not only the quality of the output but increased customer satisfaction through more efficient use of resources and participation in team decision making

trait approach to leadership a theory of leadership that rests on the belief that leaders possess certain innate traits or qualities that make them leaders

transactional communication communication going in multiple directions at all times

transition statements statements the speaker uses to notify the audience that the speech is moving from one point to another

trustworthiness the speaker's honesty with the audience

"turn system" series of nonverbal signals used by a speaker and a listener direct the flow of a conversation

unrepeatable communication communication that cannot be "staged" again

uses and gratifications theory theory that audiences select pieces of mass media to meet their own needs

values underlying principles that guide the formation of a person's personality

virtual community social groups emerging from long-term use of computer-mediated communication channels and personal attachment to co-communicators or their forums

visualization mentally picturing yourself in a certain state or performing a certain task successfully

vivid language words and phrases used to create a desired picture of an event, idea, or incident

vocabulary list of words, usually including their definitions

voir dire part of the trial known as the jury selection process

"we" role a type of group role that contributes to the group members' emotional satisfaction and social well-being

words symbols that have been developed by cultures to represent objects, concepts, actions, characteristics, and conditions

work group a group united by common desire to accomplish a task

"yes but" syndrome a mode of listener feedback that reveals a lack of empathy

References

Abramson, J. (1994). *We, the Jury. The Jury System and the Ideal of Democracy*. New York, NY: Basic Books.

Achtert, W. S., & Gibaldi, J. (1985). *The MLA Style Manual*. New York, NY: Modern Language Association of America.

Adelman, M. B., & Frey, L. R. (1994). "The Pilgrim Must Embark: Creating and Sustaining Community in a Residential Facility for People with AIDS." In L. R. Frey (Ed.). *Group Communication in Context* (pp. 3–22), Hillsdale, NJ: Lawrence Erlbaum.

Aden, R. C., Beck, C. S., & Smith, M. J. (1996). "The Co-construction and Management of Multiple Identities as Relational Bond on Lois & Clark: The New Adventures of Superman." Paper presented to the Speech Communication Association, San Diego, CA.

Aden, R. C., Rahoi, R. L., & Beck, C. S. (1995). "Dreams Are Born on Places Like This: The Process of Interpretive Community Formation at the Field of Dreams Site." *Communication Quarterly*, 4, 368–380.

Adler, S. J. (1994). *The Jury: Trial and Error in the American Courtroom*. New York, NY: Time Books.

Alberti, R. E. (1995). *Your Perfect Right: A Guide to Assertive Living (7th ed.)*. San Luis Obispo, CA: Impact.

Althen, G. (1994). "Recurring Issues in Intercultural Communication." In G. Althen (Ed.), *Learning Across Cultures* (Rev. ed., pp.185–197). Washington, DC: Association of International Educators.

Anderson, K. (1997). *Friendships That Run Deep: 7 Ways to Build Lasting Relationships*. Downer Grove: IL: Intervarsity Press.

Aristotle. (1991). *The Art of Rhetoric*. (J. H. Freese, Trans.). Cambridge, MA: Harvard University Press.

Ashenbrenner, G. L., & Snalling, R. D. (1988). "Communication with Power." *Business Credit*, 90, 39–42.

Axtell, R. E. (1993). *Dos and Taboos Around the World*. New York, NY: John Wiley & Sons.

Ayers, J., & Hopf, T. S. (1989). "Visualization: Is It More Than Extraattention?" *Communication Education*, 38, 1–5.

Ayers, J. (1986). "Perceptions of Speaking Ability: An Explanation for Stage Fright." *Communication Education*, 38, 1–5.

Bagish, H. (1981). *Confessions of a Former Cultural Relativist*. Santa Barbara, CA: University of California at Santa Barbara.

Baker, L., Edwards, R., Gaines, C., Gladney, K., & Holley, F. (1981). "An Investigation of Proportional Time Spent in Various Communication Activities by College Students." *Journal of Applied Communication Research*, 8, 101.

❖ ❖ ❖ ❖   Barker, L. L., Wahlers, K. J., & Watson, K. W. (1995). *Groups in Process: An Introduction to Small Group Communication* (5th ed.). Boston, MA: Allyn & Bacon.

Barnard, C. I. (1938). *The Functions of the Executive*. Cambridge: Howard University Press.

Beatty, R. H. (1992). *The New Complete Job Search*. New York, NY: John Wiley & Sons.

Bechler, C., & Johnson, S. C. (1995, February). "Leadership and Listening: A Study of Member Perceptions. *Small Group Communication*, 77–85.

Beck, C. S. (1997). *Partnership for Health: Building Relationships Between Women and Health Caregivers*. Mahwah, NJ: Lawrence Erlbaum.

Benne, K., & Sheats, P. (1948). "Functional Roles of Group Members." *Journal of Social Issues*, 4, 41–49.

Bennett, W. L. (1978). "Storytelling in Criminal Trials: A Model of Social Judgment." *Quarterly Journal of Speech*, 64, 1–22.

Bennis, W. (1986). *Leaders and Visions: Orchestrating the Corporate Culture*. New York, NY: Conference Board.

Bennis, W., & Namus, B. (1985). *Leaders: The Strategies for Taking Charge*. New York, NY: Harper & Row.

Berryman-Fink, C., & Brunner, C. C. (1987). "The Effects of Sex of Source and Target on Interpersonal Conflict Management Styles." *Southern Speech Communication Journal*, 53, 38–48.

Birdwhistell, R. L. (1970). *Kinesics and Context: Essays on Body Motion Communication*. Philadelphia, PA: University of Pennsylvania Press.

Bizzell, P., & Herzberg, B. (1990). *The Rhetorical Tradition: Readings from Classical Times to the Present*. Boston, MA: St. Martin's Press.

Blake, R. R., & Mouton, J. S. (1964). *The Managerial Grid*. Houston: Gulf Publishing.

Boase, P. H., & Carlson, C. V. (1989). "The School of Interpersonal Communication: An Historical Perspective." Unpublished manuscript, School of Interpersonal Communication. Athens, OH: Ohio University.

Bolles, R. N. (1997). *What Color Is Your Parachute? A Practical Manual for Job Hunters*. Berkeley, CA: Ten Speed Press.

Braiker, H. B., & Kelley, H. H. (1979). "Conflict in the Development of Close Relationships." In R. L. Burgess & T. L. Huston (Eds.), *Social Exchange in Developing Relationships*, (pp. 135–168). New York: Academic Press.

Brilhart, J., & Galanes, G. (1989). *Effective Group Discussion*. Dubuque, IA: Wm. C. Brown.

Brown, R. H. (1994). Introduction. In S. DeWine, *The Consultant's Craft: Improving Organizational Communication*. New York, NY: St. Martin's Press.

Brownell, J. (1990). "Perceptions of Effective Listeners: A Management Study." *Journal of Business Communication*, 27, 401–415.

Burgoon, J. K., & Saine, T. J. (1978). *The Unspoken Dialogue: An Introduction to Nonverbal Communication*. Boston, MA: Houghton-Mifflin.

Burns, J. M. (1978). *Leadership*. New York, NY: Harper & Row.

Burrell, N. A., Buzzanell, P. M., & McMillan, J. J. (1992). "Feminine Tensions in Conflict Situations as Revealed by Metaphorical Analyses." *Management Communication Quarterly*, 6, 115–149.

Canary, D. J., & Stafford, L. (1996). *Communication and Relational Maintenance*. San Diego, CA: Academic Press.

Cantrel, H. (1940). *The Invasion from Mars: A Study in the Psychology of Panic*. Princeton, NJ: Princeton University Press.

Carmichael, C. W. (1991). "Intercultural Perspectives of Aging." In L. A. Samovar & R. E. Porter (Eds.), *Intercultural Communication: A Reader* (6th ed.), (pp. 128–135). Belmont, CA: Wadsworth Publishing.

Cheney, G. (1995). "Democracy in the Workplace: Theory and Practice from the Perspective of Communication." *Journal of Applied Communication Research, 23*, 167–200.

Chiles, A. M., & Zorn, T. E. (1995, February). "Empowerment in Organizations: Employees Perceptions of the Influences on Empowerment." *Journal of Applied Communication Research, 23*, 1–25.

Clawson, J. G. (1992). *Self-assessment and Career Development*. Englewood Cliffs, NJ: Prentice-Hall.

Compton, C. D., White, K., & DeWine, S. (1991). "Techno-sense: Making Sense of Computer-Mediated Communications Systems." *Journal of Business Communication, 28*, 23–43.

Conley, T. M. (1990). *Rhetoric in the European Tradition*. Chicago, IL: University of Chicago Press.

Conquergood, D. W. (1994). "Homeboys and Hoods: Gang Communication and Cultural Space." In L. R. Frey (Ed.), *Group Communication in Context: Studies of Natural Groups* (pp. 23–55). Hillsdale, NJ: Lawrence Erlbaum.

Conrad, C., & Poole, M. S. (1998). *Strategic Organizational Communication Into the Twenty-first Century*. Fort Worth: Harcourt Brace.

Cooks, L., Hale, C., & DeWine, S. (1996). "Giving Voice to Sexual Harassment: Dialogues in the Aftermath of Thomas-Hill." In S. L. Regan, D. G. Bystrom, L. L. Kaid, & C. S. Beck (Eds.), *The Lynching of Language: Gender, Politics, and Power in the Hill- Thomas Hearings*. Urbana, IL: University of Illinois Press.

Cooper, B., & Descutner, D. (1996). "'It Had No Voice to It': Sydney Pollack's Film Translation of Isak Dinesen's 'Out of Africa'." *Quarterly Journal of Speech, 83*, 228–250.

Cooper, L. (1932). *The Rhetoric of Aristotle*. New York: Appleton-Century-Crofts.

Cooper, L., & Husband, R. (1993). "Developing a Model of Organizational Listening Competency." *Journal of the International Listening Association, 7*, 6–34.

Cronkhite, G. (1986). "On the Focus, Scope, and Coherence of the Study of Human Symbolic Activity." *Quarterly Journal of Speech, 72*, pp. 231–246.

Crowley, D. J., & Heyer, P. (Eds.). (1995). *Communication in History: Technology, Culture, and Society*. (2nd ed.). White Plains, NY: Longman.

Dance, F. E. X. (1970). "The 'Concept' of Communication." *Journal of Communication, 20*, (2) pp. 201–210.

Daniels, T. D., Spiker, B. K., & Papa, M. J. (1997). *Perspectives on Organizational Communication* (4th ed.). Dubuque, IA: Brown & Benchmark.

Dawson, K. M. (1996). *Job Search: The Total System*. New York, NY: John Wiley & Sons.

Deal, T. E., & Kennedy, A. A. (1982). *Corporate Cultures: The Rites and Rituals of Corporate Life*. Reading, MA: Addison-Wesley.

December, J. (July, 1997). "Notes on Defining Computer-mediated Communication." *CMC Magazine*. Online. Internet. Available: http://www.December.com/cmc/mag/1997/jan/December.html.

Deetz, S. A. (1992). *Democracy in an Age of Corporate Colonialization*. Albany, NY: State University of New York.

Dennis, E. (1988). American Media and American Values. *Vital Speeches of the Day*, 54, 349–352.

DeVito, J. A., & Hecht, M. L. (1989). *The Nonverbal Communication Reader*. Prospect Heights, IL: Waveland Press.

DeWine, S. (1994). *The Consultant's Craft: Improving Organizational Communication*. New York, NY: St. Martin's Press.

DeWine, S., & James, A. C. (1988). "Examining the Communication Audit: Assessment and Modification." *Management Communication Quarterly*, 2, 144–169.

Dindia, K. (1997). "Self-disclosure, Self Identity, and Relationship Development: A Transactional/Dialectic Perspective." In S. Duck (Ed.), *Handbook of Personal Relationships: Theory, Research and Interventions*. (2nd ed., pp. 411–426). New York, NY: John Wiley & Sons.

Doyle, M. W. (Producer). (1996). *Cyberspace: Virtual Unreality?* [Videocassette]. Princeton, NJ: Films for the Humanities and Sciences.

Duncan, S., Jr., & Fiske, D. C. (1977). *Face-to-face Interaction: Research Methods and Theory*. New York, NY: Lawrence Erlbaum.

Dutka, A. (1994). "Demographic Trends in the Labor Force." In E. Einzberg (Ed.), *The Changing U.S. Labor Market* (pp. 14–32). Boulder, CO: West View Press.

Eble, C. C. (1996). *Slang and Sociability: In-group Language Among College Students*. Chapel Hill, NC: University of North Carolina Press.

Egdorf, K. (1996). "Communicating with Co-workers During Organizational Downsizing: A Social Construction Perspective on Sense-making and Social Support Interactions." Unpublished dissertation, Athens, OH: Ohio University.

Ehninger, D. (1969). "Marshall McLuhan: His Significance for the Field of Speech Communication." *Speech Journal*, 6, 17–24.

Eisenberg, E. M., & Goodall, H. L. (1993). *Organizational Communication: Balancing Creativity and Constraint*. New York, NY: St. Martin's Press.

Ekman, P., & Friesen, W. V. (1972). "The Repertoire of Nonverbal Behavior: Categories, Origins, Usage, and Coding." *Semiotica*, 1, 49–98.

Elgin, S. H. (1993). *Genderspeak: Men, Women and the Gentle Art of Verbal Self-defense*. New York, NY: John Wiley and Sons.

Fairhurst, G. T. (1993). "Echoes of the Vision: When the Rest of the Organization Talks Total Quality." *Management Communication Quarterly*, 6 (4, May), 331–371.

Ferraro, G. P. (1990). *The Cultural Dimension of International Business*. Englewood Cliffs, NJ: Prentice Hall.

Fisher, W. R. (1985). "The Narrative Paradigm: In the Beginning." *Journal of Communication*, 35, 74–88.

Fitzpatrick, M. A. (1997). "Interpersonal Communication on the Starship Enterprise: Resilience, Stability, and Change in Relationships in the Twenty-first Century." In J. Trent (Ed.), *Communication: Views from the Helm for the Twenty-first Century*. Boston, MA: Allyn & Bacon.

Foss, S. J., & Griffin, C. L. (1995). "Beyond Persuasion: A Proposal for an Invitational Rhetoric."*Communication Monographs, 62*, 2–18.

Garner, J. F. (1994). *Politically Correct Bedtime Stories*. New York, NY: McGraw-Hill.

Gaulke, S. (1997). *101 Ways to Captivate a Business Audience*. New York, NY: American Management Association.

Gearhart, S. M. (1979). "The Womanization of Rhetoric." *Women's Studies International Quarterly, 2*, 195–201.

Gerbner, G., Gross, L., Morgan, M., & Signorielli, N. (1986). "Living with Television: The Dynamics of the Cultivation Process." In J. Bryant & D. Zillman (Eds.), *Perspectives on Media Effects* (pp. 17–40). Hillsdale, NJ: Lawrence Erlbaum.

Gergen, K. J. (1991). *The Saturated Self: Dilemmas of Identity in Contemporary Life*. New York, NY: HarperCollins.

Gerland, O. (1994). "Brecht and the Courtroom: Alienating Evidence in the Rodney King Trials." *Text and Performance Quarterly, 14*, 305–318.

Gibson, M. K. (1994, November). "In the Line of Duty: Contemporary Closing Arguments in Defense of Police Action." Paper presented to the Legal Communication Division, Speech Communication Association Convention, New Orleans, LA.

Gibson, W. (1984). *Neuromancer*. London: Grafton.

Gibson-Hancox, M. (1997). "The Mud, the Blood, and the Beer Guys: A Structurational Analysis of Organizational Power, Ideology, and Discourse in a Blue-Collar Work Community." Unpublished dissertation, Athens, OH: Ohio University.

Giese, M. (1996). "From ARPAnet to the Internet: A Cultural Clash and Its Implications in Framing the Debate on the Information Superhighway." In L. Strate, R. Jacobson, & S. B. Gibson (Eds.), *Communication and Cyberspace: Social Interaction in an Electronic Environment, 123–141*. Cresskill, NJ: Hampton Press.

Goffman, E. (1959). *The Presentation of Self in Everyday Life*. New York, NY: Anchor.

Golden, J. L., Berquist, G. F., & Coleman, W. E. (1976). *The Rhetoric of Western Thought*. Dubuque, IA: Kendall-Hunt.

Golen, S. (1990). "A Factor Analysis of Barriers to Effective Listening." *Journal of Business Communication, 27*, 25–36.

Gouran, D., Wiethoff, W. E., & Doelgar, J. A. (1994). *Mastering Communication*. (2nd ed.). Needham Heights, MA: Allyn & Bacon.

Graham, E. (1997). "Turning Points and Commitment in Post-divorce Relationships."*Communication Monographs, 64*, 1–19.

Griffin, E. (1997). *A First Look at Communication Theory*. (3rd ed.). New York, NY: McGraw-Hill.

Grimes, B. F. (Ed.). (1996). *Ethnologue: Languages of the World*. (13th ed.). Dallas, TX: Summer Institute on Linguistics.

Gudykunst, W. B. (1995). "Anxiety/Uncertainty Management Theory: Current Status." In R. L. Wiseman (Ed.), *Intercultural Communication Theory* (pp. 8–58). Thousand Oaks, CA: Sage.

Guzley, R. E. (1992). "Organizational Climate and Communication Climate: Predictors of Commitment to the Organization." *Management Communication Quarterly, 4*, 422–449.

❖ ❖ ❖ ❖

Haas, J. W., & Arnold, C. L. (1995, April). "An Examination of the Role of Listening in Judgments of Communication Competence in Co-workers." *Journal of Business Communication*, 32, 123–139.

Hacker, Diana. *A Writer's Reference* (3rd ed.). Boston, MA: St. Martin's Press.

Hackman, M. Z., & Johnson, C. E. (1991). *Leadership: A Communication Perspective*. Prospect Heights, IL: Waveland Press.

Haffner, L. (1992). "Translation Is Not Enough: Interpreting in a Medical Setting." *Western Journal of Medicine*, 157, 255–260.

Hale, C. L., Farley-Lucus, B. F., & Tardy, R. W. (1996). "Interpersonal Conflict From a Younger Point of View: Exploring the Perspectives of Children." *Qualitative Studies in Education*, 9, 269–291.

Hall, E. T. (1976), *Beyond Culture*. New York: Doubleday.

——. (1969). *The Hidden Dimension*. Garden City, NY: Anchor Press/Doubleday.

Hall, E. T., & Hall, M. R. (1987). *Hidden Differences: Doing Business with the Japanese*. Garden City, NY: Anchor Press/Doubleday.

Hauben, M., & Hauben, R. (1997). *Netizens: On the History and Impact of the Usernet and the Internet*. Los Alamitos, CA: IEEE Computer Society Press.

Heimlich, E. P.. & Mark, A. J. (1990). *Paraverbal Communication with Children: Not Through Words Alone*. New York, NY: Plenum Press.

Hersey, P., & Blanchard, K. (1988). *Management Organizational Behavior: Utilizing Human Resources*. Englewood Cliffs, NJ: Prentice Hall.

Hickson, M. L. III., & Stacks, D. W. (1985). *Nonverbal Communication: Studies and Applications*. Dubuque, IA: Wm C. Brown Publishers.

Hinde, R. A. (1981). "The Bases of a Science of Interpersonal Relationships." In S. Duck & R. Gilmore (Eds.), *Personal Relationships*. Orlando, FL: Academic Press.

Hocker, J. L., & Wilmot, W. (1985). *Interpersonal Conflict*. Dubuque, IA: Wm. C. Brown.

Hoff, R. (1992). *I Can See You Naked: A New Revised Edition of the National Bestseller on Making Fearless Presentations*. Kansas City, KS: Andrews and McNeel.

Hofstede, G. (1980). *Culture's Consequences: International Differences in Work-related Values*. Beverly Hills, CA: Sage.

Hulit, L. M., & Howard, M. R. (1997). *Born to Talk: An Introduction to Speech and Language Development* (2nd ed.). Boston, MA: Allyn & Bacon.

INXS. (1987). "Devil Inside." On *Kick* [compact disk]. New York: Atlantic.

Jablin, F. (1985). "Task—Work Relationships: A Lifespan Perspective." In M. Knapp & G. Miller (Eds.), *Handbook of Interpersonal Communication* (pp. 615–654). Newbury Park, CA: Sage Publications.

——. (1987). "Organizational Entry, a Simulation, Exit." In F. Jablin, L. Putnam, K. Roberts, & L. Porter (Eds.), *Handbook of Organizational Communication* (pp. 679–740). Newbury Park, CA: Sage Publications.

——. (1979). "Superior-Subordinate Communication: The State of the Art." *Psychological Bulletin*, l, 1201–1222.

Janis, I. (1972). *Victims of Groupthink*. Boston: Houghton Miflin.

Jarratt, S., & Ong, R. (1995). "Aspasia: Rhetoric, Gender, and Colonial Ideology." In A. A. Lunsford (Ed.), *Reclaiming Rhetorica: Women in the Rhetorical Tradition* (pp.9–24). Pittsburgh, PA: University of Pittsburgh.

Johnson, J. R., Bernhagen, M. J., Miller, V., & Allen, M. (1996). "The Role of Communication in Managing Reductions in Workforce." *Journal of Applied Communication Research*, 24, 139–164.

Johnson, E. P. (1995). "SNAP! Culture: A Different Kind of Reading." *Text and Performance Quarterly*, 15, 122–142.

Johnson, W. B., & Packer, A. H. (1984). *Workforce 2000: Work and Workers for the 21st Century*. Indianapolis, IN: Hudson Institute.

Joseph, N. (1986). *Uniforms and Nonuniforms: Communication Through Clothing*. Westport, CT: Greenwood Publishing Group.

Josipovici, G. (1996). *Touch: An Exploration*. New Haven, CT: Yale University Press.

Jourard, S. (1971). *The Transparent Self* (Rev. ed.). New York, NY: Van Nostrand Reinhold.

Kabagarama, D. (1997). *Breaking the ICE: A Guide to Understand People From Other Cultures* (2nd Ed.). Englewood Cliffs, NJ: Prentice Hall.

Kanter, R. M. (1989). *When Giants Learn to Dance*. New York: NY: Simon & Schuster.

———. (1983). *The Changemasters*. New York: NY: Simon & Schuster.

Kavanagh, K. H., & Kennedy, P. H. (1992). *Promoting Cultural Diversity*. Newbury Park, CA: Sage.

Kelly, R. M. (1997). "Gender Culture and Socialization." In D. Dunn (Ed.). *Workplace/Women's Place* (pp. 19–31). Los Angeles, CA: Roxbury Publishing.

Kim, Y. Y., & Paulk, S. (1994). "Intercultural Challenges and Personal Adjustments: A Qualitative Analysis of the Experiences of American and Japanese Co-workers." In R. L. Wiseman, & R. Shuter (Eds.), *Communicating in Multinational Organizations* (pp. 117–140). Thousand Oaks, CA: Sage.

Klapper, J. T. (1960). *The Effects of Mass Communication*. New York, NY: Free Press.

Knox, M., & Walker, M. (1995). *The Private Diary of an O. J. Juror: Behind the Scenes of the Trial of the Century*. Beverly Hills, CA: Dove Audio.

Kochman, T. (1984). *Black and White Styles in Conflict*. Chicago, IL: University of Chicago Press.

Kreps, G. L. (1986). *Organizational Communication*. New York, NY: Simon & Schuster.

Lamm, K. (1995). *10,000 Ideas for Term Papers, Projects, Reports and Speeches*. (4th ed.). New York, NY: ARCO.

Landow, G. P. (1992). *Hypertext: The Convergence of Contemporary Critical Theory and Technology*. Baltimore, MD: Johns Hopkins University Press.

Lazarfeld, P. F., Berelson, B., & Gaudet, H. (1948). *The People's Choice: How the Voter Makes Up His Mind in a Presidential Campaign*. (2nd ed.). New York, NY: Columbia University Press.

Lewin, K., et al. (1939). "Patterns of Aggressive Behavior in Experimentally Created Social Climates." *Journal of Social Psychology*, 10, 271–299.

Library of Congress. (1996). Abraham Lincoln's Gettysburg Address. Available: http://lcweb.loc.gov/exhibits/gadd/

Lowery, S. A., & DeFleur, M. (1995). *Milestones in Mass Communication Research: Media Effects* (3rd ed.). White Plains, NY: Longman.

Ludlow, P. (Ed.). (1996). *High Noon on the Electronic Frontier: Conceptual Issues in Cyberspace.* Cambridge, MA: MIT Press.

Macaulay, S. (1986). "Images of Law in Everyday Life: The Lessons of School, Entertainment and Spectator Sports." *Institute for Legal Studies* (Working Papers, Series 2). Madison, WI: University of Wisconsin-Madison Press.

Marshall, E. L. (1996). *A Student's Guide to the Internet: Exploring the World Wide Web, Gopherspace, Electronic Mail, and More!* Brookfield, CT: Millbrook.

Mathews, G. (1996). *What Makes Life Worth Living?: How Japanese and Americans Make Sense of Their Worlds.* Berkeley, CA: University of California Press.

Matlon, R. J. (1993). *Opening Statements/Closing Arguments.* San Anselmo, CA: Stuart Allen Books.

McBride, N. F. (1997). *How to Have Great Small Group Meetings: Dozens of Ideas You Can Use Right Now.* Colorado Springs, CO: NavPress Publishing Group.

McGinniss, J. (1969). *The Selling of the President, 1968.* New York, NY: Penguin Books.

McKenzie, E. C. (1990). *14,000 Quips and Quotes: For Speakers, Writers, Editors, Preachers, and Teachers.* Grand Rapids, MI: Baker Book House.

McKerrow, R. E. (1988). "Whately's Phylosophy of Language." *Southern Speech Communication Journal,* 53, 211–226.

McLuhan, M. (1964). *Understanding Media: The Extension of Man.* New York, NY: Routledge.

McNeill, D. (1992). *Hand and Mind: What Gestures Reveal About Thought.* Chicago, IL: University of Chicago Press.

McPherson, M. (1996). "Restricted Communication and Uncertainty as Predictors of Marital Satisfaction." Unpublished dissertation, Athens, OH: Ohio University.

Metts, S. (1997). "Face and Facework: Implications for the Study of Personal Relationships." In S. Duck (Ed.), *Handbook of Personal Relationships: Theory, Research and Interventions.* (2nd ed., pp. 351–372). New York, NY: John Wiley & Sons.

Miller, L. C., Cooke, L. L., Tsong, J., & Morgan, F. (1992). "Should I Brag? Nature and Impact of Positive and Boastful Disclosures for Women and Men." *Human Communication Research,* 18 (3, March), 364–399.

Milroy, L., & Muysken, P. (Eds.). (1995). *One Speaker, Two Languages: Cross-disciplinary Perspectives on Code-switching.* New York, NY: Cambridge University Press.

Modaff, D. P. (1997). "Learning from War: Stories of World War II Veterans." Paper presented to the National Communication Association, Chicago, IL.

Monge, P., Bachman, S., Dillard, J., & Eisenberg, E. (1982). *Communicator Competence in the Workplace: Model Testing and Scale Development.* In M. Burgoon (Ed.), *Communication Yearbook* 5 (pp. 502–527). New Brunswick, NJ: Transaction Books.

Morley, D. D., & Shockley-Zalabak, P. (1991). "Setting the Rules: An Examination of the Influence of Organizational Founders' Values." *Management Communication Quarterly,* 5, 379–402.

Morris, D. (1995). *Bodytalk: The Meaning of Human Gestures.* New York, NY: Crown Publishing Group.

Morrison, T., Conaway, W. A., & Borden, G. A. (1994). *Kiss, Bow or Shake Hands: How to Do Business in Sixty Countries.* Holbrook, MA: Bob Adams.

Mortensen, C. D. (1991). "Communication, Conflict, and Culture." *Communication Theory,* 1, 273–293.

Motley, M. T. (1990). "On Whether One Can(not) Communicate: An Examination via Traditional Communication Postulates." *Western Journal of Speech Communication,* 51 (1, winter), pp. 1–20.

Naisbitt, J. (1982). *Megatrends.* New York, NY: Warner Books.

Naisbitt, J., & Aburdene, P. (1990). *Megatrends 2000: Ten New Directions for the 1990s.* New York, NY: William Morrow & Co.

Nardi, P. M. (Ed.). (1992). *Men's Friendships.* Newbury Park, CA: Sage.

Neblett, P. (1996). *Circles of Sisterhood: A Book Discussion Group Guide for Women of Color.* New York, NY: Writers & Readers Publishing.

Newstrom, J., & Secunnell, E. E. (1997). *The Big Book of Presentation Games: Wake-em-up Tricks, Icebreakers, and Other Fun Stuff.* New York, NY: McGraw-Hill.

O'Hair, D., Friedrich, G. W., Wiemann, J. M., & Wiemann, M. O. (1995). *Competent Communication.* New York, NY: St. Martin's Press.

O'Hara-Devereaux, M., & Johansen, R. (1994). *Globalwork: Bridging Distance, Culture, and Time.* San Francisco: Jossey-Bass.

Ong, W. J. (1982). *Orality and Literacy: The Technologizing of the Word.* New York, NY: Methuen.

Papa, M., Auwal, M. A., & Singhal, A. (1997). "Organizing for Social Change Within Concertive Control Systems: Member Identification Empowerment, and the Masking of Discipline." *Communication Monographs,* 64, 219–249.

Parks, M. (1997). "Communication Networks and Relationship Life Cycles." In S. Duck (Ed.), *Handbook of Personal Relationships: Theory, Research and Interventions.* (2nd ed., pp. 351–372). New York, NY: John Wiley & Sons.

Patton, B. R., & Giffin, K. (1981). *Interpersonal Communication in Action.* Cambridge, MA: Harper & Row.

Peppers, D. (1995). *Life's a Pitch: Then You Buy.* New York, NY: Doubleday.

Perrow, C. (1986). *Complex Organizations: A Critical Essay.* (3rd ed.). New York, NY: Random House.

Peters, T. (1988, Spring). "Learning to Listen." *Hyatt Magazine* pp. 16–18.

Peters, T. J., & Waterman, R. H. (1984). *In Search of Excellence: Lessons from America's Best Run Companies.* New York, NY: Warner Communications.

Petronio, S., Martin, J., & Littlefield, R. (1984). "Prerequisite for Self-disclosing: A Gender Issue." *Communication Monographs,* 51, 268–273.

Pettus, A. B. (1990). "The Verdict Is In: A Study of Jury Decision Making Factors, Moment of Personal Decision, and Jury Deliberations—from the Juror's Point of View." *Communication Quarterly,* 38, 83–97.

Phillips, A., Lipson, A., & Basseches, M. (1994). "Empathy and Listening Skills: A Development Perspective on Learning to Listen." In J. D. Sinnott (Ed.), *Interdisciplinary Handbook of Adult Lifespan Learning* (pp. 301–324). Westport, CT: Greenwood Press.

Pinker, S. (1994). *The Language Instinct: How the Mind Creates Language.* New York, NY: William Morrow & Co.

Poster, M. (1990). *The Mode of Information: Poststructuralism and Social Context*. Chicago, IL: University of Chicago Press.

Publication Manual of the American Psychological Association. (4th ed.) (1994). Washington, DC: American Psychological Association.

Radway, J. (1984). *Reading the Romance: Women, Patriarchy, and Popular Literature*. Chapel Hill, NC: University of North Carolina Press.

Rawson, H. (1995). "Euphemisms." In G. Goshgarian (Ed.), *Exploring Language* (7th ed.). New York, NY: Harper Collins.

Redding, W. C. (1985). "Stumbling Toward Identity: The Emergence of Organizational Communication as a Field of Study." In R. McPhee & P. Tompkins (Eds.), *Organizational Communication: Traditional Themes and New Directions* (pp. 15–54). Beverly Hills, CA: Sage.

——. (1994). Foreward. In S. DeWine *The Consultant's Craft: Improving Organizational Communication*. New York, NY: St. Martin's Press.

Redding, W. C., & Tompkins, P. (1988). "Organizational Communication—Past and Present Tenses." In G. Goldhaber & G. Barnett (Eds.), *Handbook of Organizational Communication* (pp. 5–33). Norwood, NJ: Ablex.

Rheingold, H. (1993). *The Virtual Community: Homesteading on the Electronic Frontier*. Reading, MA: Addison-Wesley Publishing.

Rieke, R. D., & Stutman, R. K. (1990). *Communication in Legal Advocacy*. Columbia, SC: University of South Carolina Press.

Riekehof, L. L. (1987). *The Joy of Signing* (2nd ed.). Springfield, MO: Gospel Publishing House.

Robbins, S. P. (1989). *Training in Interpsersonal Skills: Tips for Managing People at Work*. Englewood Cliffs, NJ: Prentice-Hall.

Rodrigues, D. (1997). *The Research Paper and the World Wide Web: A Writer's Guide*. Upper Saddle River, NJ: Prentice Hall.

Ross, R. S. (1986). *Speech Communication* (7th ed.). Englewood Cliffs, NJ: Prentice-Hall.

Rothwell, J. D. (1995). *In Mixed Company* (2nd ed.). Fort Worth, TX: Harcourt Brace College Publishers.

Rubin, R. B., Palmgreen, P. Y., & Sypher, H. E. (1994). *Communication Research Measures: A Sourcebook*. New York, NY: Guilford.

Rubin, R. B., Rubin, A. M., & Piele, L. J. (1996). *Communication Research: Strategies and Sources*. (4th ed.). Belmont, CA: Wadsworth.

Schultz, W. C. (1958). *FIRO: A Three-dimensional Theory of Interpersonal Behavior*. New York, NY: Holt, Rinehard & Winston.

Sigal, J., Braden-MaGuire, J., Hayden, M., & Mosely, N. (1985). "The Effect of Presentation Style and Sex of Lawyer on Jury Decision-making Behavior." *Psychology*, 22, 13–19.

Simpson, T. A. (1995). "Communication, Conflict and Community in an Urban Industrial Ruin." *Communication Research*, 22, 700–719.

Singer, M. (1987). *Intercultural Communication: A Perceptual Approach*. Englewood Cliffs, NJ: Prentice-Hall.

Slezak, E. (1995). *The Book Group Book: A Thoughtful Guide to Forming and Enjoying a Stimulating Book Discussion Group*. Chicago, IL: Chicago Review Press.

Smith, L. J., & Malandro, L.A. (1985). *Courtroom Communication Strategies*. New York, NY: Kluwer Law Book Publishers.

Smith, R. C., & Eisenberg, E. M. (1987). "Conflict at Disneyland: A Root-metaphor Analysis." *Communication Monographs*, 54, 367–380.

Sorenson, S. (1981, May). "Grouphate." Paper presented to the International Communication Association, Minneapolis, MN.

Spencer, C., & Arbon, Beverly. (1996). *Foundations of Writing: Developing Research and Academic Writing Skills.* Lincolnwood, IL: NTC.

Sproule, J. M. (1997). *Propaganda and Democracy: The American Experience of Media and Mass Persuasion.* New York, NY: Cambridge University Press.

Sullivan, R. (1997). *Climbing Your Way to the Bottom: Changing the Way You Approach Your Job Search.* Chicago, IL: Pure Play Publishing.

Tarter-Hilgendorf, B. J. (1986, November). "Impact of Opening and Closing Statements." *Trial*, 79–80.

Tedesco, J. A., Spiker, J. A., & Miller, J. (In press). "Presidential Campaigning on the Information Super Highway: An Exploration of Content and Form." In L. L. Kaid, & D. Bystrom (Eds.), *The Electronic Election.* New York, NY: Lawrence Erlbaum.

Tedford, T. L. (1985). *Freedom of Speech in the United States.* New York, NY: Random House.

Thibout, J. W., & Kelley, H. H. (1959). *The Social Psychology of Groups.* New York, NY: John Wiley & Sons.

Thomas, C., Booth-Butterfield, M., & Booth-Butterfield, S. (1995). "Perceptions of Deception, Divorce Disclosures, and Communication Satisfaction with Parents." *Western Journal of Speech Communication*, 59, 228–245.

Thornton, H. (1995). *Hung Jury: The Diary of a Menendez Juror.* Philadelphia, PA: Temple University Press.

Tirkkonen-Condit, S. (1988, August). *Explicitness vs. Implicitness of Argumentation: An Intercultural Comparison.* Paper presented to the Colloquium on the Role of Argument in the Creation of Community, Venice, Italy.

Tortoriello, T., Blatt, S., & DeWine, S. (1978). *Communication in the Organization: An Applied Approach.* New York, NY: McGraw Hill.

Trenholm, S. (1995). *Thinking Through Communication: An Introduction to the Study of Human Communication.* Needham Heights, MA: Allyn & Bacon.

Turkle, S. (1996). "Parallel Lives: Working on Identity in Virtual Space." In D. Grodin, & T. R. Lindlof (Eds.), *Constructing the Self in a Mediated World* (pp.156–175). Thousand Oaks, CA: Sage.

Victor, D. A. (1992). *International Business Communication.* New York, NY: HarperCollins.

Vitanza, V. J. "Netiquette." In V. J. Vitanza (Ed.), *Cyberreader* (pp.474–475). Boston, MA: Allyn & Bacon.

Wagner, E. J. (1992). *Sexual Harassment in the Workplace.* New York, NY: Amacom—American Management Association.

Waldron, V. R., & Krone, K. J. (1991). "The Experience and Expression of Emotion in the Workplace: A Study of a Corrections Organization." *Management Communication Quarterly*, 4, Newbury Park, CA: Sage Publications.

Walther, J. B. (1996). "Computer-mediated Communication: Impersonal, Interpersonal, and Hyperpersonal Interaction." *Communication Research*, 23, 3–43.

Watzlawick, P., Beavin, J., & Jackson, D. (1967). *Pragmatics of Human Communication.* New York, NY: Norton.

Weaver, R. (1963). "Language Is Sermonic." In R. E. Nebergall (Ed.), *Dimensions of Rhetorical Scholarship.* Norman, OK: University of Oklahoma Press.

Wheeless, L. R., Erikson, K. V., & Behrens, J. S. (1986). "Cultural Differences in Disclosiveness as a Function of Locus of Control." *Communication Monographs,* 53 (1, March), 36–46.

Wheeless, V. E., Zakahi, W. R., & Chan, M. B. (1988). "A Test of Self-disclosure Based on Perceptions of a Target's Loneliness and Gender Orientation." *Communication Quarterly,* 36, 109–121.

"Whistle-Blowers on Trial" (1997, March 24). *Business Week,* p. 172.

White, K. (1987). "Influence of the Target, Agent, and Message Type on Compliance Resistance Strategies in Organizations: The Development of a Compliance Resistance Taxonomy." Unpublished dissertation, Athens, OH: Ohio University.

White, R. A. (1983). "Mass Communication and Culture: Transition to a New Paradigm." *Journal of Communication,* 33, 279–301.

Williams, A., & Giles, H. (1996). "Intergenerational Conversations: Young Adults' Retrospective Accounts." *Human Communication Research,* 23, 220–250.

Winter, R. (1976, March). "How People React to Your Touch." *Science Digest,* 46–56.

Witte, K., & Morrison, K. (1995). "Intercultural and Cross-cultural Health Communication: Understanding People and Motivating Healthy Behaviors." In R. L. Wiseman (Ed.), *Intercultural Communication Theory* (pp. 216–246). Thousand Oaks, CA: Sage.

Wolfram, W. (1991). *Dialects and American English.* Englewood Cliffs, NJ: Prentice Hall.

Wolvin, A., & Coakley, C. (1992). *Listening* (4th ed.). Dubuque, IA: Wm. C. Brown.

Wood, J. T. (1992). "Telling Our Stories: Sexual Harassment in the Communication Discipline." *Applied Communication Research,* 20, 349–362.

Wood, J. T., & Inman, C. C. (1993, August). "In a Different Mode: Masculine Styles of Communicating Closeness." *Journal of Communication Research.* 279–295.

Yamada, H. (1997). *Different Game, Different Rules: Why Americans and Japanese Misunderstand Each Other.* Oxford, England: Oxford University Press.

Zuber, S., & Reed, A. M. (1993). "The Politics of Grammar Handbooks: Generic **he** and Singular **they**." *College English,* 55, 515–525.

Subject Index

341

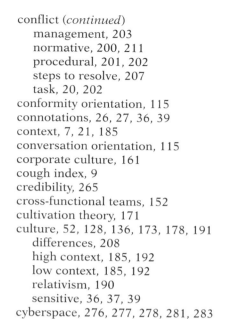

❖ ❖ ❖ ❖

❖ ❖ ❖ ❖

Author Index

347

❖ ❖ ❖ ❖